T3-BWG-867

No. 2401
$21.95

THE ANNOTATED

FAA PRACTICAL TEST STANDARDS

SINGLE-ENGINE AND MULTI-ENGINE LAND

ALBERT J. TAYLOR

Illustrations by Marjorie Taylor

 TAB BOOKS Inc.

Blue Ridge Summit, PA 17214

FIRST EDITION

FIRST PRINTING

Copyright © 1987 by TAB BOOKS Inc.

Printed in the United States of America

Library of Congress Cataloging in Publication Data

Taylor, Albert J.
    The annotated FAA practical test standards—
single-engine and multi-engine land.

    Includes index.
    1. Airplanes—Piloting—Examinations,
questions, etc.   2. Air pilots—Licenses—
United States.   I. Title.
TL710.T33   1986   629.132′52′076   86-23086
ISBN 0-8306-0701-3
ISBN 0-8306-2401-5 (pbk.)

Contents

Introduction

This guide is intended to provide the applicant for the Private Pilot's Certificate with an understanding of the requirements of the practical test, or what is popularly referred to as the checkride. Although flight instructors may find the book helpful in preparing student pilots for the test, the material will probably be most useful to the applicants.

Those flight instructors who use the book will find it a useful tool for standardizing their preparation of student pilots for the checkride as well as for administering the recommendation ride. Private Pilot Certificate applicants, on the other hand, will find the book most helpful in coming to understand more precisely what will be expected of them in order to qualify for the certificate. It should help to remove some of the trepidation with which they approach this check on flying skills.

Too often the checkride is contemplated with fear and uneasiness because applicants do not know precisely what to expect. Unfortunately, in some instances in the past, this concern has been warranted, since the practical test was a rather mysterious event. Some examiners encouraged this by refusing to reveal in advance of the practical test what was planned for the applicant. With the publication of the *Practical Test Standards*, some of this mystery should be dispelled. It should be clear to all that what is intended is for applicants to be as familiar as possible with what will be required of them.

In the first place, it should prove helpful to have the tasks specified. This guide will help to clarify what is involved in each of the tasks. Further, in presenting the tasks in terms of objectives, the guide focuses on and clarifies the outcomes—the performances—that will demonstrate the competence required for the certificate sought. Applicants should find it most helpful to learn precisely what he/she will be *doing* in demonstrating competency.

Obviously, the actual checkride may differ in some ways from the guide. The order of the tasks will vary from one examiner, or test, to another. Some tasks may be combined, or some of the tasks described in the guide may be omitted entirely if, in the view of the examiner, the skill and/or knowledge has been demonstrated in some other way. It is extremely unlikely, however, that an applicant will encounter some requirement that has not been presented herein. In other words, the scope of this guide is exhaustive in that it covers everything that an applicant will encounter on a checkride.

Since the applicant's instruction will have been directed toward preparing him/her for the Practical Test, the earlier the guide is employed, the more useful and helpful it will be. This is not to say that the private pilot applicant will not find the book helpful if he/she has waited until after the recommendation ride to begin his/her study of the content of the guide; it can be helpful at any stage. But to get the greatest benefit from the help that the guide provides, student pilots will find it most useful if they acquire the book early in their flying experience and relate it to the instruction they are receiving. In this way, the guide will help the student pilot to understand what his/her flight instructor is trying to achieve throughout the period of flight instruction. By the time he/she is ready for the practical test, the applicant should have a very clear picture of what the checkride will consist of.

If the guide simply removes some of the mystery and apprehensiveness regarding the practical test, it will have served the applicant well. If he/she is able to approach the test with a clearer understanding of the tasks to be demonstrated, the applicant should feel much more confident. This greater confidence is almost certain to be reflected in better performance of the practical test requirements.

Section 1

Single-Engine

Chapter 1

I. AREA OF OPERATION:
PREFLIGHT PREPARATION

A. TASK: **CERTIFICATES AND DOCUMENTS** (ASEL)

PILOT OPERATION – 1

REFERENCES: FAR Parts 61 and 91; AC 61–21, AC 61–23; Pilot's Operating Handbook and FAA–Approved Flight Manual.

1. **Objective.**   To determine that the applicant:

   a. Exhibits adequate knowledge by explaining the appropriate –

      (1) pilot certificate privileges and limitations.
      (2) medical certificate and expiration.
      (3) personal pilot logbook or flight record.
      (4) FCC station license and operator's permit.

    b. Exhibits adequate knowledge by locating and explaining the significance and importance of the airplane's –

        (1) airworthiness and registration certificates.

        (2) operating limitations, handbooks, or manuals.

        (3) equipment list.

        (4) weight and balance data.

        (5) maintenance requirements and appropriate records.

2. Action. The examiner will:

    a. Ask the applicant to present and explain the appropriate pilot and medical certificates and personal flight records and determine that the applicant's performance meets the objective.

    b. Ask the applicant to locate and explain the airplane documents, lists, records, and other required data, and determine that the applicant's performance meets the objective.

    c. Place emphasis on the applicant's awareness of the importance of certificates, records, and documents as related to safety.

Objective: What's expected of the applicant as regards certificates and documents.

Certificates, Privileges, and Limitations. Although this is a practical test guide, and most of the material will be related to what the prospective private pilot will be doing rather than what he/she will be saying, a part of what the applicant can anticipate will involve a demonstration of knowledge that requires telling rather than performing. In this category of tasks is the need for exhibiting knowledge regarding certificates and documents. This covers the papers that refer to both you and the aircraft you'll be flying. A thorough review of this material can be had by sifting through the appropriate sections of Part 61 of the Federal Aviation Regulations (FARs). Your ground school study will have prepared you for this part of the test, but a brief survey here of what is required may save you a more extensive review.

In the first place, temporarily, you're going to be neither fish nor fowl. You're still a student, but you expect to be a private pilot. Consequently, you can reasonably be expected to know something regarding privileges and limitations of both certificates. A significant difference between the two is that while your Student Pilot Certificate expires at the end of the 24th month in which it was issued, the Private Pilot's Certificate, like all others except the student certificate, has no specific expiration date. Also, though your Student Pilot Certificate is also your Medical Certificate, this will no longer be the case. Your Medical Certificate, which will have an expiration date, will be a separate document from your Private Pilot Certification.

The greatest privilege bestowed by your Student Pilot Certificate was that of being able to fly solo after certain other conditions had been met. Prior to such flights, of course, you demonstrated to your instructor that you were familiar with the flight rules of Part 91 that pertain to student solo flights. Having demonstrated such knowledge, your solo flights required an endorsement both on your pilot certificate and in your logbook by the flight instructor who gave you your instruction. You will recall that *each* of your cross-country solo flights also required supervision and was specifically endorsed by your CFI.

Beyond the limitations imposed by the requirement that all your flying was to be supervised by your flight instructor, a number of other restrictions limit the student pilot's privileges. You are prohibited from acting as pilot-in-command of an airplane that is carrying passengers or carrying property for which compensation is to be given. As a matter of fact, you cannot fly for hire at all, nor even fly in furtherance of a business. You are also restricted to domestic flights. The student pilot cannot even be the required pilot flight crewmember on any aircraft that requires more than one pilot.

Now that you're to be a private pilot your privileges will be increased and the limitations decreased significantly. With the acquisition of the new certificate, you will acquire the privilege of acting as the pilot-in-command of an aircraft that is carrying passengers, though you still may not carry passengers or property for hire, except in certain very limited cases. For example, your boss can pay you to fly an airplane in connection with the business, or your employment, if the flying is incidental to the business or employment and neither paying passengers nor property is on board. If you're an aircraft salesperson with at least 200 hours, you may demonstrate aircraft to prospective buyers. An additional privilege that some find very useful is that of sharing expenses of a flight with passengers. Fortunately for you, there are no specifications as to how small your share may be. You may act as pilot-in-command of a passenger-carrying airplane sponsored by a charitable organization. However, this privilege is hedged in with a number of restrictions, so you should check this out in 61.118 prior to committing yourself to such flights.

Incidentally, contrary to some popularly held notions, your Private Pilot's Certificate does *not* afford you the privilege being paid to fly second-in-command, nor can you be second-in-command in an aircraft certificated for more than one pilot when that aircraft is carrying passengers or property for compensation or hire.

However, once you've acquired that Private Pilot's Certificate, you may fly solo to your heart's content and your wallet's or purse's capabilities. No more endorsements by CFIs are required for that. And you can fly just about anywhere you please without first checking your travel plans with a CFI. You will be required to have your proficiency checked periodically, however, through a biennial flight review, which must be conducted by a flight instructor. And the flight instructor, or examiner, who provides this review must attest to your proficiency with an appropriate log book endorsement.

Although your license doesn't have an expiration date, your Medical Certification does. You will probably continue to fly under the provisions of that Third Class Medical Certificate which you acquired as a student pilot. That won't expire until the end of the last day of the 24th month after the month of the date of the examination shown on the certificate. If you decide to upgrade to a Second Class Certificate, then your "medical" will expire at the end of the last day of the 12th month after the month of the date of the examination. However, even on this certificate, your Third Class privileges will still continue as they normally would for a Third Class Certificate.

Having earned that Private Pilots Certificate, you will also have earned the privilege of keeping it current. That means simply keeping the FAA informed if you change your name or address. In the case of the name change, you'll need also to submit a copy of whatever document (marriage license, court order, etc.) affects the change. If your certificate is lost or destroyed, you are responsible for its replacement. If this happens, Part 61 (61.29) will guide you in obtaining a replacement.

One other point might be made: Having earned the certificate, it's *your* certificate and no one can take it away from you except through due process. Hopefully, it won't happen, but a circumstance could arise in which someone may *ask to see* your certificate. If a law enforcement officer believes that you've violated some law or regulation, he/she may request that you *show* your certificate. If that occurs, you're required to show it, but you are not required to *surrender* it. *Never hand your certificate over to anyone.* Even an FAA type may seem to demand that you give him/her your license for examination. *Don't do it.* Officers of the law have the privilege of seeing your license, but that does not extend to their fondling it. If you are ever in such a predicament, hang on to your certificate and seek legal counsel. But don't surrender it; you may find it more difficult to get it back again than you imagine.

Recording and Documenting Your Flying. Logbooks are funny things. On the one hand, all your training and experience used to meet the requirements for a certificate or rating or recent flight experience must be shown by a reliable record. That means a logbook. Yet, once you've acquired the certificate, you are no longer required to log your time. My advice is: Maintain a current logbook. And when you go for the practical test (checkride), know what's required in logbook entries.

Be aware that you log as solo flight time only that time when you are the sole occupant of the aircraft. As a private pilot, you may log as pilot-in-command time only that flight time when you're actually flying the airplane. You may log as second-in-command the flight time when you are second-in-command of an aircraft that by certification or regulation requires more than one pilot. Simply riding in the right seat does not qualify as second-in-command time. Also, you may record as instrument flight time only the flight time you spend actually operating the aircraft solely by reference to the instruments in either actual or simulated instrument flight conditions. Such entries must also include the name of the safety pilot accompanying you during such a flight. Instruction time will be entered by your flight instructor and specified as flight, instrument, or ground instruction.

Any pilot must present his/her logbook for inspection upon *reasonable request* by the Administrator or an authorized representative of the National Transportation Safety Board or any state or local law enforcement officer. That does *not* include the FBO, or a flight instructor, or chief pilot at any installation at which you happen to land. This applies even to student pilots, though they must carry the logbook on all solo cross-country flights as evidence of having received flight instructor clearances and endorsements. But you need let only the Administrator or NTSB reps or law enforcement officers peek inside.

Other Documents. There was a time when you were also required to carry at least a Restricted Radiotelephone Operator Permit issued by the FCC. That requirement has been eliminated. But although *you* are no longer required to have a radio license, each transmitter aboard your aircraft must be covered by an FCC station license. Make certain that this document is in the aircraft that you use for the flight check and that you can produce it readily when the examiner calls for it.

The Airplane's Certificates. The examiner will ask you to produce the papers related to the aircraft. One such document is the Airworthiness Certificate. As you will recall from your ground school instruction, this simply certifies that when the aircraft left the factory, it was deemed airworthy. For commercially built aircraft, this is essentially meaningless, but it should be on display in the aircraft that you'll be using for the checkride. Make sure it is.

The other certificate you'll be expected to point out is the airplane's registration certificate. That's usually contained in the same case that displays the Airworthiness Certificate. Beyond this, although the FAA publications do not mention it, you may be called on to prove that the airplane is registered by the state in which it is based. Be familiar with what is required in your state. This "certificate" may be in the form of a decal affixed to some external part of the airplane.

Operating Limitations. Most aircraft these days have a manual on board that lists the operating limitations of the airplane. Older airplanes might simply be placarded, but somewhere on that airplane should be something that indicates the various limitations of the airplane.

Equipment, Weight, and Balance. Generally, the equipment list and the weight and balance data are a part of the same document. Since one cannot add equipment to the basic airplane without altering the weight and balance, you'll find a document that specifies the basic information about weight and balance of the particular airplane which you're flying.

Maintenance and Other Records. Finally, although it's not necessary to carry the airplane's logs aboard the airplane, you'll need them for your practical test. There'll be separate logbooks for the engine and the airplane. Look these over before you meet with the examiner so that you can readily and easily point out the information he/she may ask you about. Locate the records of the most recent periodic check, annual inspection, and/or whatever is required for the particular airplane you are flying.

B. TASK: OBTAINING WEATHER INFORMATION (ASEL)

PILOT OPERATION – 1

REFERENCES: AC 00–6, AC 00–45, AC 61–21, AC 61–23, AC 61–84.

1. **Objective.** To determine that the applicant:

    a. Exhibits adequate knowledge of aviation weather information by obtaining, reading, and analyzing –

    (1) weather reports and forecasts.
    (2) weather charts.
    (3) pilot weather reports.
    (4) SIGMETS and AIRMETS.
    (5) Notices to Airmen.

    b. Makes a sound go/no–go decision based on the available weather information.

2. **Action.** The examiner will:

    * **a.** Determine that the applicant has obtained all pertinent weather information. (If current weather materials are not available, the examiner will furnish samples for use.)   *
    b. Ask the applicant to analyze and explain the weather data, and determine that the applicant's performance meets the objective.
    c. Place emphasis on the applicant's ability to interpret the weather data and make a sound go/no–go decision.

Objective: What's expected of the applicant regarding weather information.

Obtaining and Analyzing the Weather Data. Hopefully, you've had considerable experience obtaining weather information during your training. You should obtain a weather briefing for your practical test, just as you did for your cross-country flights during your student flying. If you're a little shaky on this procedure, practice it a few times. The briefers in the Flight Service Station will give you weather reports and forecasts even if you are not planning a flight. They would appreciate it if you would supply them with an aircraft identification number when you call, but that can be from any of the airplanes listed in your logbook.

Since the folks who people Flight Service Stations are human like the rest of us, you'll encounter all types in various moods. Some will volunteer a great deal of information and provide a very thorough briefing, while others will wait for you to specify what you want. Be prepared for the latter. Request weather for a specific location and time period. Ask for both a report of current conditions and a forecast. Record the weather that's given to you. At the conclusion of the briefing, your record should show: ceiling, visibility, and precipitation (if any is present or in the forecast), surface winds, and winds aloft. You should also be aware of any flight precautions that are available. If these are not given, ask for them. It's also helpful to have pilot's reports if conditions warrant such information. On the day of your practical test, obtain and record such a briefing and take this written record with you along with the other materials listed on the checklist.

The Various Weather Charts. It's probably unlikely that you'll be called on to read and analyze any of the various weather charts. It's possible, however, that out there somewhere is an examiner who may expect you to possess at least a nodding acquaintance with these charts. If you're shown a surface analysis chart, you may not be able to recall all the details of the station models that constitute the basic unit of information, but you should be able to identify the pressure systems and fronts that are shown and to explain the significance of these for your flight. You should also understand what the isobars represent in terms of pressure and general wind conditions. If, in addition to these, you can also describe sky cover from the appropriate symbols, you'll know all that can be reasonably expected of you.

You should also be able to sort out the radar summary chart from among the various charts and be familiar with what it shows. These are simpler than other charts and require a familiarity with very few symbols. You'll undoubtedly remember from your ground school instruction the depiction of storms, and the meaning of terms such as "NE" (no echoes). You'll recall that weather depiction charts are somewhat abbreviated analysis charts that give a quick, general picture of pressure systems, fronts, and sky cover. The "prog" charts (low-level significant weather prognosis charts) are similarly uncluttered and general, providing forecasts for 12 to 24 hours ahead. You'll need to recognize only a few symbols on such charts and, as with the others mentioned, will probably have been sufficiently prepared by your ground school instruction to handle these should they come during the preflight part of your practical test. Since it's unlikely that this will occur, a quick review of the accompanying illustrations should suffice (Fig. 1-1).

PIREPS. What you do with or about pilot weather reports may depend

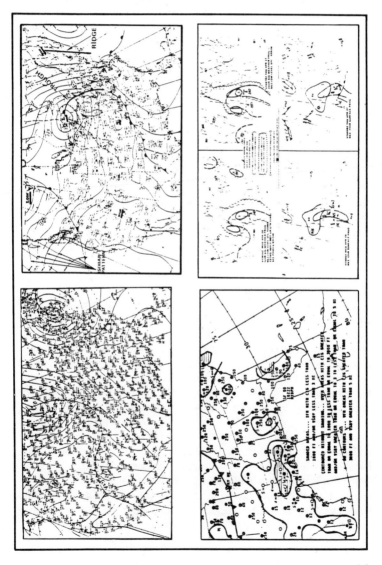

Fig. 1-1. Weather maps.

on the conditions of the day of your checkride. If you luck out and get a "severe clear" with no significant conditions, calm winds and the like, it will be pointless during your weather briefing to ask for PIREPS (pilot weather reports). If there's nothing to report, then no one reports.

SIGMETS and AIRMETS. Unless you have good reason not to, it's generally good practice to inquire about flight precautions. It might just be the case that on that bright, sunny day with all those pretty, white, puffy clouds floating around, you'll encounter some turbulence. The flight precautions may be given to you in the form of AIRMETS (advisory for light aircraft) or SIGMETS (significant meteorology). The latter, of course, will preclude your taking a checkride, since they refer to meteorological phenomena that is significant for *all* aircraft. They are issued for such things as squall lines, embedded thunderstorms, isolated severe thunderstorms or areas of such storms, hail, tornadoes, icing, severe turbulence, and the like. Since these are of significance to all aircraft, they are sufficiently serious to keep you and your airplane on the ground. AIRMETS are less severe in nature but are still potentially hazardous to aircraft having limited capabilities because of lack of equipment or pilot qualification. You need to assure the examiner that you have requested such information as a part of your weather briefing and that you understand the significance of such flight precautions.

NOTAMS. Finally, you will be expected to be familiar with what NOTAMS are (Notices to Airmen), and with any that may be applicable to the area of your flight. Such notices give you information about closed or shut-down radio or instrument facilities, runways under construction or closed, alterations in lighting, etc. These do not seem to be related to weather. Their only connection with weather is that they may be included after some surface weather reports.

You should know that NOTAMS are concerned with the types of information listed above which was not known at the time that aeronautical charts or other documents were published. They are therefore disseminated in other ways. Some notices may be significant enough to alter your go-no go decision. Airport closures or shut-down navigation aids can affect your decision. Other notices may be merely of interest to the pilot, e.g., such information as closed taxiways, workers and/or equipment near or crossing runways, etc. Still other notices may be regulatory in nature, involving amendments to charts or instrument approaches, or intended to affect restrictions to flights.

Beyond certain NOTAMS being included after some weather reports, notices will also be included in the flight publication called, appropriately enough, *Notices to Airmen.* Prior to your checkride, you should have consulted this guide for any information that might relate to your area of flight. If you locate such information, provide this to the examiner with whom you'll be taking the practical test. If the Notices contain no relevant information for you, you should still let the examiner know that you've checked the publication.

The Go/No-Go Decision. You'll then be expected to render a go/no-go decision based on all the data which you've accumulated. Don't try to read the examiner's mind on this. Make your own independent judgement. If everything looks fine for the flight, then make this pronouncement with confidence. If you have some doubt and you're concerned about the reaction of the examiner, who may seem determined to make the flight, then you can simply inform him/her that in your judgement conditions do not seem to warrant flying and that if you were making a judgement about making a flight on your own, you'd choose not to go. That leaves the final say up to the examiner who may determine that, because of his/her extensive flight experience, the flight may be made. When in doubt, make the judgement on the side of safety.

C. TASK: DETERMINING PERFORMANCE AND LIMITATIONS (ASEL)

PILOT OPERATION – 1

REFERENCES: AC 61–21, AC 61–23, AC 61–84; Pilot's Operating Handbook and FAA–Approved Flight Manual.

1. **Objective.** To determine that the applicant:

   a. Exhibits adequate knowledge by explaining the airplane's weight and balance, performance, and limitations including adverse aerodynamic effects of exceeding the limits.
   b. Uses the available and appropriate performance charts, tables, and data.
   c. Computes the weight and balance and determines that the weight and center of gravity will be within limits during all phases of the flight.
   d. Calculates the airplane's performance considering density altitude, wind, terrain, and other pertinent conditions.
   e. Describes the effects of seasonal and atmospheric conditions on the airplane's performance.
   f. Makes a sound decision on whether the required performance is within the airplane's capability and operating limitations.

2. **Action.** The examiner will:

   a. Ask the applicant to explain the airplane's performance and limitations including adverse effects of exceeding the limits and determine that the applicant's performance meets the objective.
   b. Ask the applicant to determine the airplane's performance and limitations,

and describe the effects of seasonal and atmospheric conditions on the airplane's operation, and determine that the applicant's performance meets the objective.

c. Place emphasis on the soundness of the applicant's judgment based on complete and accurate performance calculations.

Objective: What is expected of the applicant regarding determining performance and limitations.

Explaining Weight and Balance. Besides being able to complete the computation required to assure that your airplane is within the limits of weight and balance, you'll also be expected to tell the examiner about these significant factors, which affect virtually every aspect of airplane performance. You must demonstrate that you know that takeoff speed, length of takeoff run, angle and rate of climb, range, cruising speed and attitude, stalling speed, and landing roll, all are affected by the airplane's weight and by the distribution of that weight.

The weights with which you'll be concerned will fall under two categories, *empty weight* and *gross weight*. You'll explain to the examiner that the basic empty weight of the airplane is the weight of the airplane itself along with all unusable fuel, full operating fluids, full engine oil, and all optional equipment that has been added.

For more complex airplanes, other weights may have to be taken into consideration such as *maximum ramp weight, maximum takeoff weight,* etc. But for your purposes, the empty and gross weights will suffice. In relation to those, you should also demonstrate understanding that useful load is the difference between the actual weight and the basic empty weight. Payload, on the other hand, is the weight of occupants, baggage, and cargo.

The basic empty weight of the airplane you will be flying can be determined only by checking the weight and balance forms provided for that aircraft. To obtain the loaded weight of the airplane, you simply add to the basic empty weight the weight of the fuel load, the weight of the pilot and passengers, and the weight of baggage and cargo.

In computing the weight of fuel, you must recall that fuel is figured at about six pounds per gallon. As for pilot and passenger weight, you already know your own weight. If you're shy about asking the examiner for his/her weight, you can exhibit a measure of diplomacy by inquiring as to what figure he/she would recommend your using for this portion of the computation. If the examiner is shy about revealing his/her weight, you may just be reminded that it will be sufficient to use the standard average weight of 170 pounds per person.

In addition to checking the weight, you are required also to show that you understand that this weight must be appropriately distributed for your particular airplane. You'll explain that the airplane's balance is determined by locating its center of gravity (CG), which is the imaginary point where the airplane would be balanced if it were suspended from a single point. The CG limits are the locations, forward and aft of this point, within which the CG of the airplane must be located for all operations. These limits are usually specified in inches from a reference datum, i.e., another imaginary point from which all horizontal distances are measured for balance purposes (Fig. 1-2). You can't be given that piece of datum here, of course, because it varies, being located on the airplane's nose for some airplanes, or at some point forward of the nose for others, or even within the airplane itself. Make sure you have located this information on the equipment/weight and balance information for the airplane which you will be flying.

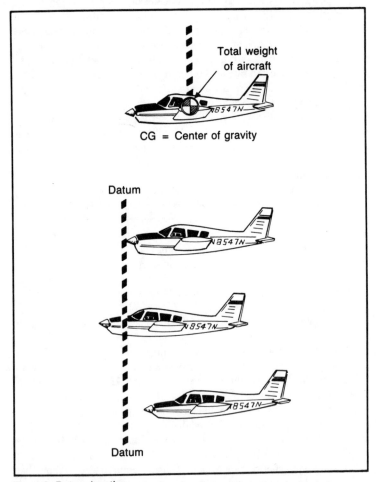

Fig. 1-2. Datum location.

Effects of Weight and Balance on Performance. In explaining the effects of weight, you'll need to discuss how weight determines the loads imposed on the airplane during takeoff, flight, and landing. You must recall from your ground school training that the term *load factor* is central to this explanation. Load factor, you'll explain, is the ratio of actual weight. You compute it simply by dividing (1) the actual load being applied to the airplane's structure by (2) the total weight of the airplane. The resultant quotient, or ratio, is expressed as "Gs," "G" being the force of gravity, or the actual weight of the airplane you'll be flying.

When the aircraft is at rest on the ground, or flying in a uniform climb or straight and level flight in smooth air, the load factor is one G, or the aircraft's loaded weight. However, because of centrifugal force, the airplane will "weigh more" in a turn. A smooth, 60-degree banked turn will impose a load of 2Gs on the airplane, i.e., cause it to "weigh" twice its normal loaded weight. Similar additional loads can be imposed when the airplane is flying in gusty air, which is why you operate at or below maneuvering speed when flying in turbulence. Consequently, overloading an airplane can either decrease the airplane's performance to a dangerous level or impose stress that risks structural damage.

Similarly, maintaining the CG limits within the recommended range assures safe airplane control through all flight speed ranges. However, attempting to fly when the limits are exceeded creates risks related to control. Locating the CG forward of the forward limit requires heavy elevator force to pull the nose up, may prohibit adequate elevator force to hold the tail down in a tail-low altitude during landing, increases stall speed significantly, etc. If the weight is distributed in such fashion that the aft CG exceeds the aft limits, then the airplane becomes tailheavy, making it difficult to recover after a maneuver. The plane also becomes more unstable, to the point of reducing chances of recovery from a stall or a spin (Fig. 1-3). The conditions created by an out-of-balance airplane are mild at first, but become increasing severe as the CG moves further from the CG range. Because of the seating arrangements and location of baggage compartments on most airplanes that you'd normally use for your checkride, the aft CG limit is more likely to be exceeded. Consequently, you should generally load the heavier passengers and cargo forward and locate the lighter loads in the aft area.

Using Charts, Tables, and Data to Compute Weight and Balance. Although the objective treats the use of charts, tables, and graphs on the one hand, and computation on the other, as separate and distinct items, we will combine them. The approach in the objectives confuses by presenting the items separately and, in addition, reverses the natural order of things. In actual practice, you'll begin by using the data provided in the tables, graphs, and charts provided in the airplane's operating limitations manual and then, on the basis of these alone, or using these and computation, arrive at the appropriate analysis of weight and balance.

The airplane's manual will generally provide a sample loading prob-

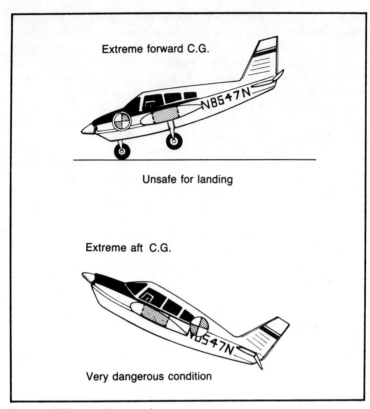

Extreme forward C.G.

Unsafe for landing

Extreme aft C.G.

Very dangerous condition

Fig. 1-3. Difficult stall recoveries.

lem alone with space for you to do the computation for your particular flight (Fig. 1-4). Item 1 will be provided in your airplane's equipment/weight and balance data. You'll simply copy this information on the table. Item 3 will require your input for weight along with the data taken from the chart (Fig. 1-5). Items 4, 5, and 6 will be completed in the same manner.

You will then total the weight and moment columns by addition. In the sample, you can see that the total weight was 1600 pounds, and the moment 57.9 inches. Now, using this data, simply look at the center of gravity moment envelope (Fig. 1-6) to see that the weight (1600 pounds) and moment (57.9 inches) fall within the envelope. Your airplane is within limits.

There may be some situations in which you may be required to do some computation. In such instances, you'll record data from the operating handbook and from the factors (pilot and passengers, fuel, baggage, etc.) of your particular flight. In such a case (Fig. 1-7), you would enter whatever items are provided by the operating handbook or the factors you provide regarding your flight. You'll notice that you must calculate the moment for each entry. (Arm aft datum will be found in the operating manual.) You must also add all the weights and moments. Next, you divide the total moment by the total weight to determine the distance of the airplane's loaded CG from the datum. Having completed all these calculations, you can now compare the aircraft's CG and weight with the limits. As you can see, the weight does not exceed the maximum and the CG is within limits.

These approaches are typical. If you find that your aircraft's manual uses tables listing useful load weights and moments, you'll not be required to do any computation. Instead, you simply pick the numbers appropriate to your actual flight and check these against the limits provided by table.

SAMPLE LOADING PROBLEM	SAMPLE AIRPLANE		YOUR AIRPLANE	
	Weight (lbs.)	Moment (lb.-ins. /1000)	Weight (lbs.)	Moment (lb.-ins. /1000)
1. Licensed Empty Weight (Sample Airplane)...	1038	34.1		
2. Oil (6 qts. - Full oil may be assumed for all flights)	11	-0.1	11	-0.1
3. Fuel (Standard - 22.5 gal at 6 lbs./gallon)...	135	5.7		
Fuel (Long Range - 35 gal. at 6 lbs./gallon). .				
4. Pilot and Passenger.	340	13.3		
5. Baggage - Area 1 (or children on child's seat)	76	4.9		
6. Baggage - Area 2.				
7. TOTAL WEIGHT AND MOMENT	1600	57.9		

8. Locate this point (1600 at 57.9) on the center of gravity moment envelope, and since this point falls within the envelope, the loading is acceptable.

BAGGAGE LOADING AND TIE-DOWN

UTILITY SHELF

BAGGAGE AREA
MAXIMUM ALLOWABLE LOADS

AREA (1) = 120 POUNDS
AREA (2) = 40 POUNDS
AREAS (1) + (2) = 120 POUNDS

✶ TIE-DOWN NET ATTACH POINTS

✶ A cargo tie-down net is provided to secure baggage in the baggage area. The net attaches to six tie-down rings. Two rings are located on the floor just aft of the seat backs and one ring is located two inches above the floor on each cabin wall at the aft end of area (1). Two additional rings are located at the top, aft end of area (2). At least four rings should be used to restrain the maximum baggage load of 120#.

If the airplane is equipped with an optional utility shelf, it should be removed prior to loading and tying down large baggage items. (Slide the tab of the locking clips on each end of the shelf to disengage the shelf from the aircraft structure.) After baggage is loaded and secured, either stow the shelf or, if space permits, install it for storing small articles.

Fig. 1-4. Loading samples.

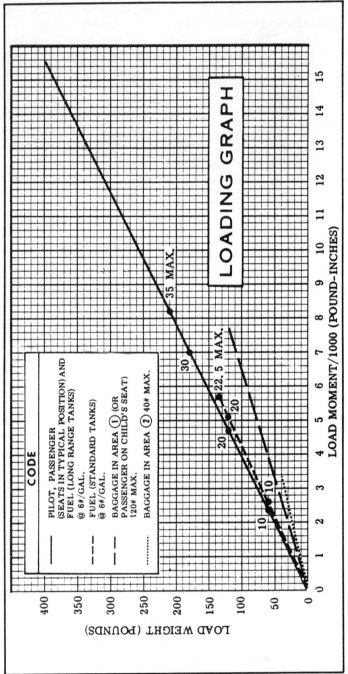

Fig. 1-5. Loading graph.

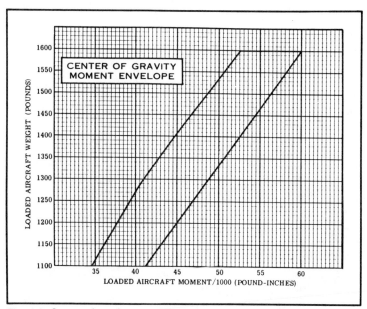

Fig. 1-6. Center of gravity moment envelope.

In any case, be sure that you check the operating manual provided for the airplane you'll be flying and familiarize yourself with whatever method is used. If it differs from the samples given above, it should be close enough to require no more than a few minutes of study. Whatever method is used, the manual will provide instructions and sample uses. Prior to meeting with your examiner, work out the weight and balance problem so that you can handle it with confidence when required to do so for the test.

The Effects of Conditions on Airplane Performance. In addition to the tables, graphs, and charts on weight and balance, the airplane's man-

CG Location Limits: 84.0 to 95.8 inches aft of datum Maximum Certificated Weight=2,150 lbs	Weight (Lbs)	Arm Aft Datum (Inches)	Moment (In-Lbs)
Basic Empty Weight	1,290	85.0	109,650.0
Pilot and Front Passenger	285	85.5	24,367.5
Passengers, Aft	290	117.0	33,930.0
Fuel (50 Gallon Maximum)	240	95.0	22,800.0
Baggage Area 1			
Baggage Area 2	45	133.3	5,998.5
Total Loaded Airplane	2150	91.5	196,746.0

Fig. 1-7. Weight and balance worksheet: (1) multiply columns; (2) and (3) add; (4) divide moment by weight and check CG.

TAKE-OFF DISTANCE — FLAPS RETRACTED — HARD SURFACE RUNWAY

GROSS WT. LBS.	IAS 50 FT. MPH	HEAD WIND KNOTS	AT SEA LEVEL & 59°F.		AT 2500 FT. & 50°F.		AT 5000 FT. & 41°F.		AT 7500 FT. & 32°F.	
			GROUND RUN	TOTAL TO CLEAR 50 FT. OBS	GROUND RUN	TOTAL TO CLEAR 50 FT. OBS	GROUND RUN	TOTAL TO CLEAR 50 FT. OBS	GROUND RUN	TOTAL TO CLEAR 50 FT. OBS
1600	68	0	735	1385	910	1660	1115	1985	1360	2440
		10	500	1035	630	1250	780	1510	970	1875
		20	305	730	395	890	505	1090	640	1375

NOTES: 1. Increase the distances 10% for each 35°F. increase in temperature above standard for the particular altitude.
2. For operation on a dry, grass runway, increase distances (both "ground run" and "total to clear 50 ft. obstacle") by 7% of the "total to clear 50 ft. obstacle" figure.

MAXIMUM RATE-OF-CLIMB DATA

GROSS WEIGHT LBS.	AT SEA LEVEL & 59°F.			AT 5000 FT. & 41°F.			AT 10000 FT. & 23°F.		
	IAS, MPH	RATE OF CLIMB FT./MIN.	FUEL USED, GAL.	IAS, MPH	RATE OF CLIMB FT./MIN.	FUEL USED FROM S.L., GAL.	IAS, MPH	RATE OF CLIMB FT./MIN.	FUEL USED FROM S.L., GAL.
1600	74	670	0.6	71	440	1.6	67	220	3.0

NOTES: 1. Flaps retracted, full throttle, mixture leaned to smooth operation above 5000 ft.
2. Fuel used includes warm-up and take-off allowances.
3. For hot weather, decrease rate of climb 15 ft./min. for each 10°F above standard day temperature for particular altitude.

LANDING DISTANCE — FLAPS LOWERED TO 40°. POWER OFF — HARD SURFACE RUNWAY - ZERO WIND

GROSS WEIGHT LBS.	APPROACH SPEED, IAS. MPH	AT SEA LEVEL & 59°F.		AT 2500 FT. & 50°F.		AT 5000 FT. & 41°F.		AT 7500 FT. & 32°F.	
		GROUND ROLL	TOTAL TO CLEAR 50 FT. OBS	GROUND ROLL	TOTAL TO CLEAR 50 FT. OBS	GROUND ROLL	TOTAL TO CLEAR 50 FT. OBS	GROUND ROLL	TOTAL TO CLEAR 50 FT. OBS
1600	60	445	1075	470	1135	495	1195	520	1255

NOTES: 1. Decrease the distances shown by 10% for each 4 knots of headwind.
2. Increase the distance by 10% for each 60°F. temperature increase above standard.
3. For operation on a dry, grassy runway, increase distances (both "ground roll" and "total to clear 50 ft. obstacle") by 20% of the "total to clear 50 ft. obstacle" figure.

Fig. 1-8. Takeoff, climb, and landing data.

ual will also provide data on performance in relation to conditions such as density altitude, wind, terrain, etc. You will be expected to read and interpret tables regarding takeoff distance, rate of climb, landing distance (Fig. 1-8), cruise performance (Fig. 1-9), and the like. Some aircraft also provide similar graphs providing data regarding the effects of density altitude (Fig. 1-10). Such graphs are not difficult to read and interpret, but you need to be familiar enough with those provided for your particular airplane so that you can perform confidently when called on to calculate your airplane's performance.

Describing the Effects. Beyond doing some actual calculations using aircraft operating charts and graphs, you may also be called on to tell about other effects that may not be present for your particular flight. For exam-

CRUISE PERFORMANCE ——— WITH LEAN MIXTURE

ALTITUDE	RPM	%BHP	TAS MPH	GAL/HR.	END. HOURS STANDARD 22.5 GAL.	END. HOURS LONG RANGE 35 GAL.	RANGE, MILES STANDARD 22.5 GAL.	RANGE, MILES LONG RANGE 35 GAL.
2500	2750	92	121	7.0	3.2	5.0	390	605
	2700	87	119	6.6	3.4	5.3	410	635
	2600	77	114	5.8	3.9	6.1	445	690
	2500	68	108	5.1	4.4	6.9	475	740
	2400	60	103	4.6	4.9	7.7	505	790
	2300	53	96	4.1	5.5	8.6	535	830
	2200	46	89	3.6	6.2	9.7	550	860
	2100	40	79	3.2	7.0	10.9	555	865
5000	2750	85	121	6.4	3.5	5.5	425	660
	2700	80	118	6.0	3.8	5.8	445	690
	2600	71	113	5.3	4.2	6.6	475	740
	2500	63	107	4.8	4.7	7.4	505	790
	2400	56	101	4.3	5.3	8.2	530	830
	2300	49	93	3.8	5.9	9.2	550	860
	2200	43	84	3.4	6.6	10.3	560	870
	2100	37	71	3.0	7.5	11.7	540	835
7500	2700	74	117	5.5	4.1	6.3	480	745
	2600	66	111	4.9	4.6	7.1	505	790
	2500	58	105	4.4	5.1	7.9	535	830
	2400	52	98	4.0	5.7	8.8	555	860
	2300	45	89	3.6	6.3	9.8	560	875
	2200	40	77	3.2	7.1	11.1	550	850
10,000	2700	68	116	5.1	4.4	6.8	510	790
	2600	61	109	4.6	4.9	7.6	535	830
	2500	54	102	4.1	5.4	8.5	555	865
	2400	48	93	3.7	6.1	9.4	565	880
	2300	42	82	3.3	6.8	10.6	555	860
12,500	2650	60	110	4.5	5.0	7.8	550	855
	2600	56	106	4.3	5.3	8.2	555	865
	2500	50	97	3.9	5.8	9.1	565	880
	2400	44	86	3.5	6.5	10.1	560	870

NOTES: 1. Maximum cruise is normally limited to 75% power.
2. In the above calculations of endurance in hours and range in miles, no allowances were made for take-off or reserve.

Fig. 1-9. Cruise performance.

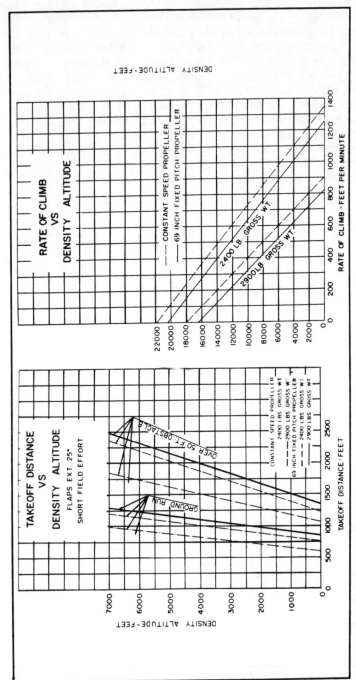

Fig. 1-10. Density altitude—feet.

ple, you may take your test on a cool, dry early winter's day when your airplane is performing exceptionally well. The examiner may reasonably expect you to know that things will be different when you're flying during the heat and humidity of a mid-summer's day. You should be able to explain the effects of conditions such as temperature and humidity on aircraft and engine performance. You should also be able to explain the effects of phenomena such as ice and frost. In addition, be prepared as well with explanations as to how you meet these conditions, such as carrying lighter loads or allowing for longer takeoff runs and landing rollouts when faced with heat and humidity, or clearing the flying surfaces of frost prior to attempting flight.

Again, on the basis of data regarding the airplane's performance as this is affected by weight and balance, by atmospheric conditions and the like, you'll be expected to make a decision as to whether or not to fly. The examiner will expect *you* to make the decision. Make it on the side of safety. If the examiner then determines that his/her experience with such conditions is such that your decision may be safely overridden, so be it, but you must make the decision that you'd make in the situation in which you are the pilot-in-command.

D. TASK: CROSS–COUNTRY FLIGHT PLANNING (ASEL)

PILOT OPERATION – 7

REFERENCES: AC 61–21, AC 61–23, AC 61–84.

1. **Objective.** To determine that the applicant:

   a. Exhibits adequate knowledge by planning, within 30 minutes, a VFR cross–country flight of a duration near the range of the airplane considering fuel and loading.

   b. Selects and uses current and appropriate aeronautical charts.

   c. Plots a course for the intended route of flight with fuel stops, if necessary.

   d. Selects prominent en route check points.

   e. Computes the flight time, headings, and fuel requirements.

   f. Selects appropriate radio navigation aids and communication facilities.

   g. Identifies airspaces, obstructions, and alternate airports.

   h. Extracts pertinent information from the Airport/Facility Directory and other flight publications, including NOTAM's.

   i. Completes a navigation log.

   j. Completes and files a VFR flight plan.

2. **Action.** The examiner will:

   a. Ask the applicant to plan, within 30 minutes, a VFR cross–country flight of a duration near the range of the airplane considering fuel and loading.

   b. Ask the applicant to explain cross–country planning procedures, and determine that the applicant's performance meets the objective.

   c. Place emphasis on the applicant's knowledge and accuracy in planning the cross–country flight.

Objective: What is expected of the applicant regarding cross-country flight planning.

Planning the VFR Cross-Country Flight. Depending on the point of view of your examiner, you may or may not know in advance the route and destination of the flight you'll be called on to plan. An examiner with whom I worked for many years did not believe in keeping such matters a secret. His use of the same airport of destination was not for the purpose of saving himself the trouble of continuously checking the planning for each new examinee; he had selected the destination with great care because it presented a real challenge to the student pilots who were taking their Private Pilot Practical Test. The airport selected required enroute and arrival planning that not only called on considerable knowledge on the part of the applicant, but also provided a rich learning experience for him/her.

The examiner's selection required the student to take into account whether or not he/she would use a Victor airway, how to use the various enroute navigation aids, such as when to change over from one VOR station to another, how to take into account the TCA that overlay the area of the destination airport but which would be avoided by the student's planning carefully, etc. His approach also seemed more realistic in view of the fact that it seems highly unlikely that a private pilot will ever arrive at an airport completely in the dark about where he/she may be flying and having only 30 minutes to plan such a flight. Hopefully, for your practical test, you'll have such an examiner as this one.

Whatever its destination or routing, you may be assured that the flight you'll be required to plan will be of such duration that it will approach the airplane's maximum range, necessitating very careful consideration of the airplane's fuel capacities and the loading arrangements that will be required. You may be placed in the predicament—for planning purposes only, of course—of having to make some choice between fuel and passengers, or fuel and luggage or cargo.

One important consideration regarding this requirement is to avoid becoming rattled. You know that there is going to be such a requirement. You'll have to do the planning just as though you were making the flight, even though you won't be making the entire flight during the flight checkride. Therefore, think the requirement through in advance and anticipate how you will handle it, rehearsing the steps that you'll be going through. In fact, since you've probably saved the materials from your cross-country instructional flights, it might be helpful to review these in advance of going for the practical test. On the day of the test, make sure that you take all charts needed, along with your plotter and computer, flight log forms, and flight plan forms.

Selecting and Using Current and Appropriate Charts. For your flight planning purposes, you'll undoubtedly be using Sectional Charts rather than WAC charts. You may also need to carry VFR Terminal Area Charts, depending on your location and that of the destination airport you'll be using for flight planning purposes. You might also find it useful to have a

VFR Planning Chart. The examiner will not expect you to carry in your head the different scales of the various charts, but he/she might expect you at least to know that you'll be using the Sectional with its scale of about eight miles to one inch rather than the WAC chart (with a scale of about 16 miles to the inch) because the former contains more of the information you'll be needing for the specific area in which you'll be flying. Besides, it's more suited for the type of flying that you would expect to be doing as a private pilot. In view of the fact that the Sectionals are revised and issued every six months, it's important that you check the expiration date of the Sectionals you'll be using to be certain that they are current. Also, it may be a good idea to have with you the Sectional that adjoins that which you'll be using for your planning. If your route passes near the edge of the chart, some features on the adjoining chart may be relevant to your projected route. Or, in planning for a diversion due to weather, you may find that the nearest airport is located on the chart adjoining the one containing the course you've laid out.

Having completed your ground school and passed the FAA written test, you'll experience no difficulty in using the Sectional Charts. Most of the information listed on them will be obvious and/or self-explanatory. Once you've selected your route, however, it is important to see all the data that the chart you're using provides. Don't inadvertently plot a course through a prohibited zone or ignore significant terrain features or obstacles. If you come across symbols on your Sectional that you're unfamiliar with, use the legend that appears on every chart to identify the feature (Fig. 1-11). **Plotting the Course.** If you need to cross over to another chart, or to move to the other side of the chart on which you're doing your planning, you'll find it helpful to fold your Sectional in such a fashion that the transition is simplified.

Your course may be a single straight line out on the Sectional using your plotter or some other straight edge, or it may be a series of such straight lines. Which it is will depend on a number of factors, including navigation aids, features such as controlled airspaces, consideration of the need for fuel stops, and the like. Since the flight proposed by your examiner will undoubtedly carry you near the range of your airplane, planning for fuel stops will be a necessary consideration. Additionally, your planning should include information on alternatives in the event that the planned flight cannot be completed. In this planning, always allow at least 45 minutes of reserve fuel. If arrival at your destination does not permit this, then it will be necessary to plan for an enroute fuel stop.

You must also clarify when your examiner makes the assignment whether he/she intends for you to do the planning necessary only to reach the destination or whether you are also to plan for a return trip.

Selection of Checkpoints. Having drawn your route of flight on the appropriate Sectional chart(s), you will examine the route of flight for checkpoints. The number of checkpoints will be determined by the distance of the flight, the availability of prominent checkpoints, and the conditions of

Fig. 1-11. Aeronautical symbols.

flight. As you select the checkpoints along the plotted course, circle them in such a manner that they can be prominently seen. Beyond being indicated on the chart(s), each checkpoint will also be recorded on the flight log. (More on the flight log later.)

A number of considerations will guide your selection of checkpoints. In the first place, keep in mind that all features shown on the charts may not be readily visible from the air. For example, in choosing towns as checkpoints, rely on those that appear as yellow extensions of color rather than as simply dots or small circles. The towns represented by patches of color will be identifiable as towns, whereas the circle or dot may represent a cluster of only a half dozen or so dwellings.

The selection of checkpoints that are both prominent and readily identifiable will not only impress your examiner, but will help instill this practice when you engage in planning on your own, adding considerably to the confidence with which you'll undertake cross-country flights.

Performing the Required Computation. Your computation will begin with the measurement of the true course. You'll of course need to measure the course in terms of distance in order to later compute flight time and fuel requirements. In addition, you'll also need to identify the true course. To do this, simply place the small hole in the center of the plotter directly over an intersection of the true course line and one of the longitude lines on the chart. Next, align the plotter edge adjacent to the protractor with the true course line that you've drawn. Now read from the scale of the protractor that lies directly over the longitude line. Use the

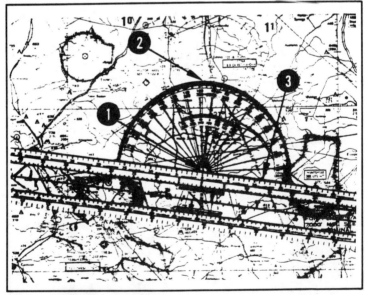

Fig. 1-12. Measuring true course.

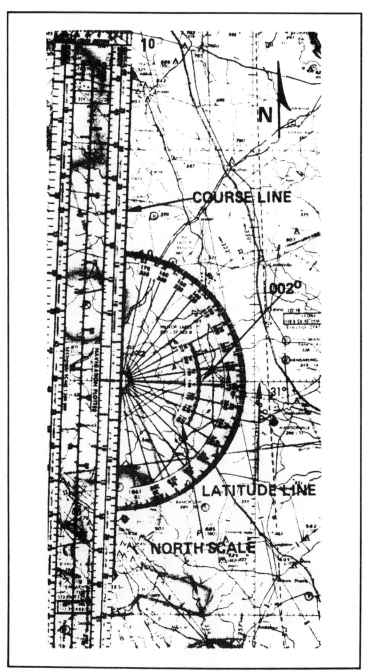

Fig. 1-13. Measuring a north-south true course line.

outside scale for measuring easterly courses, and the inside scale for westerly courses (Fig. 1-12).

If your true course is such that it lies in a northerly or southerly direction and does not cross meridian, it will be necessary to use the special innermost north-south scales on the plotter. In such a case, you'll still lay the same plotter edge along the true course that you've drawn. However, this time the hole should be placed over the intersection of the true course line and a line of latitude. You'll then read the true course using the point where the north-south scale directly overlies the latitude line (Fig. 1-13).

If your plotter is the rotating azimuth type, then use these steps: First, place the plotter parallel to the course line. Holding the plotter stationary, rotate the protractor until the arrowed lines point north, parallel to a line of longitude. Now read the true course at the "course arrow" that points in the appropriate direction. The other "course arrow," of course, gives you the reciprocal of your true course (Fig. 1-14). The true course should be recorded in the appropriate space in the navigation log.

As you've learned from your cross-country flights, the *true course* is the projected or intended direction of flight. However, the direction in which the nose of the airplane is actually pointed during flight is the *true heading*. True heading can be graphically represented by the wind triangle, which can be used to determine ground speed, heading, and time. You've probably done this during your ground school. Generally, this is done to aid the student in understanding the effects of wind.

However, for your flight planning for the practical test, it is not necessary. What you'll rely on instead is the computation that you may have done with the E6B computer or, as is increasingly likely, with an electronic navigation computer. If you are using the former, the instructions are printed

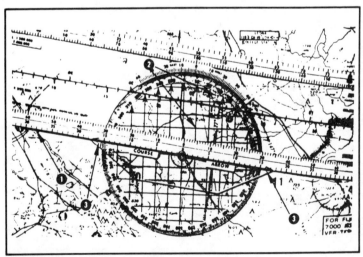

Fig. 1-14. Rotating azimuth plotter.

on the computer itself. If you haven't used it lately, a little practice with a few problems the night before your practical test would be helpful.

If you're using the electronic computer, it becomes even simpler. With the computer in the "Wind" mode, enter the information that you've obtained from your weather briefing, i.e., wind direction and wind velocity, along with the airplane's true airspeed (from the operating manual) and the true course. Now, it's just a matter pressing the "Comp" and "Hdg" keys to see the true heading displayed. This information can also be listed on the flight log. While the information is still in the electronic computer's memory, you can also obtain the anticipated ground speed by pressing "Comp" and "GS/FPH," which will also be entered in the flight log.

Use the dashed magneta lines on the Sectional Chart to obtain magnetic variation affecting your projected cross-country flight. On a long flight, crossing many such lines, compensation must be made for changing variation. On short flights, since the variation will not be changing appreciably, the variation nearest the center of the course is used. For the necessary computation to obtain the magnetic heading, keep in mind the mnemonic device you learned in ground school: "East is least and west is best," which means subtracting easterly variation or adding westerly variation to the true heading.

One of the last steps in this computation is establishing the compass heading. Remember that this is obtained for your particular airplane by reading the compass correction card attached to the plane's magnetic compass. This takes care of the compass deviation caused by the magnetic interference of parts of your aircraft. This item will also be entered in the appropriate place on your flight log.

Beyond the computations just covered, the flight time and fuel requirements must also be ascertained. If you're using the older mechanical computer, it's a simpler matter. Using the calculator side, you simply rotate the disc until the speed indicator is directly beneath and pointing to the speed at which your aircraft will be flying. Next, using that same scale on which your speed is located, follow the scale around clockwise until you come to the number that represents your distance. Now directly beneath that number you may read the figure that represents the time required (Fig. 1-15). Fuel consumption is calculated in the same manner except that "gallons per hour" and "gallons" are used instead of knots or miles per hour and miles.

Using the electronic computer for the same problem requires the use of the "T-S-D" mode. You simply enter the distance and the ground speed; then press the "Comp" and "Time" keys for your time. For fuel consumption, employ the same mode. Simply enter the hourly fuel consumption (obtained from the operating handbook) and the flight time. Now press the "Comp" and "Dst/Fuel" keys for the total fuel requirement. When computing fuel requirements, however, recall that you are to add 45 minutes reserve to the minimum requirements, even though this exceeds the amount required by FARs.

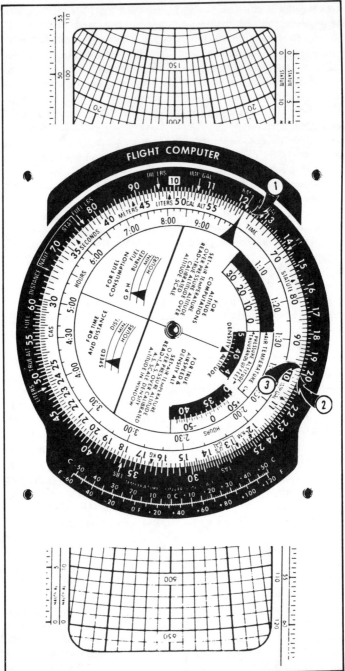

Fig. 1-15. Flight computer.

34

Radio Navigation Aids and Communications Facilities. You should now return to your charts in order to select the systems that you will use for navigation. Most likely, you'll be using whatever VOR facilities are appropriate for your route of flight, though occasionally you may be called on to utilize a Nondirectional Radiobeacon (NDB). You should note the location of those that you'll be using, listing the facilities on your flight log in the appropriate places. Include as well the frequency and the Morse code identifier. You might also note the radial(s) that you'll be using.

In addition, you should also select those communications facilities that you may be utilizing, recording the appropriate frequencies on your flight log. Minimally, this would include any communications frequencies at the airports of departure and destination. Those frequencies that are not found on the Sectional will need to be obtained from the appropriate flight publications. (More on that later.) Any enroute facilities that you might anticipate using should also be listed by name and frequency.

Identification of Special Enroute Features. As a part of your cross-country flight planning, you should also look for indicated airspaces and any possible obstructions to your route of flight. If your proposed route appears to carry you through any controlled airspaces, you will need to make note of that. If a controlled airspace is not prohibited, check the conditions under which you may fly over, under, or through such areas. Note on your flight log both the airspace and the requirements. This information, of course, may be obtained from the Sectional Chart used for your other planning. Note any terrain or other features that might have some bearing on your flight planning causing you to deviate from a straight line course to the destination airport or to the next navigation aid. You should also identify other airports that might serve as alternates to your planned flight in the event that weather or some other unforeseen circumstances causes you to deviate from your flight plan. Note such alternates on your flight log.

Using Flight Publications. In your ground school training, you'll have learned about various publications available to the pilot. One of these, the *Airman's Information Manual* of basic flight information and operating practices, is invaluable to you as a pilot, but is not useful for this type of cross-country flight planning. The publications that you'll rely on will be sections B and C, the *Airport/Facility Directory* and NOTAMS. The *Airport/Facility Directory* contains lists of airports, heliports, and seaplane bases open to the public. In the front of the volume for each region covered is a legend that clarifies the information listed including location, runway data, services available, communications facilities, navigation aids, and the like. It is essential that you consult this publication (Fig. 1-16).

It is from this publication that you'll learn about such significant matters as runways available, along with their length, surface, lighting, etc. You'll also learn about any special features of the airport, including such items as unusual traffic patterns, necessary precautions, etc. All the communications facilities will be listed, along with radio aids to navigation.

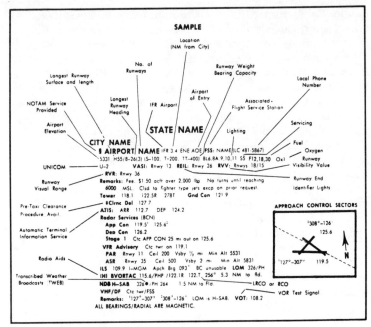

Fig. 1-16. Sample *Airport Directory* page.

You must examine very carefully and thoroughly the entries for the airports you'll be using for your flight planning.

You must also consult the Notices to Airmen. NOTAM information is regularly passed along to flyers by telephone and/or radio. However, the examiner will expect you to have consulted this publication for information that could affect your planning. You need to know about such information as airport closures, interruptions to navigation aids service, etc., which will be found in NOTAM-D. It's also useful to obtain information from NOTAM-L regarding taxiway closings, men or equipment that may be crossing runways, and similar information that will not alter your go/no-go decision but may be factors in safe operations. The latter information may have to be obtained from the FSS serving the airport concerned.

Navigation Log. Throughout this section on cross-country flight planning, references have been made to recording entries on the flight log, or navigation log (Fig. 1-17). By the time you've reached this stage of your cross-country flight planning, having completed the preceding steps, your navigation log will have been nearly completed. You need only review it now to ascertain that all necessary entries have been made and/or to add any finishing details in order to make your planning complete.

As you plotted your course, you would have listed the checkpoints for your intended route of flight. As you computed the heading (perhaps using the mnemonic device *True Virgins Make Dull Company* signifying True

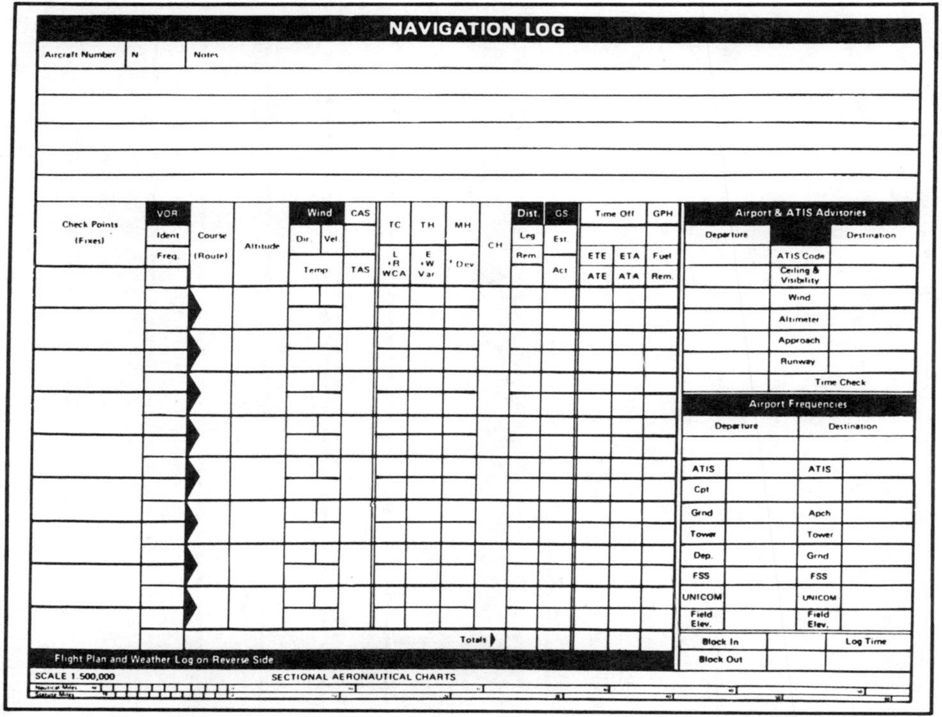

Fig. 1-17. Navigation log.

+ Variation = Magnetic + Deviation = Compass Heading), you'll have been entering these pieces of information in the appropriate columns of the navigation log. Your various speeds (true, ground), distances, times, and fuel consumption entries will have been made. You'll also have entered the various navigation aids and communications frequencies. You'll also have, in the "Notes" section, listed appropriate comments regarding airspaces, possible obstructions, and alternate airport(s). Since you'll already (prior to beginning the flight planning) have obtained a weather briefing, that data will have been entered on the weather log section.

To complete the navigation or flight log, you need only to complete the columns on altitude and estimated departure, enroute, and arrival times, checking to see that the estimated times for each leg between checkpoints actually total the time you estimated for total flying time. Having done all this, go over the navigation log one more time to make sure that the information is complete and correct. If you could make the trip relying solely on this log, then your planning is essentially complete. Of course, you won't ever make a cross-country flight relying solely on the flight log, but your planning should be thorough enough to enable you to do that. You'll always use the Sectional Charts too, because the time will come when you'll need to deviate from your projected flight and will need the Sectionals with you to enable you to do any necessary in-flight planning.

The VFR Flight Plan. The finished flight log provides nearly all the data needed for completing a Flight Plan form (Fig. 1-18). The form is, for the most part, self-explanatory. You'll check off the VFR box on the form. Item 2 calls for the N-number of your airplane. Item 3 is the type of aircraft and the equipment carried as indicated by the code selected from

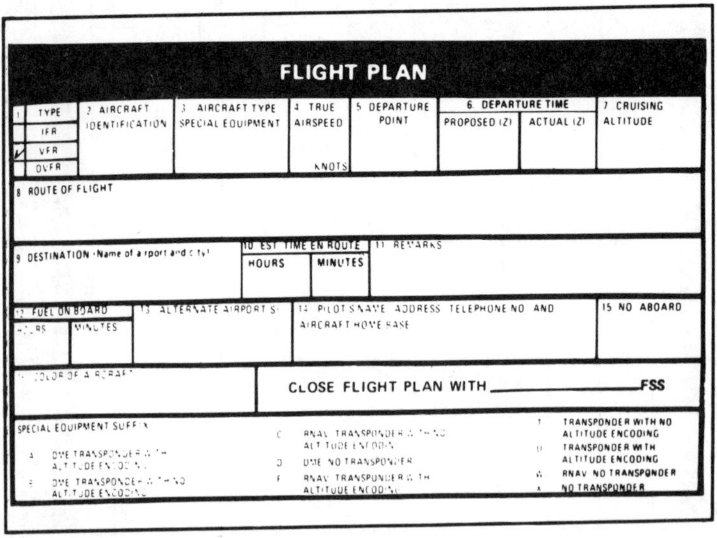
FLIGHT PLAN

1 TYPE: IFR / VFR (checked) / DVFR
2 AIRCRAFT IDENTIFICATION
3 AIRCRAFT TYPE SPECIAL EQUIPMENT
4 TRUE AIRSPEED KNOTS
5 DEPARTURE POINT
6 DEPARTURE TIME: PROPOSED (Z) / ACTUAL (Z)
7 CRUISING ALTITUDE
8 ROUTE OF FLIGHT
9 DESTINATION (Name of airport and city)
10 EST TIME EN ROUTE: HOURS / MINUTES
11 REMARKS
12 FUEL ON BOARD: HOURS / MINUTES
13 ALTERNATE AIRPORT(S)
14 PILOT'S NAME, ADDRESS, TELEPHONE NO. AND AIRCRAFT HOME BASE
15 NO. ABOARD
16 COLOR OF AIRCRAFT
CLOSE FLIGHT PLAN WITH ____________ FSS

SPECIAL EQUIPMENT SUFFIX
A DME, TRANSPONDER WITH ALTITUDE ENCODING
B DME, TRANSPONDER WITH NO ALTITUDE ENCODING
C RNAV, TRANSPONDER WITH NO ALTITUDE ENCODING
D DME, NO TRANSPONDER
F RNAV, TRANSPONDER WITH ALTITUDE ENCODING
T TRANSPONDER WITH NO ALTITUDE ENCODING
U TRANSPONDER WITH ALTITUDE ENCODING
W RNAV, NO TRANSPONDER
X NO TRANSPONDER

Fig. 1-18. Flight plan form.

the list at the bottom of the form. Items 4 through 7 need no explanation. Simply keep in mind the VFR cruising altitudes required by FARs. Also, recall that times are Zulu times. When indicating your route of flight (8), you may simply list "Direct" if that best describes it, or indicate the navigation aids and any airways you may be using. Your entry might then be a statement such as: "Dir ENO V16 VCN Dir Cross Keys." The destination entry should include both the name of the airport and the city.

Item 11 calls for remarks, but my advice is to ignore this; everyone else does. I recall trying to utilize this in the days when ATC had first switched to 360 channels for communications and my plane's equipment was limited to 180. I repeatedly informed ATC of my status in the remarks column when I filed flight plans but I was inevitably and invariably given the split channels to call when ATC communicated with me. So skip the item on alternate airports (13), since that is required only for IFR flight plans.

You can also save yourself a little time and trouble with item 14. If you contact the Flight Service Station that serves your area and enter data about yourself in their files, when you come to this portion of flight plans, you need only list your name and the remark "On file at MIV," listing, of course, the designation of your FSS.

Depending on your location, this form may be delivered by telephone or in person. If there's a Flight Service Station at your airport of departure, you can simply hand it to the person who gives you your briefing. If you need to file by telephone, you can obtain the local calling number by consulting the *Airport/Facility Directory*. Your examiner will undoubtedly advise you regarding the filing. He/she may have you go through the procedure even though the planned flight is not to be completed. You need not worry about cancelling such a flight plan, because the examiner will not have you activate it when you become airborne for your practical test and it will therefore be cancelled an hour after the proposed departure time.

* **E. TASK:** **AIRPLANE SYSTEMS** (ASEL)

PILOT OPERATION – 1

REFERENCES: AC 61–21; Pilot's
Operating Handbook and FAA–
Approved Airplane Flight Manual.

1. **Objective.** To determine that the applicant
exhibits adequate knowledge by
explaining the airplane systems
and their operation including:

a. Primary flight controls and trim.
b. Wing flaps, leading edge devices, and
spoilers.
c. Flight instruments.
d. Landing gear –

   (1) retraction system.
   (2) indication system.
   (3) brakes and tires.
   (4) nosewheel steering.

e. Engine –

   (1) controls and indicators.
   (2) induction, carburetion, and injection.
   (3) exhaust and turbocharging.
   (4) fire detection.

f. Propeller.
g. Fuel system –

   (1) tanks, pumps, controls, and indicators.
   (2) fueling procedures.
   (3) normal operation.

h. Hydraulic system –

   (1) controls and indicators.
   (2) pumps and regulators.
   (3) normal operation.   *

i. Electrical system –

   (1) controls and indicators.

(2) alternators or generators.
(3) battery, ground power.
(4) normal operation.

j. Environmental system −

(1) heating.
(2) cooling and ventilation.
(3) controls and indicators.
(4) pressurization.

k. Ice prevention and elimination.
l. Navigation and communication.
m. Vacuum system.

2. Action.   The examiner will:

a. Ask the applicant to explain the airplane systems and their operation, and determine that the applicant's performance meets the objective.
b. Place emphasis on the applicant's knowledge of the airplane systems' operation.   *

Objective: What's expected of the applicant regarding knowledge of airplane systems and their operation.

Unlike most of the practical test, this section will not be reflected in performance other than description and explanation. Your exhibition of what you know regarding airplane systems and operations will be strictly verbal. Occasionally, you may have to point to something, but essentially, you will not be doing anything other than talking.

Primary Flight Controls and Trim. The primary flight controls and trim refer to the flying surfaces that are basic or essential to flight. They are the "meat and potatoes" controls that you find on all airplanes. They consist of the ailerons, rudder, and elevators. Trim is added because you also find that control on even the simplest of trainers. You'll be expected to know that, in the case of the first three, they function by changing the shape of the flying surface, thereby altering the lift and drag characteristics.

You'll be called on to explain that the ailerons increase the lift on one

41

wing while decreasing the lift on the other. This causes the airplane to bank, you'll explain, which in turn alters the direction of lift. In its banked attitude, the lift is no longer straight up. Lift is still occurring as a consequence of the flow over the upper surface, but this surface is no longer essentially parallel to the ground. The resultant change in the forces affecting the wing causes the airplane to turn (Fig. 1-19).

The rudder, you'll point out, is the yaw control. Since the airplane banks because one wing has greater lift than the other, that raised wing, having greater lift, has greater drag as well, causing the nose of the airplane to yaw in the wrong direction. So you depress the rudder in the direction of the turn in order to overcome this adverse yaw. Assure the examiner that you recognize that the ailerons are the primary turn controls, while the rudder is simply the adverse yaw control.

There is a minor difficulty associated with the elevator (or stabilator, depending on which characterizes your airplane). The FAA would like to return to the pre-Wolfgang Langewiesche days, when this third primary control was still thought of as the up-and-down control. Some designated examiners may look for you to provide this explanation; others may want the *correct* theoretical representation. Handle it this way: Tell your examiner that the elevator is the pitch, or attitude, control. No one disputes that. The problem is that some will suggest that you use this control for climb and descent; others (like me and all True Believers) recognize that it's the primary *speed* control. Perhaps you can present it just this way—i.e., that there are these competing views—and let the examiner instruct you as to his/her views.

The other pitch control is, of course, the trim. Now, this also changes the shape of one of the flying surfaces. It may change the shape of the elevator, which in turn changes the shape of the entire horizontal tail surface consisting of the horizontal stabilizer and the elevator. Or it changes the shape of the stabilator. In either case, it increases or decreases the lift of this flying surface, which, in turn, establishes the pitch at which the airplane will fly when you are applying no forward or backward pressure on the yoke or stick.

Wing Flaps, Leading Edge Devices, and Spoilers. It's unlikely that you'll need to be concerned about anything other than wing flaps with the airplane you'll be flying for the practical test. Be sure that you explain the flaps as a device for changing the shape—and therefore the flying characteristics—of the wing. Don't make the mistake of representing flaps as brakes. Keep in mind that for many airplanes, you'll be using flaps for takeoffs as well as landings, and it wouldn't make sense to attempt a takeoff with brakes set. By altering the shape of the wing, flaps generate more lift, while creating additional drag, enabling the airplane to sustain flight at a lower airspeed, so you can use flaps to lift off in a shorter distance on takeoff or to provide a slower airspeed for landing. Beyond knowing this, you should also be familiar with the various types of flaps (Fig. 1-20).

The airplanes that are generally used for the private pilot practical test

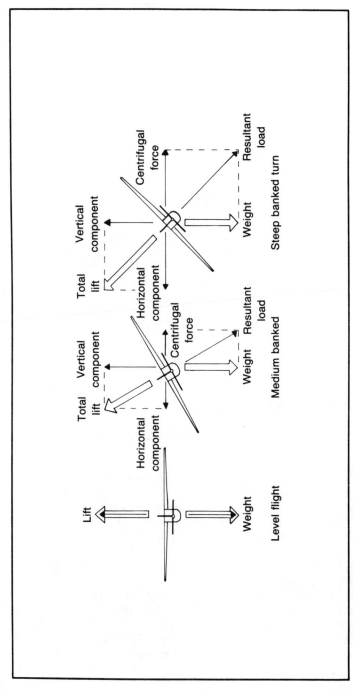

Fig. 1-19. Forces acting on an airplane in a bank.

43

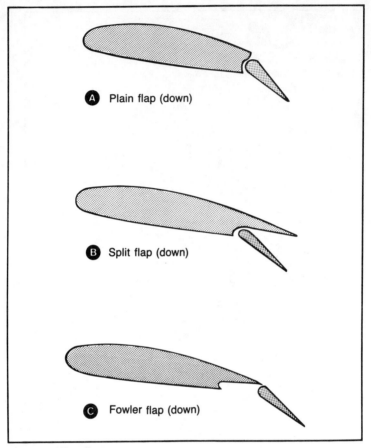

Fig. 1-20. Wing flaps.

do not have leading edge devices. If you have an airplane that does, it will not be an item over which you exercise any control. Some airplanes are equipped with slotted wings. The slot is located near the leading edge of the wing in a position that will affect the aileron. The slot is intended to allow the air to flow more smoothly over that part of the wing at a higher angle of attack, thus allowing the aileron to retain greater effectiveness when much of the rest of the wing is stalled (Fig. 1-21). Occasionally, a spoiler strip may be attached to the leading edge of the wing near the wing root. This strip breaks up the airflow at higher angles of attack, producing the desired effect of stalling the wing at the root area first (Fig. 1-21).

Flight Instruments. You're not expected to exhibit the knowledge of an instrument mechanic, but you'll be expected to know the three categories of flight instruments that are standard equipment on trainers of the type generally used for the practical test. These categories are the *pitot-*

static-associated flight instruments, the *gyroscopic flight instruments,* and *all other flight instruments,* which is the smallest group.

The pitot-static instruments are those that are in the system between the pitot tube and the static vent. The *airspeed indicator,* for example, measures the difference between the impact, or pitot, pressure and the static pressure. Obviously, the faster the airplane moves, the greater the pressure of pitot, or impact, air and the greater the difference between that and the static pressure. The difference is indicated on the face of the instrument as airspeed. You will probably be expected to recall the various airspeed indicated by colors on the indicator face. You'll recall from your ground school instruction that the white arc represents the flap operating range from the stalling speed with flaps in landing position to maximum flaps extended speed. The green represents the normal operating range

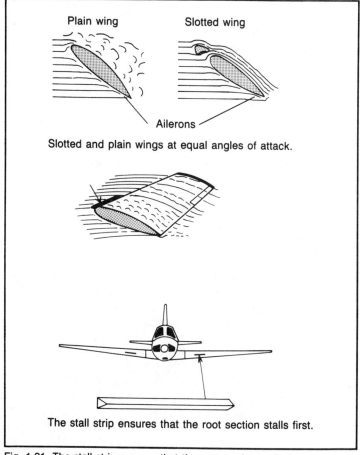

Plain wing

Slotted wing

Ailerons

Slotted and plain wings at equal angles of attack.

The stall strip ensures that the root section stalls first.

Fig. 1-21. The stall strip ensures that the root section stalls first.

from power-off stalling speed with flaps retracted to maximum structural cruising speed. The yellow range represents the caution range. (Stay out of this except in smooth air.) The red line is the never-exceed speed.

Also a part of this system is the *altimeter*. You may explain that this is really an aneroid barometer that measures the air pressure at the altitude where the altimeter is located and presents an altitude indication in feet. The largest needle represents hundreds of feet as it points towards a number, while the smaller needle represents thousands of feet as it points to a number. Some altimeters also sport a third, very tiny needle that indicates tens of thousands of feet.

The third instrument in this system is the *vertical speed indicator*. Like the altimeter, it operates strictly from the static pressure part of the system. However, this instrument is a differential pressure instrument, measuring the difference between the air in the static line and the existing atmospheric pressure. As the airplane climbs or descends, a differential pressure is created which is indicated on the instrument face as a climb or descent at a specified rate.

The gyroscopic instruments are the *turn-and-slip-indicator,* (sometimes called the *turn-and-bank indicator*), the *turn coordinator,* the *heading indicator,* and the *attitude indicator.* The airplane you'll be using for your practical test probably will use either vacuum pump or electrically driven instruments. Some older aircraft relied on a venturi tube, but this was so long ago that when today's student pilots see the venturi tube protruding from the side of one of these older airplanes, they generally have no idea what it's for and are surprised to find that instruments are operated by it. The vacuum (using a jet of air) or the electrical system spins the gyro at a high speed to establish the gyroscopic property of maintaining rigidity in space or that of precession. Some gyro instruments give their indication by remaining rigid while the airplane pitches or banks around them; others operate by precessing as the airplane moves about is axes.

The turn and slip indicator (Fig. 1-22), for example, operates by means of this latter method. When the airplane is turned or rotated about the vertical axis, a deflective force is set up causing the gyro to precess, resulting in the tilting of the gyro. As the rate of turn increases, the gyro tilts further, which is indicated on the face of the instrument as an increased rate of turn. In your explanation, you should include the information that the "doghouses" on the face of the instrument are markers for indicating turns at approximately the standard rate of 360 degrees in two minutes. (It's unlikely that your airplane's instrument will display a four-minute needle, although an occasional turn needle will. If it does, it simply means that the "doghouses" indicate a rate of turn that would require four minutes to complete 360 degrees of turn instead of the standard two minutes.) The ball part of this instrument is simply an inclinometer consisting of a sealed, curved glass tube containing kerosene and a black "aggie," or a steel ball bearing, which moves freely inside the tube. The ball seeks the lowest part of the tube unless you do something to disturb it, such as alter the balance

Fig. 1-22. Turn and slip indicator.

among the forces acting on it. If you slip or ski in a turn, the ball will tell on you. It's easy to remember what to do about this indicator; you just "step on the ball," i.e., if the ball moves to the right of center, you apply greater pressure on the right rudder, etc.

The turn coordinator, mentioned above, is simply a new version of the turn-and-slip-indicator. The needle has been replaced by a miniature airplane (Fig. 1-23). The movement of this miniature airplane about its longitudinal axis is proportional to the roll rate of the airplane. When that rate is zero—i.e., when the bank is held constant—the instrument indicates the rate of turn.

The heading indicator, or directional gyro ("DG," for short), makes it easier for the pilot to read his heading. The magnetic compass is difficult to follow with precision at times, particularly in turbulent air; the "DG" simplifies matters since it is not affected by the forces that make the compass difficult to interpret. The heading indicator, unlike the turn coordinator, depends on the principle of rigidity in space. The points of the face of the instrument (Fig. 1-24) tend to remain stationary, while the airplane rotates around them. However, since this instrument is not direction-seeking, you must provide the direction. You do this, of course, by setting the direction to correspond with that indicated by the magnetic compass. This is easy on the ground, but can get tricky in the air. However, once set, it tends to remain much more stable than the mag compass. Notice the term *tends*? Because this is a gyro instrument, it is subject to precession in response to the motion of the airplane, so you must reset it periodically. Explain to your examiner that it's necessary to keep the compass as still as possible by maintaining steady, straight and level flight while you set the DG.

The attitude indicator also operates on the gyroscopic principle of rigidity in space (Fig. 1-25). The instrument is intended to simulate outside visual references. The horizon bar and the miniature airplane portray the actual attitude of the real airplane. A knob permits adjusting the miniature aircraft upward or downward to place it on the "horizon." In a nose-high attitude, the dot representing the nose of the real airplane will be above the horizon bar. In a nose-low pitch, the miniature airplane is below the horizon bar. Similarly, in a bank to the left or right, the miniature airplane will show a similar relationship to the horizon bar. The horizon bar, of course, is maintained parallel to the actual horizon while the face of the instrument and the actual airplane revolve around it.

The "all other flight instruments" category is the easiest to handle.

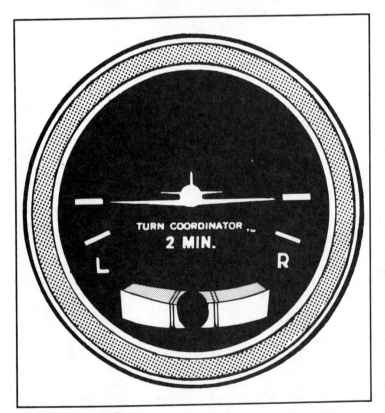

Fig. 1-23. Turn coordinator.

Fig. 1-24. Heading indicator.

It is composed of the magnetic compass. You need to recall for the examiner that this instrument is required in all airplanes, even those that are littered with sophisticated instrumentation. The advantages of the compass are: It is direction-seeking; it is reliable (though at times it may require some interpretation); it is self-contained; it is independent of external electric or vacuum power. Unfortunately, errors are associated with it and these are what you must be able to recall.

One of the errors is associated with turning. When making a turn from a heading of north (in the northern hemisphere), the compass briefly gives an indication of a turn in the opposite direction. As you continue the turn east or west, the compass will begin to indicate a turn in the right direction but will lag behind the actual turn at a diminishing rate until within a few degrees of east or west. When making a turn from a heading of south, the compass indicates a turn in the correct direction but at a faster rate than is actually being made. As the turn is continued to east or west, the indications precede the actual turn. What can I tell you that will help? Just memorize: "North lags; South leads."

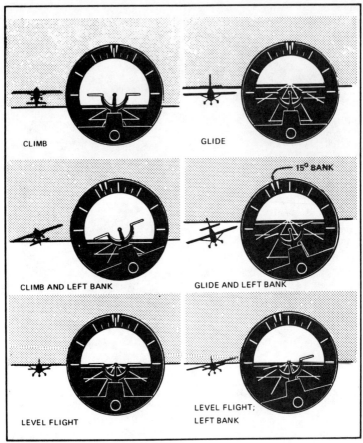

CLIMB

GLIDE

CLIMB AND LEFT BANK

GLIDE AND LEFT BANK

15° BANK

LEVEL FLIGHT

LEVEL FLIGHT;
LEFT BANK

Fig. 1-25. Relations of attitude indicator to natural horizon.

Another problem associated with the magnetic compass is that of acceleration-deceleration. Because of its pendulum-type mounting the compass card tilts during speed changes. This momentary tilting results in an error that is most noticeable on headings of east or west. When accelerating on east or west headings, the error is in the form of an indication of a turn to the north. When decelerating, the error is in the form of an indication of a turn to the south. To remember this, use the mnemonic device ANDS: Accelerate—North; Decelerate—South.

Landing Gear. The landing gear system is relatively easy to deal with. If your airplane has retractable gear (and most airplanes used for the Private Pilot Practical Test will not), then you will need to be familiar with the system. The airplane's operating handbook will tell you all you need to know. The main things the examiner will expect you to know are what makes the system operate (electricity, hydraulic fluid, a combination of these, or arm power, i.e., manual operation), and what do you do when the system fails. You will also need to explain how the indication system works, i.e., what tells you the position of the landing gear.

You should be able to explain what pilots need to look for regarding brakes and tires, i.e., how to check these externally, where you look for signs of leaks in the brake system and signs of wear on the tires, and what constitutes safety. The guide doesn't mention it, but you should also know what sort of shock system your airplane uses and how to identify both an adequate and a faulty shock system. Again, this is information that must be obtained from the operating handbook for the airplane you'll be flying. Beyond the tire itself, you should also be able to explain something about nosewheel steering. Most likely, the airplane you're using will be operated by rods and be connected to the rudder.

The Airplane Engine. You should be able to explain the engine controls that will concern you as pilot, i.e., the throttle and mixture controls and the primer. You know, of course, that the first controls the amount of fuel/air mixture that flows into the engine cylinders while the second controls the ratio of fuel to air. The primer is used to introduce vaporized fuel directly into the cylinders and its use varies with different aircraft. It is generally used to help you start the airplane engine, but you must check the operating handbook to learn the appropriate use for the particular airplane you're flying.

The indicators that will concern you will be the fuel gauge(s), oil pressure and temperature gauges, and the tachometer. You'll simply be required to know the purpose of each, what they tell you, what reading should see under various conditions, and what constitutes a warning sign. Again, you'll need to turn to the operating handbook to determine such things as the proper throttle setting and tachometer reading for the runup, etc.

You will also need to know whether your fuel system is gravity-fed (high-wing airplanes) or pump-fed (low-wing airplanes). The examiner will expect you to tell him/her what sort of induction system characterizes the engine of your plane, i.e., whether it uses a carburetor system or fuel injection system. Your knowledge of these systems will not need to go very far or deep. You already know from your ground school instruction about the role of the carburetor in mixing fuel and air properly for combustion in the combustion chamber of the cylinder. You also will recall that carburetors are subject to icing under certain conditions and you know what to do about that. Be familiar with the operation for your airplane. Cherokees, for example, need little attention because their system is less subject to icing. Cessna 150/152s, on the other hand, need to be treated very carefully. Check the operating handbook for your airplane.

Some few student pilots will be flying an airplane that uses fuel injection rather than carburetion. Several types are in use today and the operation methods are generally similar. What you should know about the system, beyond how to operate it, is that there are advantages such as a reduction in evaporative icing, better fuel flow and distribution, quicker throttle response, easier cold weather starts, and the like. There are disadvantages, too, the chief of which are troublesome hot engine starts, vapor locks on hot days, and difficulties in restarting an engine that has quit because of fuel starvation.

I recall an experience with fuel injection that impressed the last of those points on me. It was my first trip out to the practice area in an airplane that sported a fuel-injected engine. I had just completed my checkout and wanted to take a solo ride somewhere besides the airport traffic pattern. As I started to cruise along comfortably in this shiny, new Bellanca Super-viking, I confidently began to lean out the mixture, not realizing that the fuel flow gauge lagged and that the engine would not give me a warning that it was getting too lean. Carbureted engines warn you with a little initial roughness and you respond simply by enriching the mixture a bit. Since fuel injected engines feature an equal amount of fuel to all cylinders, there is no initial roughness. When you lean too far, the engine quietly and smoothly dies. That's what I accomplished. I'm not sure how long the period of relative silence lasted that day as I tried to restart, but it gave me ample time to worry about how I was going to explain an off-airport landing or, worse yet, a bent airplane. Fortunately, it restarted in plenty of time, the only consequences being a few more early grey hairs and a never-to-be-forgotten lesson about fuel injection.

You should also know a little about the exhaust system. Know where to look for the exhaust stack and what to check for. You might also explain, if your airplane is so equipped, that there's a gauge for measuring the temperature of exhaust gases at the exhaust manifold. This temperature varies with the fuel/air ration and can therefore be used to precisely regulate the fuel/air mixture. This more precise regulation can enable you to save fuel and extend engine life.

Know something about what to look for and how to respond to fire in the engine compartment. Cold weather starts with carbureted engines can create a fire hazard. We've already dealt with that. In flight, the first sign will be smoke. If it is flames, you've probably missed something and you're in graver circumstances. In any case, know what the procedures are for getting rid of any smoke in the cockpit (open a vent and let it get sucked out) and reducing whatever may be feeding the fire. Shut off electrical switches for a start and, if the situation warrants it, shut off fuel valves, too.

The Propeller. You're familiar with the fact that the prop is a rotating airfoil, another of the flying surfaces. A thorough discussion of it would be quite complex and, hopefully, beyond the scope of the practical test. The examiner will expect you to know whether your airplane has a fixed-pitched or a controllable-pitch propeller. In most cases, it will be the former. He/she may even expect you to know, in the former case, whether the airplane has a cruise prop or a climb prop. That would not be a reasonable expectation, because you can't tell by looking. (That leaves you an out. Since most trainers are equipped that way anyway, and the examiner will not be able to tell the difference, just answer with confidence, "This airplane is equipped with a climb propeller.")

If you happen to be flying an airplane with a controllable-pitch propeller, you won't be expected to know anything beyond the facts that the throttle controls manifold pressure and the propeller control regulates the rpm. Also, you should avoid high manifold pressure with low rpm settings. Know what's required for "exercising" the propeller during the runup, and know what settings are required for takeoffs and landings. In between, during cruise, you'll need to follow the recommendations in the operating handbook, although there may be a rough standard, such as "twenty-five square."

Fuel System. Much of the knowledge required here you'll have gained during preflight visual inspections of the airplane. You'll have learned how many tanks the airplane has, where they're located, drained, and strained, and where they're vented. You should also know the capacity, full and usable. The examiner will also expect you to know where fuel may be turned off, what switch positions indicate "off" and "on," and where and how to select the appropriate tank as well as what determines what. You will also, of course, be able to describe where to locate the gauges that tell you about fuel along with what they tell you.

Be familiar with refueling procedures. That involves not merely knowing where the caps are and how to take them off and put them on, but also safety requirements. It means recognizing the need for grounding before the refueling actually begins. The examiner may even expect you to know the procedures for fueling from a drum, which is essentially like refueling from any tank or tank truck. Mention that plastic or other nonconductive containers should never be used for refueling.

Hydraulic System. Probably the only hydraulic system used on the trainer you'll be flying for your practical test will be the one that operates the brakes. Check the operating manual to be sure. That handbook should contain a diagram and a brief explanation that will tell you all you'll need to know for the practical test.

Electrical System. Similarly, the airplane's operating handbook will contain a diagram, or schematic, of the electrical system (Fig. 1-26). This will show you all the components of the airplane's electrical system. The controls and indicators you'll be concerned with are the master switch, the ignition switch, and the ammeter. Be able to explain where the airplane has fuses and circuit breakers, indications of when these are "blown," and what you do about that situation. You may also be expected to know whether your airplane has an alternator or generator, though I can't imagine why. Be sure you know the voltage of the system and where the battery is located, as well as where any external power hookups are located. As for normal operation, you'll simply need to know what the indications are of any abnormality (discharging ammeter, popped circuit breaker, blown fuse, or inoperable piece of equipment). For the first, you will shut down if you're on the ground. If airborn, start turning off equipment and/or begin to plan a precautionary landing. Circuit breakers can be reset; fuses replaced. If

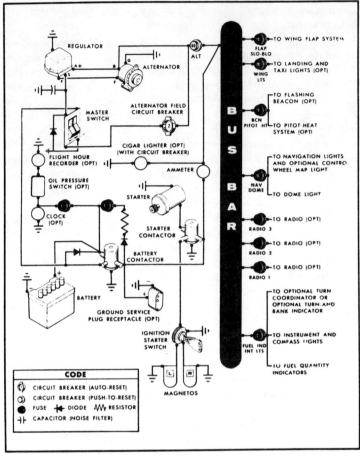

Fig. 1-26. Electrical system schematic.

they pop or blow again, then it's necessary to locate the culprit and have it checked.

Environmental System. These are the items that have to do with creature comforts. Most likely, your trainer will be warmed by heated fresh air and outside air blended in a cabin manifold somewhere aft of the firewall. Windshield defrost air is also supplied by a duct leading from the manifold. The cooling and ventilation will be provided by airflow from outside the airplane through vents that may be located in any of several locations. You'll have used these during your training and should have no difficulty describing them.

Ice Prevention and Elimination. This can have two parts—what you do on the ground and what you do in flight. If you're on the ground, you'll probably be first interested in elimination. This simply requires an explanation of the importance of ridding the airplane of ice and frost prior to flight. Prevention for most trainers means simply that you'll pull the defroster knob on to keep the windshield free. In flight, elimination means using the defroster for the windshield, pitot heat for the pitot tube, and carburetor heat to get rid of ice in the carburetor.

Navigation and Communication. There's nothing that you'll be called on to provide here that won't be covered by your preflight planning and preparation. If the examiner raises a question here that stumps you, it's a sign that your planning was inadequate, or the examiner is being unreasonable. Undoubtedly, however, you'll have dealt with this when you presented the fruits of your flight planning to the examiner.

Vacuum System. Most of the knowledge regarding this system will have been covered in your discussion of the gyro instruments. Beyond that, it's sufficient to know what drives the system and what constitutes the system. Simply check to see whether the system in your airplane operates from an engine-driven or an electric-driven pump. The only parts we haven't mentioned are the filter and the vacuum gauge. The operating handbook will give the operation range for your airplane. As a matter of fact, it's usually included on the preflight checklist. The filter is to keep the air that drives the gyros free of particles. Mention to your examiner that you know that smoke can foul up the system and that's why it's a good idea to avoid smoking in the confined interior of the airplane.

Chapter 2

AREA OF OPERATION:
GROUND OPERATIONS

A. TASK: **VISUAL INSPECTION** (ASEL)

PILOT OPERATION – 1

REFERENCES: AC 61–21; Pilot's Operating Handbook and FAA–Approved Airplane Flight Manual.

1. **Objective.** To determine that the applicant:

   a. Exhibits adequate knowledge of airplane visual inspection by explaining the reasons for checking the items.
   b. Inspects the airplane by following the checklist.
   c. Determines that the airplane is in condition for safe flight emphasizing –

   (1) fuel quantity, grade, and type.
   (2) fuel contamination safeguards.
   (3) fuel venting.
   (4) oil quantity, grade, and type.

(5) fuel, oil, and hydraulic leaks.
(6) flight controls.
(7) structural damage including exhaust system.
(8) tiedown, control lock, and wheel chock removal.
(9) ice and frost removal.
(10) security of baggage, cargo, and equipment.

d. Notes any discrepancy and determines whether the airplane is safe for flight or requires maintenance.

2. Action. The examiner will:

a. Ask the applicant to explain the reasons for checking the item during a visual inspection.
b. Observe the applicant's visual inspection procedure, and determine that the applicant's performance meets the objective.
c. Place emphasis on soundness of the applicant's judgment regarding the airplane's condition.

Objective: What's expected of the applicant regarding Visual Inspection.
Explaining the Reasons for Checking. You'll demonstrate to the examiner that you understand that safety in aviation begins on the ground. The thorough visual inspection of the airplane on the ground prior to "firing up" does more than ensure that everything is functioning. It also exhibits an attitude toward flying that you should display at all times including the occasion of your practical test. Also, generally speaking, as the pilot-in-command, you are responsible for ensuring that the airplane you are about to fly is airworthy. A part of the proficiency that you must demonstrate is preflight operations including the preflight visual inspection of the airplane.

These are general considerations. Beyond this, your performance will also include not merely looking at, nor even simply touching or manipulating, parts of the airplane. You will also provide an explanation that goes beyond the general reasons for performing the visual inspection and includes the specific reasons for checking each of the items on the checklist. As you perform each part of the inspection during the walkaround, you will tell the examiner precisely what it is you are looking for. Preflights can become rituals after a while and, as you gain more experience, much of the inspection will become second nature to you. But for the practical test, don't be content with merely silently emulating what you have seen your flight instructor doing. Be as explicit and precise as you can with your explanations.

Using the Checklist. Since you have learned that it's necessary to inspect the airplane you're about to fly before every flight, you've had plenty of practice doing this during your student pilot days. Undoubtedly, during that time, your flight instructor has made the preflight inspection so routine that you were not required to use a checklist. He/she, relying on his/her own experience and checking behind you, made the checklist unnecessary. However, for the practical test, the examiner may expect you to use a checklist. If you do not actually carry the checklist with you, make certain that your inspection follows everything that is on the list.

The surest way to make sure that you follow the checklist without carrying it with you is to establish a routine. Perform the inspection in precisely the same manner every time you do it. Also, follow some logical pattern with the visual check. I always teach my students to begin at the spot where they'll ultimately finish the inspection (Fig. 2-1).

Start with the left side of the cockpit, checking fuel quantity using the gauges. Then make sure all switches are off. Finally, before you leave the cockpit area, be sure that the gust lock, or control lock, is removed. This will enable you to move the external flight controls as you move around the airplane. Inspect those items that are in the vicinity of the door you use to enter the plane. From there, follow fuselage to the rear of the airplane, checking both fuselage and the entire empennage area. Continue around to the other side of the airplane, checking all as you go. You will then inspect the wing area on the side opposite that where you started, moving around the wing and back to the nose of the airplane. There, you'll

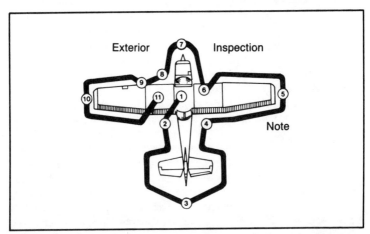

Fig. 2-1. Exterior inspection.

check all items including propeller, nose gear, engine compartment area, etc. This will bring you back to the leading edge of the wing where your inspection started. Your walkaround will take you around that wing and back to the very spot where the inspection began. Checking the plane in this same fashion every time you fly will help ensure that you follow the checklist.

Determining That the Airplane Is Airworthy. Fuel quantity will be determined in two ways: by checking the fuel gauges when you begin the visual inspection in the cockpit, and by making a visual check of the tanks. You must also determine that the proper grade of fuel is used. The proper grade and type must be obtained from the operating handbook for your particular airplane. These days, you'll usually be looking for the pale blue of 100LL for most trainers. It won't matter if it's the pale green of 100 octane and your trainer calls for 100LL, or even 80 octane. However, keep in mind that if the plane you're flying calls for 100 octane, you can't use 80. If you get anything other than the color that identifies the grade of fuel specified for your aircraft, don't go. The proper color indicates that you have both the right grade and the appropriate type.

Your inspection will also call for taking fuel samples from several locations to guard against contamination. The pilot's operating handbook will specify where the fuel drains are located. The sample should be drawn from each location into a container that permits you to actually see that the fuel is free of water, dirt, etc. If you see some of those telltale bubbles at the bottom of your sample, then empty the container and draw another sample. Continue this until the sample is entirely free of any contamination. At times you may even find it necessary simply to drain a certain amount of the fuel out of the tank before taking another sample. You're better off to run a little fuel on the ground, even if it amounts to several pints—or quarts—than to take the chance of having a quantity of water drawn into the engine's fuel system.

Similarly, you must ensure that the engine has sufficient oil for your flight. With oil as with fuel, the specifications are to be found in the operating handbook. You should know the capacity and the safe operating limits for the plane you'll be using for the test. Additionally, you must be able to tell the examiner the proper grade and the type of oil required for the airplane under the conditions you'll be meeting.

You must also be able to determine that there are no fluids leaking from the airplane. Fuel leaks can generally be recognized by discoloration around the area of the leak. As fuel leaks onto a surface and evaporates, the color remains. Where you see such discoloration, call it to the attention of whoever maintains the airplane. Oil leaks will be readily visible in the engine compartment. Look for oil on any surfaces including the firewall. Also, look for streaking along the bottom of the fuselage. Hydraulic leaks can also be located by streaking and/or discoloring. Demonstrate that you recognize these matters as you perform your walkaround.

When you examine the flight controls, you must not merely look at

59

them. What you're determining about the controls is not merely that they are sound and without damage. You are also to determine that they are properly attached and move freely.

The entire airplane must be checked for structural damage. If you come across any breaks, cracks, or wrinkles on surfaces, then call these to the attention of the person who is responsible for maintaining the airplane. Contact that person before you fly, of course.

As you proceed with the visual inspection, you will also need to untie the airplane as you come to each place where a tiedown line is attached. Similarly, when you inspect the landing gear, remove the chocks, if any are used. You'll already have removed the control lock, as we mentioned at the beginning.

Such detailed advice may seem petty, but strange things can happen. I recall watching a pilot rush to get through his preflight one day. The visual inspection was rather "hit or miss" and he was quickly aboard and starting up. What attracted my attention was his roaring engine when he tried to taxi from his tiedown spot. Unfortunately, in his haste, he'd neglected to untie the tail tiedown. It was funny to the onlookers, but embarrassing to the pilot as he engaged in his vain efforts to taxi until it finally dawned on him that he'd overlooked something. He shut down, very sheepishly got out and untied the tail, returned to the cockpit, and got out of there as fast as he could. Imagine what a hit you'd make with the designated examiner if you did something like *that*.

If you find any evidence of frost or ice on the flying surfaces of the airplane, or on the windscreen, you are responsible for seeing that this is removed. At times, it may be sufficient simply to brush away such material. At other times, where the coating is serious enough to warrant it, you may find it necessary to resort to other measures, such as using a deicer or having the airplane placed in a hanger for a time. If this last step is necessary, be sure to inspect the airplane to determine that the surfaces are dry after the ice or frost is removed in order to avoid refreezing when the airplane is in flight.

Frost on the flying surfaces is particularly hazardous because it looks so harmless. I was particularly impressed with this fact many years ago when I was working on my instrument rating and an instructor and I took off with an airplane full of frost that looked harmless. It certainly didn't add any appreciable amount of weight and didn't appear to be thick enough to cause a problem, but we ended up using nearly the entire length of a runway to lift off in a lightly loaded Cherokee 180 and barely grazed some treetops off the end of the runway. Neither of us said a word, but I think we both learned a very important lesson that day.

You must also check the inside of the cockpit and baggage area to determine that all baggage, cargo, and/or any equipment that you might be carrying are secure. It can be very distracting to find a towbar rattling or floating about the interior of the plane when you're performing some of the maneuvers required for the practical test.

Your Final Responsibility. If you note any discrepancies during your inspection—anything that does not meet the requirements of the operating handbook or anything that does not appear to be a normal condition—then you must call this to the attention of the person responsible for maintenance of the airplane. If you have *any* doubt about *anything* that you encounter, do the safe thing: Call it to someone's attention. It's much less embarrassing to make a mistake in the direction of safety than to find after you've become airborne that you've committed an error in the other direction.

Assuming that all will go well, as it usually will, your last responsibility is to pronounce the aircraft airworthy.

B. TASK: COCKPIT MANAGEMENT
(ASEL)

PILOT OPERATION – 1

REFERENCE: AC 61–21.

1. **Objective.** To determine that the applicant:

   a. Exhibits adequate knowledge of cockpit management by explaining related safety and efficiency factors.
   b. Organizes and arranges the material and equipment in a manner that makes them readily available.
   c. Ensures that the safety belts and shoulder harnesses are fastened.
   d. Adjusts and locks the foot pedals or pilot's seat to a safe position and ensures full control movement.
   e. Briefs the occupants on the use of safety belts and emergency procedures.

2. **Action.** The examiner will:

   a. Ask the applicant to explain cockpit management procedures.
   b. Observe the applicant's cockpit management procedures, and determine that the applicant's performance meets the objective.
   c. Place emphasis on safety items related to good cockpit management.

Objective: What's expected of the applicant regarding cockpit management.

Exhibiting Knowledge of Cockpit Management. This knowledge will be exhibited in two ways, explanation and performance. As with your preflight visual inspection, cockpit procedures prior to starting up can become a ritual. Consequently, beyond demonstrating by action that you know what you're doing, you'll be expected to answer any questions that the examiner may put to you about safe and efficient cockpit management. None of this will be difficult or highly technical, but you should be mindful of what you are doing and able to explain it in terms of safety and efficiency.

Organizing and Arranging Materials and Equipment. You may have a number of items to be concerned about when you enter the cockpit. If you haven't done so before, you may now be required to show the aircraft documents. If you've already gone over these with the examiner, you should know where and how to store these items. Logbooks may or may not be kept in the aircraft, but the other documents that will be carried must be taken aboard and stowed properly. For example, the examiner will not look kindly on your tossing the Airworthiness Certificate into the pile of clutter in the glovebox or the pocket behind the seat. Remember that those documents which must be carried are to be displayed, not merely stored, so take proper care of them. Also, you'll be carrying your charts, flight log, computer, etc. Arrange these in such a way that they will be accessible to you but not get in the way of your cockpit procedures.

Seatbelts and Shoulder Harnesses. Most likely the trainer that you'll be using for the practical test will be of recent enough vintage to have shoulder harnesses as well as seat belts. Keep in mind that if they're present, they must be used. You should also assume responsibility for checking the examiner's seatbelt and harness. For this part of the flight, treat the examiner like a passenger and check to see that both of you are belted and harnessed appropriately.

Seat Adjustment. Don't be shy about being comfortable. A term that seems to have become "in" with the development of computers is *ergonomics*, the relationship between people and machines. Besides being the pilot, you're the ergonomist for this flight. Adjust the seat for your comfort and ease with the controls. Also check your examiner's position. If the movement of the yoke is blocked by his/her knees, that becomes *your* problem. Look to your comfort and treat the examiner as you would a passenger.

Briefing. You're also responsible, as pilot-in-command, for instructing your passenger on the use of safety belts and shoulder harnesses. Show the "passenger" (examiner) for this flight the proper way to adjust and fasten the seat belt and shoulder harness. Also explain their use and how (and when) they may be unfastened.

You should also provide an explanation of what the passenger should do in the event of an emergency. Something that may seem obvious to you—such as keeping passenger feet free of rudder pedals, or not grabbing knobs or wheels—may require explanation for the passenger.

C. TASK: STARTING ENGINE (ASEL)

PILOT OPERATION – 1

REFERENCES: AC 61–21,
AC 61–23, AC 91–13, AC 91–55;
Pilot's Operating Handbook and FAA–
Approved Airplane Flight Manual.

1. **Objective.**   To determine that the applicant:

   a. Exhibits adequate knowledge by explaining engine starting procedures, including start-ing under various atmospheric conditions.
   b. Performs all the items on the before–starting and starting checklist.
   c. Accomplishes a safe starting procedure with emphasis on –

      (1) positioning the airplane to avoid creating hazards.
      (2) determining that the area is clear.
      (3) adjusting the engine controls.
      (4) setting the brakes.
      (5) preventing undesirable airplane move-ment after engine start.
      (6) avoiding excessive engine RPM and temperatures.
      (7) checking the engine instruments after engine start.

2. **Action.**   The examiner will:

   a. Ask the applicant to explain starting procedures including starting under various atmospheric conditions.
   b. Observe the applicant's engine starting procedures, and determine that the applicant's performance meets the objective.
   c. Place emphasis on safe starting procedures.

Objective: What's expected of the applicant regarding engine starting procedures.

Explaining Engine Starting Procedure. As with other parts of the practical test, you'll exhibit adequate knowledge by both describing and doing. Since you'll be starting the airplane under a specific set of conditions, you can demonstrate your knowledge of engine starting procedures under all conditions by saying what you'd do. If your test is on a warm, spring day, you'll also be expected to know what you'd be required to do on a very cold winter's day. The latter, for example, might have required preheating, or pulling the prop through a few times before entering the plane, or both of these. On the other hand, on exceptionally hot and humid days, when the density altitude is unusually high, you may be required to lean the mixture a bit even prior to attempting the startup. If you haven't actually experienced these variations, check them out with your instructor prior to scheduling the checkride.

Using the Checklist. Never—I say again, *never*—begin the engine starting procedures without the checklist in your hand. And *use* it. Demonstrate to the examiner that you're using it by calling out each item as you come to it. Say, "Seat belts and shoulder harness adjusted and locked," as you actually check you own and the examiner's belts and harnesses. Similarly, you'll say, "Fuel shutoff valve handle—on," as you actually check to see that it's on, or on the proper tank, as the case may be.

One important item to check is electrical equipment. Don't go over this one casually. The checklist will probably say only "All radios and electrical equipment—off." It's up to you to check *every* switch; these won't be listed on the checklist. As with the preflight visual inspection of the airplane, you can assure that nothing is omitted by establishing a routine. Start at the switch that is at the extreme right and at the highest point, most likely a radio or transponder switch. Then move systematically down and to the left, touching each switch to see that it's off, and saying "Off," as you proceed. It's particularly important in the winter to avoid any unnecessary strain on the battery, but all switches should be off at the beginning of the startup procedure at any time.

Safe Starting Procedures. Your starting procedures must be complete and efficient. They must also assure safety. As you perform the various items on the checklist, be sure to emphasize those that are required for safety. In the first place, ascertain that the airplane is in a position to avoid hazards. It should be on a smooth and level surface where debris will not be picked up or kicked up by the starting engine. It should be located where you can taxi easily and safely away at the appropriate time. It should be positioned in such a way that onlookers, or other planes, or vehicles, etc., will not be endangered by your startup, or by the addition of power when you are ready to start taxiing.

Always determine that the area is clear. You accomplish this in two ways. First, you make a visual check yourself. And you can also query your passenger with a "Clear right?" In addition, you must call out "Clear prop," to warn anyone in the vicinity that you are ready to start the engine. At night, it may be a good idea to flash your landing lights on and off once or twice to warn anyone in the vicinity.

The engine controls should be set for a safe start, too. The pilot's operating handbook will give you the appropriate throttle setting for a startup. You want the engine to come to life when you turn the key or press the starter button, but it's neither necessary nor desirable to have it roar into life at a high power setting.

A special caution is in order at this point: At times, it may be necessary to prime the engine in order to get a quick start. This can always create the chance of a fire if the engine backfires or is overloaded. If you become conscious of such a fire, *continue cranking the engine.* This continuous cranking will generally suck the flames back into the engine and extinguish them. Also, you want the engine to start in such an instance to enable the propeller to blow out any flames that may be present in the engine compartment. In the winter, when such a situation is even more likely to arise, it's always helpful to have someone present outside the airplane during the startup if that is possible.

It's advisable to set the parking brake prior to the startup, generally speaking. In some aircraft, such as the Cessna 150/152, you may not be sure that the brakes are set until the engine has started. If the airplane being used for the practical test has a separate parking brake, by all means use it. If you're using a Cessna 150/152 (or any airplane with similar equipment), then you should apply the brakes by depressing the toe pedals and then hold them on manually. Explain to the examiner that you're holding the brakes to remove all doubt. I've noticed that many students have experienced difficulty setting and releasing the parking brakes on their Cessna training aircraft. It has proved to be easier (and probably safer) simply to have them hold the brakes during the startup rather than try to set the parking brakes. Examiners will not object to this, so long as they know that you have applied brakes.

Having applied brakes, you must hold them (or keep the parking brake set) until you are ready to roll. It's very easy to become distracted or so engrossed in other items during the startup that you neglect to hold brakes and fail to notice the airplane moving. Dividing your attention between the inside and outside of the airplane will help you to avoid this difficulty.

As soon as the engine starts, you'll begin an instrument scan of the panel. For most trainers, the engine should be set at a high idle of about 800 to 1000 rpm after startup. Check this immediately. Also keep in mind that as the engine warms up, the rpm will climb, requiring some adjustment of the throttle, so monitor the tachometer.

Also, check the other engine gauges. The oil pressure should be "in the green" within about 30 seconds of startup. If it's not, then shut down immediately. You'll also, of course, need to check the fuel pressure gauge, if your airplane is so equipped. The ammeter should also be checked and indicating "in the green." Finally, turn on whatever radios you'll be needing for taxiing and tune in the appropriate frequencies. Also turn on the transponder and set it on "Standby."

D. TASK: TAXIING (ASEL)

PILOT OPERATION – 2

REFERENCE: AC 61–21.

1. **Objective.**   To determine that the applicant:

   a. Exhibits adequate knowledge by explaining safe taxi procedures.
   b. Adheres to signals and clearances and follows the proper taxi route.
   c. Performs a brake check immediately after the airplane begins moving.
   d. Controls taxi speed without excessive use of brakes.
   e. Recognizes and avoids hazards.
   f. Positions the controls for the existing wind conditions.
   g. Avoids creating hazards to persons or property.

2. **Action.**   The examiner will:

   a. Ask the applicant to explain safe taxi procedures.
   b. Observe the applicant's taxi procedures, and determine that the applicant's performance meets the objective.
   c. Place emphasis on correct airplane control, taxi speed, and avoidance of hazards.

Objective: What's expected of the applicant regarding taxiing.

Explaining Safe Taxiing Procedures. Prior to starting the taxi to the runup area, and during such taxiing, the applicant should provide explanations of what is to be expected and what is being performed. Let the examiner know what power settings you plan to use, how you will position the controls and why, what precautions must be taken, etc.

Signals, Clearance, and Routing. If your practical test is to be taken at a busy airport that lacks a control tower but includes someone who directs taxiing, you should be familiar with the uniform system of hand signals (Fig. 2-2). If your test is being taken at a controlled field, then be sure to obtain clearance to taxi prior to starting your trip to the runup area. Do not move the airplane until ground control has provided instructions.

Fig. 2-2. The uniform system of hand signals.

The procedure for obtaining clearance is simple. You'll already have set the frequency to ground control, if that is the proper frequency. Being careful not to interrupt anyone else's radio message, contact the controller with an initial callup:

"Simpla city ground control, Airchomper three six niner four Alfa, over."

"Airchomper three six niner, go ahead."

"Ground control, Airchomper three six niner on the apron ready to taxi to the active, over."

Now you simply listen for whatever instructions are issued to you. Keep in mind all that you've learned about what such clearances mean. You'll need to recall such things as where you're to hold short, whether or not your clearance is a clearance to cross a runway, etc. If you have any doubts about the instructions that you've received, the examiner would prefer that you call for clarification of instructions rather than simply plunging ahead uncertainly with the chance of not following the proper routing.

If you're at an uncontrolled field where all the decisions are yours, then you should observe the way traffic at the airport is moving. Generally, the airport will have a particular place where you're to do the runup. Generally that point is at the approach end of the active runway, but be sure you know where it is and how to get there.

Whatever the situation, as soon as the airplane starts rolling, tap the brakes lightly to ascertain that you have brakes. It's not necessary to come to a complete stop, although that's acceptable. Just exerting light pressure to assure that brakes are functioning is sufficient.

As you taxi, adjust your power for a safe and comfortable taxi. Never exceed the speed of a fast walk. Generally, this can be accomplished with a power setting of 800 to 1000 rpm. This will vary with conditions, however; if the taxi strip leading to the end of the runway is slightly inclined, you may need to increase or decrease power to adjust for the proper speed. Do not, however, use brakes to control your speed. It makes no sense to use a power setting that requires your constantly riding the brakes. A light tap occasionally may be acceptable, but power setting should be the determiner of taxi speed.

You must also indicate that you recognize hazards and avoid them. Such hazards include other taxiing aircraft, obstructions, flaws in the surface, or seasonal hazards such as snow, ice, or standing water.

As you taxi, give attention to the position of the controls. If you're taxiing to the end of the active runway, it's most likely that you'll have a tailwind. This calls for holding the yoke or stick forward. If it's a quartering tailwind, the yoke should be in a forward position and also positioned to place the aileron on the side from which the wind is blowing in a down position. That is, the yoke or stick should be moved in a direction opposite to that from which the wind is blowing, and then held in that position. In addition, the throttle should be adjusted to the requirements set by the tailwind, which usually means a slight reduction in power.

Beyond avoiding hazards, you must also avoid *creating* hazards. This means giving a wide clearance to persons and objects, avoiding sudden bursts of power or application of brakes, slowing the airplane prior to making turns, and continuously sweeping the environment to assure that you stay clear of everything. It also means that you must precisely follow any instructions that you have received by signals or from ground control.

E. TASK: PRE–TAKEOFF CHECK (ASEL)

PILOT OPERATION – 1

REFERENCES: AC 61–21; Pilot's Operating Handbook and FAA–Approved Flight Manual.

1. **Objective.**   To determine that the applicant:

   a. Exhibits adequate knowledge of the pre–takeoff check by explaining the reasons for checking the items.
   b. Positions the airplane to avoid creating hazards.
   c. Divides attention inside and outside of the cockpit.
   d. Ensures that the engine temperature is suitable for runup and takeoff.
   e. Follows the checklist.
   f. Touches control or switch, or adjusts it to the prescribed position after identifying a checklist item.
   g. States the instrument reading, when appropriate, after identifying a checklist item.
   h. Ensures that the airplane is in safe operating condition emphasizing –

      (1) flight controls and instruments.
      (2) engine and propeller operation.
      (3) seat adjustment and lock.
      (4) safety belts and shoulder harnesses fastened and adjusted.
      (5) doors and windows secured.

   i. Recognizes any discrepancy and determines if the airplane is safe for flight or requires maintenance.
   j. Reviews the critical takeoff performance airspeeds and distances.
   k. Describes takeoff emergency procedures.

l. Obtains and interprets takeoff and departure clearances.
m. Notes takeoff time.

2. **Action.** The examiner will:

  a. Ask the applicant to explain reasons for checking items on the pre–takeoff check.
  b. Observe the pre–takeoff check, and determine that the applicant's performance meets the objective.
  c. Place emphasis on the applicant's ability to recognize discrepancies and to use sound judgment in making decisions related to the flight.

Objective: What's expected of the applicant regarding the pre-takeoff check.

Providing the Explanations. You're expected not only to do the pre-takeoff check, but also to understand what you're doing. Your performance will demonstrate that you can do it; your explanations will demonstrate that you understand all that you're doing. Again, since circumstances can alter requirements, you'll need to say what you're doing, what calls for such performance and what it's intended to accomplish. You'll also be required to know what's called for under other circumstances. The pre-takeoff check would be altered to some extent for different seasons. It would also be different for night flight than for flight completed during daylight hours. Consequently, you must be sure that you understand every item on the checklist and can provide an adequate explanation of it.

Positioning the Airplane. Although the examiner will emphasize safe practices, other considerations will be relevant, too. When you prepare to do the runup, it's not merely a matter of ending the taxiing and holding brakes. You must consciously select the appropriate position for the airplane. In the first place, choose a spot that will not create a hazard. Position the plane where you will not jeopardize other airplanes. Select a spot that is free of any debris that might be kicked up by the prop during runup. Such debris could damage the propeller, some part of your airplane or another, or injure someone. You've been taught, as well, to head the airplane into the wind. This, of course, provides additional cooling for the engine as you do the runup. Additionally, always be conscious of what is behind your airplane prior to performing the runup. Even if it doesn't create a hazard, it's extremely discourteous to have the tail of your airplane pointed at another aircraft, or toward vehicles, or buildings, or people who will get the full "benefit" of your blasting them with air (and perhaps debris) as your check your mags. At times, this may preclude your heading your airplane directly into the wind, but that's of the less consequence.

Directing Your Attention. There's no question but that the checklist will occupy your main attention during the pre-takeoff check, or runup. Next in importance will be the controls, switches, instruments, etc., that are associated with the particular item on your checklist. Equally important is what is happening outside your airplane. Keep a watch out for other aircraft, people, the outside effects of what you're doing inside your airplane, etc. This will keep you and others safe from such accidental occurrences as your airplane inadvertently starting to roll while you're focusing on following the checklist.

Checking the Gauges. Normally, by the time you've completed your startup procedures and have done all that is necessary to get to the runup area, all your gauges will be in the green. Don't merely assume that they're there, however. As you get ready to do the runup, be sure that the engine has warmed up sufficiently to perform this part of the pre-takeoff check. In extremely cold weather, you may find it necessary to allow the engine fluids to warm up a bit before you strain the engine with a runup at the mag check power setting. Similarly, at completion of the pre-takeoff check, be sure the engine is sufficiently warmed up for takeoff. It generally will be, if you find that you can't advance the throttle without the engine "protesting" with some coughing and/or hesitation, then exercise a little patience and idle at 800 to 1000 rpm until the engine is ready.

Following the Checklist. Don't even think about doing the runup from memory. You may have done it enough times by this stage to have it memorized. Don't exhibit such knowledge by neglecting to use the checklist. Hopefully, your instructor will have by precept and example instilled in you the unalterable habit of using the checklist. The examiner will definitely *not* be properly impressed if you show off and do the runup without the list. Use the checklist. Use the checklist. *Use the checklist.* Don't use it merely for the practical test. *Always use the checklist.*

Identifying and Checking the Items. As you perform the runup, or pre-takeoff check, touch or indicate each control, switch, or instrument referred to. Also, adjust or position or move each item to its proper setting as you refer to it on the checklist. In addition to identifying and adjusting (where appropriate) each item on the list, call it out to the examiner as you go along. Say, "Altimeter setting to field elevation of 160 feet," as you come to this on the checklist and appropriately adjust that instrument. Handle each item in a similar manner.

Handling the Instruments. Similarly with all instruments, identify the item on the checklist, identify the instrument referred to, then say what the appropriate reading should be and what it is. If there's a difference between the two, explain the difference and what you need to do.

Pronouncing the Safe Operating Condition. As you do the preflight check, there are some items that, more than others, are related to safe operating condition. For example, you need to say—and to demonstrate—that the flight controls are moving freely and correctly. You might even specify what the correct movement is. When you set the altimeter, for example, say what you're setting it to and why. As you check the mags, specify what power setting you are using, and what we should see on the tachometer and hear from the engine compartment ("Throttle setting at 1700 rpm. Switching to the right mag; slight-drop in rpm but its less than 75 rms [or whatever is called for]. Back to both. Now, to the left mag; slight drop in rpm but the engine is running smoothly. Back to both again." etc.)

Prior to taking off, you'll also make another check of the seat adjustment and assure yourself that seats are locked into position. We don't need the thrill of a seat slipping back and someone grabbing a control just after liftoff. Do another check of seatbelts and shoulder harness—both yours and the examiner's. Be sure also that windows and doors are fully closed and locked. It can be most distracting to you and terrifying to a passenger to have a door or window pop open on takeoff or in flight.

Recognizing Discrepancies and Responding. It's unlikely that you're going to encounter any discrepancies during the runup; one seldom does. But the checklist is purposeful; it's to ensure that everything is fine. If, however, you note that (for example) the rpm drops off more than the book calls for and the engine runs rough on one of the mags, know what to do. You'll need to know what the limits are for all items on the checklist and what constitutes a discrepancy.

Critical Takeoff Performance Airspeeds and Distances. You should inform the examiner of what sort of takeoff you intend to do and what airspeed is called for when making such a takeoff. Usually, you'll begin with a normal takeoff, which will require knowing the best rate of climb airspeed. It's also important to know critical distances. At what point on the runway will you abort the takeoff if the airplane hasn't yet lifted off? How far from the airport do you expect to be before you make your first turn? Are there any noise abatement procedures that you must follow? Provide the examiner with such information.

Emergency Procedures. Aside from critical airspeed and safe distances, you need to demonstrate that you can handle emergency procedures. Hopefully, this will not be by actual demonstration but rather by explanation. You need to know what you would do if a window or door popped open on the takeoff. Your response would vary, of course, with the stage of takeoff at which such an incident occurred. You need also to be prepared for other emergencies. Explain how you would handle a failure of the airspeed indicator. ("I would maintain the proper pitch for takeoff that I have learned to associate with the best rate of climb airspeed. I would do this by using outside references such as the relationship between the nose of the airplane and the horizon.") Be prepared to say how you'd react if an airplane taxied across the active just as you reached full throttle power setting. You'll also need to know what you'd do in an engine-out emergency at various stages of the takeoff roll and liftoff.

Departure Clearances. If you get your clearance from the tower, be sure to follow it precisely. If you're at an uncontrolled airfield, then you must do your own clearance. You'll accomplish this by positioning yourself so that you can see both incoming and departing traffic. By pointing the nose of the airplane at about a 45 degree angle to the runway, heading toward incoming traffic, you should have a clear view. Then announce to the examiner (or your passenger, or yourself), "Clear left. Clear right. Okay to taxi onto the active." Follow this with an announcement to the world. Pick up the mike and on the appropriate frequency say something like, "Belchfire triple niner three ready to roll, runway two seven at Gowntown." Then do it.

Chapter 3

AREA OF OPERATION:
AIRPORT AND TRAFFIC PATTERN OPERATIONS

A. TASK: **RADIO COMMUNICATIONS AND ATC LIGHT SIGNALS** (ASEL)

PILOT OPERATION – 2

REFERENCES: AC 61–21, AC 61–23; AIM.

1. **Objective.** To determine that the applicant:

   a. Exhibits adequate knowledge by explaining radio communication, ATC light signals, and prescribed procedures for radio failure.
   b. Selects the appropriate frequencies for the facilities to be used.
   c. Transmits requests and reports using the recommended standard phraseology.

d. Receives, acknowledges, and complies with radio communication.

2. **Action.** The examiner will:

a. Ask the applicant to explain radio communication procedures, phraseology, prescribed procedures for radio failure, and ATC light signals.
b. Observe the applicant's communication procedures, and determine that the applicant's performance meets the objective.
c. Place emphasis on the applicant's phraseology, clarity, and use of appropriate frequencies.

Objective: What's expected of the applicant regarding radio communications and Air Traffic Control light signals.
Explaining Radio Communication and ATC Light Signals. It may seem as though it's taking us a long time to get to the flying part of the practical test. It will seem equally long when you take the actual test. The examiner will cover a lot of material before you take to the air.

You're about ready to take off now, having completed most of your ground operations, but you're not quite ready yet. The examiner will want to know the extent of your knowledge regarding communications. You'll begin by providing the appropriate frequencies for your situation. If you're at a controlled field, you already took care of this part a long time ago, when you were doing your paperwork and checked the information in the *Airport Facility Directory*.

On your flight plan log you have already listed the information needed now. The examiner will not mind if you check to be sure; that's why you wrote this information down. You can now check to see whether you first need to contact Clearance Delivery for instructions or should go directly to Ground Control. If the facility has an ATIS, you will tune that frequency in first so that you can inform the first controller you talk to that you have that information. Then, when you're ready, call the appropriate person.

You'll tell the examiner at this stage, after giving the proper frequencies and facility, that you're going to provide the name of the facility called followed by your identification, your location, and your intention. Whatever phraseology gets that information across is acceptable. Just don't use too many "Roger Wilcos"; the controller won't known whether you're a pilot or a movie star.

Occasionally, radios fail. The examiner will expect you to know what to do in the event your radio fails. If you're aware of a radio problem prior to even getting ready to fly, alert the tower so that they'll be expecting you to taxi and depart without radio communications. The controllers will give you all your instructions ahead of time and you'll simply wait at appropriate times for their light signals. If you're about to depart and find that you can't raise anyone and suspect that you've just lost your radio capability, then you have a different sort of a problem. The fastest way to get the attention of the folks in the tower is to start moving. Do so slowly and exercise the greatest caution. Have your strobe(s) and/or beacon on to further attract attention. If you can face the tower and flash your landing lights, do that, too. Someone will see you, realize that you have a problem, and start hunting for the old, hand-held signal light that no one's seen for a long time. Or, there's always your transponder as a possible way of communicating your problem to the tower. On the other hand, maybe you can be really resourceful at this point, and before he/she gets a chance to ask you, you address the question to the examiner. "What would I do if I were ready to taxi to the active and discovered that my radio wasn't functioning?"

You learned the light signals a long time ago in ground school as you prepared for your written. I hope that you remembered to review them before you got to the end of the runway, where the examiner will expect you to come up with the information. Look them over again. There are only six signals that you need to learn. You'll probably recite these for the examiner. You might be lucky and never see them during your flying career. (If you do see them, you'll probably not see the six. On the few occasions when I've had to resort to such communications, I've never seen anything used except flashing red or flashing green. Maybe controllers forget, too.)

Selecting the Appropriate Frequencies. As was mentioned above, during the flight planning portion of your preparations, you obtained and listed on the flight log the radio frequencies needed for this flight. At this point, you'll first select the ATIS frequency, if that's available at your location, and note the information listed. If no ATIS is available, you'll then tune in the Clearance Delivery or Ground Control frequency, whichever is required for your airport. Following this, you'll use the tower frequency for takeoff clearance. If your airport is extremely busy and fully equipped, you may also be given a departure frequency, or an enroute frequency to be contacted after takeoff. Record any such frequency that is given to you.

If you're flying from a field with an FSS (Flight Service Station), then you'll use the appropriate advisory frequency for that facility. Again, that will be a frequency that you'll have listed on your flight log during the planning phase. Or perhaps you're departing from an uncontrolled field. In that case, you'll simply need the local Unicom frequency, which you'll have jotted down during your preflight planning.

Transmitting Requests and Reports. There are terms and phrases that are generally used but, although there is a rather standardized phraseology, there is no prescribed language. When you're ready to taxi, for example, you can use something like the following:

"Pompa City Ground Control. Blastair Two Four Six Alpha, over."

Ground replies: "Blastair Four Six Alpha, Pompa City Ground. Go ahead."

"Pompa City ground, Blastair Four Six Alpha, terminal ramp, ready to taxi to the active."

Ground control will give you your instructions. Notice the information that you provided. It's not necessary for you to memorize any particular phraseology; just get your message across—completely, but *briefly*. Don't clutter the airwaves. You gave the same information here that you generally give after the initial callup, i.e., your identification, your location, and your intention.

Most of your transmissions, after the initial callup will follow that format and present those three pieces of information. For example, when you're ready to take off, you'll call up the tower and, after your callup has been acknowledged say something like the following:

"Pompa City tower, Blastair Four Six Alpha, runway one niner, ready to roll."

One word of caution here: Avoid the use of the term "takeoff." Reserve that for the tower's clearances. Your use of the term might confuse some other poor soul into thinking that he/she has been cleared for takeoff, so say "Ready to roll," or "Ready to depart," or some term that indicates your intention without actually using the term "takeoff."

Occasionally, in other circumstances, these three pieces of information—which constitute most of your transmissions—may need to be expanded slightly. At times, your identification may include the transponder code you're squawking as well as your call number. Or your location may include your altitude as well as your geographic location, but remembering that you generally will be providing those three pieces of information should help you to transmit with confidence.

Receiving, Acknowledging, and Complying. There's no trick to receiving communications. You just sit there with the noises making impressions on your nervous system via the ears. The important part is to note whatever needs to be noted. For example, if you're given a frequency, or runway, or some similar bit of information, jot it down. And let the other party know that you've heard the message. Frequently, it's sufficient simply to repeat your call sign at the termination of the message you've received. At other times—for example, when you're being given enroute clearances—you may need to repeat the message to indicate that you've received it correctly. Just keep in mind that you must acknowledge every communication that you receive.

Do you always need to acknowledge by radio? No. If your message was ". . . cleared for takeoff," you acknowledge by taking off. If the message was "Squawk two zero four zero," or "Squawk ident," you acknowledge by simply squawking the assigned frequency, or by squawking ident.

Your compliance with radio communications should be accurate, prompt, and confident. If you're given a clearance to do something, do it immediately. If you're asked to repeat a communication, or to respond with a piece of information, do it without hesitation. If it's necessary to delay at all, then respond with a "Stand by one" message. Generally, however, you should expedite your response to a communication in order to get things moving and to free the airwaves for the next person.

B. TASK: TRAFFIC PATTERN OPERATIONS (ASEL)

PILOT OPERATION – 2

REFERENCES: AC 61–21, AC 61–23; AIM.

1. **Objective.** To determine that the applicant:

   a. Exhibits adequate knowledge by explaining traffic pattern procedures at controlled and uncontrolled airports including collision avoidance.
   b. Follows the established traffic pattern procedures consistent with instructions or rules.
   c. Corrects for wind drift to follow the appropriate ground track.
   d. Maintains adequate spacing from other traffic.
   e. Maintains the traffic pattern altitude, ±100 feet.
   f. Maintains the desired airspeed, ±10 knots.
   g. Completes the pre–landing cockpit checklist.
   h. Maintains orientation with the runway in use.
   i. Completes a turn to final approach at least one–fourth mile from the approach end of the runway.

2. **Action.** The examiner will:

   a. Ask the applicant to explain airport traffic pattern operations.
   b. Observe the applicant's ability to conform with the established traffic pattern procedures, and determine that the applicant's performance meets the objective.
   c. Place emphasis on the applicant's planning and division of attention in relation to collision avoidance.

Objective: What can be expected of the applicant regarding traffic pattern operations.

Explaining Traffic Pattern Procedures. If you're taking your practical test at a non-controlled field, the examiner wants you to demonstrate that you can handle situations at a controlled field, and vice versa. The way he/she determines that you know what procedures obtain at any airport where you might be landing when you're a licensed pilot is to have you describe those situations that you won't encounter during the checkride. While taking your flight training, you'll have encountered both types of airports. When called on to explain airport procedures, recall the situations that you actually experienced during training and use them as a basis for explaining procedures. This will necessitate explaining how you determine the nature of the airport (by using the *Facilities Directory*), and what to look for at airports; e.g., wind direction indicators or other landing direction indicators such as a tee or tetrahedron, or a segmented circle with traffic pattern indicators. Include in your explanation the fact that even at controlled airports, the pilot-in-command is still the final authority and is responsible for maintaining separation and avoiding incidents. That means cooperating with advisories or instructions and not executing unexpected maneuvers.

Following Traffic Pattern Procedures. There are standard practices such as 90-degree left turns, straight-out departures or 45 degree turns from the crosswind leg, pattern altitudes generally observed, and the like. Don't get creative during the practical test. Know the established traffic pattern procedures at the airport you'll be using as well as the standard procedures and follow them as precisely as you can. If the test is conducted at an airport that you haven't customarily flown, then check the facilities directory for any specific rules or instructions which you'll follow "to a T."

Following Appropriate Ground Track. Procedures regarding departure tracks can differ. Generally, the pattern is to track straight out from the takeoff runway, which will necessitate your correcting for any wind to prevent your drifting off the track. It's very annoying to fly with someone who blithely ignores what the wind is doing to the airplane and proceeds to track wherever nature leads. The whole point of all that rectangular flight you did during your student practice sessions was to correct such tendencies and get you accustomed to flying precise traffic patterns. Demonstrate to your examiner that you are capable of that by tracking straight out from the end of the runway, unless instructed to do otherwise. If you're flying from a controlled field, you might be instructed to "Maintain runway heading." If you're departing from runway one niner, this means that you hold a heading of 190 degrees after liftoff and ignore what the wind does to you. That's okay, because everyone will be getting that instruction and flying the same track. But absent such a specific instruction, track straight out from the end of the runway. Don't be afraid to look back to see that you're doing just that.

Maintaining Adequate Spacing. The tower at a controlled field will pretty much take care of spacing for you, but keep in mind that you're pilot-in-command and therefore ultimately responsible for maintaining your own separation. At uncontrolled fields, it's all yours. Impress your examiner by not taking off if a departing aircraft is not a runway's length ahead of you when you're ready to turn on to the active, or an arriving aircraft has already turned to the final leg at the time you're ready to taxi onto the runway. In the pattern, maintain a similar separation by not turning to the crosswind leg until the preceding aircraft has turned downwind, or by delaying your turn from downwind to base until the airplane in front of you has turned from base to final. These are simply approximations, of course, and will vary with differing speeds and performance among the airplanes in the pattern.

Maintaining Pattern Altitudes. Traffic pattern altitude is normally 1000 feet above ground level (AGL). Keep in mind that your altimeter will be indicating the MSL (Mean Sea Level) altitude and you'll need to add the 1000 feet AGL to the field elevation to obtain the normally appropriate pattern altitude. This height can vary, however, to accommodate individual airport requirements, so be sure that you're using the correct altitude for the field at which you're flying.

It's recommended that you make your first turn (from the takeoff leg to the crosswind leg) at about 300 feet below pattern altitude and/or beyond the departure end of the runway. You'll continue climbing until you reach pattern altitude, of course. Once at pattern altitude, maintain that altitude precisely. It's no more difficult to fly at 1000 feet AGL than to fly at 850 feet AGL or 1150 feet AGL, maintain that pattern altitude with precision. Your descent for a landing will of course be started while still flying the downwind leg. As you know, there are not prescribed altitudes for the base and final legs but you should exercise good judgement here. Try to maintain an altitude that will enable you to reach the end of the runway in the event of engine failure.

Maintaining Desired Airspeeds. On takeoff, you'll be using either the best rate-of-climb airspeed, or the best angle-of-climb airspeed, whichever is called for. Use the former, unless there is some good reason for using the latter. Keep in mind that the airspeed will be controlled by the attitude of the airplane, so use that primary speed control, the yoke or stick, to maintain a precise airspeed. Also remember to use a visual reference, the relationship between the nose of the airplane and the horizon, to maintain that airspeed; then, simply refer to the airspeed indicator as a check of the established airspeed. I guarantee that if you try to use the airspeed indicator as the basic reference for maintaining airspeed, you'll never catch up to it. It'll always be ahead of or behind the speed that you want.

The downwind leg airspeed is, of course, the normal cruising airspeed for the trainer that you'll probably be flying. As you begin your approach to a landing by reducing the power in order to start a descent, maintain essentially the same pitch or attitude that you used for cruising downwind. This attitude, with the reduced power setting, will probably slow you down to the desired approach speed, which will most likely be the same as your best rate-of-climb airspeed. As you further reduce power, you'll find it necessary to change the attitude of the airplane, but you'll still be using attitude (the yoke or stick, not the throttle) to maintain the proper approach airspeed. Sticking to the numbers—both for altitude and airspeed—will assuredly impress the examiner favorably. Precision is the difference between the accomplished pilot and the hack.

The Pre-Landing Checklist. Some airplanes are equipped with a mounted checklist; others are not. But you won't be able to haul out the printed one while you're in the pattern, so have it clearly in mind. The checking begins, of course, on the downwind leg when you pull carburetor heat on about halfway down the downwind leg. As you accomplish each part of the list, say it aloud as you manipulate, or touch, the part of the plane that you're referring to.

Maintaining Orientation. The active runway is your reference for the rectangular flight pattern you'll be using, so don't lose sight of it. I once had a licensed pilot who'd done all his flying at loosely operated sod strips come to me for a little refresher work in order to renew his license. We had a half a dozen hard surface runways at the airport where I was instructing, all clearly marked. But he wasn't impressed with precision. As I flew with him, I insisted on precision and he reluctantly complied. I found that I always had to direct him to make 90-degree turns, and to start that turn from downwing to base when the end of the runway was at about a 45-degree angle behind him. But I finally turned him loose for a solo in the pattern one day. Much to my dismay—nay, horror—he landed on three different runways before I could get him stopped. Needless to say, we went back to circuits and bumps (takeoffs and landings) *in the pattern* until he was so impressed with it that he never forgot. Don't make such an impression on your examiner. Fly your pattern with the proper runway in sight and in mind.

The Turn from Base to Final. This turn to your final approach should be made at least one-fourth mile from the approach end of the runway. Don't overcompensate in the other direction, however, and make your turn to final out of sight of the airport. If you keep in mind the suggestion made above, i.e., starting that final turn when the approach end of the runway is at about a 45-degree angle behind you, all should turn out well.

C. TASK: AIRPORT AND RUNWAY MARKING AND LIGHTING
(ASEL)

PILOT OPERATION – 2

REFERENCES: AC 61–21; AIM.

1. **Objective.** To determine that the applicant:

   a. Exhibits adequate knowledge by explaining airport and runway markings and lighting aids.
   b. Identifies and interprets airport, runway, and taxiway marking aids.
   c. Identifies and interprets airport lighting aids.

2. **Action.** The examiner will:

   a. Ask the applicant to explain the meaning of various airport and runway markings and lighting aids.
   b. Ask the applicant to identify the various airport and runway markings and lighting aids, and determine that the applicant's performance meets the objective.
   c. Place emphasis on the applicant's ability to explain how markings and lighting aids relate to safe operations.

Objective: What's expected of the applicant regarding airport and runway marking and lighting.

Explaining Airport and Runway Markings and Lighting Aids.
There aren't many airports that sport all the runway markings and lighting aids that are available to pilots. You may be quizzed about those that are featured at the airport that is the site of your practical test; you'll also be expected to exhibit familiarity with those that might be encountered at other airports (Fig. 3-1). You should know, for example, that the numbers on the end of the runway represent, to the nearest tenth, the magnetic heading of the runway. So Runway Nineteen could give you an indication of, say, 194 degrees, or 186 degrees, when you line up on the centerline. The letters "L" or "R" are used to distinguish between paral-

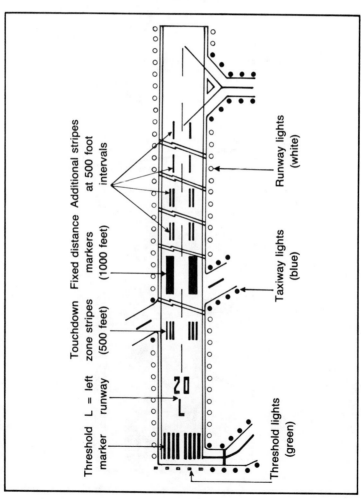

Fig. 3-1. Precision runway marking.

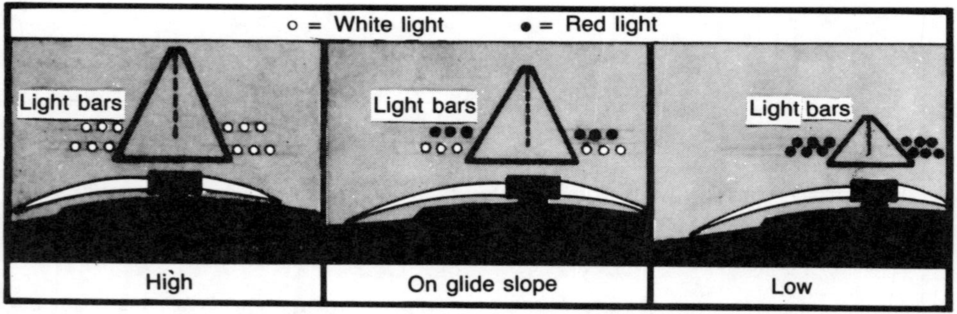

Fig. 3-2 The VASI system.

lel runways. You should also recognize the markings that indicate thresholds, displaced thresholds, and overrun areas. Explain other markings too, such as the continuous yellow line that marks the taxiway, and the "X" that indicates a closed runway or taxiway.

The lighting you'll be expected to explain will be, of course, the green/white rotating beacon and what it signifies. Though it's unlikely that you'll be taking your test at night, you should still be prepared to tell your examiner that red lights mark obstructions, green lights mark thresholds, "white" lights mark the runway, and blue lights are taxiway lights. If you're asked about VASI, say with confidence that it means Visual Approach Slope Indicator (Fig. 3-2). Recite the business about "All white is too high; all red, you're dead; but red over white is alright." You might want to review the FAA's *Pilot's Handbook* (AC 61-23), which provides much greater detail, though it's unlikely that an examiner will require more on an oral exam than we have listed here.

Identifying and Interpreting Marking Aids. Assuming that you're able to recite the various runway and taxiway markings, it seems reasonable to expect that you'll identify them when you actually see them and will interpret them appropriately. You'll taxi out following the yellow line with your nosewheel and stop at the appropriate points. If you're at a controlled field, you'll be following the controller's instructions, of course. If your test is being taken at a large and complex airport, then you'll need to follow the identifying marks for various taxiways as you follow the controller's instructions leading you to the active runway. If you become uncertain or confused, don't hesitate to check with the controller. Better to check than to blunder into a disqualifying error.

Identifying and Interpreting Lighting Aids. You will also need to identify and interpret any lighting aids that might be encountered during your checkride. This is strictly a performance requirement, since you'll already have provided an explanation of such aids. Since your test will most likely be during the day, it's unlikely that you'll encounter any lighting aids at all, let alone any that might confuse you. If the test should carry you beyond the daylight hours, just keep in mind the explanations that you provided and be prepared to respond appropriately to any lights that you might encounter.

Chapter 4

IV. AREA OF OPERATION:
TAKEOFFS AND CLIMBS

A. TASK: NORMAL TAKEOFF AND CLIMB (ASEL)

PILOT OPERATION – 5

REFERENCE: AC 61–21.

1. **Objective.** To determine that the applicant:

   a. Exhibits adequate knowledge by explaining the elements of a normal takeoff and climb including airspeeds, configurations, and emergency procedures.
   b. Aligns the airplane on the runway centerline.
   c. Advances the throttle smoothly to maximum allowable power.
   d. Checks the engine instruments.
   e. Maintains directional control on runway centerline.
   f. Rotates at the recommended[1] airspeed and accelerates to V_y.

g. Establishes the pitch attitude for V$_y$ and maintains V$_y$, ± 5 knots.

h. Retracts the wing flaps as recommended or at a safe altitude.

i. Retracts the landing gear, if retractable, after a positive rate of climb has been established and a landing can no longer be accomplished on the remaining runway.

j. Maintains takeoff power to a safe maneuvering altitude.

k. Maintains a straight track over the extended runway centerline until a turn is required.

l. Completes after–takeoff checklist.

[1] The term "recommended" as used in this standard refers to the manufacturer's recommendation. If the manufacturer's recommendation is not available, the description contained in AC 61–21 will be used.

2. Action. The examiner will:

a. Ask the applicant to explain the elements of a normal takeoff and climb including related safety factors.

b. Ask the applicant to perform a normal takeoff and climb, and determine that the applicant's performance meets the objective.

c. Place emphasis on the applicant's demonstration of correct airspeed, pitch, and heading control.

Objective. What's expected of the applicant regarding normal takeoff and climb.

Explaining the Elements of the Normal Takeoff and Climb. The point of having you explain such elements of the takeoff and climb as appropriate airspeeds, configurations, and emergency procedures is to assure the examiner that you know these procedures. Your performance may not exactly match what is called for, but if you indicate to the examiner that you at least know what is called for, it will be clearer that though your airspeed, for example, may not be precisely what is required, the requisite airspeed is at least what you are striving for. The airspeeds you'll be expected to recite will be the recommended rotation speed as indicated in the Operating Handbook (if such speed is listed), the best rate-of-climb airspeed (V_y), and the best angle-of-climb airspeed (V_x). Remember to explain that the best rate-of-climb airspeed is that which gets you to the desired altitude in the shortest *time*; the best angle-of-climb airspeed is the one that gets you to altitude within the shortest *distance* (Fig. 4-1).

As for configuration, you will provide the examiner with information on the appropriate flap setting for takeoff and also the appropriate procedure for flap retraction during the climb. If you were flying a retractable gear plane, you would also state the appropriate time (or location) for gear retraction, which is, of course, as early as possible after you have reached the point where it would not be possible to set the airplane down on the runway in the event of an emergency. We speak of this as "getting the gear up after you've run out of runway." If your plane also features cowl flaps, you'll need to specify the appropriate setting for these during taxi,

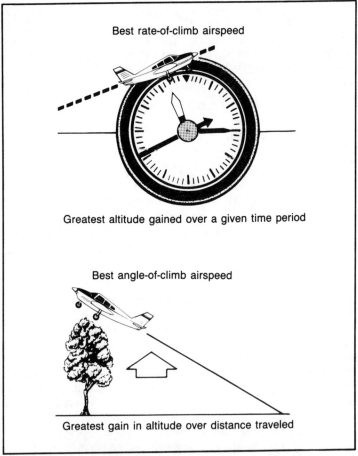

Fig. 4-1. Best rate-of-climb and best angle-of-climb airspeeds.

takeoff, and climbout. You should also advise the examiner as to when and under what conditions cowl flaps should remain open or may be closed.

You should also be able to describe the procedures to be followed in the event of an emergency. In the case of engine-out emergencies (the one that examiners are usually most concerned about), the important points to note would be the point at which you would simply abort the takeoff and remain on the runway, the point beyond which this could be accomplished and the need for continuing straight ahead as nearly as possible. Very slight turns would be permissible at low altitudes in order to avoid obstructions. You should also specify the altitude at which a turn might be attempted in order to return to the airport. When you discuss this latter point, emphasize the necessity of maintaining the airplane in a nose-low attitude and keeping the bank shallow. Also, clarify for the examiner that you clearly understand that in most instances an engine-out emergency on takeoff requires immediately dropping the nose to get the airplane into an attitude that would provide the best angle-of-glide airspeed and then maintaining flight as nearly straight ahead as possible.

Aligning the Airplane on the Centerline. When you taxi onto the active runway for your takeoff, you will have ascertained that your separation from any approaching aircraft is sufficient to permit you time to align the airplane with the runway centerline. To assure that there is such separation, I teach my students to look to the right and say "Clear right," then look to the left and say "Clear left," prior to taxiing onto the runway. They then taxi onto the active and make an effort to align the airplane with the centerline, placing the nosewheel on the center stripe. This sort of precise approach will be more impressive than that exhibited by some "hot" pilots, who jam on full throttle while still taxiing onto the active and more-or-less align themselves as they rush into the takeoff roll on the runway. That sort of thing impresses spectators, but leaves examiners a little cool.

Advancing the Throttle. Now you're lined up and ready to roll. Handle the throttle precisely as you've been instructed to do it. Even though you will probably be flying a trainer-type airplane, treat it as you would a higher performance machine. Advance the throttle steadily and smoothly to the full throttle position and hold it there. Avoid jamming it forward and then leaving it to grab the yoke in both hands. The movement should be smooth and steady; in most modern trainers, your left hand will control the yoke while your right hand remains on the throttle.

Checking the Gauges. The FAA manual calls for checking the engine instruments, and you should. Just keep in mind that most of your attention will be outside the plane. However, you will glance at the tachometer to make certain that you're getting full power. Attention is then back to the outside. Another glance to check oil pressure, sweep quickly to airspeed indicator, and then return your attention to the runway environment. The demands of the takeoff will permit little more than this, because at this crucial stage your attention must be focused on flying the airplane rather than checking gauges.

Maintaining Directional Control. Hold the airplane on the centerline. You know that as the engine reaches full power, the airplane is going to make an effort to turn to the left. Be prepared for this by maintaining the proper amount of pressure on the right rudder. If you are flying a taildragger, you also know that when the tail lifts off, gyroscopic precession is going to add to that left-turning tendency, so be prepared for it. Directional control at this phase is maintained by the rudder. At the same time that you're avoiding left-turning tendencies by maintaining pressure, you must avoid applying too much pressure and then having to correct for that. Such overcontrolling can be avoided by resting your heels on the floor, keeping the ball of the foot on the rudder pedal and steering by simply applying pressure on the ball of the foot instead of shoving the whole foot forward.

Rotation. Some airplane operating handbooks will specify a particular indicated airspeed at which you rotate, or apply back pressure to the yoke. The Cessna 150 manual, for example, specifies lifting the nosewheel at 55 mph (48 kt.). My Cherokee 235 operating handbook calls for allowing "the airplane to accelerate to 55 to 65 miles per hour, then ease back on the wheel to let the airplane fly itself off the ground." If you are not provided with such a specification, then you must follow a procedure that permits you to be sensitive to pressures. You need to avoid applying excessive back pressure that will force the airplane into the air too early. The way to avoid this is to maintain a neutral position on the control until the airplane has reached sufficient speed for you to be able to feel the pressures on the control surfaces. At that point, simply ease on enough back pressure for the airplane gradually to assume the pitch or attitude that is used for the best rate-of-climb airspeed. Hold that position and allow the airplane to lift off by itself and gradually attain the desired airspeed.

Establishing V_y Pitch Attitude. Many airplane operating manuals specify a speed at which you are to rotate, or apply sufficient back pressure to raise the nosewheel clear of the runway. However, they seem to neglect to add the additional piece of datum as to how *far* off the runway you are to lift the nosewheel. Since you will be using the best rate-of-climb airspeed (V_y), you should exert sufficient back pressure to achieve the pitch or attitude that you use in the climbout to maintain V_y. If you've practiced this during your training, then you'll recognize about where you should carry the nose of the airplane in relation to the horizon. You cannot be extremely precise about this. However, you can get close enough to enable you then to achieve V_y (or within five knots plus or minus) by making only a small adjustment in attitude after you've checked the airspeed indicator to see whether you need to add more back pressure or diminish the back pressure on the yoke or stick. Avoid staring at the airspeed indicator. Fly the airplane by pitch or attitude according to outside references and then merely—and briefly—check the airspeed indicator to see if any further adjustments are required. Do not, however, chase the needle. Simply make adjustments in pitch or attitude and hold it there.

Retracting the Flaps. As you learned in your earliest days of ground school instruction, the flap's function is to alter the shape of the wing, thereby creating or diminishing the amount of lift being generated. Retracting the flaps changes the camber of the wing, diminishing the amount of lift. As your instructor has demonstrated, the plane is going to settle slightly when you get those flaps off. Consequently, you need to be at a safe altitude when you ease off, or retract, the wing flaps. We usually advise maintaining the takeoff configuration until "clear of obstacles." That generally translates into holding them until you're at least 200 feet AGL. If there are trees or other obstructions off the departure end of the runway, then retract the flaps at a couple of hundred feet above those obstacles.

Retracting the Landing Gear. For most of you, this will not be a consideration on the private pilot practical test since you'll most likely be flying a trainer with fixed gear. If gear retraction is a part of your concern, then follow the advice listed in the FAA objective. Retract the gear after a positive rate-of-climb has been established. You can interpret this to mean after the plane has lifted off and the airspeed is approaching V_y. You may also need to touch the brakes prior to gear retraction to avoid having the wheels still spinning as they settle into the wheel wells. In freezing temperatures, if you've splashed through some water, it's best to leave the landing gear down for a bit to guarantee that everything has had a chance to dry off before retraction. In any event, don't retract the gear until it's no longer possible to accomplish a landing on whatever runway remains before you.

Maintaining Takeoff Power. What you do with the power setting will vary with different airplanes. With most small trainers, it's safe and advisable to maintain the takeoff power setting until you're at whatever altitude you intend to use for cruising. In some airplanes, it's advisable to reduce power and alter the prop setting as soon as you're clear of obstacles. There is no single rule for all planes. Therefore, prior to your checkride, be sure to check the airplane operating manual for the procedure appropriate to the particular airplane you're flying.

Tracking Out. As we mentioned before, at uncontrolled airports—and at controlled airports unless advised otherwise—you are expected to maintain a straight track over the extended centerline of the runway. Make whatever corrections are necessary to continue tracking straight out until you are ready to make the first turn in the traffic pattern.

The After-Takeoff Checklist. You won't begin any checking until you have "cleared the obstacles" (i.e., reached a safe altitude) and achieved the appropriate airspeed for the climbout. Then you'll check to make sure that you've reduced power, if that's called for. You'll also have retracted the flaps (and the landing gear, if you're in that type airplane). Most such checklists are extremely brief, enabling you to memorize them with ease. Recite it aloud for the examiner as you complete each item after the takeoff, while you continue the climbout and whatever is called for in maintaining a proper traffic pattern.

B. TASK: CROSSWIND TAKEOFF AND CLIMB (ASEL)

PILOT OPERATION – 5

REFERENCE: AC 61–21.

1. **Objective.** To determine that the applicant –

   a. Exhibits adequate knowledge by explaining the elements of a crosswind takeoff and climb including airspeeds, configurations, and emergency procedures.
   b. Verifies the wind direction.
   c. Aligns the airplane on the runway centerline.
   d. Applies full aileron deflection in proper direction.
   e. Advances the throttle smoothly to maximum allowable power.
   f. Checks the engine instruments.
   g. Maintains directional control on the runway centerline.
   h. Adjusts aileron deflection during acceleration.
   i. Rotates at the recommended airspeed, accelerates to V_y, and establishes wind–drift correction.
   j. Establishes the pitch attitude for V_y and maintains V_y, ± 5 knots.
   k. Retracts the wing flaps as recommended or at a safe altitude.
   l. Retracts the landing gear, if retractable, after a positive rate of climb has been established and a landing can no longer be accomplished on the remaining runway.
   m. Maintains takeoff power to a safe maneuvering altitude.
   n. Maintains a straight track over the extended runway centerline until a turn is required.
   o. Completes after–takeoff checklist.

2. **Action.** The examiner will:

   a. Ask the applicant to explain the elements

of a crosswind takeoff and climb including related safety factors.
- **b.** Ask the applicant to perform a crosswind takeoff and climb, and determine that the applicant's performance meets the objective. (NOTE: If a crosswind condition does not exist, the applicant's knowledge of the TASK will be evaluated through oral questioning.)
- **c.** Place emphasis on the applicant's demonstration of correct airspeed, pitch, heading, and drift control.

Objective: What is expected of the applicant regarding crosswind takeoff and climb.

Again, a part of your exhibition of what you know will be your verbal representation of what constitutes a crosswind takeoff and climb. The exception to this set of particulars will be the airplane's configuration. Even most of this will remain essentially the same. The major changes will be in how you handle ailerons and what you do after liftoff to maintain directional control (Fig. 4-2). You'll explain that the crosswind takeoff calls for cranking the ailerons into the wind. At least that's the way we instructors usually talk about it to students, confusing them until we say what we mean by such talk. What's meant, of course, is that you turn the control wheel or move the stick in the direction from which the wind is blowing. What's intended is to raise the aileron on the side from which the wind is blowing while lowering the opposite aileron. We want more lift on the downwind wing. This may even cause the downwind wheel to lift off the runway first, resulting in completing the takeoff roll on the upwind wheel. So long as directional control is maintained, this creates no problem and will put no unusual side load on the landing gear. Explain that lifting off with the proper amount of aileron turned into the wind will generally give us drift correction as the plane becomes airborne. Emergency procedures will not be altered by what we do during the crosswind takeoff.

Verifying Wind Direction. It's inconceivable that a pilot would ever take off without verifying wind direction. A different element is present when we're faced with a crosswind, however. Ideally, the takeoff would always be accomplished into the wind, but that's not always possible as you've long since learned. As a matter of fact, at airports there seems to be a universal principle at work dictating that winds must never be aligned with runways. This, of course, is particularly applicable to practical flight tests. There's *always* a crosswind, and it's *always* howling. (Or was that just my imagination on all those days when I had a student taking a checkride?) At any rate, you'll need to verify wind direction in order to be able to crank the aileron into the wind.

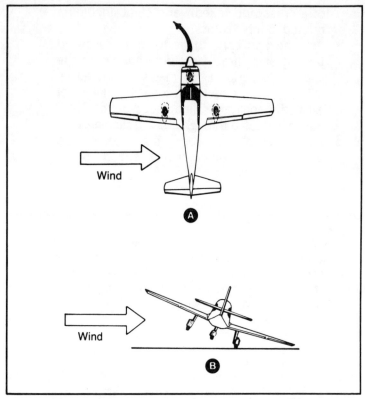

Fig. 4-2. Airplane tends to weathercock (A) as well as lean (B).

Aligning the Airplane. Nothing new here; it's mentioned just to avoid misleading anyone by omitting it. As with the normal takeoff, you align the airplane with the runway centerline, with the nose gear placed directly on that line.

Positioning the Ailerons. This is where the difference from a normal takeoff begins (Fig. 4-3). Since the wing will be developing little lift at the beginning of the takeoff roll, the aileron can have very little influence. Therefore, at the start of your takeoff roll, you will have the ailerons fully deflected in the proper direction. If the wind is from the right, then you'll crank the control wheel or push the stick all the way "to the stop," i.e., as far as it will go to the right, and you'll hold it there as the takeoff roll begins.

Advancing the Throttle. As with the normal takeoff, handle the throttle precisely. Don't jam it forward; simply advance it smoothly and steadily to the full throttle position and hold it there.

Checking the Engine Instruments. No changes here either. You'll handle this exactly as you did for the normal takeoff, remembering that most of your attention is focused on flying the airplane. You briefly glance at the instruments to verify full power, airspeed, and the like.

Maintaining Directional Control. In the tri-gear airplane, there'll be no appreciable difference since the rudder and nosewheel are generally interconnected. You'll maintain directional control just as you do for any takeoff by steering with the nosewheel. You may, however, notice some difference in the amount of pressure required to maintain alignment.

If you're taking the test in a taildragger, then the difference will be significant. In a strong crosswind, you'll find it necessary to hold considerable pressure on the downwind rudder pedal because of the airplane's tendency to weathervane.

Adjusting Aileron Deflection. You started the takeoff roll with full aileron deflection. As the airplane's speed increases, more lift will be generated and the ailerons will become increasingly effective. As they do, you adjust the deflection accordingly. This means that you will gradually move the ailerons in the direction of neutralizing them. Do not, however, remove the deflection entirely. It's desirable to maintain sufficient aileron deflection for the airplane almost to turn into the wind automatically as it becomes airborne. That aileron deflection enables you to more readily establish drift correction as you lift off.

Rotation. It may be advisable to increase the speed at which you rotate when performing a crosswind takeoff. By adding a little to the speed at which you lift off, you preclude the possibility of the airplane's settling back on the runway while moving slightly sideways. Since the airplane will start to drift as soon as it lifts off, or will be crabbing at least to some extent, settling to the runway would place an unusual side load on the landing gear. This can be avoided (and *should* be avoided) by lifting off at a slightly higher airspeed than normal. However, there will be no difference

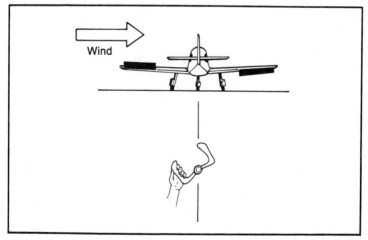

Fig. 4-3. Use of ailerons to compensate for a crosswind during takeoff roll and landing roll.

in the pitch you establish with the rotation; it still will be that which is required to achieve V$_y$ (best rate-of-climb airspeed).

As soon as the airplane is airborne, drift correction is achieved by crabbing, not by aileron deflection which lowers a wing.

Establishing Pitch or Altitude. Just as with the normal takeoff, the pitch is that which gives you V$_y$. All that's different is the heading flown in order to maintain a track straight out from the runway.

Maintaining Takeoff Power. No difference here. Follow the recommendations of the operating manual for your airplane. For most trainers, this will mean simply maintaining the full throttle setting until you reach altitude.

Maintaining a Straight Track. You will find it necessary to rely on outside references to ascertain whether or not your track is straight out from the runway. Having established a crabbing altitude on liftoff, you will now find it necessary only to make minor adjustments in the crabbing angle in order to maintain the proper track. This angle will be held until you are ready to make the first turn in the traffic pattern.

The After-Takeoff Checklist. This is no different for the crosswind takeoff than for the normal takeoff.

C. TASK: SHORT—FIELD TAKEOFF AND CLIMB (ASEL)

PILOT OPERATION – 8

REFERENCE: AC 61–21.

1. **Objective.** To determine that the applicant:

   a. Exhibits adequate knowledge by explaining the elements of a short—field takeoff and climb including the significance of appropriate airspeeds and configurations, emergency procedures, and the expected performance for existing operating conditions.
   b. Selects the recommended wing flap setting.
   c. Positions the airplane at the beginning of the takeoff runway aligned on the runway centerline.
   d. Advances the throttle smoothly to maximum allowable power.
   e. Adjusts the pitch attitude to attain maximum rate of acceleration.
   f. Maintains directional control on the runway centerline.
   g. Rotates at the recommended airspeed and accelerates to V_x.
   h. Climbs at V_x or recommended airspeed, +5, –0 knots until obstacle is cleared, or until at least 50 feet above the surface, then accelerates to V_y and maintains V_y, ±5 knots.
   i. Retracts the wing flaps as recommended or at a safe altitude.
   j. Retracts the landing gear, if retractable, after a positive rate of climb has been established and a safe landing can no longer be accomplished on the remaining runway.
   k. Maintains takeoff power to a safe maneuvering altitude.
   l. Maintains a straight track over the extended runway centerline until a turn is required.

m. Completes after–takeoff checklist.

2. Action. The examiner will:

a. Ask the applicant to explain the elements of a short–field takeoff and climb including the significance of appropriate airspeeds and configurations.

b. Ask the applicant to perform a short–field takeoff and climb, and determine that the applicant's performance meets the objective.

c. Place emphasis on the applicant's demonstration of correct airspeed control.

Objective: What's expected of the applicant regarding short-field takeoff and climb.

Exhibiting Knowledge through Explanation. As with other required takeoffs and climbs, there are many elements of the short-field takeoff and climb that are the same as those for the normal takeoff and climb. You should expect to describe whatever is unique to the short-field takeoff and climb.

Selecting the Recommended Wing Flap Setting. There is no general statement regarding flap setting that will be appropriate to all aircraft. There is no alternative to checking the operating handbook for the airplane you'll be flying for the practical test. For example, though normal takeoffs in the Cherokee are made with flaps retracted, the short field takeoff is performed with two notches (25 degrees) of flaps. In the Cessna 150/152, on the other hand, both normal takeoffs and short-field takeoffs are accomplished with flaps up. Check the operating handbook for your plane and get it right.

Aligning the Airplane with the Centerline. This is essentially the same requirement as for the normal takeoff. There is one difference here, however. Since this is to be accomplished within a short distance, you must exercise greater-than-normal care in utilizing *all* available space. Consequently, after ascertaining that all approaching and departing aircraft are clear, you will taxi onto the runway exercising care, as you align your plane with the centerline, to place the main gear at the very end of the runway. having thus positioned the airplane. You will then apply and hold brakes.

Advancing the Throttle. There may be some slight controversy here, though I doubt that it is serious. A disagreement may arise based on the way this was handled in the good old days. In those times, we lined up, applied brakes, advanced the throttle to the full open position, and then released the brakes to start the takeoff roll. We did it that way because we thought it got us into the air sooner and climbing more rapidly. When experiments demonstrated that such procedure made no significant difference in the performance of the plane, it was dropped in favor of handling the throttle precisely as one does for normal takeoffs. In recent years, however, there has been a return to the old procedure. Once again, while holding brakes at the end of the runway, we smoothly, steadily advance the throttle to the full open position. We don't do it because we expect better performance from the airplane. Nowadays, we use the procedure to give us a chance to check power. So while holding brakes at full throttle, check the tachometer. Since this is a short-field performance, we want to be certain that full power is available. Use this procedure, and if your tachometer indicates that the aircraft engine is developing less than full power, abort the takeoff. Since you presumably have a shorter-than-normal distance available to you for taking off, you can't afford the luxury of using part of the runway for checking the gauges.

Adjusting Pitch or Altitude for Maximum Rate of Acceleration. You're sitting at very end of the runway, holding brakes with full throttle applied. The ailerons will be neutral (unless there's a crosswind), as will the rudder. That's the way it is for normal takeoffs, too. In the case of the short-field takeoff, it's important to ascertain that the elevators are in neutral position, too. Maintaining this neutral position will provide the lowest angle of attack possible without exerting unusual pressure on the landing gear (Fig. 4-4). The low angle of attack creates the least amount of life possible in this situation, which also creates the least amount of drag possible, thereby enabling the airplane to accelerate at the maximum rate. At the same time that you maintain this low angle of attack (some instructors refer to it as "holding the airplane on the runway"), you must exercise care not to hold forward pressure on the yoke. Forward pressure could exert additional pressure on the nose gear, thus countering your other efforts to maximize the rate of acceleration.

Maintaining Directional Control. Again, there will be some difference in handling the plane for this type of takeoff. Since the pilot has run the engine up to full power before releasing the brakes, the airplane will have a distinct tendency to swerve to the left when the brakes are released.

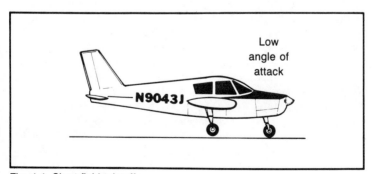

Fig. 4-4. Short-field takeoff.

Be prepared for this by holding some pressure against the right rudder prior to releasing brakes. Care must also be exercised to avoid overcontrolling, particularly at the beginning of the takeoff roll. Once the takeoff roll is established, then directional control will be no different than during the normal takeoff.

Rotating at the Recommended Airspeed. The airspeed at which you will rotate for the short-field takeoff will be few knots less than the recommended best *angle*-of-climb airspeed for your airplane. If the best angle-of-climb airspeed for the trainer you're flying is 55 knots, then at about 50 knots you'll start the rotation. By the time the plane has achieved the appropriate altitude, your airspeed, which will continue to increase, will be at the best angle-of-climb airspeed. For this takeoff, you're relying on a greater angle of attack to generate more lift than normal. Since greater lift means greater drag, the airspeed for this takeoff and climb will be lower than that for the normal takeoff and climb.

Climbing at the Recommended Airspeed. The airspeed is one of the elements that distinguishes the short-field takeoff and climb from the normal handling of this maneuver. The recommended airspeed is the best angle-of-climb airspeed (V_x) instead of the best rate-of-climb airspeed (V_y). (Review Fig. 4-1.) Since the pilot is dealing with a short field, what's called for is getting to altitude in the shortest possible *distance*, rather than in the shortest possible *time*. The pitch that maintains this airspeed—and consequently the airspeed itself—is maintained until "clear of the obstacle," or until at least 50 feet AGL. In case you're wondering about that 50 feet, that number is an arbitrary obstacle clearance figure. If there are no obstacles at all, then best angle-of-climb airspeed is maintained until that altitude is reached. If you've got trees that are 80 feet tall at the end of the runway, then you'd better make an adjustment and maintain your pitch until you're 50 feet above them. (Bader Field at Atlantic City was once a prime example of the need to ignore that "50 feet" number. In the pre-casino days, all runways were open and it used to be a fascinating experience to take off to the east, where the hotels awaited you just a short distance from the end of the runway. Both pilots and hotel guests on the upper floors were provided an interesting view of each other as lightplanes, maintaining their best angle-of-climb airspeed to several hundred feet, flew among the tall buildings and out over the ocean.) So keep in mind that it's the "clear of obstacle" (and then some) requirement that's significant. Once clear of obstacles, you then lower the nose to reduce pitch, or altitude, in order to achieve the best rate-of-climb airspeed. That is, you go from V_x to V_y, or you convert the short-field climb to a normal climb.

Retracting the Wing Flaps. There is nothing unique about getting the flaps up following the short-field takeoff. As with any takeoff, if flaps are used, they are not retracted until you've reached a safe altitude. With the climbout from the short-field takeoff, you can retract the flaps as soon as you've altered your pitch or attitude to achieve V_y. By that time, you know you're going to be high enough to make any settling that occurs with flap retraction insignificant.

Retracting the Landing Gear. If this requirement is applicable to the airplane you're flying, it may mean retracting the gear earlier than you may be accustomed to. You still will not retract gear until the airplane is really climbing and you've run out of runway, but with a short field, it's very likely that as soon as you're sure the plane has lifted off and there's no danger of settling back onto the runway, you'll be able to get the landing gear out of the way. Cleaning the airplane up a little earlier, since you run out of runway earlier, will help increase your rate of climb while you're in that best angle-of-climb attitude.

Maintaining Takeoff Power. Again, there's no significant difference from the normal climb. As a matter of fact, once you've "cleared the obstacle" and reduced the pitch in order to achieve V_y, the climb is converted to a normal climb. For most trainers, you'll simply hold full throttle until you reach your cruising, or maneuvering, altitude. Check the operating handbook if you're unsure about what to do with the particular airplane you're flying for the checkride.

Maintaining a Straightout Track. This is no different from the normal climb.

Completing the After-Takeoff Checklist. This is still the same as the normal takeoff. If you happen to be flying a plane like the Cherokee, then you have the extra business of getting a couple of notches of flaps off. Your checklist would then include checking to see that flaps are fully retracted. Otherwise, handle this the same as you do for a normal takeoff.

D. TASK: SOFT–FIELD TAKEOFF AND CLIMB (ASEL)

PILOT OPERATION – 8

REFERENCE: AC 61–21.

1. **Objective.** To determine that the applicant:

   a. Exhibits adequate knowledge by explaining the elements of a soft–field takeoff and climb including the significance of appropriate airspeeds and configurations, emergency procedures, and hazards associated with climbing at an airspeed less than V_X. #

   b. Selects the recommended wing flap setting.

   c. Taxies onto the takeoff surface at a speed consistent with safety.

   d. Aligns the airplane on takeoff path without stopping and advances the throttle smoothly to maximum allowable power.

   e. Adjusts and maintains a pitch attitude which transfers the weight from the wheels to the wings as rapidly as possible.

   f. Maintains directional control on the center of the takeoff path.

   g. Lifts off at the lowest possible airspeed and remains in ground effect while accelerating.

   h. Accelerates to and maintains V_X ±5, –0 knots, if obstructions must be cleared, otherwise to V_Y, ±5 knots.

   i. Retracts the wing flaps as recommended or at a safe altitude.

   j. Retracts the landing gear, if retractable, after a positive rate of climb has been established and a landing can no longer be accomplished on the remaining runway.

   k. Maintains takeoff power to a safe maneuvering altitude.

l. Maintains a straight track over the center of the extended takeoff path until a turn is required.

m. Completes after-takeoff checklist.

2. Action. The examiner will:

a. Ask the applicant to explain the elements of a soft–field takeoff and climb including the significance of appropriate airspeeds and configurations.

b. Ask the applicant to perform a soft–field takeoff and climb, and determine that the applicant's performance meets the objective.

c. Place emphasis on the applicant's demonstration of correct airplane control and remaining in ground effect while accelerating to climb airspeed.

Objective: What's expected of the applicant regarding the soft-field takeoff and climb.

Exhibiting Knowledge by Explanation. As with the other required takeoffs, the soft-field takeoff and climb has many similarities to normal takeoffs and climbs. For this maneuver, as with the preceding two, you're going to be describing in particular the elements that are distinctive.

The airspeeds and configurations are genuinely significant for this maneuver. The associated hazards must be fully appreciated and the emergency procedures well-known. The element that makes this takeoff unique is the low airspeed. You will be flying the airplane at a speed less than the best angle-of-climb airspeed, i.e., slower than V_x. Consequently, you must possess adequate knowledge and exhibit genuine skill. Incidentally, the procedures used for soft fields are also used in similar situations such as higher-than-normal grass on sod runways, or snowy runways.

All that seriousness aside (and I am just taking it aside and not dismissing it), this takeoff I regard as the most fun of all takeoffs. Learning to execute it well will develop more skill, probably, than any of the other takeoffs and climbs. I enjoy teaching this one, because it requires greater skill and consequently provides greater satisfaction when mastered. And you know you've *really* got it when you can combine the requirements for this with a challenging crosswind.

Selecting the Correct Flap Setting. Even the Cessna 150/152 calls for using flaps for this takeoff. It's the only time you'll be using flaps for takeoffs in that airplane. You don't use much—only 10 degrees—but this distinction tells you that there really is something different about this takeoff and climb. For planes other than the Cessna 150/152, check the operating manual; leave nothing to guesswork.

Taxiing onto the Takeoff Surface. Notice that we didn't say runway? Generally, you'll be taking off from a runway, of course. But even the FAA manual speaks differently this time. We assume that you've started from a firm, clear surface and that you've done your runup on that surface prior even to starting to taxi. You certainly don't want to do any more taxiing than is necessary on a soft field. And clearly, you're not going to choose a soft spot to stop and conduct the runup. So when you're ready to roll, all of this has already been accomplished. You then begin the taxi to the end of the "takeoff surface" using a power setting that will keep you moving at a safe speed, generally that of rapid walk. It's important to keep the airplane moving. You'll also hold the yoke all the way back to keep pressure off the nosewheel.

As you approach the end of the runway, you get the airplane into its takeoff configuration (pull on the appropriate flap setting); check the traffic as you continue to taxi right onto the end of the runway. Once you start the airplane moving, you don't stop for anything unless an emergency sends you back to the place you started from.

Aligning the Airplane on the Takeoff Path. There is no separate positioning of the airplane for this takeoff. Since your taxiing has carried you right onto the end of the runway, the alignment is all a part of the taxiing. As the airplane becomes aligned with the takeoff path, you advance the throttle as you do for a normal takeoff, smoothly and steadily to full throttle, or to whatever power setting is appropriate for the airplane which you're flying. All of this is accomplished without the airplane ever hesitating in its movement and with the taxiing being simply converted into the takeoff run with the application of power.

Adjusting and Maintaining Pitch, or Attitude. This is another element that makes the soft-field takeoff unique. At the beginning of your taxiing, the yoke or stick should have been held all the way back to keep undue pressure off the nosewheel, as was mentioned above (Fig. 4-5). That back pressure is maintained at the beginning of the takeoff roll. Now there's an additional purpose. By holding back pressure, you cause the nose of the airplane to pitch up, significantly increasing the wing's angle of attack. This increased angle of attack generates additional lift at a slower airspeed. The effect of this is to transfer the weight of the airplane from the wheels to the wings as early as possible.

The question remains as to how much back pressure you should hold. In some light airplanes, you may continue to hold the yoke all the way back "to the stop." In other airplanes, such as the Cessna 150/152, you must ease off some of the back pressure as the airplane accelerates. I have had a number of student pilots give themselves an unexpected thrill when they held too much back pressure and banged the tail tiedown hook onto the runway. In that hollow metal airplane, it's something like striking timpani.

Fig. 4-5. Soft-field takeoff.

When the student, who's concentrating everything on holding back pressure and maintaining directional control, hears that loud, hollow bang, he/she is startled to say the least, and generally convinced momentarily that he/she and the airplane have somehow been destroyed. You don't need to impress the examiner with such a performance, so do what should be done in any airplane you may be flying. Simply hold enough back pressure to achieve the attitude that will give you the best angle-of-climb airspeed (V_x) and maintain the attitude until liftoff. Even at this stage of experience, taking your private pilot flight check, it may seem sensationally nose-high, but hold it right there despite your sensations.

Maintaining Directional Control. There's an extra little challenge in maintaining directional control on the center of the takeoff path when the airplane is in the nose-high attitude that's used for the soft-field takeoff. Normally, you'd be looking out over the nose with lots of visibility. With this takeoff, the nose will be high enough to block your view of the runway straight ahead. Consequently, you must, in a manner of speaking, look around the left side of the nose instead of across the top. Don't try to look straight out the side or straight down, however. Peer out that left side and look as far ahead of the airplane as the nose permits. You'll still be using pressure on the rudder to maintain directional control; the difference is with that changed visibility. Just remember to keep your heels on the floor and to steer with pressure on the ball of your foot rather than by shoving the whole foot forward.

Liftoff Airspeed. Notice that there is no mention of a recommended speed for rotation for this takeoff. Since the yoke is held all the way back throughout taxiing and at least at the beginning of the takeoff roll, there can't be a prescribed rotation airspeed for the soft-field takeoff. There is also no prescribed liftoff airspeed. Given the attitude of the airplane, the liftoff will occur whenever the wing generates sufficient lift. As you know, this will occur at an airspeed significantly lower than the best angle-of-climb airspeed. The wing will fly at a significantly lower airspeed because of ground effect. You might wish to review ground effect in your ground school training materials prior to the checkride. However, as you have learned, the airplane will fly at a much lower airspeed just above the runway than it will fly at altitude. Therefore, it's essential to keep the airplane in ground effect until the airspeed builds to the best angle-of-climb airspeed. As soon as the airplane lifts off, the nose must be firmly but smoothly lowered to remain in ground effect and to permit a higher airspeed to develop as a consequence of this new attitude.

I recall teaching this to a student of mine who got the airplane off but was flying out of ground effect. The stall warning horn was blaring and the airplane was shuddering while he continued to hold back pressure. I finally had to yell, "Get the nose down," and accompanied it with a healthy shove forward on the yoke. He blanched as he saw that nose drop significantly toward the runway, but we had managed to catch it in time and prevented the airplane from settling back. The tendency at times is to haul farther back on the yoke, as though to pull the airplane higher, but it'll never work. So remember to ease off that back pressure after liftoff.

Accelerating to the Appropriate Airspeed. Having leveled off as soon as the airplane lifts off, you will have established a new pitch that will enable the airplane to accelerate. As the airspeed reaches the best rate-of-climb airspeed (V_y), exert sufficient back pressure on the yoke to achieve an attitude that will maintain this airspeed. By the time the new pitch, or attitude, is established, the airplane will be slightly above V_y and you will maintain this airspeed, converting the soft-field takeoff and climb at this stage to a normal climb. If the soft field happens also to be a short field, then it will be necessary to exert the back pressure at a slower airspeed, i.e., to V_x, and to maintain the best angle-of-climb airspeed until clear of the obstacles. When clear of obstacles, the climb should be converted to a normal climb. Never, however, attempt to climb out at less than V_x.

Retracting the Flaps. The flaps have contributed to your transferring the weight of the plane from the wheels to the wings so they should remain in the takeoff position until they're no longer needed. Generally, this will occur at the point where you convert the soft-field takeoff and climb to a normal climb. At that point, when you are certain that you are clear of obstacles, flaps may be eased off, a little at a time.

Retracting the Gear. For the most part, there is no difference in the point at which retractable landing gear may be "picked up." However, if water or slush has caused you to use soft-field takeoff procedures, then you may wish to let the gear hang down a little longer than normal to ensure that they are dried. Generally, with the soft-field takeoff and climb, as with other takeoffs and climbs, the gear will be retracted as soon as possible after you have lifted off and run out of runway.

Maintaining Takeoff Power. This element of the takeoff is no different for this takeoff and climb than for any other.

Maintaining a Straight Track. As with all other takeoffs, unless instructed to do otherwise, maintain a track straight out from the extended centerline of the runway until it's time for the first turn in the traffic pattern. **Completing the After-Takeoff Checklist.** As with all other takeoffs, recite the items for the examiner touching or manipulating each item as you mention it.

Chapter 5

V. AREA OF OPERATION:
CROSS–COUNTRY FLYING

A. TASK: **PILOTAGE AND DEAD RECKONING** (ASEL)

PILOT OPERATION – 7

REFERENCES: AC 61–21, AC 61–23.

1. **Objective.**   To determine that the applicant:

   a. Exhibits adequate knowledge by explaining pilotage and dead reckoning techniques and procedures.
   b. Follows the pre–planned course solely by visual reference to landmarks.
   c. Identifies landmarks by relating the surface features to chart symbols.
   d. Navigates by means of precomputed headings, groundspeed, and elapsed time.
   e. Combines pilotage and dead reckoning.
   f. Verifies the airplane's position within 3

nautical miles at all times.

g. Arrives at the en route checkpoints ± 5 minutes of the initial or revised ETA and estimates the destination, ± 10 minutes.

h. Computes the remaining fuel.

i. Corrects for, and records, the differences between preflight groundspeed and heading calculations and those determined en route.

j. Maintains the selected altitudes, within ±200 feet.

k. Maintains the appropriate power setting for the desired airspeed.

l. Maintains the desired heading, ±10°.

m. Follows the climb, cruise, and descent checklists.

2. **Action.** The examiner will:

a. Ask the applicant to explain navigation by pilotage and dead reckoning.

b. Ask the applicant to navigate by pilotage and dead reckoning, and determine that the applicant's performance meets the objective.

c. Place emphasis on the applicant's ability to locate the airplane's position at all times, and to estimate ETA's and fuel consumption accurately.

Objective: What's expected of the applicant regarding pilotage and dead reckoning.

Exhibiting Knowledge by Explanation. Despite the fact that these times are being touted as the age of the computer, and that the little black boxes seem to be taking over the cockpit increasingly, private pilots are expected to be present in the cockpit and to use their heads when engaged in cross-country flying. There's no denying that there are pilots out there whose sole approach to navigation is wandering from VOR station to VOR station, but the requirement for knowing something about pilotage and dead reckoning remains.

Pilotage is the type of navigation that you learned and used first in your flight training. When you were approaching the end of an hour of dual and the instructor said to you, "Okay, take me back to the airport," you wiped the sweat off your brow and, having been concentrating strictly on airwork, looked around to see where your maneuvers had carried you. As you looked around, you finally noticed that big lake off to your left, and then the high-speed, dual-lane highway to the right of that and said to yourself, "Oh, yeah, the airport's back *thataway*." Turning the airplane, you flew in the right direction, watching for the town with the tower and the big factory on the left and then the other town with the blue water tower that came up next on the right. From there you could see the quarry that was just to the southeast of the airport, etc. Using such familiar and visible landmarks, while flying at relatively low altitudes, you found your way back to the airport.

That's all there is to pilotage. It's just a matter of sitting there with the charts on your knees and the landscape out there, and you match 'em up and fly according to what you see. Explain to the examiner that the advantages are: It's easy to learn, easy to do, and requires no special equipment. The disadvantages are: You can use it only when prominent landmarks are available, you may be precluded from following the shortest route, and it may be impossible to use in conditions of limited visibility. Its practicality can be improved if you add the compass to your kit of equipment, because then, if some landmarks are a little far apart, the compass may carry you to the next prominent feature. But pilotage is generally limited to those flights of short duration at low altitude when plenty of prominent landmarks are available.

Nowadays, with the introduction of interstate highways, pilots can use them instead of the old "iron beam" (railroads, for the younger generation), but we generally rely on more sophisticated navigation. Don't dismiss pilotage, however. We don't rely solely on the use of pilotage, but it is a good idea to use it along with more sophisticated systems. When I'm teaching cross-country flying, I still turn off the radios at some point and force the student to navigate by eyeball.

Even dead reckoning isn't extensively used any longer. Still, you will be expected to demonstrate knowledge of this technique. In fact, the first part of the practical test required that you do all the paperwork preliminary to actually navigating by using dead reckoning. Strictly speaking, we don't use landmarks for dead reckoning. This system of navigation is based solely on airspeed, compass heading, wind direction and velocity, and elapsed time. In practical terms, however, we rely on a combination of dead reckoning and pilotage.

There really should be very little left to explain at this stage of the practical test, since you'll already have gone over all the required material and explanations during the cross-country planning part of the preflight phase of your practical test. You might add, in your discussion of this with the examiner, that even though you may rely essentially on radio navigation for cross-country flying, you also invariably do the dead reckoning preparation and couple it with radio navigation so that you always know where you are. This keeps you prepared for the day you lose your radio(s) and must rely on dead reckoning to get you to your destination.

Pilotage. Your practical test will include the requirement that you at least start to fly the cross-country flight that you've planned. It's very unlikely that you'll complete the trip, because the examiner does not generally want to make a trip but only to check your skills. Consequently, after taking off, you'll start the trip that you planned earlier. During some phase of the flight, the examiner will require you to fly the course strictly by reference to visible landmarks. He/she may even turn off the radio to simulate radio failure and force you to rely solely on landmarks. If you continuously pay attention to where you are, this should pose no difficulty.

Relating Landmarks to Chart Symbols. Since you'll be sitting there with the charts on your knees, simply point out surface features both on the map by referring to the appropriate symbols and on the ground by indicating to the examiner where these features are actually located.

Navigating by Dead Reckoning. While the radios are off, the examiner may require that you now rely on the dead reckoning that you planned during the preflight phase. This may make you a little nervous because you undoubtedly learned during your student flying days that there were times when your dead reckoning fix didn't exactly agree with your position according to radio and pilotage. Some variable wasn't appraised quite accurately and this created a difference. Admittedly, there is an element of uncertainty surrounding every position determined purely by dead reckoning. Generally, it's because dead reckoning involves computation with *approximate* data. The wind direction and velocity are never precisely as you represented them in your planning. Nor can your actual ground speed be predicted with precise and exact reliability. All of this means that any fix that you take while you're flying must also be approximate. But you're lucky. Being up there above the obstructions, you can look around a bit and find the landmarks that indicate where you're supposed to be. The lack of absolute certainty is one of the reasons you listed those checkpoints on your flight log. Instead of cranking in all the data and then flying until you reach your destination before checking, you include many "destinations" on your flight log. That way, you're never more than 15 or 20 minutes from your last known checkpoint. And with the use of dead reckoning, you've now added another element to the others that make up each checkpoint.

Combining Pilotage and Dead Reckoning. When you reach checkpoint number one, you will not only look for that intersection, railroad, and water tower that are supposed to be there; you'll also look at your watch and the flight log and see that according to the rate and time, this distance should indeed have been covered, thus verifying that those items on the ground do, without doubt, constitute the checkpoint you were looking for.

Verifying the Airplane's Position. Using the combination of dead reckoning and pilotage in this manner will assure that you know the approximate position of the airplane at all times. Instead of sleeping between checkpoints and trusting to luck to get you to the next one, you should be constantly alert to your airplane's position. The fact that you've listed particular points on your flight log for positively verifying the position of the airplane does not preclude your regularly checking as the flight progresses. Knowing precisely how long ago you passed the last checkpoint, and having a reasonably accurate idea of your rate, you should be able to very quickly calculate the airplane's position within two or three miles whenever the examiner requests such verification. Then, having made such a guess, look for something on the chart that can be used to back up your estimate.

Checking the Checkpoints. You'll be expected to arrive at each checkpoint reasonably close to the time you estimated during your flight planning. However, keep in mind that you are not wedded to those figures that you entered on the flight log. As you reach each checkpoint, you will have a newer and more accurate idea as to what the wind is doing to your rate and distance, enabling you with relatively easy calculation to correct the figures on your flight log. Consequently, the actual time at which you reach your destination may differ significantly from the time you originally entered in the flight log. But if you keep a record of what's happening as you reach each checkpoint and then revise the flight log accordingly, you should be able to arrive at the destination well within the plus-or-minus 10 minutes tolerance allowed by the examiner.

Computing Fuel. While you're making those little adjustments to your flight log by putting in the "actuals" to replace all the "estimateds," don't neglect to keep a check on what's probably happening to your fuel. If you do this at each checkpoint, you will be able to provide the examiner with a reasonable estimate of fuel remaining at any time he/she may request such information.

Making the Corrections. For the dead reckoning part of your cross-country flying, this will also include checking to see what the wind is actually doing to you so that you can include heading corrections in the changes that you make in the flight log as well as in actually flying the course.

Maintaining Altitude. While all of the navigating is going on, you'll also steal occasional glances at the altimeter to maintain the altitude that you listed on the flight log. You will need to make occasional corrections here, too. If you see that you're beginning to drift away from the altitude at which you planned to fly, don't ignore it until it gets serious. Make whatever adjustment you need to make in order to maintain a relatively constant altitude.

Maintaining the Desired Airspeed. Well, as you can see, the FAA blew it on this item. They said that you should maintain the appropriate power setting in order to get the airspeed that you want. We all know that's wrong, except for the FAA. You'll set the *attitude* that you want in order to maintain the desired airspeed. The power setting is what will maintain your *altitude*. I recommend to my students that once the airplane is at the altitude they've planned, the throttle should be locked. This will minimize the need for continuously making adjustments.

Now, you can't lock the yoke or stick in order to maintain a constant airspeed. (Well, that gust lock might do it, but it would also bust your checkride.) So, you lock onto an image; you get a picture of where that nose should be in relation to the horizon and keep it as near to that position as you can. Your airspeed will then take care of itself. All you'll need to do is monitor the airspeed indicator, just as you continuously monitor the altimeter, making whatever minor adjustments are called for. Make such adjustments rather promptly, too; don't wait until you are 500 feet or 20 knots off before you respond.

On the other hand, when you respond, do it simply by making some adjustment which you continue to maintain. Don't get in the habit of continuously chasing needles; they always win.

Maintaining Heading. Similarly, your heading should be held. The FAA manual calls for holding a heading within 10 degrees either way. You'll be better off if you keep it tighter than that. You keep it tighter by making a correction when the airplane begins to drift off. If you wait too long, i.e., until you're 10 degrees off, you'll find yourself flying an erratic course. When you see the airplane drift two or three degrees off the desired heading, just hold a little pressure on a rudder pedal to correct. Yes, I know—you'll skid a little bit. But holding that pressure will gradually bring you back to the heading without causing you to overcorrect.

Following the Checklists. You've already done the climb checklist; we took care of that in the last chapter. The cruise checklist is usually relatively simple, particularly for the trainers that most prospective pilots fly for the practical test. It generally involves no more than establishing the cruise power setting, adjusting the elevator trim (rudder trim, too, if that's available), and leaning the mixture. The latter is important; don't ignore it. Not only do you save fuel, but the engine performs better and is healthier if you lean for cruise.

Similarly, the descent checklist is generally relatively simple. It usually involves no more than returning to full rich mixture, applying carburetor heat before reducing power (if that's appropriate), and establishing a descent airspeed. More about all of that when we get to doing landings.

B. TASK: RADIO NAVIGATION (ASEL)

PILOT OPERATION – 7

REFERENCES: AC 61–21,
AC 61–23.

1. **Objective.** To determine that the applicant:

   a. Exhibits adequate knowledge by explaining radio navigation, equipment, procedures, and limitations.
   b. Selects and identifies the desired radio facility.
   c. Locates the airplane's position relative to the radio navigation facility.
   d. Intercepts and tracks a given radial or bearing.
   e. Locates the airplane's position using cross bearings.
   f. Recognizes or describes the indication of station passage.
   g. Recognizes signal loss and takes appropriate action.
   h. Maintains the appropriate altitude, ±200 feet, and desired airspeed, ±5 knots.

2. **Action.** The examiner will:

   a. Ask the applicant to explain the procedures used for radio navigation.
   b. Ask the applicant to intercept and track a given radial or bearing, and determine that the applicant's performance meets the objective.
   c. Place emphasis on the applicant's ability to identify a navigation signal and to track a radial.

Objective: What's expected of the applicant regarding radio navigation.
Exhibiting Knowledge by Explanation. There are several levels of knowledge regarding radio navigation. The level presented here is not that which is required for your private pilot practical test. But if you see how

the system works, it may help you provide an explanation that will not only get you through the checkride, but will enable you properly to use radio navigation throughout your flying in the future. Although there are various refinements and some rather complex equipment, the basic radio navigation will consist of the use of VOR—Very high frequency Omnidirectional Range.

You'll explain that the equipment consists of a VOR station, which broadcasts an infinite number of radials, and a receiver, in the airplane, which is calibrated to reflect 360 separate radials. Each radial is a magnetic direction from the VOR radio station. The radials are numbered according to the bearing from the station, with the 0- (or 360-) degree radial pointed toward magnetic north (Fig. 5-1). The airplane's receiver can detect each radial, and can therefore identify the one on which the airplane is currently located. The pilot, then, is able to determine a bearing or line of position from the VOR station.

Let the examiner know that you understand that the VOR gives bearing, or azimuth, only, not location or direction. Of course, you can use the radial from two or more stations to determine your location, but the signal from each still indicates only a bearing. You establish the location at the point of intersection of two of these radials. Clarify also that the bearing derived from the radio signal is not related to your direction of flight. You can be on the 300-degree radial regardless of the direction in which you're flying.

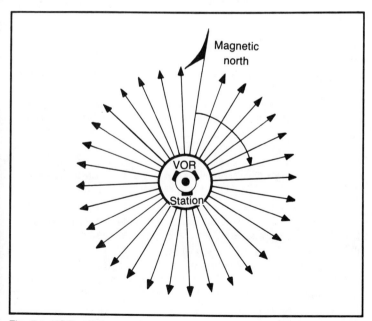

Fig. 5-1. VOR radials.

The VOR stations transmit within a VHF frequency band of 108.00 to 117.95 MHz. Being VHF, the signals are line-of-sight and subject to the restrictions imposed by such transmissions. The range varies in direct proportion to the height of the airplane receiving equipment. *Generally*, the reception range at an altitude of 1000 feet is about 45 to 50 miles. The distance increases with altitude. This can be altered, of course, by obstacles such as a hill or range of mountains. On the other hand, the advantages of the system are that the pilot can navigate on any of the 360 courses to or away from the station. Also, the VOR frequencies are free from interference caused by electrical storms. The pilot can fly straight-line courses with great accuracy. And all the VOR courses are magnetic.

Selecting and Identifying the Desired Radio Facility. You will first select the facility on the chart (Fig. 5-2). The VOR symbol (1) is surrounded by an azimuth ring (2). Information about the VOR station is given in the small box (3) near the VOR symbol within the compass rose. This information includes the name of the station (4), the station frequency in Megahertz (5), the station code letters (6), and the Morse identification (7). Transmitting and receiving frequencies are indicated above the box (8), and the controlling Flight Service Station is indicated in brackets beneath the box (9).

Having selected the appropriate facility on the chart, you must now make the selection on the NAV receiver. The first step is to turn the station selector to the proper frequency. Second, listen to the identifier code to ensure that the proper station is tuned in and that this station is functioning. Next, tune the Omni Bearing Selector (OBS) until the appropriate TO-FROM flag is displayed. Finally, continue tuning the OBS until the Course Deviation Indicator (CDI), or "needle," is centered. You now have the bearing to (or from) the station.

Locating the Airplane's Position Relative to the Facility. Keep in mind that the only data given by the procedure above is bearing. You can determine, however, which radial the airplane is on. You know that if the flag indicates TO, you are on the reciprocal of the bearing indicated. That is, if a TO flag is displayed with a 300-degree radial indicated, you are then on the 120-degree radial. If a 300-degree radial is indicated and a FROM flag is displayed, then you are on the 300-degree radial.

Intercepting and Tracking. The examiner will probably ask you to fly to (intercept) a given radial and then to track to, or on, that radial. Keep in mind that if you are asked to intercept the 300-degree radial in order to track to the station on that radial, then you must, after obtaining the TO flag as described above, tune in the reciprocal, or the 120-degree radial. The TO flag indicates that the radial you have tuned in is on the side of the station opposite that of your position. You are flying to that radial, not on it (Fig. 5-3). On the other hand, if you are asked to intercept a radial in order to track outbound from the station, then, assuming that you are on the proper side of the station and the examiner is not being tricky, simply obtain the FROM flag, tune in the radial requested, and you'll be fly-

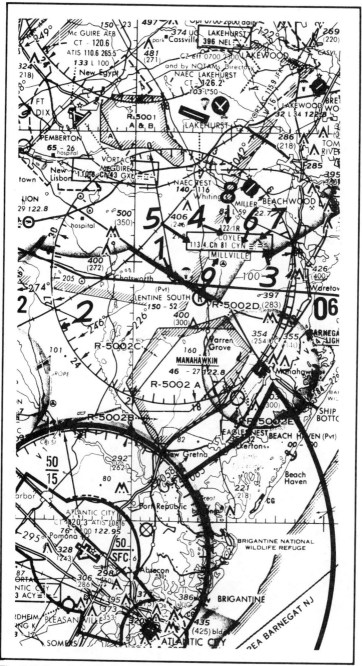

Fig. 5-2. Sample of Sectional Chart.

119

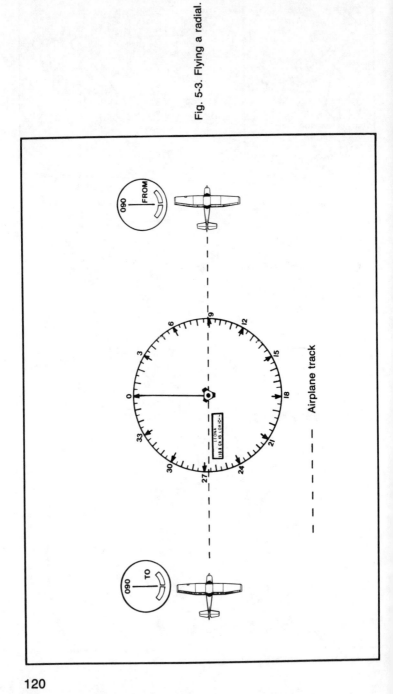

Fig. 5-3. Flying a radial.

ing on that radial.

The tracking part is simple. But it can get confusing if you forget that the VOR data simply gives you azimuth. Maybe a more accurate way to think about it is to understand that the VOR really tells you what quadrant the airplane is in. In the first place, the needle can be centered by tuning in either of two radials. For example, if you're on the 90-degree radial, then either the 90-degree or 270-degree setting will center the needle. So we add the flag to the needle. The TO-FROM flag will indicate whether you're in the hemisphere on the same side of the station as the radial tuned in or on the opposite side. The TO flag means you're on the opposite side of the station from the hemisphere in which is located the radial tuned in with the OBS. FROM means that one is located in the hemisphere in which that radial is located. This is true regardless of the heading you may be flying (Fig. 5-4).

That's half the story since it covers only hemispheres and the VOR gives you quadrants. The hemispheres must be divided in half to get the whole story. We do that, calling one the blue section and the other the yellow section. From here on it gets complicated.

Imagine looking down on the compass rose surrounding the VOR station. The yellow hemisphere is located on the left side of the station and the blue hemisphere is on the right side. Seem simple? The problem is that as you look at the VOR head on your airplane's instrument panel, the order is reversed. Fortunately, you don't have to remember that because you can see it by just looking at the VOR head (Fig. 5-5). Just keep in mind that the needle shows which hemisphere you're in, whether blue or yellow.

Now, let's try to put it all together. Remember, if you have the 90-degree radial tuned in, and the TO flag displayed, then your plane is in the hemisphere on the opposite side of the station from the 90-degree radial. (You wouldn't be flying to it if you were already on it.) Also keep in mind that the heading being flown makes no difference (Fig. 5-4, again).

Now, in addition to being in that hemisphere, suppose the needle is in the yellow section of the omni head. That tells you that you're in the yellow hemisphere section in relation to the station. Put those two pieces of data together and you know which quadrant you're in. Again, this is independent of the heading you may be flying.

Being in the yellow quadrant, you'd need to turn toward the blue quadrant in order to center the needle. Here I'm referring to the quadrant on the right side of the station, not the blue sector appearing on the face of the omni head. Consequently, if the airplane is on the side of the station opposite the 90-degree radial, and is flying a heading of approximately 90 degrees, then you would need to turn toward the right in order to fly toward the blue quadrant to center the needle, as Fig. 5-5 shows. In this instance, we "fly to the needle," because the needle shows us in which direction the radial lies in relation to our location.

Now, imagine that you're flying in the opposite direction, a heading of 270 degrees. Everything remains essentially the same. The VOR is still

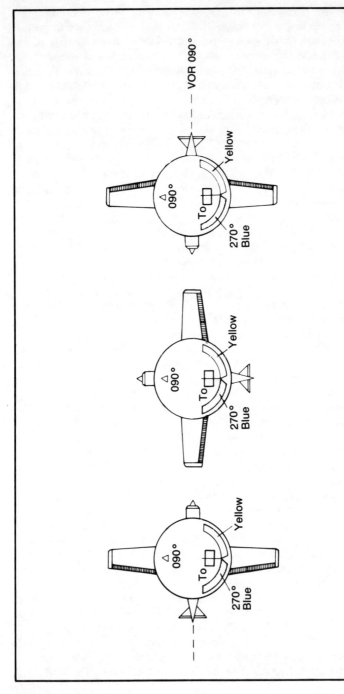

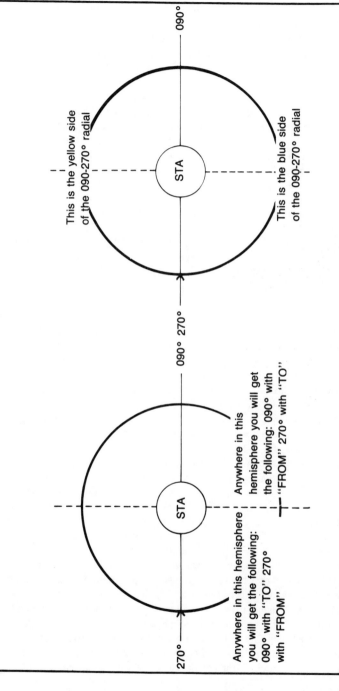

Fig. 5-4. Regardless of your heading or your location along this radial, you will get the same indications on your VOR head.

tuned to the 90-degree radial, and we still have a TO flag, even though we're flying away from the station. And since the yellow quadrant is always the left quadrant in relation to the station, and the blue is always to the right in relation to the station, we're still in the yellow quadrant, although we've reversed the direction of flight. Further, we would still need to fly toward the blue quadrant in order to return to the radial and center the needle.

But notice the difference in Fig. 5-5. The needle still shows your location in relation to the station. You're in the yellow quadrant opposite the 90-degree radial and your VOR head shows precisely that. But notice that although the needle is on the right side of the dial, showing that you're in the yellow quadrant, you must now turn toward the left in order to fly toward the blue quadrant and center the needle. You must pick up a heading to the left of the 270 degree heading you've been flying. That is, you "fly away from the needle." That's what's called *reverse sensing*. Technically speaking, "reverse sensing" is a misnomer. The VOR receives and behaves, or "senses," precisely as it always has, showing you invariably which quadrant you're located in. What gets reversed is not the sensing, but how you respond to the information the VOR is giving you.

Now, all of that is for your understanding only. Don't worry about trying to remember all of that lengthy explanation in order to recite it to the examiner. The examiner will not expect it of you. You need only to keep in mind that in order to track a given radial, you will fly to the needle when your heading is approximately the same as the radial you have tuned in. Or, conversely, you will fly away from the needle when your heading is approximately opposite the radial which you have tuned in. How approximate is "approximately"? It means anywhere within 90 degrees of the heading you've tuned in. Just keep in mind this simple rule: Heading agrees with radial, do what the needle says (i.e., needle left, fly left); heading is opposite hemisphere from radial, do opposite of what the needle indicates (i.e., needle left, fly right).

You should keep one additional matter in mind. What the examiner is looking for is tracking, not homing. You can reach a VOR station by continuously returning the OBS and flying that new heading until you drift off; then you retune and go through it again. Eventually, you'll reach the station. That's homing, and it's undesirable. Instead, after you've dialed in the radial that will take you to the station, make adjustments in the airplane's heading rather than in the radial selected with the OBS. After selecting the proper radial, turn to that heading and see what the needle tells you. If it tells you that the radial is to your right, then make a change in heading of a few degrees to the right. Fly that heading for a bit and see what happens. Usually, the needle will begin to center slowly. If it doesn't, alter your heading a few more degrees and fly that heading. As the needle begins to approach the center, take out some of your correction by now turning a few degrees back to the left and fly that new heading. In this manner, try to "bracket" the needle. Notice which heading caused you to

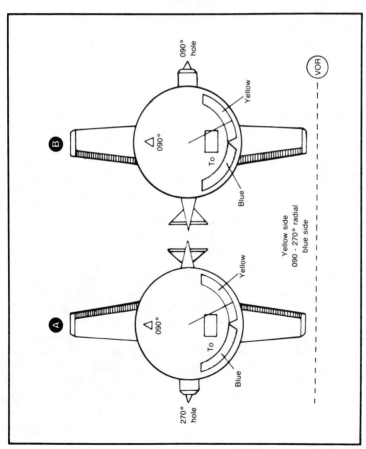

Fig. 5-5. The needle does not show that the radial is to the right. It shows that you are in the yellow quadrant. In A, you must turn left to intercept; in B, you must turn right to intercept the radial.

drift to the left, and which caused you to drift to the right. Somewhere in between will be the heading that will keep the needle centered. Because of wind, it may not be precisely the same as the radial that you've selected, but continue to fly the heading, instead of chasing the needle or retuning the OBS.

Locating the Airplane's Position. This is a relatively simple matter. Since you'll already be flying on or to a radial, you'll have one piece of required data. If you have the 90-degree radial tuned in and the needle centered, you know you're somewhere along the 90/270-degree radial. To determine precisely where you are along that radial, simply select a VOR station that's off one of your wingtips using the procedures outlined earlier and tune in the station. Now, however, instead of tuning in the TO flag, you'll tune in the FROM flag and continue tuning until the needle is centered. You now know that you are on the radial tuned in. The point at which that radial intersects the radial you're tracking is the plane's location. This should give you no problem, since you've probably practiced it several times during your training flights.

Station Passage. It's a simple matter to describe station passage to the examiner. If you're flying to a radial, the flag will switch from TO to OFF to FROM. The clue that you're getting close to the station will be the needle's increased sensitivity, indicated by somewhat erratic swinging. If you've made small corrections to keep the needle centered, the switch will not take long. Hopefully, you haven't made any wild swings in order to keep the needle centered. You've flown headings rather than chase the needle. Continue to do this as you get close to the station. If the needle starts to swing very rapidly, recognize that this means that you're close to the station and hold the heading even if the needle doesn't remain centered. As all of this is occurring, provide an explanation to the examiner. If the station is too far away and the examiner does not wish to take the time to fly there, then be prepared to give the explanation without a demonstration of your recognition of the station passage.

Recognizing Signal Loss. Signal loss is indicated by the TO-FROM flag giving a continuous reading of OFF. If this occurs (i.e., if you get an OFF indication not associated with station passage), take appropriate action. First, recycle the tuner to make sure that you have tuned in the right frequency. Listen for the station identifier. If you get no flag and no Morse code and/or voice identifier, it's safe to assume that you've lost the signal. Inform the examiner and continue the flight using the combination of dead reckoning and pilotage that you've been using. While you're doing that (since your *first* responsibility is to fly the airplane), then you may try using a different VOR than the station you had originally tuned in.

Maintaining Airspeed and Altitude. With all the attention required for radio navigation, you may tend to neglect other factors. Even with all the tuning and tracking and explaining, scan the instrument panel occasionally to see that you are maintaining altitude and airspeed within prescribed limits.

C. TASK: DIVERSION TO ALTERNATE
(ASEL)

PILOT OPERATION – 7

REFERENCES: AC 61–21,
AC 61–23.

1. **Objective.** To determine that the applicant:

   a. Exhibits adequate knowledge by explaining the procedures for diverting to an alternate airport including the recognition of conditions requiring a diversion.
   b. Selects an alternate airport and route.
   c. Proceeds toward the alternate airport promptly.
   d. Makes a reasonable estimate of heading, groundspeed, arrival time, and fuel consumption to the alternate airport.
   e. Maintains the appropriate altitude, ±200 feet and the desired airspeed, ±5 knots.

2. **Action.** The examiner will:

   a. Ask the applicant to explain the reasons for diverting and the procedures for selection of an alternate airport, estimating time en route, and estimating fuel consumption.
   b. Present a situation in which diversion to an alternate airport would be required, and determine that the applicant's performance meets the objective.
   c. Place emphasis on the applicant's judgment and performance in diverting to an alternate airport.

Objective: What's required of the applicant regarding diversion to an alternate airport.
Explaining Procedures for Diverting to an Alternate Airport. Since you won't complete the cross-country flight that you prepared for during the preflight planning portion of the practical test, the examiner has an opportunity for having you divert from that planning after you have

demonstrated the foregoing cross-country procedures. In some instances, the diversion will be simulated only. In many cases, however, the examiner may actually require that you divert to an alternate airport. An examiner with whom I worked for a number of years always had the applicant abort his cross-country after it had been demonstrated that the cross-country procedures were acceptable. He would generally work the student in the direction of a small sod strip and, setting a problem, ask the student to divert to an airport. The airport selected was to be the small sod strip, which could then be used for other parts of the test.

Explain to your examiner that a number of conditions could require diversion to an alternate airport from the planned route. For example, deteriorating weather at the destination airport might necessitate selecting an alternate. Perhaps higher-than-estimated winds have resulted in greater fuel consumption than was originally planned, requiring diversion to another airport for a refueling stop. Or an inflight emergency might require altering one's course. In the case of weather, where marginal VFR conditions might be encountered, it may be unwise to attempt to continue a flight even though legal VFR conditions may obtain. It's generally wise to have your own set of minima, and no examiner would disqualify you if you suggested that you would not continue a flight into marginal conditions, even though such flight might not violate any regulations.

The inflight plotting of the alternate course would begin with immediately and precisely locating one's present position. Then, based on the conditions creating the need for diversion, the chart should be examined for an appropriate alternate destination. The heading to the new course should next be determined and the airplane turned to the new heading. As you proceed toward the alternate, the wind correction, actual distance, and estimated time enroute can be computed.

Selecting the Alternate Airport and Route. The examiner will provide a description of the simulated conditions requiring diversion. As quickly as you can, determine your present position and give that information to your examiner. Quickly survey the chart for possible alternates and select the one appropriate to the conditions laid out by the examiner. Using your plotter, or even laying your finger along the projected course to the alternate, measure the distance on the scale at the bottom of the chart. Then, using the nearest compass rose, estimate the heading. Give the examiner the name of the alternate, the estimated distance and the estimated heading. Explain why this particular alternate was selected.

Flying to the Alternate. As soon as you've determined the heading to the alternate, turn and proceed along the new route. Note the time that you assumed this new heading. Having determined that it's necessary to divert, it would be foolish to continue on the original route until all your computation is completed. Keep in mind that your *first* responsibility is to fly the airplane.

Completing Your Planning. Established on the new route, refine your original estimates if possible. Check to make sure that your estimates of distance and heading are as accurate as you can make them. With this information you can now calculate your estimated ground speed, based on what you know about the winds in this area from your original planning and any subsequent computation. Also compute the estimated time of arrival and your fuel requirements for flying to the alternate airport and provide this information for the examiner.

Maintaining Heading and Altitude. The requirements are no different along the alternate route than they were for the original. Even as you do your inflight plotting and computing, it will be necessary to monitor the instruments to ensure that you are within the prescribed limits for altitude and airspeed.

D. TASK: LOST PROCEDURES (ASEL)

PILOT OPERATION – 7

REFERENCES: AC 61–21, AC 61–23.

1. **Objective.** To determine that the applicant:

   a. Exhibits adequate knowledge by explaining lost procedures including the following items:

   (1) maintaining the original or an appropriate heading, identifying landmarks, and climbing if necessary.
   (2) rechecking the calculations.
   (3) proceeding to and identifying the nearest concentration of prominent landmarks.
   (4) using available radio navigation aids or contacting an appropriate facility for assistance.
   (5) planning a precautionary landing if deteriorating visibility and/or fuel exhaustion is imminent.

   b. Selects the best course of action when given a lost situation.

2. **Action.** The examiner will:

   a. Ask the applicant to explain lost procedures for a given situation, and determine that the applicant's performance meets the objective.
   b. Place emphasis on the applicant's judgment in selecting the most appropriate procedure for a particular lost situation.

Objective: What's expected of the applicant regarding lost procedures.
Exhibiting Knowledge through Explanation. Hopefully, you will not be called on to demonstrate how to handle such procedures as a consequence of your actually being lost. However, at times the examiner will

divert your attention for some time by getting into other parts of the practical test. Then, allowing sufficient time for you to have become disoriented, he/she will call on you to locate your present position and/or to fly to a specified point, thus requiring some demonstration of procedures. This may or may not occur. You *will* be called on, however, to provide an explanation that will cover all the points listed under the stated objective.

First Steps. Unless there is good reason for altering your heading, it's probably best to simply maintain the original heading until you have resolved the problem. As you maintain this heading, search the appropriate area of the Sectional to locate readily identifiable landmarks. Then search the area outside the plane to see if anything matches items that you've noticed on the Sectional. At times, it may be a good idea to commence a climb, since this allows you to view a greater area, increasing the likelihood of identifying a landmark. It also provides a greater chance for radio contact and for radar and DF (Direction Finding) detection.

Rechecking Calculations. When you notice that the checkpoints you planned for have not appeared, recheck your calculations for distance, wind direction and velocity and their effect on your flight path, and your estimated time enroute. Don't dwell on this, however, since there are other procedures to be followed. But an error could mean that the sought-after checkpoints are just over the next range of hills and you need only to continue on course for a few more minutes.

Identifying Prominent Landmarks. If your survey of the terrain outside yields something prominent, such as a town with an adjacent lake and railroad and highway intersection, proceed to that landmark and, as you slowly circle it doing a 360 to maintain some orientation, try to associate it with something on your Sectional.

Using Radio Aids. The first radio aids, of course, would be the VOR equipment, if this is available to you. Taking a fix on the basis of cross-bearings could help you to quickly determine your location. If these are not available to you, then use the communication side of your transceiver to contact an appropriate facility. Using the Sectional to determine a frequency, you may try to contact an FSS, or a nearby traffic control tower.

If you cannot raise anyone on such a frequency, or if you are unable to determine an appropriate frequency, then use 121.5, the emergency frequency, to contact a facility, explain your situation, and seek help. The facility contacted may ask for as much information as you can provide, such as your flight plan destination, departure point, time enroute, etc., including any prominent landmarks in your vicinity. On this basis, the facility may be able to give your location. Or you may be advised to squawk a particular code on the transponder and/or to climb high for possible radar detection. The facility contacted might offer a DF steer, if it is so equipped. In this case, you must precisely follow the exact instructions transmitted to you.

Planning a Precautionary Landing. Faced with deteriorating weather and/or imminent fuel exhaustion, you might find it wiser to plan an immediate or early landing rather than wait until a dire emergency forces you down. A planned landing, even if it involves an off-airport landing, where the airplane is still under your complete control is preferable to being forced into a hostile environment under conditions where some factors of flight may not be controllable. A planned precautionary landing provides you with the opportunity to search for the best possible landing site, to make as thorough an examination of that site as is possible from the air, to make a go-around if that proves necessary, or to do whatever may be called for in the situation. It gives you time to communicate your intentions to whatever facility you can contact and to provide that facility with as much information as possible in order to aid in search and rescue procedures if such become necessary. Explain to your examiner that delaying a response until one is in an emergency situation—such as having exhausted fuel or having entered an area of bad weather—seriously reduces the options available and leaves fewer factors under the control of the pilot.

Selecting the Best Course of Action. It's unlikely that the examiner will require more of you than simply beginning to simulate the actions that you would take if you became lost while on a cross-country flight. As a matter of fact, you may be required only to provide an explanation. However, the examiner may have you actually go through all the procedures possible such as selecting an alternate, plotting the flight, and flying to the alternate. In such case, it will be necessary to cancel the flight plan that you have filed. You may even be called on to start the procedures for a precautionary landing. Having been given a situation, you will be required either verbally, or actually, to select the course of action that represents the safest response when lost.

Chapter 6

VI. AREA OF OPERATION:
FLIGHT BY REFERENCE TO INSTRUMENTS

A. TASK: STRAIGHT–AND–LEVEL FLIGHT (ASEL)

PILOT OPERATION – 6

REFERENCES: AC 61–21, AC 61–23, AC 61–27.

1. **Objective.** To determine that the applicant:

   a. Exhibits adequate knowledge by explaining flight solely by reference to instruments as related to straight–and–level flight.
   b. Makes smooth and coordinated control applications.
   c. Maintains straight–and–level flight for at least 3 minutes.
   d. Maintains the desired heading, ±15°.
   e. Maintains the desired altitude, ±100 feet.
   f. Maintains the desired airspeed, ±10 knots.

2. Action. The examiner will:

   a. Ask the applicant to explain flight solely by reference to instruments as related to straight–and–level flight.
   b. Ask the applicant to perform straight–and-level flight by reference to instruments, and determine that the applicant's performance meets the objective.
   c. Place emphasis on the applicant's ability to maintain altitude and heading.

Objective: What's expected of the applicant regarding straight-and-level flight by reference to instruments.

Exhibiting Knowledge by Explanation. Though you will provide some explanation of flight by references to instruments, you are not expected to cover the world of IFR. Consequently, this phase of the practical test need cover only sufficient knowledge to demonstrate that you, as a private pilot, are familiar with those instrument procedures that would be required to control the airplane adequately to remove yourself from a situation requiring flight by reference solely to instruments. For straight-and-level flight, your knowledge is limited to the instruments used and the appropriate responses to them (Fig. 6-1).

You should be able to explain, for example, that the fundamental instrument is the attitude indicator, or artificial horizon, or gyro horizon. All the outside references that are normally used during flight are represented in this little gauge. One's attention should not be riveted on this single gauge, however, despite the fact that this one instrument can help you to maintain altitude, directional control, and airspeed. Keeping the nose of that little "airplane" on the "horizon" and keeping the "wings" level in relation to the horizon can help to assure your holding altitude, heading, and airspeed fairly constant.

Explain that it's necessary, however, to scan the entire panel. There is no standard procedure for visually sweeping the entire instrument panel. Consequently, what's suggested here is illustrative only. From the attitude indicator, the gaze should move to another instrument—say the altimeter—briefly, then the heading indicator, briefly, and then back to the attitude indicator. Follow this with another scan, this time to the airspeed indicator, the vertical speed indicator, the turn-and-slip indicator, and back to the attitude indicator. These visual sweeps should also periodically check the magnetic compass and the engine instruments. For some portion of this phase of the practical test, the visual sweep might also take in the VOR, or, if your plane is so equipped, the ADF. You should be able to explain the use of the ADF, too; more about that later.

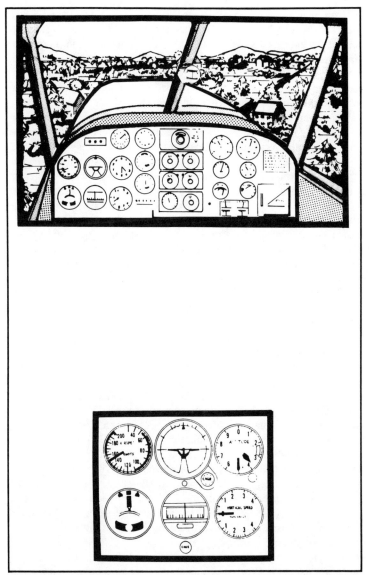

Fig. 6-1. Straight and level.

Control Applications. Though you will not be expected to perform as capably and confidently as an instrument-rated pilot, you should be able to make smooth, coordinated, and appropriate responses to the data you gather from the instruments. If you notice that the nose of the artificial airplane is too low, you simple add a little back pressure to the yoke. If the artificial wings are not parallel to the artificial horizon, you should simply apply the proper aileron and rudder pressure to level the wings. Applications or reductions of power should also avoid abruptness and roughness.

Maintaining Straight-and-Level Flight. Most private pilot applicants find it more challenging to keep all the numbers, needles, and dials still than to get them moving in the right direction. The first step is to get the nose and the wings of the little airplane in the attitude indicator on the horizon. Then check the altimeter to make certain that the airplane is neither climbing nor descending. If you detect any climb or descent, use the altimeter and the vertical speed indicator (VSI) to establish level flight and make any adjustment necessary to place and hold the little airplane on the horizon of the attitude indicator. Keep in mind, however, that the VSI generally lags significantly. With the attitude indicator properly adjusted, you need only keep the nose and wings on the artificial horizon in order to maintain straight-and-level flight. However, instead of simply staring at the attitude indicator, monitor the altimeter and the directional gyro (DG) as well. If you detect any change in either of these, make an immediate—and smooth—adjustment by applying appropriate pressure on the controls to return things to the proper readings.

The greatest problem you'll encounter will be the tendency to over-control. You notice that you've started a slight climb; instinctively you shove the yoke forward. Now you've got a shallow dive. Haul back on the yoke. In the meantime, a little glance shows you that the DG is moving. Jam the yoke and rudder in the opposite direction to stop that. Oops! There goes the nose again. Now the darned wing is low and you're turning. And so it goes.

Much of that tendency can be avoided by using the attitude indicator as the primary instrument and simply scanning the others in order to monitor the situation. When something drifts off, it generally requires only a bit of pressure to slightly alter the airplane's attitude in order to make a correction. You should also trim the airplane when you've established a stabile flight situation. That, too, aids in avoiding overcontrolling. Whatever you do, don't dismiss straight-and-level flight by reference to the instruments as unworthy of your attention. It's the heart of instrument flight. Three minutes may not seem like much time when you say it fast, but having to sit there drilling a straight hole in the sky for a full three minutes can begin to feel like an eternity.

Maintaining Heading. A tolerance of 15 degrees in either direction is a generous tolerance. When the examiner gives you the heading, note what that calls for and simply refuse to let the nose drift that far off. Here's a little trick that instrument pilots have learned but don't talk about. When they are maintaining a heading, they don't let the airplane drift off 15 degrees and then make a correcting bank and turn. As soon as they see the nose drift two or three degrees away from their heading, they simply apply a little rudder pressure to gently and gradually bring it back. That way, no other adjustments need to be made. As soon as the nose is on the heading again, release the pressure and neutralize the rudder. Yes, you get a momentary skid, but that's less serious than the problems you encounter when you begin to overcontrol as a consequence of letting things get too far off the numbers.

Maintaining Altitude. A tolerance of 100 feet up or down is not as generous as it may seem. As a matter of fact, it's very challenging to maintain altitude within those limits. Again, a part of the secret is to monitor the altimeter and make a correction as soon as you detect a change in altitude. Here too, you can violate the rules if you're simply making a small correction. If, as soon as you detect a change in the altimeter, you make a response, you'll find it necessary only to momentarily exert a little pressure on the yoke or stick. Yes, I know I told you that we use power for climb or descent, but to avoid overcorrection, it's simpler just to pull the nose up or down for a moment in order to get the airplane behaving. That way, all other controls can remain essentially the same and there's less tendency to overcontrol.

Maintaining Airspeed. The examiner will allow you ten knots on either side of the assigned airspeed. The most effective way to do this is simply to remember that the attitude indicator is your primary instrument. If you keep the "nose" of that little airplane on the horizon, your airspeed will almost take care of itself. Try using the airspeed indicator as your primary instrument and I'll guarantee that you'll never catch that needle. Instead, rely on the attitude indicator and use the airspeed indicator merely as a check on what you're doing.

B. TASK: STRAIGHT, CONSTANT AIRSPEED CLIMBS (ASEL)

PILOT OPERATION – 6

REFERENCES: AC 61–21, AC 61–23, AC 61–27.

1. **Objective.** To determine that the applicant:

   a. Exhibits adequate knowledge by explaining flight solely by reference to instruments as related to straight, constant airspeed climbs.

   b. Establishes the climb pitch attitude and power setting on an assigned heading.

   c. Makes smooth and coordinated control applications.

   d. Maintains the desired heading, ±15°.

   e. Maintains the desired airspeed, ±10 knots.

   f. Levels off at the desired altitude, ±200 feet.

2. **Action.** The examiner will:

   a. Ask the applicant to explain flight solely by reference to instruments as related to straight, constant airspeed climbs.

   b. Ask the applicant to perform a straight, constant airspeed climb to an assigned altitude by reference to instruments, and determine that the applicant's performance meets the objective.

   c. Place emphasis on the applicant's ability to maintain heading, pitch attitude, and airspeed.

Objective: What's expected of the applicant regarding straight, constant airspeed climbs.

Exhibiting Knowledge by Explanation. Be prepared to tell how you will handle climbs straight ahead. You recognize, of course, that for this maneuver the need for scanning the instrument panel does not change. Ex-

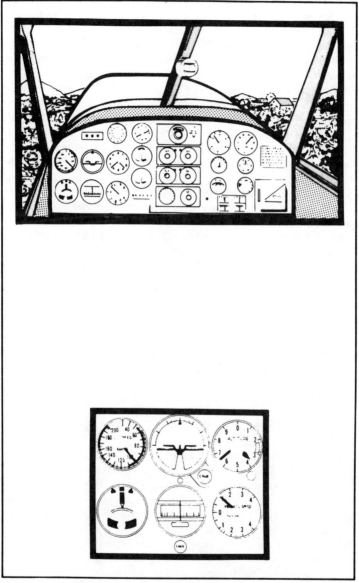

Fig. 6-2. Normal climb.

plain that certain factors will change, however. You will need to apply appropriate power, which, in most trainers used for the practical test, means full throttle. You next need to establish whatever speed the examiner calls for. This could be the normal climbout airspeed, or a cruise climb airspeed, or the airspeed that will give you a constant rate climb of 500 feet per minute. Whatever the airspeed is, assure the examiner that you understand that this will be achieved and maintained by establishing the proper attitude and maintaining that pitch. The primary instrument is still the attitude indicator, with the airspeed indicator used as a monitor to assure that you've established the correct attitude, or pitch (Fig. 6-2).

Establishing Pitch and Power Setting. When you've received the instructions from the examiner regarding the airspeed at which you're to climb, advance the throttle to the appropriate setting. Also, note the heading you've established; you'll be required to maintain that heading. Adding power will automatically begin to raise the nose. You will add sufficient back pressure on the yoke or stick to establish the proper pitch or attitude in order to achieve the assigned airspeed. The airspeed indicator will lag a bit, so keep that in mind as you establish the correct attitude. When you get it right, note where the nose of the little airplane is and hold that attitude. You may retrim, if you wish.

Control Applications. As you normally do, when you advance the throttle, do it firmly and without hesitation, yet avoid jamming it forward. As the nose begins to rise, match its tendency with back pressure on the yoke or stick sufficiently to keep it rising smoothly to the desired pitch. As you approach this attitude, simply ease off sufficient back pressure to hold the nose in the proper position.

Maintaining the Heading. Again, you have lots of leeway. Fifteen degrees on either side of the heading is a generous allowance. You know that with the addition of power the nose will have a tendency to yaw to the left. Be ready to start adding sufficient pressure on the right rudder to counteract that tendency. Your visual sweep of the panel during this maneuver should also include the turn and slip coordinator to ensure that you avoid skids. Again, avoid overcorrecting.

Maintaining Airspeed. As with straight-and-level flight, you will control airspeed with attitude.

Leveling Off. You have an allowance of 200 feet on either side of the desired altitude. You could exceed that if you begin leveling too soon or too late. About 50 feet below the assigned altitude, begin to level off by exerting forward pressure on the yoke or stick. Here, too, the attitude indicator is your primary instrument. Hold sufficient forward pressure to get the nose of the little airplane back on the artificial horizon. With the airplane in that attitude, start reducing power. As you smoothly and continuously come back on the throttle, ease off the forward pressure on the yoke in order to maintain the proper pitch and altitude.

C. TASK: STRAIGHT, CONSTANT AIRSPEED DESCENTS (ASEL)

PILOT OPERATION – 6

REFERENCES: AC 61–21, AC 61–23, AC 61–27.

1. **Objective.** To determine that the applicant:

   a. Exhibits adequate knowledge by explaining flight solely by reference to instruments as related to straight, constant airspeed descents.
   b. Determines the minimum safe altitude at which the descent should be terminated.
   c. Establishes the descent configuration, pitch, and power setting on the assigned heading.
   d. Makes smooth and coordinated control application.
   e. Maintains the desired heading, ±15°.
   f. Maintains the desired airspeed, ±10 knots.
   g. Levels off at the desired altitude, ±200 feet.

2. **Action.** The examiner will:

   a. Ask the applicant to explain flight solely by reference to instruments as related to straight, constant airspeed descents.
   b. Ask the applicant to perform a straight, constant airspeed descent to an assigned altitude by reference to instruments, and determine that the applicant's performance meets the objective.
   c. Place emphasis on the applicant's awareness of the minimum safe altitude and ability to level off within tolerance.

Objective: What's expected of the applicant regarding straight, constant airspeed descents.

Exhibiting Knowledge by Explanation. The explanations here will not differ appreciably from those that you used for the other parts of this phase of the practical test. The primary instrument remains the attitude indicator. Pitch or attitude still controls airspeed. Power controls descent, as in the preceding maneuver it controlled climb (Fig. 6-3).

Minimum Safe Altitude. This will vary, of course, with circumstances. In some instances, the examiner will assign an altitude to which you are to descend. If the judgement is left to you, then terrain and obstacle clearances will determine the minimum safe altitudes. Keep in mind that Part 91 of the FAR establishes minimum safe altitudes as 1000 feet above the highest obstacle within a horizontal radius of 2000 feet in congested areas, or 500 feet above the surface in other than congested areas, except over open water or sparsely populated areas. Hopefully, your examiner will recognize that you are applying only for a Private Pilot Certificate, not an instrument rating, and will conduct this part of the test accordingly.

Descent Configuration. This requirement calls for a controlled descent. You may be asked either to make a descent at a specified airspeed and rate of descent while maintaining a heading, or to make a descent with the throttle set at idle. Such descents will be made with the airplane in various configurations, both clean and dirty. In other words, you'll be called on to make the descents with flaps retracted and with various flap settings. If your plane features retractable landing gear, then you may also be asked to make descents with gear retracted and gear extended. In any case, the pitch will control the airspeed; use the attitude then and not the throttle. If you are asked to descend at a standard rate of descent, then gradually reduce the power until the VSI stabilizes at 50 feet per minute, whatever configuration the airplane is in. While maintaining the heading, establish the pitch or attitude which produces whatever airspeed the examiner calls for. If no airspeed is assigned, then use the normal approach airspeed, or between 1.3 and 1.4 times the power-off stalling speed in the landing configuration.

Control Application. The requirement calls for smooth and coordinated application of the controls. Following the description above should achieve this.

Maintaining Heading. This will be a little easier to achieve than was the holding of heading during the climb. With the power reduced, you do not have the same pressures exerted as with the left-turning tendency of full power. Still, it will be necessary periodically to check the directional gyro and to apply appropriate rudder pressure as soon as you see the heading start to drift off.

Maintaining Airspeed. Nothing new here either. As with the other phases, the airspeed will be controlled with pitch, or attitude. Remember that the primary instrument for maintaining a constant airspeed is still the attitude indicator with the airspeed indicator serving as a check.

Leveling Off. Just as you anticipated reaching the desired altitude with the climb, so with the descent you will begin procedures for leveling off

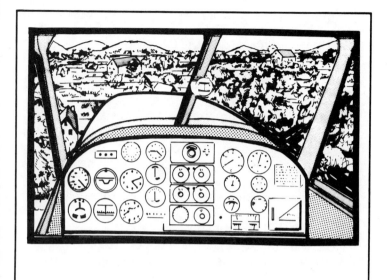

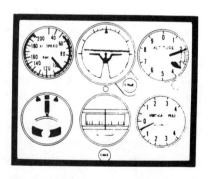

Fig. 6-3. Normal glide or descent.

before you reach that altitude. About 50 feet above the altitude you want, begin a smooth, steady application of power until you reach the normal cruise power setting. You will also gradually reduce the back pressure that you probably have been holding to maintain the proper descent airspeed. Ease off that back pressure until the controls have been neutralized. This procedure should keep you well within the allowable 200 foot tolerance.

D. TASK: TURNS TO HEADINGS (ASEL)

PILOT OPERATION – 6

REFERENCES: AC 61–21, AC 61–23, AC 61–27.

1. **Objective.** To determine that the applicant:

   a. Exhibits adequate knowledge by explaining flight solely by reference to instruments as related to turns to headings.
   b. Enters and maintains approximately a standard–rate turn with smooth and coordinated control applications.
   c. Maintains the desired altitude, ±200 feet.
   d. Maintains the desired airspeed, ±10 knots.
   e. Maintains the desired bank angle, not to exceed 25°.
   f. Rolls out at the desired heading, ±20°.

2. **Action.** The examiner will:

   a. Ask the applicant to explain flight solely by reference to instruments as related to turns to headings.
   b. Ask the applicant to turn to a specific heading by reference to instruments, and determine that the applicant's performance meets the objective.
   c. Place emphasis on the applicant's ability to maintain a constant bank and pitch attitude to avoid an uncontrolled spiral.

Objective: What's expected of the applicant regarding turns to headings by reference to instruments.

Exhibiting Knowledge by Explanation. By this time, you'll have explained all the elements of flight by reference to instruments during straight-and-level flight as well as climbs and descents straight ahead. It will not be necessary to repeat all that you've already said. Specify that essentially the same procedures obtain; that is, that the primary instrument is still the attitude indicator, power controls climb and descent, and attitude controls airspeed. Your explanation should indicate that you understand that it's still necessary to visually sweep the instrument panel with special emphasis on the directional gyro during turns. Also, explain that "standard rate turns" means a rate of turning that produces a 360-degree turn in two minutes and that the rate of turning is determined by the degree of bank. Also point out that the "doghouses" on the turn coordinator indicate the approximate bank required to achieve a standard rate turn (Fig. 6-4).

Entering the Standard Rate Turn. Handling the controls to enter a turn while you're flying on the gauges does not differ significantly from what you do when the hood is off. Use pressure on yoke and rudder together to establish the bank and turn and then essentially neutralize the controls to maintain the bank. For this turn, since it's to be standard rate, check on the DG to get the heading you're starting from and then refer to the turn coordinator to establish the degree of bank. When the little wings are on the "doghouse," hold that bank and check the attitude indicator. You'll probably see that you're in a bank of between 15 and 20 degrees, and nearer the latter. (If your airplane has a turn and slip indicator, the old "needle and ball," then put the needle on the appropriate "doghouse" and check the attitude indicator.) You can then continue to use the attitude indicator as your primary instrument, simply cross-checking with the turn coordinator occasionally. If you were an instrument pilot, you'd really time the turn, checking to see that you were getting a three-degree-per-second turn, but you won't be required to do it so precisely. So, having established a bank that approximates a standard rate turn, you can return to monitoring the instruments, primarily the attitude indicator and the DG.

Maintaining Altitude. The point in using the attitude indicator rather than the turn coordinator to make the standard rate turn to a heading is that this enables you to keep the nose of that little airplane on the horizon and thereby maintain altitude. However, since the airplane is banked (creating centrifugal force that in effect makes the airplane weigh more), you may find it necessary to add a touch of power. Monitor the altimeter to see what it takes.

Maintaining Airspeed. Again, using the attitude indicator as your primary reference aids in maintaining the desired airspeed. Since, in a bank, the forces acting on the airplane change, you may find it necessary to hold a little back pressure to keep the nose of the little airplane on the artificial horizon. As long as you maintain essentially the same attitude during the turn, your airspeed will not appreciably change.

Maintaining the Desired Bank Angle. Since you're approximating a standard rate turn, you'll keep the wings of the little airplane just shy of the 20 degree marker on the attitude indicator. Keep the bank within that 15 to 20 degree limit and you will not exceed the limits allowed for the turn to a heading. Just be sure that, as you visually sweep the instrument panel and monitor the DG to see when to roll out, you don't let the airplane roll into a steeper bank or roll out of the turn.

Rolling Out on the Heading. If you're going to roll out on the approxi-

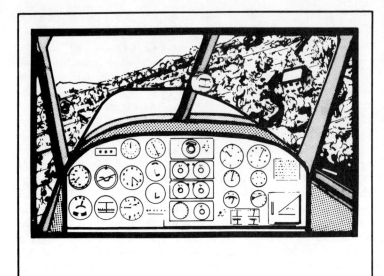

Fig. 6-4. Level turn.

mate heading to which you're turning without exceeding the 20-degree tolerance, it will be necessary to begin the rollout before you reach that heading.
Start the rollout between 5 and 10 degrees before reaching the heading
assigned. Do it gradually. Cross-checking the instruments becomes very
important now, because you may have added a bit of power and held some
back pressure on the yoke during the turn. Now all of this has to be gradually changed back as you return to straight-and-level flight. The tendency
generally will be to climb; so, equipped with that knowledge, be prepared
to compensate in order to roll out on the approximate heading without exceeding the limits for maintaining altitude.

E. TASK: CRITICAL FLIGHT ATTITUDES
(ASEL)

PILOT OPERATION – 6

REFERENCES: AC 61–21,
AC 61–23, AC 61–27.

NOTE: Critical flight attitudes, such as a start of
a power-on spiral or an approach to a
climbing stall, shall not exceed 45° bank
or 10° pitch from level flight.

1. **Objective.**   To determine that the applicant:

   a. Exhibits adequate knowledge by explaining
   flight solely by reference to instruments as
   related to critical flight attitudes.
   b. Recognizes critical flight attitudes promptly.
   c. Interprets the instruments.
   d. Recovers to level flight by prompt, smooth,
   coordinated control, applied in the proper
   sequence.
   e. Avoids excessive load factors, airspeeds, or
   stalls.

2. **Action.**   The examiner will:

   a. Ask the applicant to explain the instrument
   indications of critical flight attitudes and
   proper recovery procedures.
   b. Maneuver the airplane into a critical flight
   attitude and ask the applicant to recover to
   straight–and–level flight, and determine
   that the applicant's performance meets the
   objective.
   c. Place emphasis on the applicant's ability to
   interpret instruments and promptly recover
   avoiding excessive load factors.

Objective: What's expected of the applicant regarding critical flight attitudes.
Exhibiting Knowledge by Explanation. By now, you'll have ex-

plained most of what's required in handling flight solely by reference to instruments. Regarding critical attitudes, you can indicate that you realize that focusing on one or two of the instruments, or devoting your attention to radio communications, or to charts, can lead to the airplane's getting into an unusual attitude. Convey your understanding of the need to avoid stalls, spirals, or situations that produce excessive airspeeds and/or load factors. Let the examiner know that you also realize that when one is in that situation of having allowed the airplane to assume an unusual attitude while flying on the gauges, the only one of the senses that can be relied on is the sense of sight. You understand that you must rely solely on what the instruments are telling you.

Recognizing Critical Flight Attitudes. The examiner will not wait for you to get into a critical situation. Instead, he/she will have you remove your hands and feet from the controls. (I generally have the student fold his hands on his lap and place his feet flat on the floor. The head is bowed to remove the instruments from view. Examiners generally operate this way, too.) Then, after a few maneuvers to "fake the applicant out," the airplane is put into an unusual attitude, maybe a nose-high, banked attitude with the power reduced. The applicant is then required to recover. Or perhaps the examiner will put the plane in a spiral (Fig. 6-5). Spirals are always used because that seems to be the fix pilots who cannot fly instruments find themselves in when they "lose it." Most instances of flying into instrument conditions without adequate training end with the power-on spiral and a panicked pilot who is doomed. It's important for you to recognize this or any critical attitude promptly by reference solely to the instruments.

I once had a student, John Something-or-Other, who claimed to be capable of controlling the airplane in instrument conditions without reference to the gauges. "I'm like a cat," he used to say. "I always land on my feet." Since I was the Senior Flight Instructor at the flight school, I could choose my students, so I elected to give John, a commercial pilot student, a little workout under the hood.

After a few preliminary maneuvers, I had John bow his head, fold his hands in his lap, and put his feet flat on the floor. We tried a few unusual attitudes with John recovering by doing a little cheating, peeking out from under the hood. Finally, I gave him a little case of vertigo, put the airplane into a spiral, reached over and jammed John's hood over this whole face so that he could see nothing. "Okay, John," I told him, "it's your airplane. Recover."

He hesitated a moment. "Like this?" He said shakily. "I . . . I can't see."

"You don't need to see, John. Remember? You're like a cat. You always land on your feet. Recover."

For a few moments John wrenched the controls this way and that. We were tossed about a bit, but the spiral continued and tightened. John could hear the engine winding up. It popped a couple of times and our gyrations got worse. Suddenly John grabbed the hood and flung it off in panic, over-

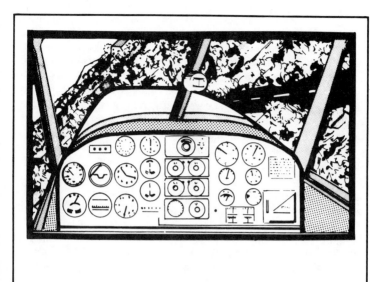

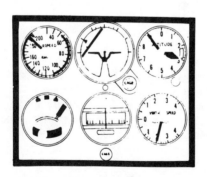

Fig. 6-5. Power-on spiral.

controlling with gusto as he desperately tried to right the airplane. I sat in the right seat, howling with laughter.

By the end of the day, most of the students at the flight school had heard about my "craziness," and John's close encounter with "death." But

I don't think he ever again bragged about being capable of instrument flight without reference to the instruments.

Interpreting the Instruments. The first instrument that should get your attention is the attitude indicator, but you must understand what you see there. You're going to have some real problems if you see the artificial horizon as the wings of your airplane; everything you do will be the exact opposite of what you should do. Consequently, get that one right first. Then start the visual sweep of the panel. Check airspeed; if it's excessive, your nose is probably low. Raise it, and check the power setting. Continue the scan, using each instrument as a cross-check on what the others seem to be telling you. For example, if you have misinterpreted the attitude indicator, the DG will seem to show you turning the wrong way. When you get such an impression, go back and check the other gauges. It's vital that your interpretation be correct; cross-checking among the instruments will help correct any incorrect interpretations you may have made.

Recovery to Straight-and-Level Flight. Your tendency will be to make quick and abrupt responses to unusual attitudes. Avoid that tendency; it could cause you to overload the flying surfaces and create unwanted stress on the airplane. If the nose is low and the speed excessive, simply apply enough back pressure to the yoke to correct the problem. If you find yourself in a power-on spiral, reduce the power immediately—but do it easily and smoothly. Then bring the wings and the nose of the little airplane back to the artificial horizon. Notice that this refers to leveling the wings first. Now, check your airspeed, then your altitude. Return to the way you generally scan the instruments. If you're on the verge of a stall in a climbing turn, relax the back pressure, level the wings, add power if it's available, and start the scan again. Then, when you're back to straight-and-level cruise, make whatever adjustments you need to make regarding power, altitude, and heading.

Avoiding Excess. It will do you little good to recover from a critical flight attitude if you overstress the airplane through excessive load factors or airspeeds. Also, if you manage to get yourself into a stall, it may be disqualifying. If you manage a spin, the examiner will probably have you fly right back to the airport from that spot, figuring on the way exactly how to word the pink slip. That's why your interpretation of the instruments must be correct, and your application of the controls smooth, coordinated, and applied in the proper sequence. Anyone can find him/herself in an unusual attitude as a consequence of a distraction. What's called for is recognizing the critical attitude and making the appropriate responses.

F. TASK: RADIO AIDS AND RADAR SERVICES (ASEL)

PILOT OPERATION – 6

REFERENCES: AC 61–21,
AC 61–23, AC 61–27.

1. **Objective.**   To determine that the applicant:

   a. Exhibits adequate knowledge by explaining radio aids and radar services available for use during flight solely by reference to instruments under emergency conditions.
   b. Selects, tunes, and identifies the appropriate facility.
   c. Follows verbal instructions or radio aids for guidance.
   d. Determines the minimum safe altitude.
   e. Maintains the desired altitude, ±200 feet.
   f. Maintains the desired heading, ±15°.

2. **Action.**   The examiner will:

   a. Ask the applicant to explain radio aids and radar services available for use during flight solely by reference to instruments under emergency conditions.
   b. Ask the applicant to use radio aids or radar services for guidance, and determine that the applicant's performance meets the objective.
   c. Place emphasis on the applicant's knowledge of the services available and ability to follow the instructions.

Objective: What's expected of the applicant regarding radio aids and radio services.

Exhibiting Knowledge by Explanation. You should be able to list and describe the major radio aids and radar services that would be available to the pilot who, in an emergency situation, is flying solely by reference to instruments. Notice that "an emergency situation" was specified. It's there to remind you that you are not an instrument pilot and you should never consider yourself such unless/until you acquire the rating.

I have a little test that I administer to applicants when I'm giving them the recommendation ride. I tell them to imagine that they've left their "home" airport under beautiful VFR conditions for a trip and have now been flying for whatever time we've been in the air. I then place the hood over their head and say, "You've flown into an area that is below VFR minima. What are you going to do?" They are now under the hood and flying solely by reference to instruments.

I get all sorts of responses, such as: "Well . . . uh . . . I would keep flying toward my destination and . . . uh . . . I'd call the nearest Flight Service Station and . . . uh . . . I'd . . . " Or, maybe they'd respond: "I guess I'd . . . uh . . . try to get on top. Or no. Maybe I'd try to get below it, real easy-like, while I watch the attitude indicator to make sure I'm straight-and-level." And so forth.

I respond to any of these with: "Are you instrument rated?"

"Well, no."

I then ask: "Is this airplane legal for instrument flight?"

"Well, it's . . . uh . . . it's got all the gauges, so I guess . . . "

Finally, I ask them: "Are you on an instrument flight plan?"

"Well, gee. No, I'm not."

"There's only one thing to do, then," I tell them. "Do a 180-degree turn and get back to the good weather that you just left behind. You have no business being here unless you can answer Yes to all three of those questions."

But you're still expected to know enough to be able to extricate yourself from trouble. So you should be able to explain a little about VOR, a little about ADF, something about DF steers and other radar services available to someone who's on the gauges and shouldn't be.

You'll have been using VOR for a part of the practical test, so no more may be required here than to recognize that you can rely on VOR to locate yourself using cross-referencing, and you can use VOR to navigate out of trouble.

Most training airplanes are not ADF-equipped, and you probably have never had experience with ADF (Fig. 6-6). You've probably at least read about these low- or medium-frequency radio beacons. Hopefully you'll remember that their range is usually limited, particularly those used with Instrument Landing Systems. The latter are called Compass Locators. They all work in the same manner. You tune the frequency in and listen for the identifier code. If you're receiving the signal, the needle will point toward the station and you simply turn the airplane until the needle points straight up. (If it points straight down, then the station is directly behind the tail of the airplane.) You continue to fly the course that keeps the needle pointing straight up until you reach the station. At that point, as you overfly the station, the needle swings from pointing straight up to pointing straight down.

Aside from its limited range, other limitations of the ADF are its be-

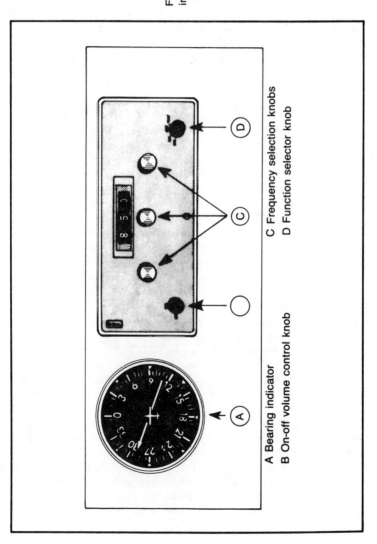

Fig. 6-6. ADF receiver and indicator.

A Bearing indicator
B On-off volume control knob
C Frequency selection knobs
D Function selector knob

ing affected by electrical storms, and the difficulty in tracking for the uninitiated. You can also use the ADF to track on commercial broadcasting stations. The problem with such stations is that they so seldom identify themselves that you can't be sure that you've got the right station.

If you've ever used a DF steer, you're a rare applicant. This VHF/UHF ground-based receiver is usually tied into radar these days. The display indicates the magnetic direction of the airplane from the station each time the plane transmits. The important thing to remember about the DF steer is to do precisely as you're instructed. When the controller asks for information, you provide that information. When you're asked simply to key the mike without speaking for a particular length of time, you do precisely that. Keying the mike without speaking transmits a carrier wave received by a special antenna. The controller will ask for this a number of times, picking up a new bearing each time and figuring how long it took you to fly through a certain number of degrees. On such bases, the DF controller will be able to pinpoint your location and give you directions for reaching a specified facility or location.

Radar services are also available to you, whether you're transponder-equipped or not. If you find yourself in a situation that requires flight solely by reference to instruments, you should contact some facility immediately. Radar is so generally available these days that it's very likely that someone is going to have the capability of getting you as a blip on a radar screen. Again, it's important to follow instructions very precisely. If you're transponder-equipped, you'll be given a frequency to tune in. Also, you'll probably be told to "Squawk ident," which means simply hitting the ID button. If your plane does not sport a transponder, then you will probably be requested to turn to particular headings for identification. Do precisely as you're instructed; the controller is watching his screen for a blip that does what he tells you to do. You may also be asked to climb to a higher altitude. This would be the case if you were low and the controller's radar were not picking you up.

Reaching the Appropriate Facility. Using your chart, you will select a facility to contact. If you've been performing some maneuvers under the hood and are not sure of your location, the first thing you may do is pick two VOR stations, get a cross bearing, and determine your location. As you tune in each station, remember to check the identifier to make sure that you have the right station(s), and that the signal is reliable.

Next, since you're simulating being on the gauges in an emergency, select the nearest facility that can give you aid. This might mean talking to a Flight Service Station that has a remote located at one of the VOR stations you used to determine your location. The important thing is to communicate with someone. Perhaps a controlled field is in the vicinity, in which case you might talk to approach control, or to the tower. Select a facility that offers you not only aid in your present circumstance, but also the opportunity to get on the ground as quickly and as safely as possible—or at least gets you out of the situation requiring you to fly solely by reference to the instruments.

If all else fails, you know that you can switch to the emergency frequency, 121.5, and broadcast your plight. You should contact someone promptly. Keep in mind that you'd be tooling around illegally in such a case and there may be lots of other shiny metal objects in those clouds who don't know you're there.

Following Instructions. If you're using VOR for aid, then use it to get out of the situation you're in; i.e., use the VOR facility that will get back into VFR conditions or on the ground the soonest. If you're talking to a radar controller, or tower controller, or getting a DF steer, then it's important for all the reasons given above for you to follow instructions *very precisely*. To ascertain that you heard the instructions given, you should repeat them as they are given to you. Since you won't actually be in an emergency under IFR conditions, your examiner will be simulating the situation. Treat it as real; repeat his/her instructions. If there's an instruction that is not clear, ask for it to be repeated, or ask for clarification.

Minimum Safe Altitude. The requirement here is the same as for the preceding section. You will need to consult your Sectional to determine what's called for in the area in which you're flying. Keep in mind those minima that we mentioned earlier. In this phase, you may need to keep another factor in mind. Since you'll be relying on radio aids or radar services, you must maintain sufficient altitude for signals to be clear.

Maintaining Altitude. There's a generous allowance of 200 feet in either direction for this phase of the checkride, too. Recall the advice given earlier; examiners will generally prefer that you stay on the high side of the allowance.

Maintaining Heading. This may be a part of following instructions intended to guide you. It would do little good for someone to give you a heading to fly if you allowed yourself to drift far enough off the heading to continue in the very conditions you're using radio and/or radar to get out of.

Chapter 7

VII. AREA OF OPERATION:
FLIGHT AT CRITICALLY SLOW AIRSPEEDS

A. TASK: FULL STALLS – POWER OFF
(ASEL)

PILOT OPERATION – 4

REFERENCE: AC 61–21.

1. **Objective.** To determine that the applicant:

   a. Exhibits adequate knowledge by explaining the aerodynamic factors and flight situations that may result in full stalls – power off, including proper recovery procedures and hazards of stalling during uncoordinated flight.

   b. Selects an entry altitude that will allow the recoveries to be completed no lower than 1,500 feet AGL.

   c. Establishes the normal approach or landing

configuration and airspeed with the throttle closed or at a reduced power setting.

d. Establishes a straight glide or a gliding turn with a bank angle of 30°, ±10°, in coordinated flight.

e. Establishes and maintains a landing pitch attitude that will induce a full stall.

f. Recognizes the indications of a full stall and promptly recovers by decreasing the angle of attack, leveling the wings, and adjusting the power as necessary to regain normal flight attitude.

g. Retracts the wing flaps and landing gear (if retractable) and establishes straight–and–level flight or climb.

h. Avoids secondary stalls, excessive airspeed, excessive altitude loss, spins, or flight below 1,500 feet AGL.

2. **Action.** The examiner will:

a. Ask the applicant to explain the aerodynamic factors associated with, and the flight situations that may result in, full stalls – power off.

b. Ask the applicant to perform full stalls – power off, in normal approach or landing configuration from straight glides and gliding turns, and determine that the applicant's performance meets the objective.

c. Place emphasis on the applicant's ability to promptly recognize and recover from the stall.

Objective: What's expected of the applicant regarding power-off, full stalls.

Exhibiting Knowledge through Explanation. Your explanation will include the aerodynamic factors and flight situations that may result in stalls. You should demonstrate that you understand that stalls are a factor of angle of attack and not of airspeed, meaning that stalls can occur at any airspeed, not simply that which is listed as the stalling speed in the airplane's operating handbook. Explain that angle of attack means the angle at which

157

the wing meets the relative wind, which may be only grossly and indirectly related to the airplane's pitch or attitude in relation to the horizon.

Explain that other things can accompany the stalling of the wing. For example, if the controls are not perfectly coordinated, or the angle of attack is different on each wing, the nose of the plane may tend to yaw one way or the other, or one wing may stall before the other. Or the airplane may be in some configuration that requires attention to some control other than the yoke, or stick, alone. Still, the first thing that must be done in recovering is to reduce the angle of attack. Then other matters may be attended to.

Display your understanding that there are hazards associated with a stall occurring during uncoordinated flight. Principally, this means that instead of simply stalling straight forward, the airplane may spin. In fact, in a climbing turn, since the "outside," or high, wing will generally stall

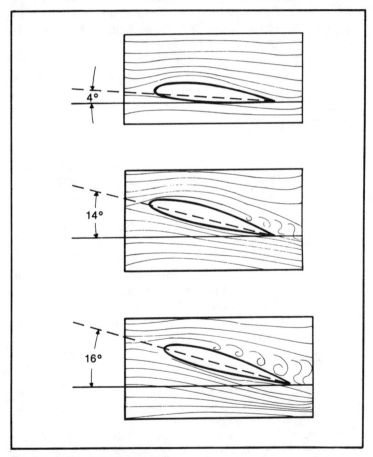

Fig. 7-1. Angle of attack and stall.

first, the airplane might roll over the top and then enter a spin, completely disorienting the unprepared pilot. In other words, you may end up not knowing which end is up or what to do about it.

Selecting a Safe Altitude. The standard calls for a recovery to be completed at no lower than 1500 feet above ground level. Sometimes the examiner will suggest an altitude. If this doesn't occur in your case, then choose 2500 feet—and be sure that it's 2500 feet above the *ground*, not 2500 feet MSL. That will be sufficiently high to meet the standard, yet not so high that it will consume a great deal of time to get to altitude.

Establishing the Approach. The FAA's handbook on the practical test doesn't refer to this as anything other than a "full stall—power off." However, the examiner may not ask for it that way. If he/she requests an "approach stall," you'll know that a "full stall—power off" is being requested. Since it's a simulation of your experiencing a stall during an approach to a landing, you'll use such a power setting and probably be called on to do stalls in landing configurations and situations. What constitutes the "normal approach or landing configuration" would vary with which part of the approach to landing you're in. On a downwind leg, you might not yet have applied any flaps at all. Consequently, you may be asked for a power-off, straight-ahead, no-flaps, full stall. In such a case *after making clearing turns to the right and the left*, you would reduce the power, or close the throttle, and establish the attitude or pitch that would give you the normal approach speed, i.e., 1.3 to 1.4 times the published landing configuration stalling speed.

Establishing the Glide. With the throttle closed and the airplane at such a pitch or attitude that it produces the normal approach airspeed, you will be in a normal glide. Or the examiner may request, as you proceed through a series of stalls, that you enter a gliding turn to simulate a turn from downwind to the base leg, or from base to final, on a landing approach. He/she may also request the appropriate application of flaps to match the situation being simulated. Perform whatever maneuver is called for with a smooth—not an abrupt—application of the controls.

Inducing the Stall. Once established in the straight-ahead, or in the turning, glide, begin to apply back pressure to the yoke or stick. This should not be sudden, or abrupt; it should simulate the way you would handle the controls during a landing. Keep the yoke or stick coming back until you achieve a full stall. The full stall will be indicated either by a sudden "break", i.e., the nose will suddenly pitch down, or by the plane's "mushing down" in a nose-high attitude as you hold the yoke or stick all the way back.

Recovering from the Stall. When you recognize that the full stall has occurred, based on the description in the preceding paragraph, release the back pressure to decrease the angle of attack. Do not pop the yoke or stick forward; simply release the back pressure to "unstall" the wing. If you did stall the wing on a real approach, you would already be low and you would therefore want to hold your altitude loss to a minimum. So when performing this maneuver, keep in mind that you want to do just that. Jamming the stick forward would, at best, simply put you into a dive that would cost you altitude. As the wings "unstall," level the wings and add full power by steadily and smoothly advancing the throttle until you regain a normal flight altitude, which will generally be a normal climb back to the altitude where you commenced the procedures for entering the stall.

Cleaning the Airplane Up. By now, the wing is no longer stalled and the airplane is in normal flight. This is the time for you to clean it up. Retract the wing flaps—in comfortable increments, rather than all at once. That helps you to maintain normal flight. Finally, get the gear up, if your plane features retractable gear. Continue your climb back to the altitude where it all began unless the examiner gives you a different set of directions.

Avoiding Excesses. Holding altitude loss to a minimum has already been mentioned. There's no standard mentioned, but you should be able to keep it to less than 200 feet. You must also avoid allowing the airspeed to become excessive. That can be accomplished simply by easing off back pressure on the yoke as you recover rather than jamming the yoke all the way forward.

Spins are also to be avoided. Generally, that's no big problem either, and can be accomplished merely by glancing at the turn and slip indicator to see that the ball is centered as you enter the maneuver. If one wing should drop before the other, respond by applying opposite rudder. *Do not use ailerons.* That would merely aggravate the situation. If you've entered the maneuver at the altitude suggested, there should be no problem in staying above 1500 feet AGL.

B. TASK: FULL STALLS – POWER ON
(ASEL)

PILOT OPERATION – 4

REFERENCE: AC 61–21.

1. **Objective.** To determine that the applicant:

   a. Exhibits adequate knowledge by explaining the aerodynamic factors and flight situations that may result in full stalls – power on, including proper recovery procedures, and hazards of stalling during uncoordinated flight.

   b. Selects an entry altitude that will allow recoveries to be completed no lower than 1,500 feet AGL.

   c. Establishes takeoff or normal climb configuration.

   d. Establishes takeoff or climb airspeed before applying takeoff or climb power (reduced power may be used to avoid excessive pitch–up during entry only).

   e. Establishes and maintains a pitch attitude straight ahead that will induce a full stall.

   f. Establishes and maintains a pitch attitude that will induce a full stall in a turn with a bank angle of 20°, ±10°.

   g. Applies proper control to maintain coordinated flight.

   h. Recognizes the indications of a full stall and promptly recovers by decreasing the angle of attack, leveling the wings, and adjusting the power as necessary to regain normal flight attitude.

   i. Retracts the wing flaps and landing gear (if retractable) and establishes straight–and-level flight or climb.

   j. Avoids secondary stalls, excessive airspeeds, excessive altitude loss, spins, or flight below 1,500 feet AGL.

2. **Action.** The examiner will:

   a. Ask the applicant to explain the aerodynamic factors associated with, and the flight situations that may result in, full stalls – power on.

   b. Ask the applicant to perform full stalls – power on, in a takeoff or normal climb configuration, from straight climbs and climbing turns, and determine that the applicant's performance meets the objective.

   c. Place emphasis on the applicant's ability to promptly recognize and recover from the stall.

Objective: What's expected of the applicant regarding full stalls—power on.

Exhibiting Knowledge through Explanation. Much of the required explanation for this maneuver will have been covered previously. The aerodynamic factors that result in a "full stall—power on" are essentially the same as for the approach stall, i.e., too great an angle of attack. Proper recovery procedures will differ, however. Since power is already on, the addition of power is not a part of the recovery procedures. Other than this, the procedures remain the same as those used for the power-off stall. Similarly, the hazards of stalling during uncoordinated flight remain the same. One difference, however, is that the likelihood of uncoordinated flight is greater with power on because of the left-turning tendency of the airplane, among other things. The pilot, therefore, will need to exercise even greater care in order to avoid the sort of uncoordinated flight that could result in a spin.

Selecting Entry Altitude. What was said about altitude under the preceding objective is applicable here, too. As a matter of fact, with the addition of power, the airplane will climb even further before the stall occurs, giving greater latitude for recovery above 1500 feet AGL. Still, for the same reasons given before, unless the examiner specifies a different altitude, plan on beginning this series of stalls at 2500 feet AGL or higher.

Establishing the Appropriate Configuration. The power-on stall is intended to simulate what can happen during the takeoff climbout. Consequently, it's called a *departure stall*. The normal configuration for this maneuver would be with gear and flaps retracted. Since some airplanes, under certain circumstances, may use flaps on takeoff as well as landing, you may be asked to perform some stalls with flap settings appropriate to the airplane you're flying.

Establishing Airspeed. The objective suggests that reduced power may be used during entry for this maneuver in order to avoid excessive pitch-up. Following your clearing turns, then, reduce the power to about the power setting normally used when you first reduce power while flying on the downwind leg for an approach to a landing. In a Cessna 150/152, for example, this would be about 1500 rpm. Then slow the airplane until you achieve the takeoff or climbout airspeed. At that point, begin to very smoothly advance the throttle and at the same time begin to apply back pressure to the elevator control. So, as the throttle goes forward, the yoke comes back.

Establishing Pitch or Attitude. Continue to add power and apply back pressure until you get a full stall. This will generally occur at slightly less than full throttle and will give you a positive break without excessive pitch-up. Here and there, an examiner may insist on getting the throttle full forward before achieving a full stall, despite the fact that the objective does not require this. One examiner I worked with required this. Consequently, I always instructed my students to do it my way and, when he criticized that approach, to ask for a demonstration. They would inevitably return with a story about cruising around with full throttle and the Cessna 150 in a nose-high position and mushing while the examiner cursed and tried to get an abrupt break. He never changed his approach, so I never changed mine. Fortunately, he never "busted" any of my students on the checkride, either.

You will probably be asked to do departure stalls both clean and dirty and straight ahead as well as from climbing turns. Let us hope that you don't draw one of those examiners who insists on full throttle and excessive pitch-ups, however. All that this maneuver is intended to show is that just as stalls can occur at any airspeed and any attitude, they can also occur at any power setting. Incidentally, one of the signs of an imminent stall in a climbing turn will be the tendency of the outside (or high) wing to begin to show signs of stall first. For some examiners, that will be sufficient to begin the recovery; others will require a fairly abrupt break to demonstrate how much the control of the airplane erodes in this situation.

Maintaining Coordinated Flight. You know already that you will encounter some differences with power-on stalls that make them a bit more challenging. In the first place, with power on, the stalling speed is lowered, so you'll need to maintain that nose-high attitude longer than with power-off stalls. Also, the nose must be raised higher to get the stall. And, while rudder and elevator seem to retain their effectiveness longer, aileron control seems to diminish, allowing for a tendency for the airplane to fall off on a wing. The pitch-down is also generally a little more abrupt. All of this means that your hands are just a little fuller with this than with the preceding maneuver. Keep one point in mind, however: As you were directed previously, if one wing does stall before the other, do not attempt to pick it up with the aileron, since this merely aggravates the situation. Instead, use opposite rudder. Also, you should monitor the turn and slip indicator to maintain coordinated control.

Recovering. When the full stall occurs, begin the recovery promptly, but not abruptly. In other words, when the break or pitch-down occurs, or when you have the yoke or stick all the way back with airplane mushing down in a nose-high attitude, start the recovery. Since power is already being applied. the only thing you can do here is lower the nose sufficiently to "unstall" the wing. That does not mean jamming the stick forward; it simply means easing off the back pressure until the nose is in a normal climb—or at most a normal cruise—altitude. Then level the wings, and finally adjust the power either to normal climb power setting, or to normal cruise power setting, whichever the examiner stipulates. If he/she suggests nothing, then use the normal climb power setting in order to climb back to the altitude at which the maneuver began.

Cleaning the Airplane Up. Now that the altitude and power setting are taken care of, and the airplane is in essentially normal flight, retract the wing flaps, in increments, and the gear, if retractable.

Avoiding Excesses. If you have performed the maneuver as recommended above, you will have avoided all excesses. Prompt recovery holds altitude loss to a minimum. Monitoring (not staring at) the turn and slip indicator to maintain coordinated flight will avoid spins. And simply lowering the nose sufficiently to "unstall" the wing without jamming the yoke forward to enter a screaming dive will avoid excessive speed and permit recovery well above the 1500-foot limit, if you entered the maneuver at 2500 feet AGL.

C. TASK: IMMINENT STALLS – POWER ON AND POWER OFF
(ASEL)

PILOT OPERATION – 4

REFERENCE: AC 61–21.

1. **Objective.** To determine that the applicant:

   a. Exhibits adequate knowledge by explaining the aerodynamic factors associated with imminent stalls (power on and power off), an awareness of speed loss in different configurations, and the procedure for resuming normal flight attitude.
   b. Selects an entry altitude that will allow recoveries to be completed no lower than 1,500 feet AGL.
   c. Establishes either a takeoff, a climb, or an approach configuration with the appropriate power setting.
   * d. Establishes a pitch attitude on a constant heading, ±10°, or in 20°, ±10°, bank turns that will induce an imminent stall. *
   e. Applies proper control to maintain coordinated flight.
   f. Recognizes and recovers from imminent stalls at the first indication of buffeting or decay of control effectiveness by reducing angle of attack and adjusting power as necessary to regain normal flight attitude.
   g. Avoids full stalls, excessive airspeeds, excessive altitude change, spins, or flight below 1,500 feet AGL.

2. **Action.** The examiner will:

   a. Ask the applicant to explain the aerodynamic factors associated with imminent stalls, power on and power off.
   b. Ask the applicant to perform imminent

stalls, both power on and power off, in a specified configuration and maneuver, and determine that the applicant's performance meets the objective.

c. Place emphasis on the applicant's ability to promptly recognize and recover from imminent stalls.

Objective: What's expected of the applicant regarding imminent stalls—power on and power off.

Exhibiting Knowledge by Explanation. The description that you'll provide for imminent stalls will not differ appreciably from those you presented for full stalls. Generally, you'll simply need to demonstrate your awareness of the earliest signs of a stall, i.e., what occurs as the first indications that the wing is about to stall. In most airplanes, the earliest sign will be the stall warning light or horn. Next will come a buffeting, caused by the way the air strikes the airplane's tail surfaces. Though it may seem that the wing is buffeting, it's the tail that produces this "stall warning." The pilot should also notice a diminution in the effectiveness of the airplane's controls. Explain that at the first signs that a stall is about to occur, the pilot must employ the same procedures as those used for a full stall.

Selecting an Entry Altitude. Since you'll be making the recovery before a stall actually occurs, there will be even less loss of altitude. Consequently, it would seem that there is less need for concern about recovering above 1500 feet AGL. However, keep in mind that all the objectives call for recovery above this altitude. You might as well use 2500 feet for imminent stalls, too.

Establishing Configuration and Power Setting. The examiner will have you doing both approach and departure imminent stalls. The configurations and power settings will be precisely those that you used for approach and departure stalls when you performed full stalls.

Establishing Attitude. Again, as with full stalls, you'll be required to do the imminent stalls both straight ahead and in climbing and descending turns, depending on whether you're performing departure or approach stalls. Once that attitude is established, you'll perform exactly as you did for full stalls, i.e., you will begin to apply back pressure to increase the angle of attack until the critical angle of attack is approached.

Maintaining Coordinated Flight. Nothing different about this, either. Generally, it will mean maintaining neutral ailerons and using sufficient rudder pressure to keep the ball centered.

Recognizing the Signs and Recovering. The objective calls for you to recognize and recover at the first indication of buffeting or decay of control effectiveness. That's all very well and good. However, as a practical matter, it turns out that these signs must be evident to the examiner, too. So although you should begin the recovery early, too quick a response may

166

not do the trick. The examiner may get the impression that you recovered prior to the onset of the stall unless he/she also feels those first signs. So rather than beginning the recovery at the first sign of decay of control effectiveness, which the examiner will not be able to detect since you'll be handling the controls, wait for the onset of the buffet, or a sign that will be apparent to the examiner. Occasionally an examiner will allow the stall warning light or horn to be used as the first sign of an imminent stall and will look for a recovery at that point. Your recovery will, of course, be the same as for the full stall. It's always: Reduce the angel of attack first, then adjust power, and then whatever else is required to regain normal flight.

What to Avoid. No mysteries here; the objective is very clear in specifying that you must avoid full stalls, excessive airspeeds or excessive altitude changes, spins, or flight below 1500 feet AGL. Whatever kept you from these prohibited practices in full stalls will also do the trick for imminent stalls.

D. TASK: MANEUVERING AT MINIMUM CONTROLLABLE AIRSPEED
(ASEL)

PILOT OPERATION – 4

REFERENCE: AC 61–21.

1. **Objective.** To determine that the applicant:

   a. Exhibits adequate knowledge by explaining the flight characteristics and controllability associated with maneuvering at minimum controllable airspeeds.
   b. Selects an entry altitude that will allow the maneuver to be performed no lower than 1,500 feet AGL.
   c. Establishes and maintains the airspeed at which any further increase in angle of attack, resulting from an increase in load factor or reduction in power, would result in an immediate stall while –

      (1) in coordinated straight and turning flight in various configurations and bank angles, and
      (2) in coordinated departure climbs and landing approach descents in various configurations.

   d. Maintains the desired altitude, ±100 feet, when a constant altitude is specified, and levels off from climbs and descents, ±100 feet.
   e. Maintains the desired heading during straight flight, ±10°.
   f. Maintains the specified bank angle, ±10°, in coordinated flight.
   g. Maintains minimum controllable airspeed, +5, –0 knots.

2. **Action.** The examiner will:

   a. Ask the applicant to explain the flight

characteristics and controllability involved in flight at minimum controllable airspeed.

b. Ask the applicant to perform flight at minimum controllable airspeed, specifying the configuration and maneuver, and determine that the applicant's performance meets the objective.

c. Place emphasis on the applicant's ability to recognize minimum controllable airspeed and to maintain correct airplane control.

Objective: What's expected of the applicant regarding maneuvering at minimum controllable airspeed.

Exhibiting Knowledge through Explanation. You first explained stalls, both power-on and power-off. This was followed by your explanation of "almost stalls," a sort of step back from full stalls. Now you'll take a further step back and explain what happens in flight at airspeeds that are maintained with pitch and power setting such that any increase in pitch would cause an almost immediate stall, i.e., flight at an airspeed, pitch, and power setting that are close to imminent stalls. And that's how you can introduce your explanation. Follow this by detailing the airplane's response to this situation. Recognizing that lift is related to the speed at which the relative wind moves over the wing, it should be apparent that as this speed is diminished, lift will also diminish.

Explain, too, that with a lower power setting, the nose will need to be held higher in relation to the horizon. This increases the angle of attack—not because of the position of the nose in relation to the horizon, but because the airplane is now in "mushing" straight and level flight with the relative wind striking the flying surfaces at a different angle, coming more nearly at the bottom part of the leading edge. This increased angle of attack causes the air to start to tear away from the wing, beginning at the trailing edge, and at the wing root. As this "burbling" increases, the portion of the wing providing lift gradually diminishes. Your role is to diminish the amount of lift to the point where flight is barely sustained.

Demonstrate your understanding that as the lift diminishes, control of the airplane also diminishes. The flow over the control surfaces of all the flying surfaces is affected by the increase in angle of attack, too. Just as the wing and other flying surfaces become less effective, so, too, do the control surfaces. This makes the plane more difficult to control and makes careful control more critical. Assure the examiner that you understand that any further increase in angle of attack will further erode both airspeed and controllability. Ultimately, if the back pressure on the stick or yoke were increased, the airplane would start to lose altitude, stall, or spin—or all three.

Selecting an Altitude. You're not going to stall or spin the airplane, of course; you're too competent for that. But just to keep the examiner feeling more secure, use the same entry altitude for these maneuvers that you used for stalls, unless the examiner specifies an altitude.

Establishing and Maintaining Minimum Controllable Airspeed.
This sort of thing used to be called slow flight, and it made more sense then. Is that a sign that I'm aging and getting cantankerous? I don't think so. When we called it slow flight, we taught student pilots the various "gaits" of the airplane and taught them to fly the airplane at those varied airspeeds. Slow flight meant selecting one of the useful "gaits" and checking one's skill in that. We might, for example, use a slow airspeed such as that used for approaches. We'd teach it and then check to see that student pilots could handle the airplane in varied and appropriate configurations and attitudes related to real flying needs. Then we'd select another "gait" and do the same thing with that airspeed. It seemed so practical.

Now the requirement is for "minimum controllable" airspeed. No question about it, pilots should be able to control the airplane at all its gaits. But, hopefully, they are not going to do much flying at minimum controllable airspeed. Still, it's on the test; so . . . To achieve that airspeed, start to exert back pressure on the yoke or stick. Then, to keep the airplane from climbing, reduce the power. Keep these two motions going until you have stabilized the airplane at the airspeed and altitude that the examiner calls for. One practical benefit that practicing this maneuver has is that it teaches students very clearly and undeniably that attitude controls airspeed and power controls climb and descent.

With the airplane stabilized at minimum controllable airspeed, you'll first be required to maintain altitude and heading. This will be followed by, first, 90-degree turns in both directions, followed by 180-degree turns in both directions, all accomplished while maintaining that slow airspeed and the assigned altitude. You may find it necessary to increase power in order to maintain altitude during turns, since the airplane "weighs more" then. You may also be required to run through this series of maneuvers clean and dirty, i.e., with no flaps and with flaps extended. You might also have to drop the gear for these maneuvers, if your plane is equipped with retractable gear.

Still maintaining that same slow airspeed, you'll next be required to run through a similar series of maneuvers as you climb the airplane. The pitch, or attitude, won't be changed. To climb the airplane, you'll simply increase power. Attitude will be used to control airspeed, just as it always is. Similarly, you'll run through the same operations while doing descents. Descents, of course, will be accomplished simply by reducing power until you get the desired rate of descent.

Maintaining Altitude. During the level flight phase of this part of the practical test, you'll use power to maintain the desired altitude. Monitor the altimeter; if it begins to drop off, add a touch of power. If the airplane starts to climb, ease off power. In the climbing portions, as you approach the new altitude, begin to reduce power until the climb ceases. You can begin this about 50 feet below the altitude to which you're climbing. Similarly, during a descent, start adding power about 50 feet early in order to check your descent at the altitude called for.

Maintaining Heading. In order to hold the nose of the airplane in the right direction, you'll need also to monitor the DG. If the airplane begins to drift off, use a small amount of aileron and rudder to bring it back. The application of pressure on these controls should be smooth and light. It won't take much of a bank to bring you back if you start correcting promptly.

Maintaining Bank Angle. You'll be using relatively shallow banks for all your turns during this maneuver. Be prepared for the airplane to respond very sluggishly; you may need to wait it out a little. But if the bank starts to drift from, say 20 degrees, simply use a little aileron and rudder pressure in the opposite direction. Apply a bit of pressure and then wait for the airplane to respond.

Maintaining Airspeed. There's a little tolerance in airspeed and it's all on the high side. That's because at minimum controllable airspeed, if your airspeed diminishes, you "lose control." Just keep in mind at all times that it's the airplane's attitude that will control its airspeed.

Chapter 8

VIII. AREA OF OPERATION:
TURN MANEUVERS

A. TASK: CONSTANT ALTITUDE TURNS (ASEL)

PILOT OPERATION – 10

REFERENCE: AC 61–21.

1. **Objective.** To determine that the applicant:

   a. Exhibits adequate knowledge by explaining the performance factors associated with constant altitude turns including increased load factors, power required, and overbanking tendency.
   b. Selects an altitude that will allow the maneuver to be performed no lower than 1,500 feet AGL.
   c. Establishes an airspeed which does not exceed the airplane's design maneuvering airspeed.
   d. Enters a 180° or 360° turn maintaining a

bank angle of 40° to 50° in coordinated flight.

    e. Divides attention between airplane control and orientation.

    f. Rolls out at the desired heading, ±20°.

    g. Maintains the desired altitude, ±200 feet.

2. Action. The examiner will:

    a. Ask the applicant to explain the performance factors associated with constant altitude turns.

    b. Ask the applicant to perform constant altitude turns and specify degree of turn and roll–out heading, and determine that the applicant's performance meets the objective.

    c. Place emphasis on the applicant's ability to control pitch and bank, and maintain coordinated flight.

Objective: What's expected of the applicant regarding constant altitude turns.

Exhibiting Knowledge through Explanation. Since these turns will involve factors and requirements other than those practiced earlier, your explanations will differ. Prior to this phase of the test, you've used medium, or even shallow, banked turns. Since these turn maneuvers call for bank angles of 40 degrees to 50 degrees, a different description will be needed.

In the first place, as a consequence of the centrifugal force resulting from the curved flight, the airplane will "increase its weight." In straight-and-level flight, your trainer may weigh 1600 pounds. The centrifugal force from the curving flight will increase as the bank (and the rate of turning) increase until, in a 60-degree bank, the wing loading has been increased to the point that they are now supporting 3200 pounds. As you sit in the airplane, you realize from your contact with the seat of the airplane that your seat has also doubled in weight; you can feel yourself being shoved down in the seat. Many people can also feel their stomach (and whatever they had for lunch) weighing down on them, too. Since the load has doubled, twice as much lift is required to sustain level flight. Further, without going into the mathematics of it, as the load on the airplane increases, the "stalling speed" also increases significantly; it's not doubled, but it's significantly higher than in straight-and-level flight. Also, since the airplane now "weighs more," its airspeed will also be reduced, all other factors being equal.

Since the airplane requires greater lift to keep it flying level, and since it will tend to slow down, something must be done to respond to these changes in the airplane's flight characteristics. It's quite apparent that in order to keep the airplane from descending, power must be added. Further, a part of the reason for the lower airspeed is that in the turn, with its tendency for the airplane to start a descent because of the forces acting on it, the pilot must hold some back pressure to maintain normal pitch, or attitude. This back pressure, of course, has the effect of slowing the airplane. Now, to overcome this, you may increase the power a little beyond that required to maintain level flight. This will enable you to ease off some of that back pressure on the yoke, which will help to maintain the airplane's airspeed.

Finally, explain to your examiner that you have learned that in turns with shallow banks, the wings of the airplane have a tendency to level themselves because of the airplane's designed-in lateral stability. So you have to hold pressure on the aileron on the inside of the turn to overcome this. Now, in any turn, there's a difference in the distance traveled by the inside wing and the outside wing, which means that since they complete the turn at the same time, the outside wing must be traveling somewhat faster to cover its greater distance (Fig. 8-1). The slight extra speed of the outside wing increases as the bank increases.

In medium turns, because the outside wing in the turn is moving faster than the inside wing, the bank has balanced the inherent lateral stability of the plane and there is no need to hold the aileron pressure that is required for shallow banked turns. (I knew an airplane salesperson who used to employ this little bit of aeronautical knowledge to demonstrate to prospective customers that the airplane he was selling was a very stable craft. He'd trim the airplane for a little nose-up flight, add a touch of power, and roll into a medium bank. Then he'd take his hands and feet off the controls to demonstrate that his airplane was the most stable airplane in the stable. He sold more airplanes that way.)

The turns for this phase of the practical test, however, are steep turns. Since the bank is greater, it goes beyond what happens with medium banks, and overcomes the inherent lateral stability of the airplane. The consequence of this is that the airplane has a tendency to overbank, requiring the pilot to hold opposite aileron pressure, once the bank is established, in order to keep the airplane from overbanking.

Selecting a Proper Altitude. If your turns are not perfectly executed, you may gain or lose some altitude. Figuring that you could lose as much as 200 feet and still not be disqualified, it's best not to begin these maneuvers at 1500 feet AGL. Give yourself a safe margin; start the procedures at no less than 2000 feet AGL, or whatever altitude is assigned by the examiner.

The Right Airspeed. The maneuvering airspeed may be less than normal cruising airspeed for the airplane you're flying. If so, slow the airplane to the maneuvering speed published in the operating handbook or placarded

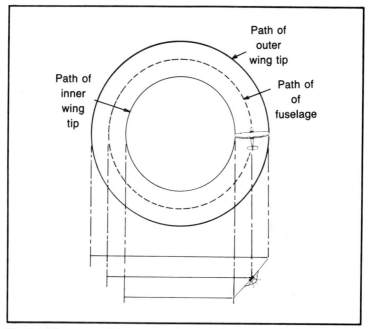

Fig. 8-1. The cause of the overbanking tendency in steep turns.

on the panel before starting this series of turns. If your plane permits you to maneuver at higher than cruising airspeeds, then you have no problem. Simply enter all the maneuvers at normal cruising airspeed.

Performing Steep Turns. You will be required to do 180-degree turns in both directions. Similarly, you will be required to perform 360-degree turns to the left and to the right. The turns will be made with a bank angle of 40 to 50 degrees. The objective also calls for coordinated flight. So, having checked traffic in the direction of your turn, go ahead and roll into a turn with a bank of about 45 degrees. But knowing what forces will be acting on the airplane, begin to apply back pressure to the yoke, and to advance the throttle as you roll into the turn. This should keep you in level and coordinated flight. Once you're established in the turn with the proper bank, and holding some back pressure and a little more power, you need to monitor both outside and inside references.

Dividing Your Attention. For these maneuvers, most of your attention should be on outside references. If you use the horizon to keep your bank steady and to keep the nose of the airplane in the same place in relation to the horizon all the way through the turn, then altitude, airspeed, and other factors will nearly take care of themselves. But pilots don't have built-in altitude and airspeed and degree-of-bank sensors, so you'll need to check the gauges occasionally to see that you are at the right altitude, that the bank really is about 45 degrees, and that the airspeed is not excessive. Having checked those factors on the instruments, you redirect your attention to the outside references again.

One of the difficulties associated with steep turns is that what's up and down in relation to the horizon is no longer quite up and down to the pilot. What's "up" to the pilot is no longer just the sky but a point that's somewhere between the zenith and the horizon, and what's "down" is not simply the ground but a location between nadir and horizon that—like "up"—includes both earth and sky. Shallow banks (or even medium banks) don't seem to have this effect, but steep banks can cause some problems with orientation. There are even weird myths associated with this maneuver, such as "the rudder becomes the elevator," etc. Just remember to use *all* your references and you should be able to maintain your orientation, which will help you to control the airplane.

Rolling Out of the Turns. Since you're in a steep turn, the rate of turning is going to be greater, and it will take slightly longer to roll to straight-and-level flight. Similar to what you did with turns in other phases, start your rollout before reaching the heading. As you reach about 10 degrees short of the heading that will complete your 180-degree or 360-degree turn, start to increase the aileron pressure you've been holding. As the rollout is completed, you'll be right on the heading—or close enough to be within tolerances.

Maintaining Altitude. Since you've been holding back pressure on the yoke, and using a little extra pressure, you know what to do now. As the airplane rolls back to straight-and-level flight, it will "weigh less." Since this doesn't happen all at once, your response shouldn't be all at once. As you begin to roll out of the steep turn, ease off the back pressure you've been holding and gradually reduce power to the normal power setting. Continue to divide your attention between outside and inside references during the rollout, just as you did throughout the rest of the turn. As a matter of fact, this attention to references will be even more critical at this stage than while you're in the midst of the turn. It's usually at the end that applicants will "bust it," turning past the heading or climbing beyond the 200 feet tolerated.

B. TASK: DESCENDING TURNS (ASEL)

PILOT OPERATION – 10

REFERENCE: AC 61–21.

1. **Objective.**   To determine that the applicant:

   a. Exhibits adequate knowledge by explaining the performance factors associated with descending turns while maintaining the airplane's position in relation to the surface.
   b. Establishes a glide at the recommended airspeed when power loss is simulated.
   c. Selects a suitable area over which a descending turn can be performed.
   d. Enters the descending turn, not to exceed a bank angle of 40° at the steepest point, over the selected area with the desired radius of turn.
   e. Maintains a radius which is approximately constant over the selected area.
   f. Divides attention between airplane control, planning, flightpath, and orientation.
   g. Maintains the desired airspeed, ±10 knots.
   h. Recovers at a safe altitude and position from which an emergency landing could be accomplished.

2. **Action.**   The examiner will:

   a. Ask the applicant to explain the performance factors associated with descending turns while maintaining the airplane's position in relation to the surface.
   b. Ask the applicant to perform a descending turn combining this task with high altitude simulated emergencies, and determine that the applicant's performance meets the objective.

c. Place emphasis on the applicant's ability to plan and maintain the desired flightpath in relation to the surface.

Objective: What's expected of the applicant regarding descending turns. **Exhibiting Knowledge through Explanation.** Well, they've done it again and you must undo it. The FAA has changed the name and made less clear the maneuver they have in mind . . . So you must exhibit your understanding here that the FAA doesn't really mean descending turns, even though that's what they say. "Descending turns" is simply too vague to do the job. You understand that what they're referring to here is what used to be called *spirals*. Let the examiner know that you understand that. You can even ask why the FAA decided to refer to it the way they do, though I'm sure no one knows. Maybe it's just too simple to say "spiral" instead of saying "descending turns while maintaining the airplane's position in relation to the surface." As a matter of fact, "the airplane's position in relation to the surface" changes during this maneuver—the airplane gets *continuously closer to* the surface.

Clear this up for the examiner. Let him/her know that this maneuver involves several important factors. For one thing, it may be seen as related to emergency procedures since it does provide practice in maintaining a steep gliding turn at a controlled airspeed over a particular point. It's just the procedure you might use for an engine-out emergency. The spiral as required here is also a ground reference maneuver, since you'll have the task of keeping the course you'd be describing on the surface an equal distance from a point on the surface. It's also an exercise in dividing your attention between inside and outside references.

When power is reduced, you will use the airplane's pitch or attitude to maintain a constant airspeed, generally the best angle-of-glide airspeed. Since the bank angle may at times be as much as 40 degrees, there will be times when the plane may have a tendency to overbank, meaning that you cannot simply set the controls and hold them in the same position throughout. As a matter of fact, you will need to vary the bank in order to keep the airplane "over the spot" as you compensate for any wind. This will require steepening the bank on downwind headings and shallowing the bank on upwind headings. Explain that although the airspeed remains relatively constant, the ground speed varies. Since you're going faster downwind, the radius of the turn would increase, requiring a steeper bank in order to increase the rate of turning and keep the airplane as close to the center here as at other points. On upwind legs, where ground speed would be slower, the opposite is required, of course.

As you probably realize from having practiced this with your instructor, the fairly steep bank while you're descending alters the outside references that you normally see and this can lead to disorientation. Couple this with the successive turning and the need to continuously check references inside the airplane and you also have a situation that can cause vertigo. Hopefully, your earlier practice has helped you to overcome this.

Clarify that you understand that the points to be kept in mind for this maneuver are the constant airspeed, the need to keep a constant radius, and the requirements that you roll out at a safe altitude on the proper heading.

Selecting a Suitable Area. The objective lists this point after mentioning the requirement to establish a glide, but you'll select the area for the maneuver first. Or perhaps the examiner will select the point and give you a heading, or specify the number of complete turns for this maneuver. If he/she leaves the selection up to you, you might choose an intersection with one of the highways lined up with the wind as closely as possible.

Establishing the Glide. Begin the entry to the maneuver downwind from the point over which you intend to spiral. Flying upwind, cut the throttle to simulate loss of power right over the point and immediately roll into your descending turn. You may be required to perform this maneuver in both directions, but if the choice is yours, choose a spiral to the left. It's easier for you since the point below around which you're spiraling will be more readily visible to you, and (you may tell the examiner) most traffic patterns are to the left and you can therefore simulate entering a traffic pattern from the spiral. Since you're headed upwind, the bank will not be steep. That helps you maintain orientation while you get the proper attitude, or pitch, in order to control your airspeed. Keep in mind at all times that it's the pitch or attitude of the airplane that will control the airspeed.

Entering the Descending Turn. As we've already pointed out, the initial bank angle will not be steep, since you're headed upwind and your ground speed is therefore relatively slower. In order to stay fairly close to the point around which you're going to be turning, make your initial bank at least 20 degrees—preferably more.

Maintaining a Constant Radius. In order to maintain the radius you've established, it will be necessary to gradually steepen the bank as you come around to a downwind heading. Your downwind bank angle will be about 40 degrees, the steepest bank permitted for this maneuver. Then, as the turn continues and you come around to an upwind heading, the bank will be gradually shallowed with the shallowest bank occurring on the upwind portion of the spiral.

Dividing Attention. This is a demanding maneuver. There is no alternative to dividing your attention between outside and inside references. The outside references are important to holding proper attitude or pitch in order to keep the airspeed under control and also to check the radius of the spiral by noting distance from the point. Outside references are also essential to maintaining orientation. Still, you cannot guess at airspeed and heading, so the airspeed indicator and DG must be monitored. Similarly, you must keep a check on the attitude indicator to ensure that your bank angle does not exceed 40 degrees. And, as though all of that were not enough to totally occupy one person, it's also necessary to plan ahead to avoid rolling

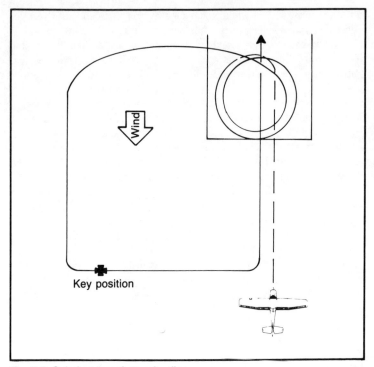

Fig. 8-2. Spiral approach to a landing.

out too early or too late, or descending too low.

Maintaining the Desired Airspeed. Unless the examiner specifies otherwise, use the best rate-of-climb or rate-of-glide airspeed. As with the other maneuvers, rely on the attitude of the airplane; a constant attitude will give you a constant airspeed. Do not rely on the airspeed indicator to hold a constant airspeed; start chasing that needle and you will never hold the airspeed constant. However, this does not relieve you from monitoring the airspeed indicator to assure that the airspeed you're holding is appropriate.

Recovery. Although the objective specifies no altitude, most maneuvers must be completed above 1500 feet AGL. At times, examiners will suggest descending to pattern altitude for this maneuver to simulate preparing to enter a traffic pattern. Also, now and again an examiner will have you treat this as an emergency landing and from the spiral, or descending turns, have you simulate an approach to an emergency landing (Fig. 8-2).

Chapter 9

IX. AREA OF OPERATION:
FLIGHT MANEUVERING BY REFERENCE TO GROUND OBJECTS

A. TASK: RECTANGULAR COURSE
(ASEL)

PILOT OPERATION – 3

REFERENCE: AC 61–21.

1. **Objective.**   To determine that the applicant:

   a. Exhibits adequate knowledge by explaining wind–drift correction in straight and turning flight and the relationship of the rectangular course to airport traffic patterns.
   b. Selects a suitable reference area.
   c. Enters a left or right pattern at a desired distance from the selected reference area and at 600 to 1,000 feet AGL.
   d. Divides attention between airplane control

and ground track, and maintains coordinated flight control.

e. Applies the necessary wind–drift corrections during straight and turning flight to track a uniform distance outside the selected reference area.

f. Maintains the desired altitude, ±100 feet.

g. Maintains the desired airspeed, ±10 knots.

h. Avoids bank angles in excess of 45°.

i. Reverses course as directed by the examiner.

2. **Action.** The examiner will:

a. Ask the applicant to explain wind–drift correction as it relates to the rectangular course and airport traffic patterns.

b. Ask the applicant to perform flight around a suitable rectangular area course, and determine that the applicant's performance meets the objective.

c. Place emphasis on the applicant's correct airplane control and proper wind–drift corrections.

Objective: What's expected of the applicant regarding rectangular course.
Exhibiting Knowledge through Explanation. Clarify that, like all ground reference maneuvers, rectangular course is intended to prepare student pilots for maneuvering that is related to takeoffs, landings, and other aspects of traffic pattern flying. Through these maneuvers, the pilot is to develop proficiency in dividing attention between inside and outside references while handling the airplane safely and with coordination. Specifically, the rectangular course flying will allow you to demonstrate your ability to fly a definite ground track while maintaining a specified altitude. It simulates a trip around the airport and requires recognizing the effects of wind and the means of counteracting those effects.

Explain that in order to fly a particular track in relation to the field chosen, the pilot must crab, i.e., hold the nose of the airplane into the wind sufficiently to produce the desired track. Turns must be planned and entered at the proper time in order to keep the airplane the same distance away from all boundaries of the field. While maintaining the proper distance from all edges of the field, the pilot must also avoid gain and/or loss of altitude, using the rudder alone to crab, poor planning resulting in flying legs too close to or too far away from the field, and skidding or slipping in turns.

Selecting a Field. This sometimes constitutes one of the more challenging parts of rectangular flight. There may be a large number of fields in the area where the practical test is being conducted, but depending on the area of the country, these may be too small, too large, or not rectangular. Pilot training manuals generally recommend the selection of a field having sides no greater in length than a mile nor less than a quarter mile. It doesn't have to be a field, of course; it can be any area. You should, however, select a site well away from areas of air traffic. Obstructions such as towers or power lines should be avoided as well, since the ground reference maneuvers are performed at relatively low altitudes. And, out of consideration for those on the ground, look for an area with as few residences, schools, and the like as possible. Ideally, a field or area with the long side of the rectangle lined up with the wind should be used. Keep in mind also that with such low-altitude flying, it's always a good idea to have an emergency landing site within easy gliding distance from any point of the rectangular course.

Entering the Pattern. It won't matter much whether you choose to enter a left or right pattern, since the examiner will probably require that the rectangular course be flown in both directions. More important is to enter at an appropriate distance from the field. You definitely do not want to be over the edge of the field or course, or even so close that it makes it difficult to keep the edge in sight. You need to keep the boundaries of the course far enough away to enable you to easily keep them in clear view as you divide your attention between inside and outside references. Flying too close not only creates the problem of keeping the boundaries in sight, but also requires turns that are too steep, and may result in flying an oval rather than a rectangular course. Since the maneuver simulates flying an airport traffic pattern, something close to the distance you normally fly from the active runway should be appropriate.

Entry altitude also needs consideration. The examiner may select an altitude. If not, then you select an altitude that approximates a normal traffic pattern altitude. Establish the selected altitude prior to entering the rectangular course, just as you get down to pattern altitude when you are approaching an airport for a landing. You should not be still descending as you begin flying the rectangular coarse.

Dividing Attention. This is at the heart of the maneuver. As in traffic pattern flying, most of your attention will be on outside references in order to maintain flight properly in relation to references on the ground. You must devote a great deal of attention to the course you fly in relation to the rectangular reference. At the same time, however, it will be necessary to maintain a relatively constant altitude, requiring that you monitor the altimeter. Strange things can happen when the major part of your attention is outside the airplane, so you must also periodically check the tachometer for your power setting, and your airspeed indicator to assure a constant and safe airspeed. In addition, while you're tracking along a boundary in a crabbing attitude, as well as during turns, tension may lead you to hold rudder pressure, creating a continuous skid. You can detect that by periodic checking of the turn and slip indicator to see that the ball is centered. If it's not, remember that you center it by "stepping on the ball."

Wind Drift Corrections. If there's little wind, or a steady, relatively light wind blowing when you take the practical test, rectangular flight will not offer a great challenge. Be prepared, however, for problem wind conditions, because some law of the universe guides gusty conditions to areas of practical tests. One phase of wind correction requires the proper amount of crabbing on the straight part of the rectangular flight. As you well know, this means yawing the nose sufficiently in the direction from which the wind is blowing to enable you to maintain a track parallel to the boundary of the site you've chosen.

The other consideration is the planning required for turns that will keep your track a uniform distance from the edge of the selected reference area. Turns will be started at the same point at each corner, namely, at an imaginary line extended from the edge of the field. However, you must recall that when you are flying downwind, your ground speed will be greater, requiring the steepest bank at the beginning of these turns and gradually shallowing the bank as you come about. Conversely, upwind turns will be shallower initially and gradually become steeper prior to your rolling out (Fig. 9-1).

Maintaining Altitude. While all of the above is going on, you'll also be expected to maintain a relatively constant altitude—either one selected by the examiner or normal pattern altitude. Maintaining a constant power setting will help maintain constant altitude, but tension can cause throttles to creep. There is no alternative to regularly monitoring the altimeter and the tachometer among other instruments as you periodically switch your attention from outside references to those inside the airplane.

Maintaining Airspeed. You'll also need periodically to check the airspeed indicator. The ground reference maneuvers may be conducted at normal cruise airspeed or at a lower airspeed selected by the examiner. He/she may choose the airspeed that you would normally use for the base leg or final approaches to landings. As with other maneuvers, the airplane's attitude will determine the airspeed. Maintaining a constant attitude will keep your airspeed constant. The attitude can be checked by attention to outside references other than the selected reference area, namely the horizon. But you must also monitor the airspeed indicator.

What makes this airspeed requirement somewhat tricky is the problem created by flight at a lower-than-normal altitude. It gives the illusion that you are flying much *faster* than normal. There is a tendency, therefore, to fly the airplane at a lower airspeed than normal to keep all references the same as they appear in flight at cruising or practice altitudes as well as to allow more time for planning. This is what necessitates peri-

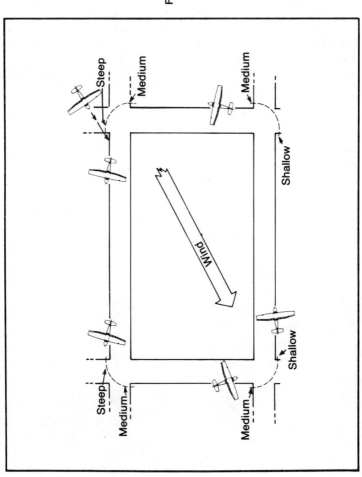

Fig. 9-1. Rectangular pattern.

185

odic checking of the airspeed indicator; slower flight may seem quite normal because of the lower altitude.

Avoiding Excessive Banks. Excessively steep banks during rectangular flight are to be avoided. In the first place, it's more difficult to maintain orientation when banks of more than 45 degrees are used. Further, such steep banks are generally the result of flying a pattern too close to the reference area, resulting in an oval instead of a rectangular course. Also, since the flight is at a lower-than-normal altitude, an error such as slipping, or overcorrections resulting in a stall, can be very dangerous. Therefore, steep banks should be avoided. The objective sets the limit at 45 degrees. You would be better to set your own personal limit of 30-degree banks for this maneuver.

Reversing the Course. Regardless of which direction you entered the pattern for rectangular flight, you will be required at some point to reverse the course. The examiner wants to know that you are capable of flying both right- and left-hand patterns. Be prepared for the fact that you may find it a little more challenging to fly the rectangular course using right turns than you found flying to the left. This is the consequence, of course, of the fact that most of your pattern flying has involved left turns.

B. TASK: S–TURNS ACROSS A ROAD
(ASEL)

PILOT OPERATION – 3

REFERENCE: AC 61–21.

1. **Objective.**   To determine that the applicant:

   a. Exhibits adequate knowledge by explaining the procedures associated with S–turns, and wind–drift correction throughout the maneuver.
   b. Selects a suitable ground reference line.
   c. Enters perpendicular to the selected reference line at 600 to 1,000 feet AGL.
   d. Divides attention between airplane control and ground track, and maintains coordinated flight control.
   e. Applies the necessary wind–drift correction to track a constant radius turn on each side of the selected reference line.
   f. Reverses the direction of turn directly over the selected reference line.
   g. Maintains the desired altitude, ±100 feet.
   h. Maintains the desired airspeed, ±10 knots.
   i. Avoids bank angles in excess of 45°.

2. **Action.**   The examiner will:

   a. Ask the applicant to explain wind–drift correction as it relates to S–turns across a road.
   b. Ask the applicant to perform a series of S-turns across a selected reference line, and determine that the applicant's performance meets the objective.
   c. Place emphasis on the applicant's correct airplane control and wind–drift corrections.

Objective: What's expected of the applicant regarding S-turns across a road.

Exhibiting Knowledge through Explanation. You'll discuss the procedures associated with S-turns along with the purposes of this ground reference maneuver. As with rectangular course flight, S-turns provide the opportunity for you to demonstrate your ability to conduct maneuvers that require attention to references outside the airplane, particularly points on the ground. Such maneuvers are intended to improve a pilot's general plane-handling capabilities as well. For S-turns, the object is to fly a pattern of two perfect half-circles of equal size on each side of a road. Essentially the same procedures for wind drift correction will be utilized for S-turns across a road as were required for flying the rectangular course. One must take into account the effects of wind and the proper responses in order to fly the desired track.

Selecting a Site. Keeping in mind the need to select a site well away from air traffic as well as clear of obstacles and residences, try to locate a road that is perpendicular to the direction of the wind. As with other low-altitude maneuvers, the selected site should also be in the vicinity of a field that can be available as an emergency landing field.

Entering the Pattern. The objective calls only for entry at an altitude between 600 and 1000 feet AGL, perpendicular to the road you've chosen. If the examiner does not assign an altitude, fly the S-turns at an altitude that approximates an airport traffic pattern altitude. It is generally a good idea to make the entry flying downwind, since that allows you to select the steepest bank needed for the maneuver, helping you to avoid excessively steep banks as the maneuver progresses.

Dividing your Attention. The requirements here are essentially the same as those for flying a rectangular course. It is necessary for most of your attention to be on the references outside the airplane. You must check to see that your track describes half-circles and that the radii of those half-circles are the same on both sides of the road. There is no way to check this except to closely monitor your position in relation to the selected reference.

While this use of outside references is necessary to fly the desired pattern, there is also a need for maintaining a relatively constant altitude as well as for keeping the airspeed within limits. This requires regular and frequent checking of the tachometer (for power setting) and the airspeed indicator. You will also need to periodically check the turn-and-slip indicator to ascertain whether or not you are misusing the rudder.

At the same time that you are dividing your attention between the inside and outside references mentioned above in order to fly the desired pattern, you must also give attention to controlling the airplane. Tension produced by trying to meet the requirements can cause you to attempt to fly the airplane with the use of "body English" instead of the flying controls. Consequently, some attention will also need to be given to what you are doing to the attitude of the airplane by tensing up with your grip on the yoke. You may also find yourself unconsciously retarding or advancing the throttle. Even more likely will be your misapplication of rudder pressure alone in order to correct for wind drift. Try consciously to sit relaxed so that you can "ride with the airplane;" this will go far toward helping you to relax your grip on the controls and to use the controls rather than "body English." You must also regularly check to see that the ball is centered.

Applying Wind Drift Correction. To achieve a constant radius for the turn on each side of the road, you will need to alter the angle of bank. If you begin the maneuver by flying downwind across and perpendicular to the road, your first turn will use the steepest bank. Again, this is related to ground speed, which will be greatest flying downwind. As you make the turn, the bank may be gradually shallowed until you roll out in order to again fly across and perpendicular to the road. Since you're flying upwind, your ground speed will be reduced, requiring a lower rate of turning in order to fly a half circle with the same radius as the preceding one. Therefore, flying upwind, the bank used for entering the turn will be the shallowest, gradually increasing until you are ready once more to roll out and again fly across and perpendicular to the road (Fig. 9-2). And so it will go, until your examiner is satisfied. If you run out of road, the examiner may call on you to reverse the course.

Keep in mind also that a certain amount of crabbing will be needed when you are flying the crosswind portion of the turns. On the downwind side of the road, it will be necessary to hold the nose of the airplane toward the inside of the circle a bit. Upwind, of course, the opposite will be true.

Reversing the Direction of Turns. During this maneuver, the airplane will only momentarily be straight and level. You commence the S-turns by flying straight across the road that serves as your reference line. Immediately roll into a turn. Your rollout should be planned to enable you to roll out just prior to recrossing the road. Again, you will momentarily fly straight and level across the road and immediately roll into a turn in the opposite direction. The rollout of a turn as well as banking into the turn in the opposite direction should be done smoothly. Do not handle the controls abruptly at any point of the maneuver.

Maintaining Altitude. Although this is a ground reference maneuver, you will need to monitor certain instruments, though the main part of your attention will be outside the airplane. But while flying those perfect half-circles, you will also be expected to maintain a relatively constant altitude. This will require periodic checking of the altimeter and the power setting.

Maintaining Airspeed. You may perform the S-turns at normal cruising airspeed, or the examiner may assign a somewhat slower airspeed to simulate pattern flying. Whatever the requirement, you will need regularly, as you check the references inside the airplane, to monitor the airspeed indicator. A combination of eyeing the horizon and checking the attitude indicator will help you to keep the airspeed within acceptable limits.

Avoiding Excessive Banks. In entering the maneuver, you can con-

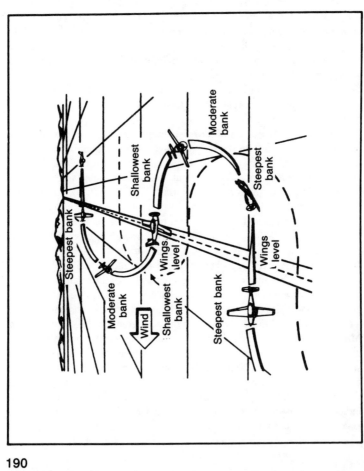

Fig. 9-2. S-turns across a road.

trol the angle of bank by starting downwind where the steepest angle of bank is required. If your first bank is about 30 degrees, that will establish the radius of the first turn and therefore of each turn that you make, guaranteeing that you will not exceed the 45-degree limit. However, it will be necessary to include the attitude indicator as one of your inside references in order to ensure that you do not exceed the limit for bank angles.

C. TASK: TURNS AROUND A POINT
(ASEL)

PILOT OPERATION – 3

REFERENCE: AC 61–21.

1. **Objective.** To determine that the applicant:

   a. Exhibits adequate knowledge by explaining the procedures associated with turns around a point and wind–drift correction throughout the maneuver.
   b. Selects a suitable ground reference point.
   c. Enters a left or right turn at a desired distance from the selected reference point at 600 to 1,000 feet AGL.
   d. Divides attention between airplane control and ground track, and maintains coordinated flight control.
   e. Applies the necessary wind–drift corrections to track a constant radius turn around the selected reference point.
   f. Maintains the desired altitude, ±100 feet.
   g. Maintains the desired airspeed, ±10 knots.

2. **Action.** The examiner will:

   a. Ask the applicant to explain the procedures associated with turns around a point and necessary wind–drift corrections.
   b. Ask the applicant to perform turns around a point, and determine that the applicant's performance meets the objective.
   c. Place emphasis on the applicant's correct airplane control and wind–drift corrections.

Objective: What's expected of the applicant regarding turns around a point.

Demonstrating Knowledge by Explanation. Your description will show that you appreciate the fact that the turn around a point is one of the more demanding ground reference maneuvers. Such turns require planning, timing, maintaining your orientation, and the ability to divide your attention between inside and outside references while you also attend to properly handling the airplane. So far, this would seem an apt description of all ground reference maneuvers. What makes the turn around a point more demanding is the fact that, unless in a no-wind condition, you must maintain a constant radius, which requires a constantly changing angle of bank.

The constantly changing angle of bank is required because, in order to fly a circle pattern with a uniform radius, you must continuously change the rate of turning to correct for wind drift. The steepest angles of bank will occur when the airplane is on downwind headings, while the shallowest banks will be required when on the upwind headings of the circle.

Selecting a Site. Begin by selecting a prominent reference point that is well away from traffic, obstacles, residences, and the like. The site should, as with the other maneuvers, be within easy gliding distance of an area that would allow a landing should the need arise. The point you choose should be sufficiently prominent to be easily seen by both you and the examiner.

Entering the Turn. As with the S-turns, you should begin this maneuver by flying downwind. Just past the reference point, at a distance equal to the intended radius of the turn, roll into a bank of about—but not more than—45 degrees. Entering the turn downwind will, of course, allow you to use the steepest bank required for keeping the radius constant and guarantee that you will not use excessively steep bank angles. Also, the radius of the turn established by using a bank angle of about 45 degrees will keep you close enough to the reference point to permit you to see the point from a high-wing airplane even when the bank is the steepest. Some advise using a lateral distance from the point that is about the same as your height above it, but I have found that even experienced pilots have difficulty making a judgement like that. If you have practiced turns around a point using a bank angle of about 45 degrees for the downwind turns, then you will have some sense of the proper distance to maintain from the reference point. As for the altitude, unless the examiner specifies otherwise, use an airport traffic pattern altitude.

Applying Wind Drift Corrections. Having entered the turn downwind, your ground speed will be greatest at this point, requiring the greatest rate of turning. Consequently, your angle of bank will be greatest at this point. Keep in mind also that as you turn, you may gradually shallow the bank, but it will also be necessary to turn far enough to keep the airplane from drifting away from the reference point on this downwind portion of the circle. Therefore, the point will appear to be ahead of the wingtip as you fly crosswind, meaning that the nose of the airplane is pointed toward the inside of the circle.

As you come about, the bank angle will be decreased until, during the upwind portion of the circle (since the ground speed will be slowest at this point), the angle of bank will be shallowest. As the turn continues from

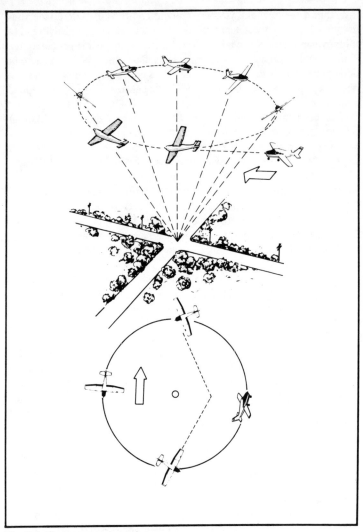

Fig. 9-3. Turns around a point.

that point, the angle of bank must be gradually and continuously increased. Also, on this upwind portion of the circle, the reference point will seem to move gradually behind the wingtip, meaning that the nose of the airplane is pointed outside the circle, allowing you to crab in order to maintain a uniform radius (Fig. 9-3).

Maintaining Altitude. While all of the above is going on, you will also need to maintain that pattern altitude—or whatever altitude you used to enter the maneuver. A part of this will be accomplished by holding a constant power setting, but you must also check inside the airplane, glancing at the altimeter and the tachometer periodically to make sure that all is going well.

Maintaining Airspeed. By now, you'll know what airspeed satisfies your examiner for these ground reference maneuvers. Whatever it is, you'll be aided in maintaining that airspeed by using the horizon as one of the outside references. Although the angle of bank will be continuously changing, the pitch or attitude will remain the same. This should take care of most of your airspeed problems. However, there is no substitute for glancing at the airspeed indicator and the attitude indicator as parts of your inside references. The latter instrument, of course, is checked not only for attitude, but also to help you avoid excessively steep angles of bank.

Chapter 10

X. AREA OF OPERATION:
NIGHT FLIGHT OPERATIONS[2]

A. TASK: **PREPARATION AND EQUIPMENT** (ASEL)

PILOT OPERATION – 9

REFERENCES: AC 61–21, AC 67–2.

1. Objective.   To determine that the applicant exhibits adequate knowledge by explaining:

a. Preparation and equipment essential for night flying.
b. Factors related to night vision including those which will change night vision.
c. Airplane, airport, and navigation lighting.
d. Weather conditions, terrain features, and unlighted areas that may affect night flight operations.

[2]This area of operation will not be evaluated if the applicant does not meet night flying regulatory requirements. If this area of operation is not evaluated, the applicant's certificate will bear the limitation, "Night Flying Prohibited."

2. **Action.**   The examiner will:

   a. Ask the applicant to explain preparation essential for night flying, characteristics of night vision, lighting, weather conditions, terrain features, and effect of unlighted areas on night flight operations, and determine that the applicant's performance meets the objective.

   b. Place emphasis on the applicant's knowledge of the hazards of night flight into areas of deteriorating weather and areas devoid of lights.

Objective: What's expected of the applicant regarding night flight operations.

Exhibiting Knowledge through Explanation. Unlike most of the other parts of the practical test, the night flying requirements usually involve only your coming to the test prepared (which will be dealt with shortly), and your discussion of matters related to flying at night. There is no requirement for a flying performance phase for the private pilot practical test; the judgement about whether or not to make actual night flying a part of the checkride is the individual examiner's. Consequently, this part of the practical test generally involves no actual practice.

Preparation and Equipment. A part of the preparation for the night flight operations portion of the practical test involves your preparation. If you have not had at least three hours of flight intruction at night, including at least 10 takeoffs and landings with the proper entries in your logbook, then you will not need to be concerned with this section. The examiner will simply note that you do not meet night flying regulatory requirements and your certificate will bear the limitation, "Night Flying Prohibited."

Assuming that you have met the preparation requirement, we can next direct our attention to the airplane. Part 91 of the FARs informs us that the airplane must have at least all the instrumentation and equipment required for day VFR flight and, in addition, must have position lights and an anti-collision light, usually referred to as a rotating beacon unless it happens to be a strobe. If the airplane is operated for hire, then an electric landing light must be included in the list of required equipment. There must also be an adequate source of electrical energy for all installed electrical and radio equipment. You're required as well to carry a spare set of fuses, unless you have three spare fuses of each kind required. These requirements will add to the items to be checked during your preflight inspection of the airplane. Also keep in mind that those lights that are required should be on any time the airplane is moving between sunset and sunrise, whether flying or merely taxiing.

Although the FARs don't refer to it, you'd be very foolish to attempt night flying without adequate cockpit lighting. Not only is there the possibility of encountering lowered visibility at night, which would restrict visual references and require you to rely heavily on instruments (would that the FAA would require that all night flight be IFR), but you'll have a tough time flying a traffic pattern if you can't read the altimeter. Included in the list—your personal list—of requirements should be a flashlight, preferably with a red lens. (You can always cover the lens with a piece of red transparent plastic.) You may carry that flashlight for years and not use it, but if the need ever arises, you'll bless who/whatever made you carry it along on the flight.

I was transporting a colleague of mine from Morristown, NJ to Bridgeport, NJ late one night when I gave thanks for a flashlight. We had left Morristown to return home late that night. The tower had told us as we were going in that our transmission was weak, but I had made this trip so many times that I paid little heed to equipment. I noticed, however, that I also had difficulty raising Flight Service to activate my flight plan.

Once we were under way, I slouched down, turned the lights very low, and cruised along without much attention to anything. We turned the ADF on and picked up a commercial station in order to get a couple of ball scores, and then turned some music on so low we could barely hear it. I intended to stay under the TCA floor until we reached Solberg VOR, where I knew I would be clear of NYC's TCA and could do pretty much as I pleased.

After boring a hole in the night sky for a while, it gradually dawned on me that we had been going for quite a while and should be past Solberg. I squinted at the VOR head and tried to make out whether the flag said TO or FROM. Lo and behold, it said OFF. Uttering a mild expletive over having lost my number one radio, I tuned in number two. Same problem—an OFF flag. We hadn't even noticed that we weren't getting music any more on the ADF set. I was still a little dense; I couldn't believe that both radios had conked out. I turned up the rheostat switch for the panel lights to full bright. Nothing. A light slowly came on inside my head. Adding a little to my earlier profanity, I dug around for my trusty five-year flashlight. Sure enough, the little bugger worked. I was not at all surprised to see that my ammeter was pegged. I had no electrical system. I turned everything off—including even the lights—except for one radio. I could raise no one. I was totally without electricity. Did I give thanks for the trusty flashlight? You bet I did.

In case you're wondering, it all turned out all right. Using old reliable, the magnetic compass, I just held a generally southerly heading and scanned the horizon for airport beacons. I finally located one and landed. (There's another whole story there, too, since the field's lights were not on and I had no radio to activate them, but we got in without undue difficulty.) I even got a magazine article out of the experience—but I got a lesson, too. *Always* include at least one flashlight on your list of required night flying equipment.

Night Vision Factors. You may be a creature of nocturnal habits in some ways, but when it comes to the eyes, the owls have it all over you. Fortunately, you're not completely ill-equipped for night vision. You remember from the medical facts section of the private pilot ground school that the retinas of your eyes have two kinds of cells, called cones and rods. The cones are in the center and pick up color, details, and distant objects. You use them for day viewing of whatever you view during your days. The rods are arranged around the cones and detect color only as shades of gray. They don't help much with detail or distance, but they certainly are helpful at night. In fact, they're what you use for night vision. You obviously don't see as well at night, but you'll see some things better if you remember about cones and rods.

In the incident I related above about losing my electrical system at night, my first view of the airport beacon that I located was out of the corner of my eye. I thought I had seen the green flash, but when I stared at the spot where I thought I had seen it, it wasn't there. Then I remembered rods and cones. I looked straight ahead again, so that the beacon could catch the corner of my eye. Sure enough, there it went again. Remember that when you're looking for a beacon. Just think to yourself, "What was it that Al Taylor said about cones and rods? Oh, yeah, because the rods see it, don't look directly at the object at night." You can tell that to the examiner, too.

You should also tell the examiner that preparation for night vision should begin, if possible, at least 30 minutes prior to boarding the airplane, since that's how long it takes for eyes to become night-adapted. Red lights will not adversely affect your night vision, but I've never known anyone who took the trouble to don red goggles a half-hour before going night flying. As a matter of fact, I've never met anyone who even *owns* a set of red goggles. Probably, the best you can do is to try to avoid bright white lights before flying insofar as that is possible. At any rate, you can keep the lights low in the cockpit.

It's also a good idea to scan the instruments rather than to stare at them; staring supposedly "tires" the eyes. Probably more important is to avoid alcohol and tobacco, since these impair night vision.

Include in your explanation the understanding that at night, distances can be deceptive. It's more difficult to judge the size, which is one basis for assessing distance. It is probably this difference in vision that causes most student pilots (and others) to make approaches and attempt landings at higher-than-normal speeds. This tendency calls for a greater reliance on instruments than may be required for daylight flying. An effort should be made to make normal approaches. If there is any variation, it may be to use power during the approach in order to be able to land more slowly and use less runway. In using such a technique, the power is cut as soon as you feel the wheels on the runway.

Airplane, Airport, and Navigation Lighting. Lighting for the airplane was discussed above; there is nothing to add here. Airport lighting is important—not simply as an aid to vision, but because the lighting system gives you information. Airports at night are beautiful places with all those lights of varied hues, but you must sort them out. Let the examiner know that you realize that the blue lights are taxiway lights, while the "white" lights are runway lights. Green lights may mark the threshold; red lights mark obstructions. The airport beacon will alternate green with white flashes, though military airports separate the green flashes with *two* white flashes. Airports use various types of approach light systems, but since these are for the use of IFR types, the examiner will not test you on them.

The major navigation lighting aids you'll be concerned with are the rotating beacons of airports. To those mentioned above may be added the flashing white and yellow beacon of lighted water airports. Flashing red lights are generally used to mark enroute obstructions, with steady-burning red lights employed to mark obstructions near airports. High-intensity flashing white lights are also used to mark some obstructions.

Other Factors Affecting Night Flight Operations. Let your examiner know that you recognize that certain features are significantly different at night. Weather is one of those. During the day, it's generally easy to see approaching clouds or to recognize that ceiling and visibility are lowering. At night, it's possible to suddenly notice that you can see a glow of green and/or red around your navigation lights that wasn't visible before, telling you that you've inadvertently entered a cloud. Or in limited visibility on a hazy night with few ground lights beneath you, it's easier than you may think to become disoriented as the ground lights give the illusion of being continuous with the stars. Recognize that if you notice that lights are beginning to disappear, this is a sign that weather is deteriorating. Your response, of course, is to do a 180 and get back to the good weather you left behind—and to get on the ground, since you're not an instrument pilot on a filed IFR trip.

Terrain can also create another problem, since some higher terrain may not be visible. The very limited illumination can cause errors in judgement of surfaces, particularly in judging distances. Further, the terrain in the vicinity of airports creates a special problem because of its being a potential hazard during takeoffs and landings. Also, there is no reliable way to make judgements about the terrain beneath you in the event that an emergency arises. It's not even possible in such instances to rely on large unlighted areas as suitable emergency landing areas, since such an area could be heavily forested land or a body of water. There's an old story that pilots tell (or maybe it's just a story that old pilots tell) regarding night emergencies. They like to say to novice pilots: If you find yourself facing a night emergency, turn on the landing light as the descent is being made. If you don't like what you see, just turn the light off. It's funnier in the hangar than it is during a night emergency, as I can testify from having had a couple of night emergencies.

B. TASK: NIGHT FLIGHT[3] (ASEL)

PILOT OPERATION – 9

REFERENCE: AC 61–21.

1. **Objective.**   To determine that the applicant:

   a. Exhibits adequate knowledge by explaining night flying procedures including safety precautions and emergency actions.
   b. Inspects the airplane by following the checklist which includes items essential for night flight operations.
   c. Starts, taxies, and performs pre–takeoff check adhering to good operating practices.
   d. Performs takeoffs and climbs with emphasis on visual references.
   e. Navigates and maintains orientation under VFR conditions.
   f. Approaches and lands adhering to good operating practices for night flight operations.

2. **Action.**   The examiner will:

   a. Ask the applicant to explain or demonstrate (as required by the examiner) essential elements relating to night flight operations, and determine that the applicant's performance meets the objective.
   b. Place emphasis on the applicant's knowledge of the factors affecting safety during night flight operations including emergency procedures.

[3] When, in the judgment of the examiner, the demonstration of night flight is an impracticable task, competency may be determined by oral testing. If night navigation is required by the examiner, the applicant is expected to follow procedures similar to those described in this standard under "Cross–Country Flying."

Objective: What could be expected of the applicant regarding night flight pilot operations.

Exhibiting Knowledge through Explanation. The explanation given for the preceding part will probably constitute your entire night flight operations check. But what happens if you get an examiner who wants to schedule your practical test at a time that will permit night flying? The first thing that will happen will be the same sort of explanation given by those who don't do the night flying—no point in repeating it all here. Having given the explanations, you'll get right into the flying part of the checkride.

Preflight Inspection. This will be accomplished in about the same manner as any other preflight inspection. You simply add the items that are required for night operations. Your inspection must include checking to see that the required lights are actually functioning. Although it's not listed on the set of requirements, reassure the examiner by showing him/her that the instruments are lighted and that you carry a flashlight. Be sure that you know where the spare fuses are located, too, prior to taking the practical test.

Startup and Taxiing. The night startup is very similar to what you normally do for flight during the day. The difference is that during the day, people in the vicinity of your airplane can generally see that you are preparing to start the engine. Generally, they will be visible to you, too. Despite that, you always clear the area as an extra precaution. Extra precautions must be taken at night, too. It's not sufficient simply to shout "Clear!" Normal airport noises may prevent someone's hearing you. In addition, the darkness may prevent your seeing someone nearby, just as *they* may miss seeing *you* preparing to start. It's a good idea, therefore, to flash your lights on to signal to all that a startup is imminent. Using your landing light will also help you see others in the area.

Having turned your lights on as a warning, you may turn them off again for the actual startup in order to save the battery. For cold weather starts you may need all the energy the battery can give. After the engine is running, you can turn on whatever equipment is needed in addition to the lights. The taxi light, or landing light, will, of course, be on for taxiing. It helps your visibility and makes you more visible to others who may also be taxiing. Even with the lights on, you must taxi very slowly at night. In the first place, your judgement of distances is not as good at night. Further, your visibility is limited pretty much to the area that is illuminated by your taxi or landing light.

When you reach the runup area, the taxi or landing light may be turned off to conserve energy. The pre-takeoff check will not be appreciably different from a check conducted during the day. However, in the subdued lighting of the airplane's interior, the checklist may be difficult to see. Also, some controls and switches that are readily visible in daylight may be difficult to locate or check at night. If you must turn up the interior lights, do so; but you know what bright lights do to night vision. Aren't you already glad that you thought to bring along that flashlight with the lens covered with clear red plastic? Prior to takeoff, turn your taxi light back on, stow the flashlight, and make sure the cockpit lighting is at an appropriate level—relatively low.

Takeoff and Climb. This is the point where your visual references really change. The examiner may even include some takeoffs without the landing light. (Is it a takeoff light at that stage?) Your references will be the runway edge lights. That distant object that you've always used during the day is no longer there. Distances seem different, making it more difficult to judge speed and altitude. As a matter of fact, because of the darkness, you will have a tendency to pick references that are closer, which will have the effect of making your airspeed seem greater than it really is. This will require greater reliance on instruments than for daylight flights. But you cannot stare at them, just as you cannot fix your vision on the area illuminated by the landing/takeoff lights. You must scan the references both inside and outside the airplane, with most of your attention directed to the outside.

You rotate only when you're sure your airspeed is sufficient for liftoff and climb. Do not rely solely on the sensations you receive from outside references; give a quick check of the airspeed indicator. Then, when you have the proper airspeed, rotate and hold the nose of the airplane in about the same attitude that you normally use for a short-field liftoff and climb. This will assure your clearing obstacles beyond the end of runway. Be prepared as well for a moment of "blindness," particularly if you are taking off from a runway with runway lights of relatively high intensity. There's just a moment during the takeoff when you may lose outside references until you've climbed above the effects of the runway lights. So, momentarily, you may need to rely on the instruments until you're high enough above the runway lights to clearly pick up outside references again.

Navigation and Orientation. To the uninitiated, and to those with little experience, night flying presents an entirely new challenge. Not only are you precluded from flying at night unless you've had the prescribed instruction, but for your own safety and that of others, you should not attempt night flight without a thorough checkout. The problem with orientation and navigation at night is that nearly all the references that you use for daytime VFR flight are gone. You are above a sea of black velvet set with thousands of lights indistinguishable from one another until you are accustomed to the new element. As the note under the objectives indicates, the same requirements that obtain for cross-country flying apply to this phase of the practical test. What makes it different is that you rely on a different set of references for checkpoints. Generally, it will be combinations of lights that will be used rather than railroads, power lines, lakes, etc.

Another aspect of night flying that is not spelled out in the objectives is the need to orient yourself in relation to other aircraft. Other airplanes will probably be even more evident to you at night; those lights in the sky seem to get your attention more readily than another aircraft during the day. However, beyond simply seeing other aircraft, you must be aware of their position and direction of travel in relation to your own. If you see only a green light, a white light, and a rotating beacon, that conveys a different message than if you see red, green, white, and the rotating beacon. It may be helpful to you to develop some mnemonic device for remembering what the position lights signify when you see them in the night sky in which you're flying.

Approaching and Landing. You may want to exercise even greater care than in the daytime when completing the landing checklist. Say each item on the list for the examiner to hear as you go down the list. It may also be advisable to fly a somewhat larger pattern at night, too, starting by flying a downwind leg a little farther out than usual. This will help compensate for the greater difficulty in judging distance and provide a more leisurely pattern, allowing more time for planning and preparation. Many pilots plan a pattern that permits the use of power all the way around, including the final leg. Carrying power enables you to make a slower, steeper approach to the runway.

Landing lights may be turned on at any point in the pattern, but most pilots prefer to make that a part of the final leg checklist. The limitations of visibility compared to daylight approaches will be evident. On hazy nights, visibility will be reduced even further, though you will probably notice that it will improve as you begin to round out for the landing. Generally, you will still be carrying power even at this point. Since there is a tendency for night approaches to be at a higher airspeed, check your airspeed indicator to ensure that you have the proper airspeed.

If you continue to hold power through the roundout until touchdown, cutting power as soon as you feel the main wheels on the runway, you will find that a much shorter rollout is required, provided that you have not used excessive airspeed during the approach and your landing is a full stall landing.

Chapter 11

XI. AREA OF OPERATION:
EMERGENCY OPERATIONS

A. TASK: EMERGENCY APPROACH AND LANDING (SIMULATED)
(ASEL)

PILOT OPERATION – 10

REFERENCE: AC 61–21.

1. **Objective.** To determine that the applicant:

   a. Exhibits adequate knowledge by explaining approach and landing procedures to be used in various emergencies.
   b. Establishes and maintains the recommended best–glide airspeed and configuration during simulated emergencies.
   c. Selects a suitable landing area within gliding distance.
   d. Plans and follows a flight pattern to the selected landing area, considering altitude,

wind, terrain, obstructions, and other factors.

e. Follows an appropriate emergency checklist.
f. Attempts to determine the reason for the simulated malfunction.
g. Maintains correct control of the airplane.

2. **Action.** The examiner will:

a. Ask the applicant to explain emergency approach and landing procedures.
b. Simulate emergencies at various altitudes and in various situations, and determine that the applicant's performance meets the objective. (Examiner should terminate the emergency approach at or above minimum safe altitude.)
c. Place emphasis on the applicant's judgment, planning, and control during the simulated emergencies.

Objective: What's expected of the applicant regarding emergency approaches and landings.

Exhibiting Knowledge through Explanation. Hopefully, your practical test will not include any genuine emergency operations. However, you will be required to explain how you would handle certain emergency procedures related to landings. Since this phase of the test has to do with approaches and landings, your explanations will deal only with emergencies occurring while the airplane is in flight. You could lose an engine while on the takeoff roll, or immediately upon liftoff, but this phase doesn't address that. Be prepared, though, to provide explanations for situations occurring at *any* phase of flight. You will, for example, be asked about emergencies such as an engine-out situation while climbing out and at other locations in the traffic pattern. Consequently, you need to be prepared to provide explanations for such situations.

Suppose you lost your engine—or had a partial power loss, or detected smoke—shortly after liftoff. What would be your response? Essentially, it would be to get the airplane back on the ground as quickly and as safely, and with as little damage to occupants and airplane, as possible. In some instances (such as loss of power) this would mean, of course, simply continuing straight ahead, essentially, to the best of what fate had put in your path. A very slight turn (to an open area, for example) might be possible, but *under no circumstances* would you attempt a return to the field if you were past the point of simply settling back onto the runway. If your problem were a *partial* loss of power, you would still continue straight ahead, monitoring airspeed as you try to gain altitude. If sufficient altitude could be gained—say 700 or 800 feet AGL—then you might try easing your way back to the airport.

There are those who frown on presenting the notion of not turning back as a hard and fast rule. There is no denying that there may be situations in which some other procedure might seem at least as desirable as landing straight ahead. Studies have been done to show how much altitude loss occurs from gliding straight ahead, as opposed to making shallow turns, or steep turns. Some pilots even talk about the possibility of wingovers or skidding turns in order to get back to the field. What most of that talk overlooks is the fact that the airplane will stall at higher airspeeds in a bank, and the steeper the bank, the higher the airspeed at which wings will stall. Studies of accidents associated with such emergencies seem to indicate that it's much safer to have "unlearned" that instinct to return to the airport. When an emergency occurs in a tight spot like the climbout, there's not time for figuring things out; instincts take over. *I hope your instructor has instilled the instinct for continuing straight ahead.*

Similar emergencies at altitude would call for different procedures, but you must have a set procedure in mind. The objectives statement lists the order in which you would proceed.

The very first response to an engine-out emergency would be to establish the proper glide attitude. It should happen automatically; *get the nose down.* Then, and only then, would you begin to look for a suitable place to land. This site should be as nearly directly under you as you can make it. Having picked the site, you should plan your approach, taking into account such factors as wind, obstructions, terrain, and the like. While you're carrying out this plan, you could go through a checklist and attempt a restart, but the first rule of this game is: *Fly the airplane.*

Aside from emergencies associated with total or partial loss of power, other situations could arise that would lead to landings that were not included in your flight plan. For example, as a private pilot with a shiny new license, you might encounter rapidly deteriorating weather on your VFR flight. An emergency landing with the airplane under full control might be preferable to continuing into a situation that could get completely out of hand. Or unanticipated winds and/or other conditions might have used up more fuel than usual, leaving you with serious doubts as to whether or not you can reach your destination airport. A planned off-airport landing with the airplane under control would be better than a forced landing without power in whatever situation obtained when the fuel was exhausted. These would be precautionary landings, but such matters should be a part of your explanation of emergency landings.

A visible oil leak or an indication of low oil pressure might also call for a landing that was not a part of your original planning. Similarly, low fuel pressure, excessively high oil temperature, or cylinder head temperatures might require getting the airplane on the ground earlier than sched-uled. Indications of some sort of structural damage (such as a serious birdstrike, or airplane or engine vibrations) could also be signs of serious trouble. Even becoming totally lost might be an occasion for a landing that could be regarded as an emergency situation.

Many of the matters in the preceding paragraph will be covered in more detail in the following section. The possibilities that could arise need only be mentioned in this phase. The major concern at this point will be with the procedures, outlined in the first four paragraphs, concerned with ap-proach and landing procedures.

Establishing and Maintaining Proper Airspeed and Configura-tion. Airspeed gets priority over all other matters during an emergency approach and landing. The very first step is to establish the airspeed that gives you the best-glide airspeed. *Best-glide airspeed* is that which provides the longest glide in terms of time. In a sense,this is also the glide that pro-vides the greatest distance, but since airplanes are flying *in* air as well as *through* the air, that distance would have to be measured as the greatest distance through the relative wind. Whether you were flying more nearly upwind or more nearly downwind may not alter the distance you travel through the relative wind, but it would certainly make a significant differ-ence in the distance over the ground that you would cover. Airplane hand-books will generally include a chart or graph to give you the best-glide airspeed (Fig. 11-1). If none is provided (or you've forgotten what it says, since you've not had that many occasions to use the best-glide speed), then establish the attitude that gives you the best rate-of-climb airspeed and use that for your gliding descent.

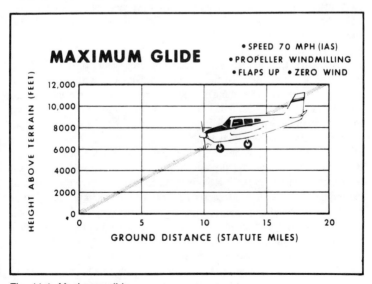

Fig. 11-1. Maximum glide.

The preceding procedures are those associated with an engine out or similar emergency in which you wish to have the greatest amount of time to prepare for the emergency landing. Another type of emergency, such as a fire, might call for the fastest practical rate of descent. The point is to get the airplane on the ground in the shortest possible time. It's still important to pick the best possible site for the emergency landing, but if the airplane turns into a puff of smoke and a cinder while you're getting to that beautiful field, you'll have *no* more worries about landing.

For the time being, let's skip by the steps such as getting switches and fuel shutoff valves off and concentrate on what gets the airplane on the ground quickly. The first step in such a maneuver is to reduce the power to idle and, if the airplane has a constant-speed prop, to place the propeller control for high rpm. The latter allows the propeller to provide maximum drag for the rapid descent. Next, the flaps should be fully extended. If your airplane has retractable landing gear, lower the landing gear, too. With the plane thus configured, establish a bank of 30 to 45 degrees for at least 90 degrees of heading change. The turning descent will allow you to clear the area and use turning to increase the rate of descent without increasing airspeed. In attempting the rapid descent, however, it is important never to exceed the airplane's never-exceed airspeed for flaps extended (and gear extended, if applicable). It's equally important to avoid reducing the airspeed below a safe speed. You must keep in mind that in a turn, the steeper the bank, the higher the airspeed at which the airplane will stall.

Selecting a Suitable Landing Area. The size and condition of the area selected for an emergency landing are very important, of course. Wind speed and direction are also important factors in selection of a landing area. The latter affect the airplane's gliding distance over the ground and could require that you pick the smaller, rougher field simply because the large, smooth one is beyond gliding distance, given your position and the speed and direction of the wind.

Obviously, the ideal emergency landing area would be a large, level field, free of surrounding obstacles, ditches, boulders, and the like, with a residence within easy walking distance to provide you with a way of communicating your plight and seeking assistance. More likely, you'll have to select from among a very few possible landing areas, each with its peculiar problems. Certainly you would select the site that is most nearly free of obstacles and possible hazards and which is of sufficient length to enable you to land and get the airplane stopped. If possible, it is also advisable to select a field that is relatively wide so that you have the option of extending the base leg if necessary to correct for error in planning. Your selected site would also allow you to land as nearly upwind as possible, enabling you to approach at a slower ground speed and to shorten your rollout after landing.

The area selected should be as nearly directly under the airplane as possible. The closer you are to the landing area, the more control you will generally have over the landing. An area near your location gives you more time to prepare for the landing, provides a better chance of using the wind to your advantage, allows more time to inspect the site and plan the approach as you descend and, providing more time, will allow you to attempt a restart. But at least as important as any of these—perhaps *more* important—a landing area close by will reduce your tendency to stretch the glide. This is a rule that is hard and fast; *never* deviate from it: *Never attempt to stretch the glide.* You would always be better off to land in a less desirable area, even among trees, with the airplane under your control than you would be if you attempt to glide too far and have the airplane impact out of control. So select a site as close to you as possible and, having once selected the area, do not change your mind.

Planning the Approach. The altitude at which the simulated emergency landing is begun is probably the single most important controlling factor. Wind direction and speed must next be considered. These three factors will have been the chief determinants of your landing area selection. Terrain and obstructions have also been considered.

Your selection having been made, your next consideration is to get the airplane to the approach end of that field. It is preferable that your planning be based on maneuvering to use a 360-degree overhead approach, a 180-degree side approach, or a 90-degree approach, modifying your choice as necessary.

You may read or hear about aiming for a key point and planning your approach from there. I've even seen diagrams indicating where the key point is to be, depending on which approach you use. I've noticed, however, that those airplanes in the diagrams always seem to make it, wherever that key point is. My advice to you is to make the key point the touchdown spot of the emergency landing site. When the emergency occurs and you select the site for landing, point the nose of the airplane at the approach end. When that spot is beneath you, you have the best possible chance of putting the airplane down on it. As you make your turns, notice what's happening to your altitude and plan accordingly. Flying a beautiful pattern is not what this exercise is about. If your examiner allows you to continue the approach until it's evident whether or not you could accomplish a successful landing, that's the only part he/she will remember. One point you might keep in mind: In your planning, aim to reach the approach end of the landing area (i.e., going "over the fence") a little high. You can always trade off a little excess altitude to get down, but you can never buy back the altitude that's above you.

Lest you get the notion that whatever gets you on the ground without harm or damage is a good pattern, that's right in a real situation. In this simulation, however, try to get over the spot so that you can use a 360-degree overhead approach, if altitude permits. Your chances of performing satisfactorily are improved using such an approach. And it also demonstrates to the examiner that you really have done some planning.

The flight pattern you've planned and used should bring you over the edge of the emergency landing area at the proper altitude to enable you to clear all obstacles and land near enough the approach end to permit a safe rollout to a stop. If your planning and pattern are well done, you should be a little high as you enter the final leg to the touchdown spot. That extra altitude is insurance. When you are absolutely certain that you have the field made, then you can begin to put down flaps, slip the airplane (if that's permissible), or perform S-turns in order to get rid of excess altitude and touch down as near as possible to the spot you've picked out. Incidentally, the flaps should *not* be extended until you are certain that you've got the field made. Once you begin to extend flaps, *never retract them* until you're on the ground.

Using the Checklist. Having started the approach, the next step is to try to avoid the emergency landing. A part of this procedure, of course, will also include a check to make sure that you're prepared if a landing is necessitated. The first item on this checklist has already been mentioned several times. Establish the proper attitude to get the appropriate airspeed, the best-glide airspeed. The next steps may not be exactly right for every situation, but they're suggested as a basis for emergency landing situations. Commit the list or something like it to memory and go through this while you're making the emergency approach on the practical flight test.

Having picked the field, established the proper airspeed, and planned your approach, you will next check the fuel selector to ensure that it's on the fullest tank. You might even wish to recycle the selector. Then turn the fuel pump on. Check that the mixture is on full rich. Pull on the carburetor heat. Touch the ignition and make certain that it is on BOTH. Make sure the flaps are retracted at the beginning. Gear should also be up. Seat belts should be fastened. The propeller would still be windmilling, even if the engine had quit, so you could get a restart. If you were in an actual engine-out emergency and trying for a restart, you might, in addition to the above, give the engine a shot or two or prime. I can recall one occasion when the only way I could keep the engine running was to continuously prime it. The music it made sounded so beautiful, compared to the previous sound of silence, that I didn't mind the extra work at all. (The engine finally had enough of that and began to run on its own without my help.)

Your emergency checklist will be essentially the same as the pre-takeoff checklist if the emergency is an engine-out situation. In the case of fire, however, it would be different. You would then need to get everything off— all electric switches and the fuel selector, or fuel shutoff, valve. If you have an engine fire, you should also close the cabin heat and cabin air controls. Then, if you have overhead or cabin window vents, open those. In this situation, of course, you would not be interested in attempting a restart, so that checklist would not be included here.

Finally, just as there is an absolute first item on the checklist for an emergency landing, there is also a last item. After everything else has been accomplished through the attempted restart, and while you're still on the emergency approach, get on the radio and talk to someone. Don't worry about whether to call the local FSS, a nearby tower, an enroute controller, or some other airplane. As fast as you can, switch to 121.5 and give a call. The *Mayday! Mayday!* will get everyone's attention. Then identify yourself, cite the nature of the emergency and give your location and intention. For the test, be sure to let the examiner know that this final item is included on your checklist.

Guessing at the Cause. You might run through the possibilities of the causes of various emergencies that would lead to emergency landings. The cause of an engine-out emergency could be fuel starvation from drawing on an empty tank, a clogged fuel line, contaminant in the fuel, carburetor icing, or the like. It's not possible to give an exhaustive list, since trouble could be caused by any of scores of problems. A partial loss of power could be the result of plug fouling, magneto problems, icing, or a breakdown of some part. Again, the number of possibilities makes it impossible to present an exhaustive list. An electrical malfunction could be the consequence of a short circuit in a piece of equipment, which you might identify by turning on one piece of equipment at a time. It would be only the more obvious items that an examiner would want you to recognize—and, in particular, those that you could do something about in the air. You will not need to be concerned about doing a complete engine or electronic analysis.

Maintaining control—there's no secret as to what this requirement is about. It's what you've been told many times. Your first, primary, major function is to *fly the airplane.* That means, in this case, avoiding excesses in maneuvering and airspeeds. The most basic part of this is maintaining the appropriate airspeed.

B. TASK: SYSTEMS AND EQUIPMENT MALFUNCTIONS (ASEL)

PILOT OPERATION – 10

REFERENCES: AC 61–21; Pilot's Operating Handbook and FAA–Approved Airplane Flight Manual.

1. **Objective.** To determine that the applicant:

   a. Exhibits adequate knowledge by explaining causes, indications, and pilot actions for various systems and equipment malfunctions.

   b. Analyzes the situation and takes appropriate action for simulated emergencies such as –

   (1) partial power loss.
   (2) rough running engine or overheat.
   (3) carburetor or induction icing.
   (4) loss of oil pressure.
   (5) fuel starvation.
   (6) engine compartment fire.
   (7) electrical system malfunction.
   (8) gear or flap malfunction.
   (9) door opening in flight.
   (10) trim inoperative.
   (11) loss of pressurization.
   (12) other malfunctions.

2. **Action.** The examiner will:

   a. Ask the applicant to explain causes, indications, and remedial action for various systems and equipment malfunctions.

   b. Simulate various equipment malfunctions, and determine that the applicant's performance meets the objective.

   c. Place emphasis on the applicant's ability to analyze the situation and take action appropriate to the simulated emergency.

Objective: What's expected of the applicant regarding systems and equipment malfunctions.

Exhibiting Knowledge through Explanation. During this phase of the test on emergencies, you will be presented with a variety of problems and expected to speculate as to the probable cause(s) and the appropriate pilot reactions to the situation. Some of these items may be handled by your action in the preceding section, i.e., by the simulation of an emergency landing. Others may call for another pilot action. Further, some of the situations may be presented in simulation calling for you to engage in some action. Others may simply be presented verbally for your explanation. Most of the items on the list under objectives will be in the latter category.

Analyzing Situations and Taking Appropriate Action. Faced with the problem of partial power loss, you have so many possible causes that you will not be expected to list them exhaustively. The most common problem of power loss that you can do something about in the air may be due to carburetor icing, or inadvertently leaving the carburetor heat on. The proper action in either case is quite evident. In other cases of partial power loss, analysis of cause is rather pointless. The appropriate pilot action is the same, however: You would make a precautionary landing. If the problem occurs on takeoff, you would continue straight ahead, just as with total power loss. However, it would be appropriate to attempt to gain altitude, keeping a very careful check on airspeed. If sufficient altitude could be gained, a return to the airport could be attempted using very shallow turns. If the problem occurred while enroute, or at higher altitude, then your precautionary landing would be made either as quickly as possible or at the nearest airport, depending on the seriousness of the power loss and your distance from an airport. With a partial power loss, the pilot must keep in mind that the engine could quit at any time and it is that eventuality which one must be prepared and plan for.

In the case of an engine running rough or overheating, a number of possibilities also exist. The engine's running rough may be merely a fouled plug. In this case, one could increase the power setting to full power, lean the mixture to the point where additional roughness occurs, and then, after briefly holding such settings, return power setting and mixture to normal. Roughness could also be the result of improper mixture control. Generally, this is the consequence either of a too-rich mixture at higher altitudes or neglecting to enrich the mixture when descending from high altitudes. The appropriate action in either instance is quite obvious.

In the case of engine overheating, a combination of causes could be present. The appropriate action would be to run through those procedures that could lower the temperature. The pilot would reduce power, enrich the mixture, and increase airspeed. But in the case of either of these malfunctions, the ultimate response is, again, a precautionary landing—either as soon as possible or at the nearest airport, depending on the seriousness of the situation.

Carburetor or induction icing is caused by the vaporization of fuel and the consequent cooling of the mixture of air and fuel. Temperatures can drop as much as 15 degrees Celsius (60 degrees Fahrenheit). The conditions that are conducive to icing are temperatures between −7 degrees and 21 degrees Celsius with visible moisture or high humidity. Low throttle settings make an engine particularly susceptible to icing. The signs of carburetor icing are reduced rpm for a fixed propeller, or a reduction in the manifold pressure for a constant-speed prop. The appropriate action is to apply full carburetor heat immediately. It's also a good idea to increase the power setting to get more heat and to allow more air-fuel mixture to get to the engine. Keep in mind, however, that the use of carburetor heat reduces power and can cause detonation if used at full power.

As with most engine-related problems, apparent loss of oil pressure can be apparent only. It's fortunate that this is not a common problem because most pilots check oil pressure when the runup is being performed and then don't bother to check it again until the next runup. It's a good idea to give the gauge a glance as your gaze sweeps the panel. When the gauge indicates a loss of oil pressure, the next thing to do is check the oil temperature gauge. If that doesn't go up in a couple of minutes, you may merely have a faulty oil pressure gauge. However, if the oil temperature starts for the red, then you had better start looking for a field. In either case, you're going to make a landing. The situation will determine whether it's a precautionary or an emergency landing.

Fuel starvation can also have variety of causes. You may simply have neglected to switch tanks. It sure does get quiet when *that* happens. The engine says nothing. The pilot and passengers say nothing; the latter turn a little pale. If the pilot also turns pale, then there's a real problem. Yes, I've done what every instrument pilot has done—stretched the range to the maximum by, in turn, intentionally running a couple of tanks dry when I've had four to draw from. It still gets awfully quiet, even when you do it on purpose.

But I've also had a problem with a fuel selector valve in which the engine continued to draw from a nearly empty tank even though I'd switched to a fuller tank. In any case, whatever the cause, engines do not run well without fuel. Your initial reaction to this problem is to get the nose down and establish the best-glide airspeed. Then you can recycle the fuel selector valve, or go to another tank altogether, if that's an option. (I also, on one occasion, had an apparent clog in the fuel line, because I not only recycled the fuel selector valve but, when that didn't work, primed the engine. Pumping the primer kept the engine running for a bit and then the problem corrected itself. I still headed for the old home base, which was close by.)

I suppose you explain an engine compartment fire by saying that something got too hot and ignited. When this occurs during a startup, from overpriming on a cold morning, just keep right on cranking to suck the flames into the engine. If it occurs in flight, then there are some specific procedures to be followed. Start emergency landing procedures first. Follow this by turning the mixture control to idle cutoff. Next, turn the fuel selector valve off and turn the master switch off. Shut off the cabin heat and the cabin air. Open any overhead or window vents to clear out any smoke that may be in the cockpit. Some also recommend increasing the glide speed to find a speed at which combustion cannot occur. In the meantime, use the procedures outlined earlier to get the airplane on the ground as quickly as possible.

What you do about an electrical system malfunction depends on what occurs and the situation in which it occurs. If you lose a generator or alternator, or if you simply see the ammeter showing discharge, then you need only to shut off all except essential equipment. Normally, the battery will sustain you and meet your needs for a while, but the more equipment you can shut off, the longer the battery will stay with you. If the electrical system malfunction causes an electrical fire, then you may have a whole new ballgame. You should first turn off the master switch. Follow this by turning off all the avionic and other electrical equipment. If the malfunction occurs while you're enroute, check to see if any circuit breakers have popped out, again after turning all electrical switches off. If you see a guilty circuit breaker protruding, leave it out and turn the master back on. One by one, turn on each item, pausing for a moment to see the result before turning on the next one. If nothing else occurs, you've identified the problem and will respond accordingly. It may be something so simple and unnecessary that the flight can continue uninterrupted. More serious concerns might be the basis for a precautionary landing.

Gear or flap malfunction may mean either that you cannot retract one or the other, or both, or that you can't extend landing gear or flaps. If the problem is with landing gear that won't fold for you, then you'll simply need to continue in the pattern and return for a landing. Similarly, if you've taken off with flaps extended for some purpose (as with a soft field takeoff) and you find that they can't be retracted, you might check circuit breakers, if the flaps are operated electrically. At any rate, as with gear that can't be retracted, your best bet is simply to continue in the pattern and return for a landing.

If the gear malfunction occurs while making an approach, you have a more serious problem. The indication, of course, will be the gear warning horn or lights, indicating that gear are not down and locked. If a gear-up landing is necessary, look for the smoothest, softest surface that you can find and fly the airplane in; do not make a full stall landing. It may also be advisable to shut the engine off when you're certain you have the field made, and to crank the engine to get the propeller in a horizontal position. *Don't*, however, follow the advice given to a pilot at one field where I instructed. He couldn't get his gear down and came in for a landing on the sod between the runway and the taxiway. This seemed like a good choice and the airplane would have suffered very little damage. However, when the airplane touched down, it cartwheeled down the runway. The airplane was totalled, though the pilot and passenger avoided serious injury. Later, when he was asked what happened, he related that as he was making the approach, he had recalled having been told one time that in a gear-up landing, one should touch a wingtip down first in order to slow the airplane. He followed the advice and wiped out an airplane that might have otherwise suffered only very minor damage.

If your flaps refuse to extend, the problem is not nearly as severe. Keep in mind that the stalling speed will be higher and you'll need more runway to get the airplane stopped after touchdown. Then use a forward slip to increase the rate of descent without a corresponding increase in airspeed. If there is a crosswind, lower the wing on the upwind side. At the same time, use the rudder to yaw the nose of the airplane in the opposite direction (Fig. 11-2). The airplane's longitudinal axis will be at an angle to the flight path, so the airplane must be aligned with the runway immediately prior to touchdown. All in the same motion, you must level the wings, release the rudder pressure you've been holding, and assume a normal touchdown attitude. This will align the airplane with the flight path and avoid the imposition of sideloads on the landing gear.

You probably will have the opportunity to demonstrate your reaction to a door opening in flight. Most examiners seem to enjoy popping a door just about the time you lift off, or just at the point after liftoff when you cannot return to the runway. Simply continue the climb at full throttle and fly a normal pattern. Some will recommend an approach at a slightly higher airspeed to compensate for the turbulence created by the open door. The wing on the open door side may tend to drop out early, it is said. My experience with popping doors is that they don't pop very far—just enough to make an unusual and distracting noise. But I have never noticed any significant difference in the way the airplane performs. You should not, however, allow the door to distract you so, nor should you get so engrossed in attempting to shut it in flight that you forget to *fly the airplane*. Remember that first rule: Fly the airplane.

A problem with the trim should not cause you great difficulty. As a matter of fact, many pilots fly airplanes with the trim set for cruise and seldom touch it. If the examiner requires that you fly the airplane through maneuvers without adjusting the trim, including even takeoffs and landings, you will find that the airplane will seem somewhat out of balance or out of rig. If the airplane you use for the test has a rudder trim, the nose will tend to yaw in one direction or the other. You obviously overcome the tendency with additional pressure on the appropriate rudder pedal. If the elevator trim is inoperative, it simply calls for sufficient pressure on the yoke or stick to overcome whatever pressures are created.

"Other malfunctions" is a catchall that enables the examiner to raise whatever questions he/she may find appropriate. The list presented in the objective section is rather extensive. Some malfunction could occur with a constant-speed propeller, or a cylinder head or exhaust gas temperature gauge could indicate a malfunction. If the examiner adds to the list specified, it will most likely be an item related to the particular airplane you're

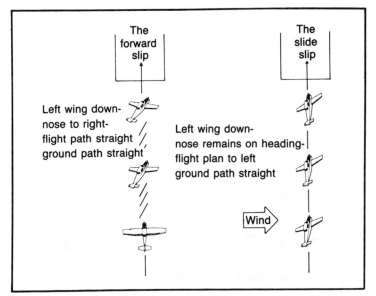

Fig. 11-2. Forward slip and side slip.

flying and will involve something with which you are familiar. It is possible that you may be asked to provide an explanation regarding causes of malfunctions in certain instruments or in a piece of avionics equipment and to describe an appropriate pilot response.

Chapter 12

XII. AREA OF OPERATION:
APPROACHES AND LANDINGS

A. TASK: NORMAL APPROACH AND LANDING (ASEL)

PILOT OPERATION – 5

REFERENCE: AC 61–21.

1. **Objective.** To determine that the applicant:

   a. Exhibits adequate knowledge by explaining the elements of a normal approach and landing including airspeeds, configurations, and related safety factors.
   b. Maintains the proper ground track on final approach.
   c. Establishes the approach and landing configuration and power required.
   d. Maintains the recommended approach airspeed, ±5 knots.
   e. Makes smooth, timely, and correct control application during the final approach and

transition from approach to landing roundout (flare).

f. Touches down smoothly at approximate stalling speed, beyond and within 500 feet of a specified point, with no appreciable drift, and the airplane's longitudinal axis aligned with the runway centerline.

g. Maintains directional control during the after–landing roll.

2. **Action.** The examiner will:

a. Ask the applicant to explain the elements of a normal approach and landing including airspeeds, configurations, and related safety factors.

b. Ask the applicant to perform a normal approach and landing, and determine that the applicant's performance meets the objective.

c. Place emphasis on the applicant's demonstration of correct airplane control particularly during the after–landing roll.

Objective: What's expected of the applicant regarding normal approaches and landings.

Exhibiting Knowledge through Explanation. You will be required to talk accurately about landings and also to perform approaches and landings. During your discussion, present the procedures for the entire approach, even though the objectives seem to focus only on the final leg through the rollout. Your explanation should begin with the point at which carburetor heat is applied while on the downwind leg. If the examiner doesn't want those details, let him/her tell you that.

Unless directed otherwise, then, begin by pointing out that carburetor heat is pulled on about midway down the downwind leg on those airplanes where carburetor heat is required. Following this, power is reduced at a point opposite the numbers—or whatever serves as the touchdown spot. Explain that approaches can be made with power off or merely reduced. The descent path desired determines how power is handled. After the power is reduced, a notch, or about 10 degrees, of flaps will generally be applied. All of this is done, of course, on the downwind leg.

When the end of the runway is at about a 45-degree angle behind the airplane, the turn is made from downwind to base leg. The airplane is still descending with power reduced. The flaps may be extended an additional notch, or 10 degrees. Power may be adjusted as needed to increase or decrease the rate of descent. Also, the airplane should by now be slowed to 5 to 10 knots above the over-the-fence airspeed. The turn from base to final will depend on wind. If the wind will be blowing from your left on final, then start the turn earlier. If it will be from the right, start the turn a little later. This descending turn should be made with a shallow bank at an altitude sufficient to clear all obstacles and allow the glide to be maintained to the touchdown spot without adding power.

On final, essentially the same glide and power setting will be maintained. Compensation must be made for any crosswind (to be explained later). Throughout the approach, the rate of descent will be controlled with the throttle alone. Never try to control the rate of descent by altering the pitch or attitude, and *never* try to alter the descent angle by retracting flaps. This is yet another of those situations where it becomes quite evident that pitch controls airspeed and power controls rate of descent. If any drift correction has been used, the longitudinal axis of the airplane must be aligned with the runway centerline prior to touchdown. Back pressure on the yoke is steadily applied to gradually slow the airplane to that point that stalling speed and attitude are reached just as the main gear touch the runway. At this point, power should be completely off. In a taildragger, the tailwheel should touch the runway at the same time that the main gear touch down. Some pilots even suggest aiming to have the tailwheel touch down slightly *ahead* of the main gear. Following touchdown, flaps are retracted, carburetor heat is shoved off, and the airplane is steered with rudder pedals alone. The airplane should be allowed to slow naturally with as little application of brake as possible.

Maintaining Proper Ground Track. The proper ground track for any landing will be aligned with the centerline of the runway. If there is no wind, or the wind is straight down the runway, the airplane's longitudinal axis should be aligned with the runway centerline through the final approach and the landing and rollout. The proper handling of crosswinds will be covered in a later portion of the approach and landing area of operation.

Establishing Proper Approach and Landing Configuration and Power. By the time you are on the final leg, flaps will have been extended two notches, or about 20 degrees, depending on the type of airplane you're flying. The flap setting established on the base leg will generally be maintained until the airplane is at a point where you are sure the runway can be reached without adding power. You may then apply full flaps. Keep in mind that extending flaps fully will significantly increase the angle of descent in most airplanes. Consequently, it's best not to apply flaps too early, since flaps should never be retracted to correct for any undershooting of the runway that may occur from too-early extension to full flap setting. There are those pilots who do not use full flaps under some circumstances. However, unless there is some good reason for not using flaps (e.g., a manufacturer's recommendation), every landing should be a full-flap landing.

The power required for a landing will be that which is required to control the descent angle in order for the airplane to land at about the midpoint of the first third of the runway. Unless you are in a no-wind situation, you will not be able to set the power once and never touch it again. It's desirable to stabilize the power setting to the extent that you can, but a number of factors will cause you frequently to increase or decrease power in order to achieve the proper angle of descent. This is another instance where, as you discovered with flight at minimum controllable airspeed, throttle controls descent. Consequently, if you're too low, check further descent by adding power. If you're too high, further reduce the power. Whatever you do, never attempt to use the yoke or stick to control your descent.

Maintaining the Proper Approach Airspeed. The airplane operating handbook will generally give you a range for the normal approach airspeed. Normally, this allows a range of about 10 knots. However, the examiner may want you to specify an airspeed. What he/she is looking for is a demonstration that you understand that the standard approach speed is 1.3 V_{so}. Now, everybody seems to remember the 1.3, but they sometimes forget *which* airspeed they're to multiply by that number. The standard approach airspeed is 1.3 times the airspeed at which the airplane will normally stall in the landing configuration. What controls that airspeed, of course, is the pitch, or attitude, of the airplane. Power may be held until you are fairly certain that you've got the runway made; then reduce power to idle. Aim then to establish the attitude, or pitch, that gives you the proper over-the-threshold airspeed.

If you've committed to your memory the point that it's power and not pitch, or attitude, that controls your descent until that's a part of your nervous system, you'll never have that problem of trying to keep the airplane in the air by hauling back on the yoke or the stick. You recognize that the application of such pressure on the controls simply increases the rate of descent as the airspeed decreases. So *never, never, never attempt to control descent with the elevators.* You'll use power for that. If you see that the *airspeed* is too high, then you can slow the airplane with the application of back pressure. Conversely, if airspeed is too low, get the nose down, even if you're low. The application of power will keep you from going any lower. So on final, use pitch, or attitude, to maintain the airspeed that is appropriate for the airplane you're flying.

Rounding Out or Flaring. As the airplane gets down to about the height of half a wingspan above the runway (generally), you will begin to apply back pressure to the yoke or stick in order to further slow the airplane. This application of back pressure will be smooth, gradual, and as nearly continuous as you can make it. The power will normally have been reduced to idle before the flare. As you begin to apply back pressure to the yoke or stick, you never shove it forward again except for a go-around, or aborted landing. If you see that the continuous application of back pressure will cause the airplane to stall before touchdown, simply relax the pressure.

The airplane will continue to settle at a normal, acceptable rate. If it is still settling too fast, then you simply add a touch of power. Even the FAA types who try to hold hard and fast to the notion that pitch controls climb and descent will specifically advise that in this situation, descent is controlled by the application of power. Do not jam the stick or the throttle forward. Holding the yoke or stick steady for a moment while you increase the power setting slightly will provide you with a smooth, appropriate flare. You'll flare with flair.

Touching Down. This application of back pressure will continue until four things occur simultaneously. The yoke or stick will be all the way back, the nose of the airplane will be at about the same position in relation to the horizon that you use for a normal climbout, the wing will stall, and the landing gear will touch down on the runway. In a tri-gear airplane, only the main landing gear will touch down; in a taildragger, all three wheels will touch down simultaneously. This should occur within 500 feet of the numbers or whatever point you specified. Further, the airplane's longitudinal axis should be aligned with the centerline of the runway, and you should not have any drifting. (We'll cover controlling drift when we do crosswind landings.)

One additional point should be made: If you feel the wheels touch the runway before your back pressure has pulled the yoke or stick all the way back, continue to smoothly, slowly, and steadily add back pressure until the stick is full back. Do not, however, yank it all the way back on contact. Such a reaction may cause a quick change in the angle of attack, increase lift, and cause the airplane to "bounce." Those things that are referred to as "bounces" on a landing are not, properly speaking, bounces. They occur because the airplane has been descending at a particular angle of attack. When the wheels touch the runway, the descent, of course, ceases. This causes a change in the angle of attack, increases lift, and the wing starts flying again, lifting the airplane into the air and creating a "bounce."

If that should occur with you, do not push the stick or yoke forward! Simply add a touch of power so that the airplane will not descend too rapidly and you will sink gently to the runway. Remember, power controls climb and descent. When you're in that nose-high attitude of the "bounce," you have the proper attitude for a landing. You just need to slow your descent.

Of course, all of this can be avoided if you've learned to make full stall landings. With full stall landings, the wing is through flying when the wheels touch the runway.

Maintaining Directional Control. Most examiners do not regard the landing as completed until the airplane has decelerated to the speed normally used for taxiing. You will have touched down with no sideways drift and with the airplane's longitudinal axis aligned with the runway centerline. If you alertly continued to keep that alignment, you will avoid problems.

Taildraggers require more care, because the center of gravity is behind the main landing gear. Consequently, if the airplane is allowed to begin a swerve from the intended track, that weight behind the main landing

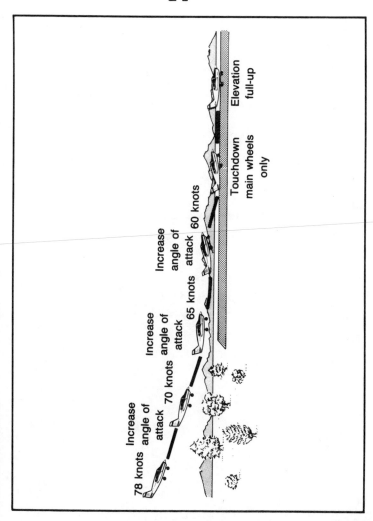

Fig. 12-1. Approach, flare or roundout, and touchdown.

gear will aggravate the tendency and make the airplane more difficult to control. It may be necessary then to use a touch of brake as well as the rudder to control any such tendency. However, brakes should be applied cautiously and sparingly.

B. TASK: FORWARD SLIPS TO LANDING (ASEL)

PILOT OPERATION – 5

REFERENCE: AC 61–21.

1. **Objective.**   To determine that the applicant:

   a. Exhibits adequate knowledge by explaining the elements of a forward slip to a landing including the purpose, technique, limitation, and the effect on airspeed indications.
   b. Establishes a forward slip at a point from which a landing can be made in a desired area using the recommended airspeed and configuration.
   c. Maintains a ground track aligned with the runway centerline.
   d. Maintains an airspeed which results in little or no floating during the landing roundout.
   e. Recovers smoothly from the slip.
   f. Touches down smoothly at approximate stalling speed, beyond and within 500 feet of a specified point, with no appreciable drift and the airplane's longitudinal axis aligned with the runway centerline.
   g. Maintains directional control during the after–landing roll.

2. **Action.**   The examiner will:

   a. Ask the applicant to explain the elements of forward slips to a landing including the purpose, technique, limitation, and the effect on airspeed indications.
   b. Ask the applicant to perform a forward slip to a landing, and determine that the applicant's performance meets the objective.
   c. Place emphasis on the applicant's demonstration of airspeed control and correct airplane control.

Objective: What's expected of the applicant regarding forward slips to landings.

Exhibiting Knowledge through Explanation. The first thing you'll be expected to do is distinguish between a *forward slip* and a *side slip*. These were illustrated in Fig. 11-2 in the preceding chapter. Look at the diagram again and fit your explanation to the diagram. Explain that the forward slip is used to steepen the glide angle without a corresponding increase in airspeed. They may be required in a landing approach over an obstacle, or in an emergency landing when you've maintained a little extra altitude as a margin of safety.

The maneuver is accomplished by lowering one wing and yawing the nose of the airplane in the opposite direction by applying opposite rudder. The airplane's longitudinal axis will then be at an angle to the centerline of the runway although the ground track will continue in line with the runway centerline. Prior to touching down, the wings will be leveled and the rudder released simultaneously to ensure that the airplane touches down with the longitudinal axis again aligned with the runway centerline.

The technique is not normally used. Indeed, the *need* to use a forward slip may be an indication of poor planning. There are some dangers involved since, given the airplane's unusual attitude, the pitot tube and static port will not be in their normal position in relation to the relative wind, giving airspeed readings that may be incorrect. Further, some manufacturers warn against forward slips in certain airplanes when flaps are fully extended. Make sure you've checked the airplane operating handbook for this prior to the practical test. (Incidentally, contrary to popular belief, slips may be performed in a Cessna 150/152 with flaps extended. I have a letter from the manufacturer regarding that, so let's lay that myth to rest.)

Establishing the Forward Slip. The point at which the forward slip is established will vary with circumstances. Generally, the pilot would begin the slip at the point at which he/she determines that altitude must be dissipated without increasing the airplane's airspeed. At that point, a wing is lowered and opposite rudder is applied. What governs which wing is lowered? There are those who recommend that the upwind wing be lowered since (it is claimed) the slip is more effective if it is made into the wind. On the other hand, there are those who suggest that the left wing be lowered and right rudder pressure applied since this provides the pilot with greater visibility. You should be able to perform the slip in either direction, since you cannot know in advance what a flight examiner may require. Be certain that whichever wing is lowered, you don't simply allow the airplane to dive at the runway.

Maintaining the Correct Ground Track. Although the longitudinal axis of the airplane is at an angle to the centerline of the runway, the original flight path, or ground track, must remain aligned with the centerline of the runway. Proper flight path will be maintained by holding an appropriate amount of opposite rudder pressure. The amount of rudder pressure will vary, of course, with the amount of bank that is being used. Although you may have observed some pilots using a relatively steep bank and a considerable amount of yaw, this should not be necessary unless planning is really poor. There should be no need for more than a moderate slip if good judgement has been exercised.

Maintaining Airspeed. A common error with this maneuver is the failure to maintain proper airspeed. Occasionally a pilot trying to use the forward slip allows the nose of the airplane to drop. This results in merely diving the airplane toward the runway with an accompanying increase in airspeed. As the wing is dropped and opposite rudder applied, it is also important to hold back pressure on the yoke or stick in order to raise the nose of the airplane and prevent the airspeed from increasing. Keep in mind, however, that you may not be getting an accurate airspeed indication so you should avoid slowing the airplane to a dangerously low airspeed. It's necessary, however, to rely on the airspeed indicator, since the very low altitude will give you a sensation of greater-than-normal speed. If the proper airspeed is maintained, there should be no floating as the airplane is flared for the landing. If the airplane has a tendency to float, it means that the airspeed was excessive.

Recovering from the Slip. If you establish a moderate slip, rather than entering a slip violently, then there will be no need for an abrupt recovery. Simultaneously, the wings should be leveled and the rudder pressure released to continue to keep the ground track aligned with the centerline of the runway. Again, as this recovery is made smoothly, continue to hold back pressure on the yoke or stick to prevent an increase in airspeed. The recovery from the slip should be followed in a continuous motion by flaring the airplane for touchdown.

Touchdown. If all has gone well, the recovery from the forward slip and the flare to a landing should be all one motion, resulting in your touching down very quickly after the recovery. The touchdown following a forward slip should be essentially the same as for a normal landing. The yoke or stick should be all the way back, the nose at the same point on the horizon that you use for a climbout, the wing stalled, and all of this happening just as the main gear touch the runway. Further, as with all landings, the touchdown should be made with no drift and with the airplane's longitudinal axis aligned with the centerline of the runway.

Maintaining Directional Control. Using a forward slip changes nothing else about the landing. The rudder—and a touch of brake, if necessary—should be used to continue the rollout straight down the centerline of the runway until the speed of the airplane is naturally dissipated and you can turn off at a normal taxiing speed.

C. TASK: GO–AROUND FROM A REJECTED LANDING (ASEL)

PILOT OPERATION – 5

REFERENCE: AC 61–21.

1. **Objective.**   To determine that the applicant:

   a. Exhibits adequate knowledge by explaining the elements of the go–around procedure including timely decision, recommended airspeeds, drag effect of wing flaps and landing gear, and coping with undesirable pitch and yaw tendencies.
   b. Makes a timely decision to go around from a rejected landing.
   c. Applies takeoff power and establishes the proper pitch attitude to attain the recommended airspeed.
   d. Retracts the wing flaps as recommended or at a safe altitude.
   e. Retracts the landing gear, if retractable and recommended, after a positive rate of climb has been established.
   f. Trims the airplane and climbs at V_Y, ± 5 knots, and tracks the appropriate traffic pattern.

2. **Action.**   The examiner will:

   a. Ask the applicant to explain the elements of a go–around from a rejected landing including timely decisions, recommended airspeeds, drag effect of wing flaps and landing gear, and coping with undesirable pitch and yaw tendencies.
   b. Present a situation in which a go–around from a rejected landing would be required, and determine that the applicant's performance meets the objective.
   c. Place emphasis on the applicant's judgment,

prompt action, and ability to maintain correct
airplane control during the go–around.

Objective: What's expected of the applicant regarding go-arounds.

Exhibiting Knowledge through Explanation. You'll be required to
demonstrate familiarity with the procedures involved in executing a go-
around from a rejected, or aborted, landing. In discussing a timely decision, point out that timeliness is related to the situation that calls for aborting
a landing. An excessively high approach may require discontinuing a landing
approach. In such an instance, the decision would be made as soon as it
became apparent that the landing could not be made within the first third
of the runway—or whatever would be safe considering both runway length
and the airplane you were flying. Overtaking another airplane on final may
require a go-around. The appearance of an unexpected obstacle on the runway or the need to avoid wake turbulence would also constitute conditions
calling for going around again.

Having made the decision to abort the landing, takeoff power should
be applied immediately. Point out that this could create both an undesirable pitchup and an undesirable yawing of the nose of the airplane to the
left. The pilot must anticipate these effects and be prepared to take cor-
rective action immediately. The application of power would be followed
by getting carburetor heat off. Then flaps should be retracted, but only
in increments in order to allow airspeed gradually to increase and also to
prevent the airplane's settling onto the runway. Finally, and only after the
possibility is past of the airplane's touching down, the landing gear should
be retracted. Once the go-around is underway, the airplane may be
retrimmed.

Making a Timely Decision. The timeliness of the decision will depend
on the circumstances creating the need for a go-around. Normally, as soon
as it becomes evident that the approach is too high, the decision should
be made to go around. A good general rule to follow is: When in doubt,
go around again.

Establishing Proper Power and Pitch. The throttle should be advanced immediately to full power when the decision is made to discontinue
a landing. This is the first step, followed immediately by getting rid of carburetor heat in order to get full power. It's also necessary to counter the
left-turning tendency with the proper amount of right rudder. Rudder should
be applied quickly and sufficiently to maintain a ground track straight ahead
and avoid swerving to the left.

There may also be a tendency for the nose of the airplane to pitch up
with this rather sudden application of power. The pitch, or attitude, that
should be established is that which will permit you to achieve the airspeed
called for—either best rate-of-climb or best angle-of-climb airspeed. As you
know by this time, it may require considerable pressure on stick and rudder to maintain proper tracking and establish proper attitude.

Retracting Flaps. Only after full power has been applied, the descent has been stopped, and the climb begun should the flaps be partially retracted. Initially, the flaps should be retracted only from full flaps to the recommended flap setting for takeoff. Even this may need to be done intermittently. Retracting the flaps, of course, alters the camber of the wing and decreases the amount of lift being generated. Consequently, care must be exercised to avoid causing the airplane to settle to the runway. In some airplanes (for example, the Cessna 150), it is essential to retract some flap because the airplane simply will not climb with full flaps. However, having cautiously retracted the flaps by increments to a setting permitting a reasonable rate of climb, the setting should be maintained until a safe altitude is reached. This may require maintaining some flaps until the airplane is completely clear of all obstacles before fully retracting flaps.

Retracting Landing Gear. If your airplane has folding gear, their retraction will be about the last item on the go-around list. On most airplanes, it's more important to retract flaps than to retract landing gear. After all chance of settling onto the runway is past—in other words, after a positive rate of climb is established—the landing gear may be retracted. This could mean that, on some airplanes, landing gear may be retracted prior to the final flap retraction.

The Climbout. Having "cleaned up" the airplane and established a positive rate of climb, the go-around becomes a normal takeoff. Since everything else has been completed, you would then trim the airplane for a normal climbout, establish the appropriate pitch, or attitude, for V_y (best rate-of-climb airspeed), and track outbound maintaining a straight climb aligned with the runway centerline. At this point you would simply be back in the traffic pattern as for any normal takeoff.

D. TASK: CROSSWIND APPROACH AND LANDING (ASEL)

PILOT OPERATION – 5

REFERENCE: AC 61–21.

1. **Objective.** To determine that the applicant:

   a. Exhibits adequate knowledge by explaining the elements of a crosswind approach and landing including crosswind limitations, and related safety factors.
   b. Maintains the proper ground track on final approach.
   c. Establishes the approach and landing configuration and power required.
   d. Maintains the recommended approach airspeed, ±5 knots.
   e. Makes smooth, timely, and correct control application during the final approach and transition from approach to landing roundout (flare).
   f. Touches down smoothly at approximate stalling speed, beyond and within 500 feet of a specified point, with no appreciable drift and the airplane's longitudinal axis aligned with the runway centerline.
   g. Maintains directional control, increasing aileron deflection into the wind, as necessary, during the after–landing roll.

2. **Action.** The examiner will:

   a. Ask the applicant to explain the elements of a crosswind approach and landing including crosswind limitations and related safety factors.
   b. Ask the applicant to perform a crosswind approach and landing, and determine that the applicant's performance meets the objective. (NOTE: If a crosswind condition

does not exist, the applicant's knowledge of the TASK will be evaluated through oral questioning.)

c. Place emphasis on the applicant's control of wind drift during the approach and landing.

Objective: What's expected of the applicant regarding crosswind approaches and landings.

Exhibiting Knowledge through Explanation. As with every other part of the practical test, you will be expected to provide a complete and thorough description of the crosswind approach and landing. Simply explain that when wind was created, it was devised to blow across runways rather than down them. Since it's often necessary to land on a runway while the wind is not blowing parallel to that runway, a pilot must be prepared to cope with the situation that he/she finds. Since many elements of the crosswind approach and landing are the same as for normal approaches and landings, you'll need only to provide an explanation of the techniques called for to correct for wind drift.

You should be familiar with the two methods utilized for crosswind approaches the landings, i.e., the crabbing or "kickout" method, and the wing-low method. The latter is the one most generally taught because it is effective and it is much easier to accomplish. In another sense, however, a combination of the two methods is used.

The former technique calls for the pilot to crab in order to compensate for drift and to hold the crabbing angle right down to the runway. Then, just before touchdown, the pilot "kicks out" the crab, or neutralizes the rudder in order for the airplane's longitudinal axis to be aligned with the centerline of the runway. This is the way the "big kids" do it, since low-wing airplanes with jet engines slung beneath the wing do not permit landing with one wing low.

The wing-low method does not require any last-minute change. Generally, it is begun with the crabbing method on final approach in order to correct for drift initially. However, it can be instituted as soon as the turn is made to final and the airplane is aligned with the runway. The upwind wing is lowered to correct for drift, with the amount of bank varying with the wind. The greater the drift, the further the wing is lowered. But, as we all know, the bank is used for turning the airplane; consequently, the airplane will tend to turn in the direction of the bank. To compensate for this, opposite rudder must be applied using sufficient pressure to keep the airplane's longitudinal axis aligned with the centerline of the runway. In other words, the airplane is sideslipped toward the runway. The advantage of this method is that there is no need suddenly to change the position of the controls. The side slip may be continued through the flare, with the upwind main wheel touching down first. Gradually, the other wheel will sink to the runway, with the nosewheel touching down last.

There are limitations on the use of either crosswind method. Any crabbing angle can be used to keep the ground track aligned with the runway centerline, but if the crabbing angle becomes excessive because strong winds cause a great deal of drift, it will not be possible to "kick out" and still avoid the sideward contact of the wheels with the runway. Similarly, if the wing-low method is used, a very strong crosswind will require an increased slip into the wind, achieved by lowering the upwind wing considerably. The lower the wing is held, the greater the tendency becomes for the airplane to turn into the wind. The greater the tendency to turn, the more rudder pressure the pilot must hold. If the wind is extremely strong, the tendency to turn may be so great that there may not be sufficient rudder travel to keep the airplane's longitudinal axis aligned with the runway. Consequently, there is a possibility of exceeding the airplane's ability to respond to the conditions encountered on a runway. In such an instance, another runway—or even another airport—must be found.

Maintaining Proper Ground Track. The ground track for the crosswind landing is the same as for any other type; i.e., it is aligned with the centerline of the runway. As was mentioned above, there are two methods, the crabbing approach and the wing-low technique. For either method, the appropriate procedure is to turn from base to final and align oneself with the runway centerline. Generally, pilots will begin the final approach with the crabbing method and then, about a wingspan's height above the ground, change to the side slip.

Establishing Configuration and Power Setting. The configuration of the airplane for crosswind approaches and landings is not generally a special concern. That is to say, the configuration will generally be the same for all landings, crosswind or otherwise; every landing is generally a full flap landing. However, the pilot's operating manual for some airplanes may call for a different configuration for crosswind landings, particularly in turbulent air. But unless the operating handbook specifies otherwise, the configuration will include using full flaps for crosswind landings.

Similarly, the power setting will not generally be different for crosswind landings except during gusty or high wind conditions. Under such circumstances, power-on approaches at an airspeed slightly above normal are used. Carrying the additional power provides for more positive control when strong horizontal gusts or up- and downdrafts are encountered. Carrying the extra power will, of course, enable you to land at a lower airspeed, since the addition of power lowers the normal stalling airspeed. However, instead of using the lower airspeed, you will use the same attitude that you normally use for an approach. This attitude, since it is the same, will result in a normal approach airspeed, but because the power lowers the stalling airspeed, you will now have a greater margin of safety. If the wind is significantly turbulent, then you may find it wise to use an attitude with the nose somewhat lower to provide greater-than-normal airspeed. The amount of power applied will vary with the airplane and circumstances and the operating handbook should be consulted for such information.

It is unfortunate that the FAA still insists on associating power setting with airspeed and pitch with climb and descent. You may encounter an examiner who insists on presenting it this way. In such cases, you have little choice but to go along with it. When FAA types try to explain away their inappropriate views on this matter, they frequently brush the issue aside by saying that we all do the same thing, but merely talk about it differently. However, such a notion unnecessarily creates dangerous possibilities for pilots. When any pilot gets into a tight situation where it becomes necessary to react quickly without sufficient time to think through an appropriate action, he/she responds on the basis of perceptions carried in one's head. This is why we still find students who attempt to stretch a glide by raising the nose instead of adding power. They entertain the false notion that they can stop the airplane from going down merely by pointing the nose up, which, of course, is precisely the opposite of what will occur. If your perception is that power is related to climb and descent while pitch is related to airspeed, you will automatically get the nose down when the speed is low, or add power when the rate of descent is too high, or the approach is too low. So carry this in your nervous system for greater safety: Despite what the FAA says, power controls climb and descent; pitch controls airspeed. Reacting automatically on the basis of those perceptions will help you to avoid trouble. There is simply no advantage to explaining it the FAA way, except that they don't have to change the manuals from the way they've written them for several decades.

Maintaining the Recommended Approach Airspeed. Again, unless the operating handbook specifies differently, or unless gusty and/or strong winds dictate otherwise, the approach airspeed for crosswind landings is the same airspeed used for normal approaches and landings. When gusts call for a higher airspeed, the airspeed generally used is based on the normal approach speed plus one-half the wind gust factor. In other words, if your normal approach airspeed is 60 knots and the wind gusts increase 16 knots, then the appropriate approach airspeed would be 68 knots. The objective permits a variation of 5 knots in either direction, but in turbulent or strong winds requiring a higher approach speed, it's best to stay on the *plus* side of the recommended airspeed.

Transitioning from the Approach to the Landing Flare. If you are using the crabbing crosswind approach, then it's necessary to carry the crab until the last possible moment before transitioning to the flare, or roundout, for touchdown. This can be difficult, particularly in a light trainer. As the airspeed decreases prior to touchdown, the controls become less effective, requiring increasing rudder deflection. Then, an instant before touchdown, the crab angle must be removed by applying sufficient rudder pressure in the opposite direction to align the airplane's longitudinal axis with the runway centerline. Failure to do so—either because your correction was too early, allowing drift, or too late, also allowing drift—

can result in severe sideloads being imposed on the landing gear.

How much simpler to use the wing-low, or sideslip, method. Using this method, the crosswind correction (upwind wing low and opposite rudder) would be maintained throughout the flare, allowing touchdown on the upwind main wheel and avoiding both the need for a sudden change in the controls and the danger of imposing sideloads.

Touching Down. As with the normal landing, touchdown should occur at approximately the stalling airspeed. It should occur without any side drift and with the airplane's longitudinal axis aligned with the runway centerline. If the sideslip has been used, the downwind main wheel should be allowed to touch down normally as the forward speed decreases, rather than forced down. After this wheel has touched down, the nosewheel should be held off as long as possible. In airplanes having the nosewheel steering interconnected with the rudder, it will be necessary to neutralize the rudder in order for the wheel to be aligned with the runway on touchdown.

Check the airplane handbook for any instructions peculiar to the airplane you are flying. The Cessna 150 handbook, for example, calls for the nosewheel to be lowered firmly to the ground after the initial contact. This action partially compresses the nose strut, allowing nosewheel swiveling and more positive steering.

Maintaining Directional Control. As with any landing, directional control during the rollout is maintained by use of the rudder. More attention may be required during a crosswind landing, however, to prevent the airplane's tendency for weathercocking. Further, the upwind wing must be kept from rising by applying proper aileron pressure. Turn the yoke or push the stick in the direction from which the wind is blowing. And, as the airplane's speed decreases, apply increased aileron until, at taxiing speed, full deflection may be held.

E. TASK: SHORT-FIELD APPROACH AND LANDING (ASEL)

PILOT OPERATION – 8

REFERENCE: AC 61–21.

1. **Objective.** To determine that the applicant:

   a. Exhibits adequate knowledge by explaining the elements of a short–field approach and landing including airspeeds, configurations, and related safety factors.
   b. Considers obstructions, landing surface, and wind conditions.
   c. Selects a suitable touchdown point.
   d. Establishes the short–field approach and landing configuration, airspeed, and descent angle.
   e. Maintains control of the descent rate and the recommended airspeed, ±5 knots, along the extended runway centerline.
   f. Touches down beyond and within 200 feet of a specified point, with minimum float and no appreciable drift and the airplane's longitudinal axis aligned with the runway centerline.
   g. Maintains directional control during the after–landing roll.
   h. Applies braking and controls, as necessary, to stop in the shortest distance consistent with safety.

2. **Action.** The examiner will:

   a. Ask the applicant to explain the elements of a short–field approach and landing including airspeeds, configurations, and related safety factors.
   b. Ask the applicant to perform a short–field approach and landing, and determine that the applicant's performance meets the objective.

c. Place emphasis on the applicant's control of descent rate, airspeed, and use of flight controls.

Objective: What's expected of the applicant regarding short-field approaches and landings.

Exhibiting Knowledge through Explanation. Those elements of approaches and landings that have already been covered in the preceding maneuvers need not be explained again for this part of the practical test. Instead, you'll be required to describe only the parts that are unique to short-field approaches and landings. The airspeed will need to be specified, since it will generally be different from that used for the preceding approaches. The airplane's configuration may be different, although that is unlikely since, in nearly all instances, all landings will be full flap landings. Important to your explanation will be the clarification that the obstacles, or the length of the runway, or the combination of these that limit the available landing area are not the only crucial items. This is a maximum performance operation calling for operating the airplane at crucial performance capabilities while close to the ground. In fact, if the steep descent is required in order to clear obstacles and still "land short," it may be necessary to operate on the "back side of the power curve."

A lot of pilots talk about the back side of the power curve and lots of others wonder what they're talking about. You, of course, know what it's all about. You know that it's involved with a technique that we use to fly slower and with a higher angle of attack than normal (Fig. 12-2). There is a range of power settings (A) such that as we increase the power setting the airplane will tend to climb and, if we use forward pressure on the yoke or stick to prevent that climb, the airplane will accelerate. Holding that forward pressure against the tendency to climb is, in effect, the same thing as diving the airplane, thus increasing the airspeed. It's in that range that we do most of our flying.

However, as Fig. 12-2 shows, there is also a power setting range (B) where, as power is added, we decrease rather than increase the airspeed. In this range, we use a lower power setting to go faster and a higher power setting to go slower. That's what we call the "back side of the power range" and it's what we use for the short-field approach.

Suppose you're on final at the airspeed indicated in Fig. 12-2 by point B. You have the proper configuration and a power setting that gives a comfortable rate of descent. Then, you realize that, at the present rate of descent, you'll undershoot the runway. Trying to hold the airplane in the air, you mistakenly exert back pressure on the yoke, thereby reducing the airspeed (B1). Now you have a deficiency in power. Raising the nose increases rather than decreases the rate of descent. The only way to overcome the higher descent rate is to increase the power setting, and it must be increased significantly. In other words, in order to fly slower on the back side of the power curve, it is necessary to increase power.

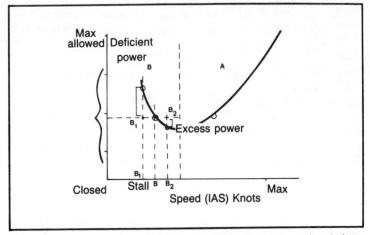

Fig. 12-2. In power setting range A as we increase the power, the airplane wants to climb; holding forward pressure increases airspeed. In range B, we increase the power in order to fly slower.

It should be pointed out that there's a point where the speed could get low enough that insufficient power would remain to check the airplane's descent. That's why speed must be very carefully controlled. As the airplane moves further back on the back side of the power curve, the reserve of power available is increasingly and rapidly diminished. Provide that kind of explanation and you'll really impress the examiner.

Considering Obstructions and Other Factors. You should be able to provide the examiner with an estimate of the altitude required in order to clear obstacles on the Approach. In some instances the examiner may actually have you fly to a field that presents a genuine short-field problem. In the absence of such real factors, assume that the obstacle to be cleared at the approach end of the runway is 50 feet.

The nature of the landing surface must also be taken into account. This generally refers to the length of landing space available rather than other conditions. The figures should be related to the performance characteristics of the airplane you're flying. For example, if your airplane, under the conditions faced, requires 1075 feet of landing distance to clear a 50-foot obstacle, and you have a total of 1700 feet of runway, you'll then have an idea of the point at which you must touch down in order to land safely. So you should know both the length of landing surface available and what's required for the airplane you're flying.

The objective requires that you also take wind conditions into account. Wind speed and direction obviously affect the distance within which you can touch down and have a safe margin for the ground roll. Other factors, such as temperature, will also need to be considered. All of this suggests that for this part of the test, you should be familiar with what is called for by the manufacturer of your airplane. Generally, you'll find a table in the operating handbook that will provide the information you'll need (Fig. 12-3).

Selecting the Touchdown Point. This will involve working out a safe compromise. You'll want to select a point near enough to the approach end of the runway to allow a very comfortable margin of safety for the ground roll following touchdown, so you'll select a point that allows the greatest possible practicable distance for the rollout. The other factor that comes into play, of course, is the distance required in order to clear an obstacle. There would be little point to picking a point close to the approach end of the runway that would require you to fly through the tops of trees in order to hit the touchdown point (though such a maneuver would be guaranteed to impress any designated examiner!), so you will select a point that allows a reasonable angle of descent yet allows the greatest possible distance for ground roll after touchdown.

Establishing Approach, Configuration, Airspeed, and Angle of Descent. The approach to a short-field landing will be started at least 500 feet above the touchdown area. Beyond that, you may also find it helpful to extend the downwind leg a little in order to give yourself more time and space to "set up" for this maximum performance maneuver. Don't fall into the trap that too many student pilots fall into. Many think that a short-field landing means a short approach and they inevitably end by overshooting the field and being forced to go around. Use an approach that gives you a little more time for getting things under control.

The landing configuration will almost certainly include full flaps. Full flaps should be extended as soon as the turn from base to final is completed. This allows you more time to adjust power and attitude for the proper angle of descent and airspeed. Check the operating handbook for your airplane for the manufacturer's recommended airspeed. If it's not listed for a short-field approach, then use the standard approach speed of not more than 1.3 V_{so}. Generally, the manufacturer's recommended airspeed for a short-field approach will be lower than this. Adjustment must be made, of course in gusty air. In the meantime, power should be maintained to permit an appropriate angle and rate of descent. This requires not merely setting the throttle, but making proper adjustments during the descent (Fig. 12-4).

Maintaining Descent Rate and Airspeed. The crucial control required for this type of approach and landing is what makes this a maxi-

—**LANDING DISTANCE**—							FLAPS LOWERED TO 40° - POWER OFF HARD SURFACE RUNWAY - ZERO WIND	
		AT SEA LEVEL & 59° F.		AT 2500 FT. & 50° F.		AT 5000 FT. & 41° F.		AT 7500 FT. & 32° F.	
GROSS WEIGHT LBS.	APPROACH SPEED. IAS. MPH	GROUND ROLL	TOTAL TO CLEAR 50 FT. OBS	GROUND ROLL	TOTAL TO CLEAR 50 FT. OBS	GROUND ROLL	TOTAL TO CLEAR 50 FT. OBS	GROUND ROLL	TOTAL TO CLEAR 50 FT. OBS
1600	60	445	1075	470	1135	495	1195	520	1255

NOTES:
1. Decrease the distances shown by 10% for each 4 knots of headwind.
2. Increase the distance by 10% for each 60° F. temperature increase above standard.
3. For operation on a dry, grassy runway, increase distances (both "ground roll" and "total to clear 50 ft. obstacle") by 20% of the "total to clear 50 ft. obstacle" figure.

Fig. 12-3. Landing distance.

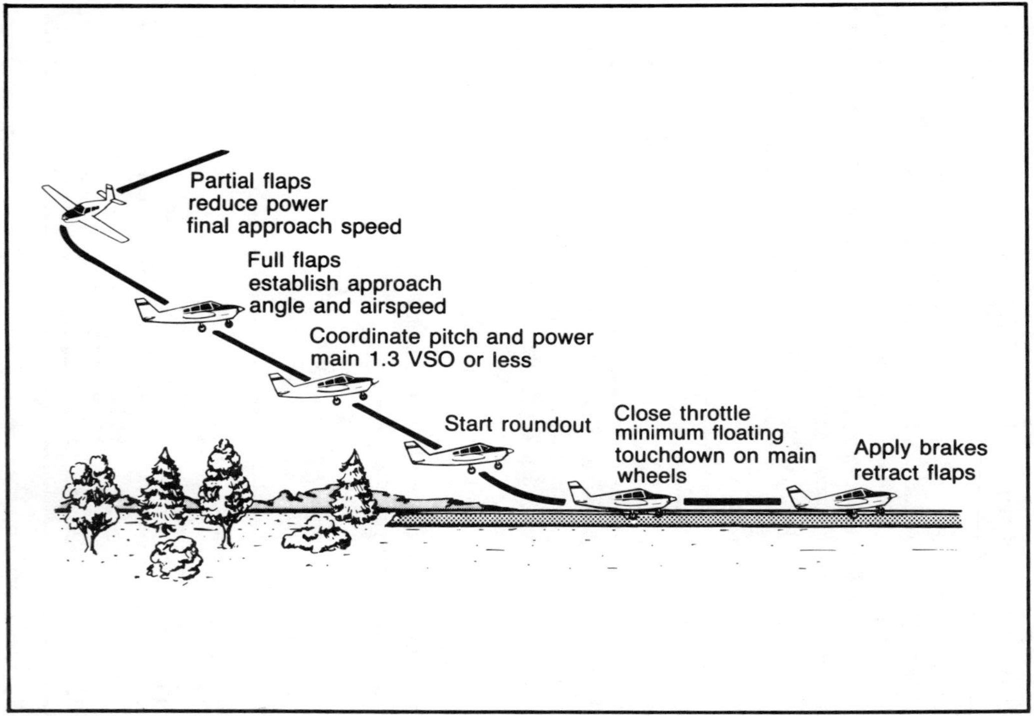

Fig. 12-4. Short-field approach and landing.

Partial flaps
reduce power
final approach speed

Full flaps
establish approach
angle and airspeed

Coordinate pitch and power
main 1.3 VSO or less

Start roundout

Close throttle
minimum floating
touchdown on main
wheels

Apply brakes
retract flaps

mum performance maneuver. The airspeed will probably be lower than that used for any other type of approach. The combination of full flaps and lower airspeed will give an unusually nose-high attitude. Once airspeed is established, this attitude may remain fairly constant. The power setting, of course, will be used to control the angle and rate of descent. Even the FAA grants that if the descent angle appears to be too great to allow obstruction clearance, power must be added. On the other hand (they grant) if obstruction clearance appears to be excessive, then you will need to reduce power to avoid touching down beyond the selected touchdown point.

Touching Down. You will be expected to touch down beyond but within 200 feet of the selected touchdown point. This is to be accomplished with no sideways drift, of course, and with the airplane's longitudinal axis aligned with the centerline of the runway. That's true of all landings. Further, the examiner will expect a minimum of float. To accomplish the latter, power should be carried until just before the touchdown. If your planning has been well done and well executed, cutting the power at this point will result in the airplane's immediately touching down, since the power setting has been the factor that held the airplane off. Handled in such fashion, there should be little or no floating, followed by a short ground roll after touchdown.

Maintaining Directional Control. This is where the short-field landing becomes like any other landing. There is no difference regarding maintaining directional control among any of the various types of landings, although crosswind landings do have their own concerns.

Stopping Short. In order to keep the ground roll after touchdown to a minimum, brakes should be applied immediately upon touchdown. Avoid jamming the brakes on, however. Application means simply that you will begin to apply sufficient pressure to slow the airplane down and minimize the rollout. The yoke should also be held all the way back to make certain that the airplane's weight is on the main landing gear in order to maximize braking effectiveness. Also, flaps should be retracted immediately. This helps transfer the weight of the airplane from the wings to the wheels more quickly and aids in stopping in the shortest possible distance. Just make sure it's the *flap* lever you grab and not the gear retracting handle.

F. TASK: SOFT–FIELD APPROACH AND LANDING (ASEL)

PILOT OPERATION – 8

REFERENCE: AC 61–21.

1. **Objective.**   To determine that the applicant:

   a. Exhibits adequate knowledge by explaining the elements of a soft–field approach and landing procedure including airspeeds, configurations, operations on various surfaces, and related safety factors.
   b. Evaluates obstructions, landing surface, and wind conditions.
   c. Establishes the recommended soft–field approach and landing configuration and airspeed.
   d. Maintains recommended airspeed, ±5 knots, along the extended runway centerline.
   e. Touches down smoothly at minimum descent rate and groundspeed with no appreciable drift and the airplane's longitudinal axis aligned with runway centerline.
   f. Maintains directional control during the after–landing roll.
   g. Maintains proper position of flight controls and sufficient speed to taxi on soft surface.

2. **Action.**   The examiner will:

   a. Ask the applicant to explain the elements of a soft–field approach and landing procedure including airspeeds, configuration, operations on various surfaces, and related safety factors.
   b. Ask the applicant to perform a soft–field approach and landing, and determine that the applicant's performance meets the objective.

c. Place emphasis on the applicant's demonstration of touchdown at minimum descent rate, proper airspeed, and use of flight controls on a soft surface.

Objective: What's expected of the applicant regarding soft-field approaches and landings.

Exhibiting Knowledge through Explanation. Your description of the soft-field landing will focus mainly on distinguishing this maneuver from the short-field landing. Many of the elements are the same. As a matter of fact, you can point out to the examiner that the approach procedures for these two types of landing are essentially the same until very near the end. There are similar considerations of airspeed, configuration, and the like. The differences begin to occur when the airplane is about a wingspan height above the runway. At that point, since you want to touch down at the slowest possible airspeed, you'll begin to slow the airplane by adding back pressure to the yoke or stick. Then, whereas just before touchdown during the short-field approach, power was pulled off, for the soft-field landing you'll do the opposite. In other words, as you get close to touchdown, power will slowly and steadily be added to enable you to slow the airplane. As with the short-field landing, safety considerations are paramount since you'll be operating at lower-than-normal airspeeds very close to the ground. You should also clarify your understanding that the soft-field procedures are used not only for soft runways, but also for conditions such as snow, deeper-than-normal grass on a sod strip, and the like.

Evaluating Conditions. The same considerations that are your concern for other landings will be present here. One difference is that you assume that the landing surface is soft regardless of appearance or actual conditions. Wind also becomes somewhat more significant than for a normal landing, since you'll be operating at exceptionally low ground speeds prior to touchdown.

Establishing Configuration and Airspeed. The configuration and airspeed for the soft-field approach and landing will be the same as those used for the short-field.

Maintaining Airspeed. Although the approach airspeed will be the same as that used for a short-field, a significant difference will occur prior to touchdown. As the airplane settles toward the runway, back pressure will continue to be exerted on the yoke or stick in order to continue slowing the airplane. Now you're really on the back side of the power curve, which requires continuously adding power as the airplane flies at a diminishing airspeed, very gradually descending to the runway (Fig. 12-5). At this stage, just above the runway, you cannot give any attention to the airspeed indicator. Your concern is with controlling the airplane at its increasingly nose-high attitude and decreasing airspeed. Besides, there's no need to check airspeed, because you know from prior practice that at this stage the airplane is already flying more slowly than the book says it's supposed to.

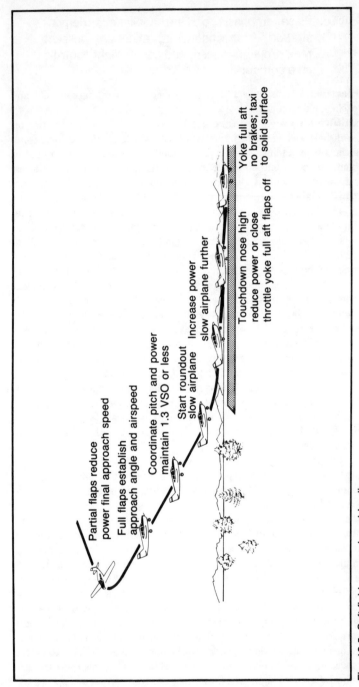

Fig. 12-5. Soft-field approach and landing.

Partial flaps reduce
power final approach speed

Full flaps establish
approach angle and airspeed

Coordinate pitch and power
maintain 1.3 VSO or less

Start roundout
slow airplane

Increase power
slow airplane further

Touchdown nose high
reduce power or close
throttle yoke full aft flaps off

Yoke full aft
no brakes; taxi
to solid surface

246

Touching Down. If you've handled the controls appropriately, this will be the gentlest touchdown and the slowest groundspeed of any of your landings. Moving so slowly with an exceptionally nose-high attitude will make it somewhat more challenging to avoid drift and keep the airplane aligned with the runway, but this is a part of the challenge. Once this technique is mastered, you need never again make a hard landing and you can, in fact, impress your passengers with the gentleness of your landings.

Some years ago, a friend of mine purchased a then-new Grumman American Tiger. He was thrilled with it, and it was a very nice airplane that made him the envy of many pilots. Since I was the Senior Flight Instructor at the flight school where he tied down, he offered me the opportunity of trying out the new craft. I loved it, but there was a method in all this; he wanted to watch me land his new airplane. It seems that he was experiencing constant difficulty—nothing serious, just an annoying little "skip" each time he attempted to land. Not a real bounce, mind you, but just this little "skip" off the surface before the airplane really settled down on the runway. He confessed to the difficulty and asked for help.

So I flew with him and found him to be a competent pilot. It's difficult to analyze such a problem, so instead of trying to arrive at an explanation of the difficulty, I taught him to avoid it. I simply reviewed with him the techniques for a soft-field landing. It solved the problem like magic and he continuously "greased it on" after that.

Done well, this is a maneuver that will enable you really to impress the examiner. When that touchdown is so soft that neither of you is really sure you're on the runway, you'll be impressive.

As soon as you are sure that you've touched down, you can cut the power. However, you must continue to hold the yoke all the way back in order to keep the weight on the main wheels. If the surface is really soft, it may be advisable to hold some power on, however, to keep the airplane light until you are certain that you're on a solid surface. Also, it's a good idea to clean the airplane up (retract the flaps) to ensure that mud, slush, or the like will not strike the extended flaps.

Maintaining Directional Control. As with all landings, rudder is used to maintain directional control. However, though some differential braking may also be used for some landings, it is not generally advisable for soft surfaces. As a matter of fact, it's usually best to avoid all use of brakes for this type of landing.

Maintaining Proper Position of Controls and Sufficient Speed. As was indicated above, the yoke or stick should be held all the way back whether you're in a tri-gear or a taildragger. It may also be necessary to carry some power in order to keep the airplane moving. Be cautious, however, about the speed used. I recall seeing an airplane damaged when the owner decided that the best way to handle a soft surface was with an exceptionally fast taxi. That's a mistake. Sufficient speed to taxi should be interpreted to mean carrying sufficient power simply to keep the airplane moving at a speed equivalent to a brisk walk and no faster.

Section 2
Airplane Multiengine Land
(AMEL) Practical Test Standard

NOTE: An applicant seeking initial certification as a private pilot in a multiengine land airplane will be evaluated in all TASKS within this standard including those referenced to the Private Pilot Single-Engine Land Practical Test Standard.

If an applicant holds a private pilot certificate with an airplane rating other than multiengine land, the applicant may be evaluated in only those TASKS described within this standard.

Chapter 13

I. AREA OF OPERATION:
PREFLIGHT PREPARATION

A. TASK: CERTIFICATES AND DOCUMENTS (AMEL)

PILOT OPERATION – 1

REFERENCES: FAR Parts 61 and 91; AC 61–21, AC 61–23; Pilot's Operating Handbook and FAA–Approved Flight Manual.

1. **Objective.** To determine that the applicant:

   a. Exhibits adequate knowledge by explaining the appropriate –

     (1) pilot certificate privileges and limitations.

     (2) medical certificate and expiration.

     (3) personal pilot logbook or flight record.

     (4) FCC station license and operator's permit.

b. Exhibits adequate knowledge by locating and explaining the significance and importance of the airplane's –

    (1) airworthiness and registration certificates.

    (2) operating limitations, handbooks, or manuals.

    (3) equipment list.

    (4) weight and balance data.

    (5) maintenance requirements and appropriate records.

2. Action.   The examiner will:

a. Ask the applicant to present and explain the appropriate pilot and medical certificates and personal flight records, and determine that the applicant's performance meets the objective.

b. Ask the applicant to locate and explain the airplane documents, records, and other required data, and determine that the applicant's performance meets the objective.

c. Place emphasis on the applicant's awareness of the importance of certificates, records, and documents as related to safety.

Objective: What's expected of the applicant regarding certificates and documents.

Exhibiting Knowledge through Explanation. In the unlikely case that you are seeking your Private Pilot Certificate in a multiengine airplane, you will be expected to provide all those explanations that were set forth in the section on single engine private pilot requirements. There is no need to repeat here the knowledge that is required regarding certificates and documents, since it is identical to that listed for single engine land airplanes. Consequently, you may refer to the lengthy explanations already provided at the beginning of the book. Nothing will be expected of you beyond what is presented there.

If, on the other hand, you already hold the Private Pilot Certificate with a single engine land airplane rating, then you will be required to deal only with the tasks that apply to the multiengine land airplane rating. Still, a little review of the material you already know might be in order in the unlikely event that an examiner cares to make a spot check of your knowledge of such matters. However, it seems very unlikely that any examiner will treat a licensed pilot who is simply adding a rating to his/her certificate as though he/she were an initial applicant. In any case, the materials presented in the opening section of the book will suffice for this section as well.

Exhibiting Knowledge by Locating and Explaining the Airplane's Certificates and Documents. Again, there will be no materials required in addition to those described in the single engine section of this book. The fact that you already hold a Private Pilot's Certificate, however, will not excuse you from providing the documents called for in the objective. The fact that you are taking the practical test in a multiengine airplane alters nothing. However, those explanations that served for the single engine rating are sufficient for the multiengine rating as well. Therefore, if you have any doubts, questions, or concerns about the airplane's certificates and documents, you may turn to the early section of the book and find these items adequately explained.

Chapter 14

II. AREA OF OPERATION:
MULTIENGINE OPERATION

NOTE: Because elements of aeronautical knowledge important for safe multiengine operation may not have been previously demonstrated, all items contained in this area of operation that are applicable to the airplane used will be evaluated through oral questioning.

A. TASK: AIRPLANE SYSTEMS (AMEL)

PILOT OPERATION – 1

REFERENCES: AC 61–21; Pilot's Operating Handbook and the FAA–Approved Flight Manual.

1. **Objective.** To determine that the applicant exhibits adequate knowledge by explaining the airplane systems and their operation including:

a. Primary flight controls and trim.

b. Wing flaps, leading edge devices, and spoilers.

c. Flight instruments.

d. Landing gear –

   (1) retraction system.
   (2) indication system.
   (3) brakes and tires.
   (4) nosewheel steering.

e. Engines –

   (1) controls and indicators.
   (2) induction, carburetion, and injection.
   (3) exhaust and turbocharging.
   (4) fire detection.

f. Propellers –

   (1) constant–speed control.
   (2) feather, unfeather, autofeather, and negative torque sensing.
   (3) synchronizing, synchrophasing.

g. Fuel system —

   (1) tanks, pumps, controls, and indicators.
   (2) crossfeed and transfer.
   (3) fueling procedures.
   (4) normal operation.

h. Hydraulic system —

   (1) controls and indicators.
   (2) pumps and regulators.
   (3) normal operation.

i. Electrical system —

   (1) controls and indicators.
   (2) alternators or generators.
   (3) battery, ground power.
   (4) normal operation.

j. Environmental system –

   (1) heating.

(2) cooling and ventilation.
(3) controls and indicators.
(4) pressurization.

k. Ice prevention and elimination.
l. Navigation and communication.
m. Vacuum system.

2. Action. The examiner will:

a. Ask the applicant to explain the airplane systems and their operation, and determine that the applicant's performance meets the objective.
b. Place emphasis on the applicant's knowledge of the airplane systems' operation.

Objective: What's expected of the applicant regarding the airplane systems and their operation.

Exhibiting Knowledge through Explanation. As the FAA document notes, all elements of aeronautical knowledge have been included. However, if the applicant for the multiengine rating is simply adding this rating to the Private Pilot Certificate, then only those elements applicable to the airplane being used will be discussed. For example, the first four sections, "a" through "d," are not unique to multiengine operations and have been previously covered. The applicant may refer to the appropriate part of Section 1 (ASEL) for any information required.

The requirements for engines, however, are a different story. The controls and indicators are clearly going to differ from those for a single engine trainer. Since the multiengine airplane will include constant-speed propellers, the throttles will be used differently than on the single engine trainer. There will be additional instrumentation, such as fuel flow as well as fuel pressure gauges, exhaust temperature gauges, cylinder head temperature gauges, and the like. Since the engine instrumentation can vary from one make and/or model to another, there is no alternative to familiarizing yourself with the instrumentation of the particular airplane that you're using for the practical test. Such familiarization should include thorough familiarity with the operating handbook.

The other items mentioned in this section (carburetion, injection, fire detection, and the like) will not differ appreciably from that presented in the single engine portion of the book and that section can therefore serve as a reference for these items.

Propellers. You will be called on to explain the constant-speed propellers of the multiengine airplane that you're flying. The airplane equipped with constant-speed propellers will, of course, have two controls for each engine, the throttle and the propeller control. The throttle still controls the power output of the engine, but it will, in this case, be measured by manifold pressure rather than the rpm used with single engine trainers. You will need to point out that the power will be read on manifold pressure gauges. The propeller control regulates the rpm, which is registered on the tachometer.

Your explanation should include the information that a combination of manifold pressure and rpm is used for setting the engine's output. The pilot is able to control both the power and the rpm. However, at a particular propeller setting, governors will automatically keep the props turning at the same rpm though power may be increased or decreased. Further, certain settings are used for various purposes. For example, the pilot will set the propeller control at low pitch, or high rpm, for takeoff in order to reduce propeller drag and allow more engine power for takeoff. In cruise, however, the control will be set at a higher pitch (lower rpm), allowing the propeller to take a "bigger bite" at a lower power setting, thus making flight more efficient.

There are limits, of course, on power settings and the relationship between rpm and manifold pressure. These relationships exist for cruising and will be found in a table in the pilot's operating handbook for your airplane. Also, proper control handling is necessary in order to avoid overstressing engines. In adding power, for example, the rpm is increased first, followed by the increase in manifold pressure. For reducing power settings, the reverse is true: Reduce manifold pressure before rpm.

You will also need to discuss all elements of feathering. Since procedures vary from one make and/or model to another, you will need to be thoroughly familiar with the procedures for your airplane. In some airplanes, for example, feathering is accomplished by simply pulling the propeller control all the way back to the stop, while in other planes the procedure is done with a feathering button. Familiarization should include checking out the operating handbook prior to the practical test. Regardless of make or model, however, feathering an engine has the same purpose, the reduction in the drag that is caused by a windmilling propeller. In some instances, there may also be the additional factor of reducing risk of engine damage.

Your explanation will include the specific procedures for the airplane you will be flying for the practical test. You'll also be expected to provide the general explanation that the failed engine is **absorbing** rather than **delivering** energy because of the windmilling propeller. Further, the increased drag causes the airplane to yaw toward the dead engine. Feathering—which means streamlining the blades of the propeller in the direction of flight and halting the windmilling—diminishes the yawing tendency of the airplane.

Feathering will not completely remove the tendency to yaw, but it certainly helps. I still recall my first experience with a twin. The instructor pilot cut the power on the left engine, advising me to hold opposite rudder to prevent the airplane's yawing. As I held full right rudder, I recalled the operating handbook's mentioning that if an engine failed, the airplane would "have some slight tendency to yaw in the direction of the failed engine." Well, as I sat there holding that right rudder pressure, my flight instructor proceeded to deliver a leisurely lecture on the proper engine-out procedures. My right leg began to quiver from the pressure of holding rudder against that "slight tendency to yaw." I wanted to plead with the instructor to please hurry up and get to the feathering part of the explanation. My right leg went from quivering to shaking. In fact, before long I was shaking all over from the pressure of holding that right rudder against the "slight tendency to yaw." Finally, to my great relief, the instructor reached the feathering part of his lecture and permitted me to go through the feathering procedure. There was still a slight tendency to yaw into the dead engine, but I could control it with much less rudder pressure after feathering.

A part of your explanation for this part of the discussion will also include the procedures for unfeathering and restarting an engine. Since procedures vary, your explanation will need to be the one appropriate to your airplane.

Propellers will also need to be synchronized and this is not done simply by referring to and aligning the tachometers. Keep in mind the significance of that uneven beat, recognizing that the faster the beat, the more the engines are "out of synch." To correct this, the propeller controls are set at the same rpm. If the uneven beat is heard, then one prop control only is moved. If the beat becomes slower, the control is being moved in the right direction. Continue to move it slightly, wait for a change, and finally the beat will be gone.

Fuel System Requirements. Most of this remains the same. The explanation given under the ASEL section will suffice for much of this section. However, you will need to know about the number and location of tanks, pumps, etc., for your particular airplane. What you will need to describe are the procedures related to the fact that you now have more than one engine guzzling gas. This may require crossfeeding. Normally, each engine will use fuel from the tanks in its own wing. However, if an engine should fail, there may be a great deal of fuel available to the operating engine by drawing on the failed engine side. Some airplanes will have a crossfeed valve; others allow the pilot simply to select the tank from which to use fuel. Check the operating handbook for your airplane to be sure of the appropriate procedures so that you can be sure that your explanation is the correct one.

Hydraulic System. Again, your explanation will need to be related to your particular airplane. To avoid additional weight, pumps and other paraphernalia might not be duplicated. Consequently, you will need to know the situation presented by your airplane. Losing a particular engine may also mean loss of the hydraulic pump. Such information, as well as how to handle related emergencies, will be presented in the operating handbook for your airplane.

Electrical System. The same thing that is true for the hydraulic system may be true for the electrical system. Your airplane may sport one alternator or generator, which operates only so long as the associated engine is operating. You'll need to explain what's lost besides power when a particular engine goes, and you will have to explain what to do about such problems. Usually, such matters also determine which engine is started first, since such procedures are not based merely on personal whim.

The other parts of the required explanation will either not be required of you since you already have a private license or, in the event that you don't, they have been covered in the appropriate part of the single engine section.

Regarding the Explanation. As was pointed out previously, if you do not already own a Private Pilot Certificate and plan to use a multiengine airplane for the practical test, then expect the complete works. The examiner will quiz you regarding all the items in the preceding section, along with those discussed briefly in this section. If you're simply adding the rating to the ticket that you already possess, then expect to be quizzed only on those items that apply to multiengine requirements and to your particular airplane.

The Emphasis. You'd better know the operations of the systems of your airplane. Examiners will not readminister the written exam, but they do expect you to know your airplane. Particularly in the case of multiengine airplanes, it is important to safe and confident flying to know how the systems operate and what your role as pilot is in relation to them. You simply must know about the operation of constant-speed props and the related controls and requirements. It's equally important to know about crossfeeding, and where various pumps and generators or alternators are located. Knowing the airplane does not mean knowing it as your local A & P knows it, mechanically. But it *does* mean knowing it as *you* must know it to operate capably and safely as a pilot.

B. TASK: EMERGENCY PROCEDURES
(AMEL)

PILOT OPERATION – 1

REFERENCES: AC 61–21; Pilot's Operating Handbook and FAA–Approved Flight Manual.

NOTE: Demonstration of intentional spins and recovery are not required on the practical test and are prohibited in most multiengine airplanes. However, the examiner will ask the applicant to explain the recommended spin recovery procedure for the particular airplane used. This knowledge is essential for recovery if an unintentional spin occurs. This is a knowledge requirement *ONLY*. It is not intended that spins be practiced in multiengine airplanes.

1. **Objective.** To determine that the applicant exhibits adequate knowledge by explaining the airplane's emergency procedures including:

   a. Emergency checklist.
   b. Partial power loss.
   c. Engine failure –

      (1) engine failure before lift–off.
      (2) engine failure after lift–off.
      (3) engine failure during climb and cruise.
      (4) engine securing.

   d. Single–engine operation –

      (1) approach and landing.
      (2) restart.

   e. Emergency landing –

      (1) precautionary.
      (2) without power.
      (3) ditching.

f. Engine roughness or overheat.
g. Loss of oil pressure.
h. Smoke and fire —

   (1) engine.
   (2) cabin.
   (3) electrical.
   (4) environmental.

i. Icing.
j. Crossfeed.
k. Pressurization.
l. Emergency descent.
m. Pitot static system and instruments.
n. Electrical.
o. Landing gear.
p. Wing flaps (asymmetrical position).
q. Inadvertent door openings.
r. Emergency exits.

2. Action. The examiner will:

a. Ask the applicant to explain the airplane's emergency procedures, and determine that the applicant's performance meets the objective.
b. Place emphasis on the applicant's knowledge of the correct emergency procedures.

Objective: What's expected of the applicant regarding emergency procedures.

Exhibiting Knowledge through Explanation. This part of the practical test is simply a continuation of the oral examination that precedes your flight check. Notice that the objective specifies that spins are not required in multiengine airplanes. That's not different or unusual, since they're not required for single engine airplanes either. However, for the multiengine rating, you will be asked to explain spin recovery for the particular airplane you'll be flying. If you check the operating manual for your airplane, you will most likely find that spins are prohibited, but an explanation will still be provided as to how to recover should an inadvertent spin occur. Be familiar with that procedure for the oral part of the practical test.

The objective lists "Emergency checklist" as though there were only one type of emergency—and, consequently, one such checklist to deal with. Probably your best approach for handling this section is to be familiar with the various emergencies that are dealt with in the operating handbook for the airplane you'll be flying. Similarly, with "partial power loss," this could be the consequence of one engine's total failure, partial power loss on one or more engines due to a malfunction, or as a consequence of icing. It could also be the result of a number of other factors too numerous to consider. Therefore, you can only offer some general statements regarding partial power loss. Any partial power loss would generally involve starting preparations for a precautionary or an emergency landing. Beyond that, you would need to relate any explanation to the specific circumstances presented by the examiner.

Engine failure is another matter. Although procedures would vary at least to some extent from one make and/or model to another, there are some generalizations that could be offered. In most light twins, an engine failure early in the takeoff run usually means one thing: Get rid of all power and keep it on the ground. Now, some manuals may make a distinction between engine failure before or after attaining engine-out minimum control speed (V_{mc}), but I have not met a multiengine pilot who would want to lift the airplane off if an engine failed before liftoff. If a failure occurs after becoming airborne, then one's concern would be attaining single-engine best rate-of-climb airspeed (V_{yse}) and holding that until a safe maneuvering altitude is reached or a landing approach initiated. If obstructions must be avoided, then best single-engine angle-of-climb airspeed (V_{xse}) must be attained and maintained until all obstacles are cleared and you can go for best rate-of-climb. The airplane's configuration is also a factor. These details will be covered later in the practical test under the Emergency Operations portion of the actual flight check.

Engine failure during climb and cruise will also need to be discussed in fairly general terms. You can explain that engine failure during these phases of flight is not as critical as during takeoff. Still, if the problem cannot be corrected, a landing must be made as soon as practical. In the instance of loss of an engine during either climb or cruise, the pilot must identify the dead engine and then go through the appropriate procedures for maintaining control and holding sufficient altitude to be able to continue the flight to a safe landing. Again, the details will be presented in a later section. At this stage, your comments can be fairly general regarding handling of mixture, throttles, props, and the general configuration of the airplane. If there is no possibility of restarting a failed engine, then you will also need to be familiar with what the manufacturer of your airplane calls for in order to secure the dead engine.

Your oral examination will also include the procedures for making an approach and landing with a single engine operating. The performance and limitations of light twins vary so greatly that no single set of procedures can be proposed that would be adequate to all. In most cases, the approach and landing procedures would involve essentially the same flight path and procedures as those used for normal approaches and landings. However, you will need to study the operating manual for the airplane which you will be flying for specifics. It would be safe, however, to suggest that in any airplane it would be desirable to avoid low, flat approaches with high power output on the operating engine, or excessive approach speeds that simply result in floating prior to touchdown. Also, allowances should be made for the reduced drag that results from having one engine feathered. Further, in any airplane one should maintain V_{yse} until you've got the runway made. Also, flaps must be extended judiciously because of the dangers involved in the event that a go-around should be required. You can provide this sort of explanation, but I've never met a person yet who says he/she would try a go-around on a single engine.

The discussion of precautionary landings or landings without power would not differ from that offered in the single engine part of the guide, so there is little point in repeating it here. Similarly, ditching is ditching, whether you have one engine or several.

Similarly, the remainder of this part of the oral—dealing as it does with engine roughness, loss of oil pressure, smoke and fire, icing, and problems with various systems—would not contain anything distinctive. It would be advisable, however, to compare the list of items with the index of the operating handbook for your airplane to see if something may be offered that is unique to your airplane. It's unlikely that such would be the case, but it's worth checking well in advance of the practical test.

C. TASK: NORMAL PROCEDURES
(AMEL)

PILOT OPERATION – 1

REFERENCES: AC 61–21; Pilot's Operating Handbook and FAA–Approved Flight Manual.

1. **Objective.** To determine that the applicant exhibits adequate knowledge by explaining the airplane's normal operating procedures including:

   a. Airspeeds for safe operations, airspeed symbols and definitions.
   b. Airplane limitations, reasons for limitations.
   c. Applicable warnings, cautions, or placards.
   d. Use of external power for starting.
   e. Taxi procedures and precautions.
   f. Takeoff profile.
   g. Pressurization, heating, cooling, and ventilation.
   h. Noise abatement procedures.

2. **Action.** The examiner will:

   a. Ask the applicant to explain the airplane's normal operating procedures, and determine that the applicant's performance meets the objective.
   b. Place emphasis on the applicant's knowledge of correct normal procedures.

Objective: What's expected of the applicant regarding normal procedures. **Exhibiting Knowledge through Explanation.** Although a great many people regard the multiengine test as similar to multiengine instruction, in that both consist of single-engine procedures in a multiengine airplane, you will also be expected to know something about normal flight procedures. It's important that you be familiar with the airspeeds for your particular airplane. They cannot be listed here, of course, but you should know what the precise airspeed markings are on the airspeed indicator of the multiengine airplane which you'll be flying (Fig. 14-1). As with any

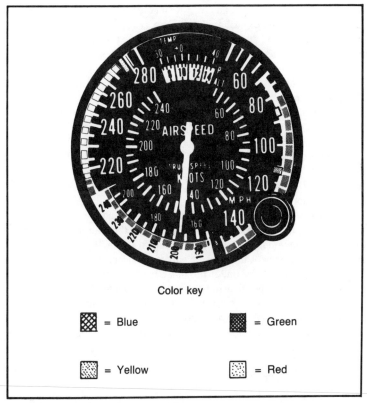

Color key

▨ = Blue   ▦ = Green

▧ = Yellow   ▢ = Red

Fig. 14-1. Airspeed markings for twin-engine airplane.

airplane, the white arc represents the normal operating range with flaps extended, ranging from the power-off stalling speed with gear and flaps in landing configuration to the maximum flaps-extended airspeed. The green arc is for airspeeds with flaps and gear retracted ranging from power-off stalling airspeed to the maximum structural cruising speed. The yellow arc is the caution range, avoided unless in smooth air. The red line marks that airspeed which should never be exceeded. To this arrangement has been added, for multiengine airplanes, a red line and a blue line. The red line at the low end represents the minimum controllable airspeed with the critical engine out. The blue line marks the best rate-of-climb airspeed with an engine out.

For some reason, you're also required to memorize the various symbols and accompanying definitions. We include them here for your convenience. V_y and V_x have the same meaning except that they apply only when all engines are operating. They mean, respectively, the airspeed at which the airplane will gain the maximum altitude in the shortest time or in the shortest distance. The speed is different with an engine out and the airspeeds then become V_{yse} and V_{xse} with essentially the same meaning, the best rate-of-climb or best angle-of-climb, respectively, with an engine out. V_{mc} is unique to multiengine aircraft, meaning the minimum airspeed at which the airplane is controllable when the critical engine suddenly becomes inoperative with the remaining engine(s) producing takeoff power. The FAA has a lot of other speeds that you can learn by reading Part 1 FAR, Definitions and Abbreviations. In addition to those that we've mentioned you probably wouldn't be called on to recall any others than—perhaps—V_a, maneuvering speed; V_{ne}, never exceed speed; V_{so}, stalling speed in landing configuration. In the event that anyone is worried about it and can't get his/her hands on Part 1, I might include the following, though it's unlikely that they'd be called for. V_1 means critical-engine-failure speed, V_2 means takeoff safety speed. I can't even imagine an examiner calling for more than that.

As for limitations, warnings, cautions, placards and the like, these will vary from one airplane to another. Simply check the operating handbook for the airplane you'll be flying for the checkride for these items. They are meaningless except in terms of particular airplanes.

The rest of the items under the objective for normal procedures are items that are either peculiar to particular airplanes or are covered in the single engine section of the manual. Therefore, if you are familiar with the operating handbook for your airplane, you'll be covered for anything the examiner might require on the oral part of the test regarding normal procedures.

D. TASK: DETERMINING PERFORMANCE AND FLIGHT PLANNING (AMEL)

PILOT OPERATION – 1

REFERENCES: AC 61–21; Pilot's Operating Handbook and FAA–Approved Flight Manual.

1. **Objective.** To determine that the applicant exhibits adequate knowledge by explaining and using the airplane's performance data for flight planning including:

   a. Accelerate–stop distance.
   b. Accelerate–go distance.
   c. Takeoff performance, all engines, single engine.
   d. Climb performance, all engines, single engine.
   e. Service ceiling, all engines, single engine.
   f. Cruise performance.
   g. Fuel consumption, range, endurance.
   h. Descent performance.
   i. Go–around from rejected landings.
   j. Landing distance.

2. **Action.** The examiner will:

   a. Ask the applicant to explain the airplane's performance data.
   b. Ask the applicant to plan a flight using specified data, and determine that the applicant's performance meets the objective.
   c. Place emphasis on the applicant's knowledge of airplane performance and correct flight planning procedures.

Objective: What's expected of the applicant regarding performance and flight planning.

Exhibiting Knowledge through Explanation. This part of your oral examination has to do with many of the numbers for your airplane. Some of the description will be general, demonstrating that you understand what various items refer to; other parts may be specifically applicable to the airplane you'll be flying, requiring that you check these numbers in the operating handbook since they cannot be provided here.

One of the critical times for facing loss of an engine is that very brief period—two to three seconds only—after the takeoff roll has started while the airplane is accelerating to a safe engine-out speed. Manuals can discuss V_{mc}, but control of airplanes close to that speed is marginal or, in some airplanes, precludes continued flight. Some manufacturers include a minimum safe single-engine speed that allows for maintaining altitude while the landing gear is being retracted and the dead prop feathered. There is, in other words, an "area of decision," where the pilot must decide what to do if an engine fails after liftoff.

Entering into the decision are factors such as remaining runway length, field elevation and density altitude, wind direction and speed, and the airplane's gross weight. This "area of decision" is located between the point at which V_y is reached and the point where obstruction clearance altitude is reached (Fig. 14-2).

Now, to get to items listed in the objective, the pilot in making his/her decision must know the accelerate-stop and accelerate-go distances. The former is the total distance required to accelerate to a specified speed and, faced with an engine failure at precisely that point, to bring the airplane to a stop on the runway that remains. The latter is the total distance required to accelerate to a specified speed and then, facing an engine out at that point, to continue the takeoff and climb on the remaining engine to a height of 50 feet AGL. The only way you can know this is to consult the appropriate graph in the operating handbook. Consequently, this item on the oral requires that you be able to interpret that chart in the handbook.

Similarly, you will need to be familiar with the takeoff performance with all engines operating and also with only a single engine operating. As with the preceding matter, there is no way this can be stated for all aircraft. The requirement then, once again, is that you be able to read and interpret the appropriate graph in the operating handbook for your airplane. The same is true for climb performance, service ceiling, cruise performance, and the like. These are particular matters that have meaning only in terms of specific airplanes.

As for the go-around from rejected landings, there is little that is different from the procedures discussed in the single engine section. Since you will be flying a more complex airplane, the go-around becomes more critical since it generally involves more complex procedures to change from landing airspeed and configuration to the requirements for climbing out. Consequently, the decision should be made well in advance of touching down. Go-around procedures vary, of course, and will be discussed in the operating handbook. The examiner will expect you to be familiar with what

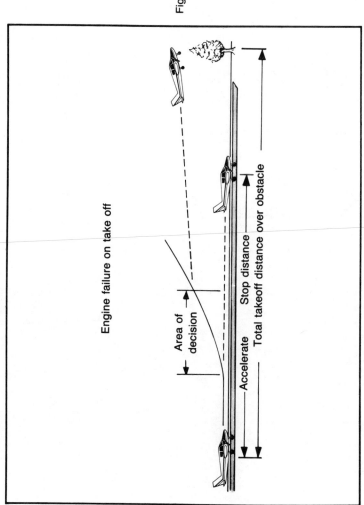

Fig. 14-2. Area of decision.

the manufacturer calls for with your airplane, but the general considerations of application of power, flap and gear retraction, and retrimming the airplane as these were discussed for single engine go-arounds apply to multiengine airplanes as well.

E. TASK: WEIGHT AND BALANCE/EQUIPMENT LIST
(AMEL)

PILOT OPERATION – 1

REFERENCES: AC 61–21,
AC 61–23; Pilot's Operating
Handbook and FAA–Approved Flight
Manual.

1. **Objective.** To determine that the applicant exhibits adequate knowledge by explaining the airplane's weight and balance procedures, the effects of exceeding the limits, and equipment list including:

   a. Use of weight and balance data.
   b. Loading recommendations and adverse effects of exceeding limits.
   c. Baggage/cargo loading.
   d. Weight and balance determination for flight.
   e. Required equipment list.

2. **Action.** The examiner will:

   a. Ask the applicant to explain the airplane's weight and balance procedures, the effects of exceeding the limits, and the equipment list.
   b. Ask the applicant to compute the weight and balance for a flight, and determine that the applicant's performance meets the objective.
   c. Place emphasis on the applicant's knowledge of correct weight and balance procedures.

Objective: What's expected of the applicant regarding weight and balance/equipment list.
Exhibiting Knowledge through Explanation. If you already pos-

sess a Private Pilot Certificate, it will not be necessary for you to again explain the business about empty weight, gross weight, useful load, or any material regarding the need to keep within load limits. Nor will you be required to review the general discussion regarding center of gravity, datum line, or other items related to balance. If you are obtaining a Private Pilot's Certificate in a multiengine airplane, then your general discussion of these matters will be the same as that required for the single engine rating. All of this material has already been presented in the first section of the book and there is no need simply to repeat it here.

There is one item regarding center of gravity and balance that you will need to explain. The single-engine minimum control speed (V_{mc}) is affected by the distribution of weight and the location of the center of gravity. What is meant by V_{mc}, as you know, is the minimum control airspeed with the critical engine out. What this refers to is the fact that a certain velocity of air movement over the rudder is required in order for the fully deflected rudder to have the desired effect of countering the asymetrical thrust occurring when an engine becomes inoperative. The velocity of that air is determined by the airplane's airspeed. Consequently, the airspeed can decrease to the point that the rudder, even fully deflected, can no longer adequately balance the airplane's asymetrical thrust with the result that directional control is lost.

To relate this to balance, recall that an airplane yaws around its center of gravity. When an engine becomes inoperative, the moment created by the still-functioning engine must be overcome by the moment created by the pilot's deflecting the rudder. The farther aft the center of gravity is located, the shorter the moment arm becomes for overcoming the asymetrical thrust created by the operating engine. That is to say, the rudder becomes less effective, meaning that a higher airspeed is required in order for the rudder to effectively counter asymetrical thrust. Point out to the examiner that as the CG moves rearward, V_{mc} increases. A shallow bank into the operating engine can help make the rudder somewhat more effective, a point that will be dealt with later. For the present, keep in mind the effect of CG on V_{mc}.

Performance. Although the objective does not specify it, there is a performance part to this "explanation" or oral phase. You will be called on to do a weight and balance computation for your particular airplane. This procedure was discussed in general terms in the single engine section. The requirement here is no different. You will, of course, do a weight and balance based on the graphs and/or charts in the operating handbook of the airplane which you'll be flying. You may also be required, having done that, to discuss how passengers, fuel, and baggage/cargo can be arranged to stay within loading recommendations. You will probably also be required to indicate that you are familiar with the required equipment list for your particular airplane.

F. TASK: FLIGHT PRINCIPLES — ENGINE INOPERATIVE (AMEL)

PILOT OPERATION – 1

REFERENCES: AC 61-21; Pilot's Operating Handbook and FAA-Approved Airplane Flight Manual.

1. **Objective.** To determine that the applicant exhibits adequate knowledge by explaining the flight principles related to operation with an engine inoperative including:

   a. Factors affecting single–engine flight –

       (1) density altitude.
       (2) drag reduction (propeller, gear, and flaps).
       (3) airspeed (V_{SSE}, V_{XSE}, V_{YSE}).
       (4) attitude (pitch, bank, coordination).
       (5) weight and center of gravity.
       (6) critical engine.

   b. Directional control –

       (1) reasons for loss of directional control.
       (2) reasons for variations in V_{MC}.
       (3) indications of approaching loss of directional control.
       (4) safe recovery procedure if directional control is lost.
       (5) V_{MC} in relation to stall speed.
       (6) whether an engine inoperative loss of directional control demonstration can be safely accomplished in flight.

   c. Takeoff emergencies –

       (1) takeoff planning.
       (2) decisions after engine failure.
       (3) single–engine operation.

2. **Action.** The examiner will:

a. Ask the applicant to explain engine inoperative flight principles, and determine that the applicant's performance meets the objective.

b. Place emphasis on the applicant's knowledge of correct procedures.

Objective: What's expected of the applicant regarding operation with an engine inoperative.

Exhibiting Knowledge through Explanation. Keep in mind that all of this is still part of the oral examination. If you are the owner of a Private Pilot Certificate and are simply embellishing it with another rating, then you'll already have done some of the explanation and will not need to repeat it. The examiner will simply look for general knowledge of the effects of certain factors on single-engine flight. There is nothing unique to single-engine flight regarding density altitude. Regarding drag reduction, the factor unique to single-engine flight in a multiengine airplane is the effect of the drag of a windmilling propeller on the directional control of the airplane.

You'll be expected to be able to explain the meanings of the various airspeed symbols listed in the objectives. These have already been presented and briefly discussed. Beyond knowing what these mean generally, the examiner will also require that you recite the various airspeeds for your particular airplane. As with most such items, this will require checking the operating handbook for your airplane.

Attitude is treated somewhat differently in a multiengine airplane with an engine out. In a single engine airplane, the attitude when the engine dies is simply nose-down. That means nosing down to whatever maintains the best gliding speed. In the multiengine airplane, it means different things under different circumstances. For example, climbing out after takeoff, it means getting the nose down to the attitude that provides V_{sy} or V_{sx}, depending on circumstances. In straight-and-level cruise, an inoperative engine probably means establishing the attitude that enables you to maintain altitude. In some light twins, close to gross, it means the attitude that gives you the airspeed that permits continued controlled flight with a minimum but steady loss of altitude while you look for a place to put it down.

Another aspect of attitude was mentioned earlier. In addition to lateral attitude, single-engine flight in a multiengine airplane also means establishing the appropriate longitudinal attitude. In addition to establishing the appropriate pitch and holding heading with the rudder, the pilot should also roll into a bank of about five degrees toward the operating engine. Establishing such an attitude will tend to turn the airplane toward the operating engine at the same time that the asymetrical thrust resulting from engine failure tends to turn the airplane toward the dead engine. This attitude makes it somewhat easier to maintain directional control. Keep in mind as well that the value of V_{mc} in your airplane is based on a maximum five degree bank into the good engine. Remember also what you were taught about wings-level flight and the fact that such flight, with the ball of the turn-and-slip indicator centered, significantly increases V_{mc}.

The considerations regarding weight and balance are essentially the same as for the single engine trainer. At least one item regarding weight should be kept in mind. The weight of the airplane accompanied by density altitude will determine whether or not you are able to maintain altitude. The effect of the location of center of gravity on V_{mc} has already been discussed.

Demonstrate your understanding that on most light twins there is a critical engine. Hanging more engines on an airplane does not remove the effects of P-factor. Remember that stuff? It's the difference in "lift" (thrust) between the downward and upward moving blades of the propeller. It's a part of what makes the airplane tend to yaw to the left at full throttle. Since most light twins have propellers turning clockwise (as seen from behind them), both engines are going to have more thrust on the right side than on the left side. Since the right side of the right engine is farther away from the centerline of the airplane than the right side of the left engine, the yawing force of the right engine is going to be greater. This means that when you lose the left engine and the right engine is still turning, the yawing force is greater than when the opposite situation occurs. Since it is therefore more difficult to control the airplane when the left engine is lost, this is regarded as the critical engine.

You'll have to talk about directional control with an engine out, covering such items as reasons for loss of directional control. This was already discussed when you explained about V_{mc}. In that same section reasons for variations in V_{mc} were also discussed. Remember that talk about CG and V_{mc}?

The indications of the approaching loss of directional control are not limited to the diminishing ability to maintain a heading with an engine inoperative. As the airspeed drops below V_{mc}, the airplane also wants to roll into the dead engine. The lower the airspeed, the greater the tendency to roll, which spells trouble. The way to counteract this rolling tendency is with the aileron. The trouble increases with that because the down aileron, while creating more lift to raise the lower wing, also increases the already present tendency to yaw toward the dead engine. Stall the airplane in this condition and a violent roll into the dead engine may occur.

Recovering from loss of directional control would require reducing the power on the good engine and reducing the angle of attack. In addition to these measures, the airplane should also be banked about 5 to 10 degrees into the operating engine to achieve greater control.

You will be expected to understand that one must determine the relationship between V_{mc} and stall speed. Explain to the examiner that this can be done by establishing a normal climb with both engines operating at takeoff power. Then power on the critical engine is reduced to idle. The airspeed is gradually reduced with back pressure on the yoke until directional control can no longer be maintained. Recovery, as described above, would then be made. However, if signs of a stall begin to appear prior to reaching the speed at which directional control is lost, recovery should be initiated immediately. Such a situation would wash out V_{mc} demonstrations.

In discussing takeoff emergencies, takeoff planning will be considered. The planning will begin with the pilot's familiarizing him/herself completely with the airplane's performance capabilities and limitations. Also to be taken into account are such factors as runway length and condition, obstructions, terrain, nearby landing areas, and the climbout path.

The pilot should also have some idea of plans to be executed at various stages of takeoff and climb in the event that an engine becomes inoperative. He/she would also keep in mind the fact that altitude is more essential to safety than excessive airspeed. However, this should never be taken to mean that airspeed should be traded for altitude to the point where safety is being sacrificed. The pilot should have in mind, before the takeoff roll begins, the altitude, airspeed, and airplane configuration required in order to attempt to continue flight in the event that an engine is lost. If these conditions cannot be met, then the situation must be treated the same as though the engine had been lost on a single engine airplane.

The pilot's decisions after an engine dies will depend on the circumstances in which this occurs. If the airplane has not yet become airborne, the decision must be made as to whether or not to continue the takeoff. If V_{mc} has not been attained, the decision is automatic: Stay on the ground. Similarly, if the airspeed is below V_{xse} and the gears are still down, the takeoff must generally be abandoned. This is not an exhaustive consideration, but simply demonstrates that one decision facing the pilot is whether or not to continue takeoff and/or flight. This is such a particular decision related so closely to the airplane being flown that the operating handbook should be consulted regarding such decisions. If a flight is continued, a decision must be made as to whether to continue to climb straight ahead or to begin a gentle turn. Generally, the former is the better course, but many factors enter into such a decision.

Enroute, an engine failure calls for a decision as to whether to attempt to continue flight or to prepare for an immediate precautionary landing. Judgements must also be made regarding whether or not to secure the failed engine or when this is to be done. The pilot also will have some determinations to make regarding the treatment of the operating engine in order to avoid abusing it, unless you're interested in flight experience in a multiengine glider.

Assuming all has gone well to this stage, a number of decisions will be required for landing with an engine inoperative. You must decide when and to what extent to lower flaps and when to drop the landing gear. An approach airspeed must also be selected; V_{yse} is the generally recommended airspeed, but again the operating handbook for the airplane you're flying should be consulted. The type of pattern to be flown must also be determined. The only generalizations that can be made here are that you must select a pattern that avoids radical or excessive maneuvering. The pattern and approach speed selected should be such as to avoid being forced into attempting a single-engine go-around. The pilot must be absolutely, thoroughly familiar with the procedures required for attempting to take the airplane around on one engine. It may turn out that for a number and variety of reasons the procedure will simply be too demanding to be attempted.

One other factor has not yet been mentioned. At some point during your efforts to work your way safely out of the single-engine dilemma, you should let someone in on your predicament. Obviously, the first rule is to "fly the airplane." You'll be very busy with that. But at some point, you should clutch that mike or depress the talk button on the yoke and tell someone that you've got problems. So there's yet another judgement to make: who to call and when to make such radio contact.

Single-engine operation in a multiengine airplane is more difficult than many realize. Losing an engine on a light twin does not mean that you've lost merely half your power. Rather, it means that you've lost 80 percent or more. Most of that excess power that two throbbing engines provided is going to be lost. Tests have indicated that in some current twins, the rate of climb on one engine is only 10 percent of that with both engines operating.

Actual single-engine procedures vary among various makes and models and from one situation to another. Some generalizations can be offered, however. Mixture, propeller controls, and throttles should be positioned for maximum power to maintain at least V_{mc}. The airplane should be cleaned up (flaps and landing gear retracted). The pilot should determine which engine is inoperative and then verify it by closing the throttle on the dead engine. If it gets awesomely quiet, you've "verified" the wrong engine, but you would also have identified the dead engine. The airplane should be banked at least five degrees into the operating engine. Then you can make some effort to determine the cause of the failure and try a restart or feather the dead engine. This is followed by heading for the nearest airport or safest landing area. The dead engine may then be secured. As the flight continues, the operating engine instruments should be monitored, power adjusted appropriately, proper configuration set and airspeed established. Then, depending on circumstances, climb established, altitude maintained, or descent controlled.

Chapter 15

III. AREA OF OPERATION:
GROUND OPERATIONS

A. TASK: VISUAL INSPECTION (AMEL)

PILOT OPERATION – 1

REFERENCES: AC 61–21; Pilot's Operating Handbook and FAA–Approved Flight Manual.

1. **Objective.**   To determine that the applicant:

   a. Exhibits adequate knowledge of airplane visual inspection by explaining the reasons for checking the items.
   b. Inspects the airplane by following a checklist.
   c. Determines that the airplane is in condition for safe flight emphasizing –

      (1) fuel quantity, grade, and type.
      (2) fuel contamination safeguards.
      (3) oil quantity, grade, and type.
      (4) fuel, oil, and hydraulic leaks.

(5) flight controls.

(6) structural damage.

(7) tiedown, control lock, and wheel chock removal.

(8) ice and frost removal.

(9) security of baggage, cargo, and equipment.

d. Notes any discrepancy and determines whether the airplane is safe for flight or requires maintenance.

2. Action. The examiner will:

a. Ask the applicant to explain the reasons for checking the items during a visual inspection.

b. Observe the applicant's visual inspection procedure, and determine that the applicant's performance meets the objective.

c. Place emphasis on soundness of the applicant's judgment regarding the air-plane's condition.

Objective: What's expected of the applicant regarding visual inspection.

Exhibiting Knowledge through Explanation. There is little difference between the visual inspection for multiengine airplanes and that for single engine planes. The explanation that precedes the actual inspection will be rather brief. As a matter of fact, if you are simply adding the multiengine rating to your private license, the only explanation the examiner will look for will be that which accompanies each part of the visual inspection. That is to say, your reasons for checking items will accompany each item as you check it. You will not be called on to go over the checklist prior to doing the actual inspection.

Determining That the Airplane Is Airworthy. The list of items to be checked does not differ from that required for the single engine practical test. These materials have been covered in the single engine section and will not be repeated here. The operating handbook will contain a preflight checklist nearly identical to that illustrated in the single engine section indicating the items to be checked and the sequence of the steps (Fig. 15-1).

Performance. Expect to be observed for the thoroughness of your preflight check of the airplane. Keep in mind that the items listed in the Objective section of the FAA guide are illustrative only. Certainly nothing

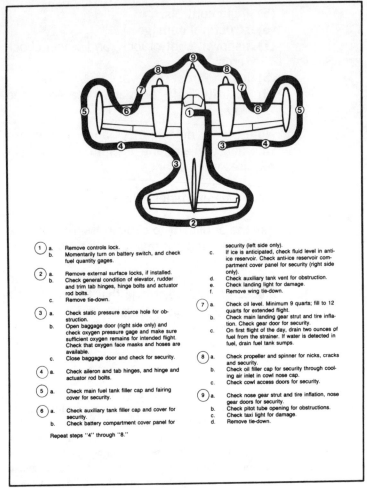

Fig. 15-1. A typical preflight inspection.

1 a. Remove controls lock.
b. Momentarily turn on battery switch, and check fuel quantity gages.

2 a. Remove external surface locks, if installed.
b. Check general condition of elevator, rudder and trim tab hinges, hinge bolts and actuator rod bolts.
c. Remove tie-down.

3 a. Check static pressure source hole for obstruction.
b. Open baggage door (right side only) and check oxygen pressure gage and make sure sufficient oxygen remains for intended flight. Check that oxygen face masks and hoses are available.
c. Close baggage door and check for security.

4 a. Check aileron and tab hinges, and hinge and actuator rod bolts.

5 a. Check main fuel tank filler cap and fairing cover for security.

6 a. Check auxiliary tank filler cap and cover for security.
b. Check battery compartment cover panel for

Repeat steps "4" through "8."

security (left side only).
c. If ice is anticipated, check fluid level in anti-ice reservoir. Check anti-ice reservoir compartment cover panel for security (right side only).
d. Check auxiliary tank vent for obstruction.
e. Check landing light for damage.
f. Remove wing tie-down.

7 a. Check oil level. Minimum 9 quarts; fill to 12 quarts for extended flight.
b. Check main landing gear strut and tire inflation. Check gear door for security.
c. On first flight of the day, drain two ounces of fuel from the strainer. If water is detected in fuel, drain fuel tank sumps.

8 a. Check propeller and spinner for nicks, cracks and security.
b. Check oil filler cap for security through cooling air inlet in cowl nose cap.
c. Check cowl access doors for security.

9 a. Check nose gear strut and tire inflation, nose gear doors for security.
b. Check pitot tube opening for obstructions.
c. Check taxi light for damage.
d. Remove tie-down.

on that list should be omitted but it may not precisely fit the airplane you'll be flying for the checkride. The examiner will expect you to rely on the checklist in the operating handbook rather than the Objective list of items. **Emphasis.** What constitutes sound judgement regarding the airworthiness of the airplane depends on the thoroughness of the preflight inspection and the correct assessment of what is observed. With multiengine, as with single engine, if there is doubt, don't go. Get it checked. Also, unless you are very familiar with the checklist—and very confident—it's best to rely on the operating handbook checklist rather than trying to do the inspection from memory, since multiengine airplanes are generally more complex than the single engine trainer.

B. TASK: COCKPIT MANAGEMENT
(AMEL)

PILOT OPERATION – 1

REFERENCE: AC 61–21.

1. **Objective.**   To determine that the applicant:

   a. Exhibits adequate knowledge of cockpit management by explaining related safety and efficiency factors.
   b. Organizes and arranges the material and equipment in a manner that makes them readily available.
   c. Ensures that the safety belts and shoulder harnesses are fastened.
   d. Adjusts and locks foot pedals or pilot's seat to a safe position and ensures full control movement.
   e. Briefs the occupants on the use of safety belts and emergency procedures.

2. **Action.**   The examiner will:

   a. Ask the applicant to explain cockpit management procedures.
   b. Observe the applicant's cockpit management procedures, and determine that the applicant's performance meets the objective.
   c. Place emphasis on safety items related to good cockpit management.

Regarding the Explanation. The examiner will look for essentially the same sort of explanation that you provided during the preflight inspection when it comes time to explain why you are doing whatever it is that you do regarding cockpit management.

The Performance. Although much of what you do will be covered in the pre-starting checklist, some items may not be included. Things like stowing gear, checking location of passengers and baggage/cargo, adjusting and locking aircrew members' seats and the like generally will not be found on the pre-start checklist but still must be accomplished. If your performance is orderly and appears to be based on a regular routine, your demonstration of cockpit efficiency should satisfy the examiner's expectations.

The Emphasis. What the examiner looks for here is different only in degree from that which was described in the single engine section. The difference in degree is related to the greater complexity of the multiengine airplane.

C. TASK: STARTING ENGINES (AMEL)

PILOT OPERATION – 1

REFERENCES: AC 61–21,
AC 91– 13, AC 91–55; Pilot's
Operating Handbook and FAA–
Approved Flight Manual.

1. **Objective.** To determine that the applicant:

   a. Exhibits adequate knowledge by explaining engine starting procedures, including starting under various atmospheric conditions.
   b. Performs all the items on the before–starting and starting checklist.
   c. Accomplishes safe starting procedures with emphasis on –

      (1) positioning the airplane to avoid creating hazards.
      (2) determining that the area is clear.
      (3) adjusting the engine controls.
      (4) setting the brakes.
      (5) preventing undesirable airplane movement after engine start.
      (6) avoiding excessive engine RPM and temperatures.
      (7) checking engine instruments after engine start.

2. **Action.** The examiner will:

   a. Ask the applicant to explain starting procedures including starting under various atmospheric conditions.
   b. Observe the applicant's engine starting procedures, and determine that the applicant's performance meets the objective.
   c. Place emphasis on the applicant's safe starting procedures.

Objective: What's expected of the applicant regarding engine starting procedures.

Exhibiting Knowledge through Explanation. Your explanation may include some general considerations regarding starting the engines but there is no substitute for the operating handbook for your particular airplane. For example, it's safe to say that on any airplane, the landing gear switch should be checked for the down position before turning the master on if the gear is operated electrically, or before cranking up if the gear is operated hydraulically. Also, it's good practice to touch or point to or operate each item on the checklist as the item is checked. But these matters don't get at the particulars required for your airplane.

Other generalizations might include the fact that normally the left engine of a light twin is started first. On some airplanes there is only one generator and it is on the left engine. Starting that engine first means that the generator is working to help start the right engine. On other airplanes where this is not the case, the left engine is started first because the battery is located on the left side and the battery cable to the engine on that side is therefore shorter, providing more electrical power for the start. Also, since safety is a factor, just as it is in starting a single engine airplane, the pilot must clear the propeller area. When the pilot of a single engine airplane yells "Clear!" it's quite apparent what he's clearing. Since there are multiple possibilities in a multiengine airplane, some pilots specify which engine they're cranking up by yelling, for example, "Clear left!"

Once you got one mill turning, it should be revved up sufficiently to have the alternator cut in to give some additional juice for starting the second engine. Since in cold weather it's not a good idea to run an engine at too high a power setting too soon, it's necessary to exercise a little patience for cold weather starting. You may need that extra boost in cold weather since it's a greater strain on the battery.

Just as with a single engine airplane, it's best to have all electrical equipment off until after all engines are running. That saves more electrical power for starting and saves electronics from damage that might occur from a sudden surge of power when an engine is started. It's also a good idea to limit cranking periods to 30 seconds. If that 30 seconds doesn't get an engine running, skip it and go to the other one. Then, after a couple of minutes, you can come back to number one again. Such a procedure will help give your starters a longer life. If it becomes necessary to use external power to get going, make sure all avionic switches are OFF and check the operating handbook for proper setting of the master switch. Just make sure that the master is turned on after you get a start.

Using the Checklist. No matter how proficient you think you are, use the operating handbook checklist. To make sure that nothing is omitted, slide your finger down the list item by item, reciting the item name and pointing to, touching, or operating each as you name it. If you have a second pilot, have him/her call out the checklist while you repeat what's called out and perform the appropriate chore.

Using Safe Starting Procedures. These are the same considerations that are called for in starting a single engine airplane. As with any airplane, position the airplane to avoid kicking up dust, stones, or other litter that can damage your airplane or one behind it. When you clear the area, clear it visually as well as verbally. Engine controls and brakes should be set appropriately for starting. And since you'll need to check some gauges after you get the start, your attention can be diverted from the airplane itself. Don't become so engrossed in scanning the panel that you relax brake pressure and allow the airplane to start rolling. Your attention must be divided between the interior of the airplane and the area outside. The rest of the list is the same as for the single engine airplane. Where there are differences, they will be covered in the operating handbook.

D. TASK: TAXIING (AMEL)

PILOT OPERATION – 2

REFERENCE: AC 61–21.

1. **Objective.**   To determine that the applicant:

   a. Exhibits adequate knowledge by explaining safe taxi procedures.
   b. Adheres to signals and clearances and follows the proper taxi route.
   c. Performs brake check immediately after the airplane begins moving.
   d. Controls taxi speed without excessive use of brakes.
   e. Recognizes and avoids hazards.
   f. Positions controls for existing wind conditions.
   g. Uses differential power when necessary.
   h. Checks instruments for proper operation.
   i. Avoids creating hazards to persons or property.

2. **Action.**   The examiner will:

   a. Ask the applicant to explain safe taxi procedures.
   b. Observe the applicant's taxi procedures, and determine that the applicant's performance meets the objective.
   c. Place emphasis on the applicant's correct airplane control, taxi speed, and avoidance of hazards.

Objective: What's expected of the applicant regarding taxiing.
Exhibiting Knowledge through Explanation. The explanation that is provided for safe taxiing procedures in the single engine section is minimally adequate for multiengine requirements. A few items may need to be added, such as the possibility of using power differential between the individual engines for directional control and the resulting need to avoid taxiing too fast as one adds power to one engine or the other. On taildragging multiengine airplanes, tailwheel locks may be used to taxi in a straight line and offset the tendency to weathervane, but this requires remember-

ing to unlock the tailwheel when a turn is required. Also, the multiengine airplane is generally larger than singles, requiring extra alertness to guarantee clearances because of the greater wingspan and length of the plane. The operating handbook for your airplane should be consulted for any specific taxiing instructions.

Heeding Directions and Other Matters. The need to adhere to signals and directions and to follow proper routes is the same for multiengine airplanes as for single engine craft. Similarly, brakes should also be checked as soon as the airplane begins moving. It is probably more important to avoid braking in the multiengine airplane, however, since it is heavier and brake wear would be greater. Riding the brakes is to be avoided altogether. Speed should be controlled with power setting to the extent possible rather than relying on brakes.

Control Positions. As for positioning controls for existing wind conditions, this requires attention to throttles as well as to ailerons and elevator. The latter are positioned in precisely the same way they would be for taxiing in a single engine airplane. The multiengine airplane, however, has the advantage of differential power between engines, which can be an aid in taxiing in a crosswind. Increasing the power setting of the upwind engine can prevent the airplane's tendency to weathervane.

Use of Differential Power. Differential power can be used as an aid in taxiing, but in most current light twins it's not essential. Throttles can be set on both engines for a safe taxi speed and directional control maintained by the use of the rudder pedals for the most part. Where differential power is used, the throttle on the inside of the turn should be pulled back to idle in order to avoid increasing the taxiing speed.

Checking Instruments Is Not Significantly Different in a Multiengine Airplane. There will be duplicates of some instruments, since there are more engines, but that hardly even needs to be called to attention. Because of the greater complexity, there may be some additional instruments to be checked, but this will not constitute a problem if the operating handbook checklist is used.

About the only difference between the multiengine airplane and the trainer regarding hazard avoidance is that the former generally sports significantly greater power, requiring even greater concern for people and objects that may be behind the airplane whenever power is advanced.

Regarding the Explanation. The oral examination part of taxiing will involve the general types of observations set out at the beginning of this task description. Beyond this, any items that need to be covered will be those items in the operating handbook, which you should be familiar with.

Procedures. The examiner will look for your recognition of the special requirements of taxiing a multiengine airplane. In the multiengine airplane, particular care must be taken to avoid excessive speeds if differential power is used to aid directional control.

The Emphasis. As the above statements suggest, the focus will be on control. This involves related matters of directional control and taxi speed.

When differential power is needed for a turn, power on the engine inside the turn needs to be reduced to keep taxi speed down. Incidentally, braking should also be avoided for directional control or taxi speed control except for occasional "nudges." And when differential braking is used to aid directional control, the examiner will expect you to avoid pivoting on one wheel.

E. TASK: PRE–TAKEOFF CHECK (AMEL)

PILOT OPERATION – 1

REFERENCES: AC 61–21; Pilot's Operating Handbook and FAA–Approved Flight Manual.

1. **Objective.**   To determine that the applicant:

   a. Exhibits adequate knowledge of the pre–takeoff check by explaining the reasons for checking the items.
   b. Positions airplane to avoid creating hazards.
   c. Divides attention inside and outside of the cockpit.
   d. Ensures that the engine temperatures and pressures are suitable for run–up and takeoff.
   e. Follows the checklist.
   f. Touches the control or switch, or adjusts it to the prescribed position after identifying a checklist item.
   g. States the instrument reading, when appropriate, after identifying the checklist item.
   h. Ensures that the airplane is in safe operating condition emphasizing –

      (1) flight controls and instruments.
      (2) engine and propeller operation.
      (3) seat adjustment and lock.
      (4) safety belts and shoulder harnesses fastened and adjusted.
      (5) doors and windows secured.

   i. Recognizes any discrepancy and decides if the airplane is safe for flight or requires maintenance.
   j. Reviews the critical takeoff performance airspeeds and takeoff distances for existing operating conditions considering engine malfunction.

k. Describes takeoff emergency procedures with emphasis on —

(1) engine inoperative cockpit procedures.
(2) engine inoperative airspeeds.
(3) engine inoperative route to follow considering obstructions and wind conditions.

l. Obtains and interprets takeoff and departure clearance.
m. Notes takeoff time.

2. Action. The examiner will:

a. Ask the applicant to explain reasons for checking items on the pre–takeoff check.
b. Observe the pre–takeoff check, and determine that the applicant's performance meets the objective.
c. Place emphasis on the applicant's ability to recognize discrepancies and to use sound judgment in making decisions related to the flight.

Objective: What's expected of the applicant regarding the pre-takeoff check.

Regarding the Explanation. As with the preflight inspection of the airplane, the explanation of the pre-takeoff check will involve little more than general observations regarding the purpose of the check and the use of a checklist. The reasons for checking the items will be related to each item as the pilot procedes through the checklist.

Performing the Pre-Takeoff Check. Doing a runup in a multiengine airplane involves all the elements of the runup in a single engine airplane. Because of the greater power, and as a consequence of having more than one engine, a little greater care may need to be exercised in positioning the airplane, dividing attention, and the like, but the general considerations will be the same.

The items in the objective list are illustrative only and need be of no particular concern because they will be covered by the operating handbook checklist that you will be using.

Takeoff Airspeeds and Distances. Although the critical airspeeds may have been covered during the oral examination phase of the practical test, you will be expected to review these prior to takeoff. They cannot be listed here, since they are particular to your airplane, but you will be expected to tick off such critical speeds as V_y, V_x, V_{mc}, and the like. You should also specify the speed at which you intend to rotate. Similarly, you will need to give the examiner some idea of critical distances involved. Again, these will have been discussed in the oral phase when you explained accelerate-stop and accelerate-go distances. As a part of the preflight check, speed and distance requirements will be related to the conditions that obtain at the time of your flight and include such factors as wind velocity and direction and density altitude.

Emergency Procedures. This will be a review of the takeoff procedures to be employed in the event of an engine-out emergency. The review will require familiarity with the operating handbook for your airplane. You will need to have clearly in mind the cockpit procedures to be followed in the event that you lose an engine on takeoff. Although some generalizations can be and have been offered, the operating handbook is indispensable. You can speak generally about what to do regarding the application of power, what to do about landing gear and flaps, and similar concerns, but you must know precisely what's required for your airplane. For example, if your airplane has only one hydraulic pump and that engine goes out, you need to be familiar with what's required of you in order to get the gear up. You must rely on the operating handbook for these procedures.

You'll already have discussed the normal operating airspeeds and, during the oral phase, the engine-out airspeeds. The examiner will expect you to review these—V_{mc}; V_{xse}; V_{yse}—immediately prior to taking off, not only to be sure that you know them, but also to ascertain that you're thinking about them at this point.

You should also have in mind—and specify for the examiner—the takeoff route that you would follow should an engine become inoperative during takeoff and after liftoff. The route should be very specific and described in detail to the examiner in order to clarify how you would plan to avoid any obstructions.

The balance of the pre-takeoff check is essentially the same as that required for any takeoff in any type of airplane.

Chapter 16

IV. AREA OF OPERATION:
AIRPORT AND TRAFFIC PATTERN OPERATIONS

A. TASK: RADIO COMMUNICATIONS AND ATC LIGHT SIGNALS
(AMEL)

> **NOTE:** Refer to the Private Pilot – Airplane Single–Engine Land Practical Test Standard.

B. TASK: TRAFFIC PATTERN OPERATIONS (AMEL)

> **NOTE:** Refer to the Private Pilot – Airplane Single–Engine Land Practical Test Standard.

C. TASK: AIRPORT AND RUNWAY MARKING AND LIGHTING
(AMEL)

NOTE: Refer to the Private Pilot – Airplane Single–Engine Land Practical Test Standard.

Chapter 17

V. AREA OF OPERATION:
TAKEOFFS AND CLIMBS

A. TASK: **NORMAL TAKEOFF AND CLIMB** (AMEL)

PILOT OPERATION – 5

REFERENCE: AC 61–21.

1. **Objective.** To determine that the applicant:

    a. Exhibits adequate knowledge by explaining the elements of a normal takeoff and climb profile including airspeeds, configurations, and emergency procedures.
    b. Aligns the airplane on the runway centerline.
    c. Advances the throttles smoothly to maximum allowable power.
    d. Checks the engine's instruments.
    e. Maintains directional control on the runway centerline.
    f. Rotates at the airspeed to attain lift–off at V_{MC} +5, V_{SSE}, or the

recommended [1] lift–off airspeed.

g. Establishes the single–engine, best rate–of–climb pitch attitude and accelerates to V_Y.

h. Establishes the all–engine best rate–of–climb pitch attitude when reaching V_Y and maintains $V_Y \pm 5$ knots, or $V_Y + 10$ knots, to avoid high pitch angles.

i. Retracts the wing flaps as recommended or at a safe altitude.

j. Retracts the landing gear after a positive rate of climb has been established and a safe landing cannot be made on the remaining runway, or as recommended.

k. Climbs at V_Y to 400 feet AGL or to a safe maneuvering altitude.

l. Maintains takeoff power to a safe maneuvering altitude.

m. Uses noise abatement procedures as required.

n. Establishes and maintains a cruise climb airspeed, ± 5 knots.

o. Maintains a straight track over the extended runway centerline until a turn is required.

p. Completes after–takeoff checklist.

2. Action. The examiner will:

a. Ask the applicant to explain the elements of a normal takeoff and climb profile including related safety factors.

b. Ask the applicant to perform a normal takeoff and climb, and determine that the applicant's performance meets the objective.

c. Place emphasis on the applicant's demonstration of correct airspeed, pitch, and heading control.

---

[1] The term "recommended" as used in this standard refers to the manufacturer's recommendation. If the manufacturer's recommendation is not available, the description contained in AC 61–21 will be used.

Objective: What's expected of the applicant regarding normal takeoffs and climbs.

Exhibiting Knowledge through Explanation. Most elements of a normal takeoff are the same whether in a multiengine or single engine airplane. At whatever airspeed is appropriate, the airplane is rotated, lifted off, and the proper attitude to achieve V_y is established. If obstacles must be cleared, then the attitude for V_x is established until obstacle clearance, at which point the V_y attitude is established. Flaps are retracted as recommended. Landing gear are retracted when a positive rate of climb is established and there is no longer any possibility of landing safely on the remaining runway. A straightout climb is continued at the recommended power setting. Finally, the after-takeoff checklist is completed.

Starting the Takeoff Roll. Power should be applied smoothly and steadily to maximum allowable power, as with a single engine airplane. The two (or more) throttles can be operated as a unit, so there's really no difference; it's essentially everything full forward: mixture, props, and throttle. If your bird has superchargers, then you must monitor the manifold pressure gauges during takeoff and set the throttles as recommended by the manufacturer. You have a few more gauges to watch now, because engine instruments are multiplied.

Maintaining Directional Control. As with single engine airplanes, directional control is generally maintained with the rudder and steerable nosewheel. At the very beginning of the run, some slight differential braking may be used. If the airplane is a taildragger, then the tailwheel may be locked after the airplane has rolled for a few feet in a straight line. As the airplane gathers speed and momentum increases, the pilot's heels should be on the floor and brakes should no longer be used. If a serious swing should begin, there's no alternative but to cut the throttles and bring the airplane to a stop. You can taxi back and try again; it's not a ride-busting maneuver.

Rotation. The speed at which you rotate is definite. While in a single engine airplane, you can simply establish the attitude for climbing and hold it while the airplane flies itself off the runway, no such practice can occur with the multiengine plane. The latter must be held on the runway until rotation speed is achieved. The objective also lists V_{sse}; that's the minimum steady flight airspeed at which the airplane is controllable on one engine. Check the operating handbook and use the speed recommended by the manufacturer. If no separate V_r is listed for your airplane, then use $V_{mc} + 5$ mph, which is the number recommended in AC61-21A.

Establishing Rate of Climb. In a single, you use just one attitude to establish V_y. In the multiengine airplane, you'll use the attitude that gives you V_{yse}, even though both mills are churning, and with that attitude you'll accelerate to V_y. Once you've achieved V_y, you can then alter the attitude a little to maintain V_y for all engines going. In order to provide better engine cooling and better visibility, the objective suggests adding 5 or 10 knots to V_y.

296

Retracting Flaps and Gear. The retraction of flaps and landing gear will follow the manufacturer's recommendations. But, as in any airplane, flaps will be retracted only at a safe altitude and then in increments. Landing gear will be retracted only after a positive climb rate has been established and there is insufficient runway remaining to put the airplane down again. These are generalizations and should not substitute for the manufacturer's recommendations.

Continuing the Climbout. The remainder of the requirements for the normal takeoff and climb are essentially the same as those for single engine airplanes. Where there are differences, such as reducing power from maximum takeoff power to METO, they will be covered in the operating handbook for your airplane. (In case you've forgotten, METO is the maximum climbing power, or maximum continuous power. The acronym represents "maximum except takeoff.")

B. TASK: CROSSWIND TAKEOFF AND CLIMB (AMEL)

PILOT OPERATION – 5

REFERENCE: AC 61–21.

1. **Objective.** To determine that the applicant:

    a. Exhibits adequate knowledge by explaining the elements of a crosswind takeoff and climb profile including airspeeds, configurations, and emergency procedures.

    b. Verifies the wind direction.

    c. Aligns the airplane on the runway centerline.

    d. Applies full aileron deflection in proper direction.

    e. Advances the throttles smoothly to the maximum allowable power using differential power as necessary to aid directional control.

    f. Checks the engines' instruments.

    g. Maintains directional control on the runway centerline.

    h. Adjusts aileron deflection during acceleration.

    i. Rotates at the airspeed to attain lift–off at V_{MC} +5, V_{SSE}, or the recommended lift–off airspeed and establishes wind–drift correction.

    j. Establishes the single–engine, best rate–of–climb pitch attitude and accelerates to V_Y.

    k. Establishes the all–engine best rate of climb pitch attitude when reaching V_Y and maintains V_Y, ±5 knots, or V_Y, +10 knots, to avoid high pitch angles.

    l. Retracts the wing flaps as recommended or at a safe altitude.

    m. Retracts the landing gear after a positive rate of climb has been established or a safe landing cannot be made on the remaining runway or as recommended.

n. Climbs at V_Y to 400 feet AGL or to a safe maneuvering altitude.

o. Maintains takeoff power to a safe maneuvering altitude.

p. Uses noise abatement procedures, as required.

q. Establishes and maintains a cruise climb airspeed, ±5 knots.

r. Maintains a straight track over the extended runway centerline until a turn is required.

s. Completes after–takeoff checklist.

2. Action. The examiner will:

a. Ask the applicant to explain the elements of a crosswind takeoff and climb profile including related safety factors.

b. Ask the applicant to perform a crosswind takeoff and climb, and determine that the applicant's performance meets the objective. (Note: If a crosswind condition does not exist, the applicant's knowledge of the TASK will be evaluated through oral questioning.)

c. Place emphasis on the applicant's demonstration of correct airspeed, pitch, heading, and drift control.

Objective: What's expected of the applicant regarding crosswind takeoffs and climbs.

Exhibiting Knowledge through Explanation. Most of the elements of crosswind takeoffs were presented in the single engine section. Since the multiengine is still an airplane, all of the steps described for single engine airplanes are applicable here as well. Crosswinds do not alter airspeeds; V_y, V_x, and V_{mc} remain the same. The configuration for the multiengine airplane is the same as for any other airplane. If there are any special precautions, they will be covered in the operating handbook for your airplane. Emergency procedures are not changed by the fact that you have a crosswind.

Accommodating to the Crosswind. As with any airplane, wind direction must be verified. The airplane will still be aligned with the runway centerline as it would be for any takeoff. The takeoff roll will begin with full aileron deflection. It is only when we come to the application of power that a difference emerges. In flying a multiengine airplane, the use of differential power is permissable and sometimes recommended. Particularly in the case of a tailwheel-type airplane, the power on the downwind engine may be reduced to overcome the tendency of the airplane to weathervane. But this use of differential power occurs only at the beginning of the takeoff roll. As the airplane attains the speed where controls are fully effective, full allowable power should be applied to both engines.

Continuing the Crosswind Takeoff and Climb. Aside from the application of differential power, the crosswind takeoff and climb in the light twin is the same as in other airplanes. Once the airplane has lifted off and a crabbing attitude is established to take care of wind drift, the crosswind takeoff and climb are essentially the same as any other. Hence, there is no need for repeating here the material that has been presented previously.

C. TASK: SHORT–FIELD TAKEOFF AND CLIMB (AMEL)

PILOT OPERATION – 8

REFERENCE: AC 61–21.

1. **Objective.** To determine that the applicant:

   a. Exhibits adequate knowledge by explaining the elements of a short–field takeoff and climb profile including the significance of appropriate airspeeds, configurations, emergency procedures, and expected performance for existing operating conditions.

   b. Positions the airplane at the beginning of the takeoff runway aligned on the runway centerline.

   c. Advances the throttles smoothly to maximum allowable power.

   d. Checks the engines' instruments.

   e. Adjusts the pitch attitude to attain maximum rate of acceleration.

   f. Maintains directional control on the runway centerline.

   g. Rotates at the airspeed to attain lift–off at V_{MC} +5 knots, V_X, or at the recommended airspeed, whichever is greater.

   h. Climbs at V_X or the recommended airspeed, whichever is greater (no lower than V_{MC}) until obstacle is cleared, or at least 50 feet above the surface, then accelerates to V_Y, and maintains V_Y, ±5 knots, or V_Y, +10 knots to avoid high pitch angles.

   i. Retracts the wing flaps as recommended or at a safe altitude.

   j. Retracts the landing gear after a positive rate of climb has been established or a safe landing cannot be made on the remaining runway or as recommended.

k. Climbs at V_Y to 400 feet AGL or to a safe maneuvering altitude.

l. Maintains takeoff power to the safe maneuvering altitude.

m. Uses noise abatement procedures as required.

n. Establishes and maintains a cruise climb airspeed, ±5 knots.

o. Maintains a straight track over the extended runway centerline until a turn is required.

p. Completes after–takeoff checklist.

2. Action. The examiner will:

a. Ask the applicant to explain the elements of a a short–field takeoff and climb profile including expected airplane performance for takeoff.

b. Ask the applicant to perform a short–field takeoff and climb, and determine that the applicant's performance meets the objective.

c. Place emphasis on the applicant's demonstration of correct airspeed, pitch, and heading control.

Objective: What's expected of the applicant regarding short-field takeoffs and climbs.

Exhibiting Knowledge through Explanation. Your explanation of short-field takeoffs will exhibit some differences from that for normal takeoffs and climbs. You must let the examiner know that you understand that the airspeed that you'll climb at will be V_x rather than V_y. You must also demonstrate awareness that on some light twins, V_x is less than V_{mc}. Now, this poses a real problem since, if you were to lose an engine, you would not be able to maintain control unless you reduced power on the good engine—not a happy situation. You'd simply have to resort to V_{mc} + 5, even if that doesn't completely solve the problem. Remember, when the manufacturer sets the V_{mc}, it only means that the airplane can be controlled at that airspeed; it doesn't mean that the plane will climb. And, if you're at gross, and the density altitude is . . . well, let's not get morbid. This explanation is about possibilities. But you'd better have read the operating handbook so that you know what the possibilities are for your airplane.

Accommodating to the Short Field. Much of the short-field takeoff and climb is the same for the multiengine as it is for the single engine airplane. It's essential to be at the end of the runway, so line that airplane up with the main wheels right on the very edge of the runway. Don't sacrifice an inch. Power is applied steadily and smoothly to maximum allowable power. Sounds pretty much the same, doesn't it?

As with a single engine airplane, you'll establish a pitch, or attitude, that gives you the lowest possible angle of attack in order to attain the maximum rate of acceleration. Directional control for this procedure is essentially the same as for all takeoffs and climbs.

Rotation. For the short-field takeoff, rotation will be at V_x rather than V_y, if such a speed is possible. However, if the manual indicates that V_x is a lower airspeed than V_{mc}, then you have no alternative but to use the standard $V_{mc} + 5$. Now, it's one thing to say "rotate," and quite another matter to say what you rotate to. In this case, when you rotate, you raise the nose to the attitude that gives you V_x, if that's above V_{mc}.

Climbing Out. Having rotated to establish the attitude for best angle-of-climb airspeed (or $V_{mc} + 5$), you maintain that attitude in order to lift off and climb at the appropriate speed. The attitude, which results in your climbing out with the nose somewhat higher than usual, should be maintained until the airplane is clear of the obstacle. At safe maneuvering altitude, the nose can be pitched down in order to allow the airplane to accelerate to V_y or to enroute climb speed. At this point, power controls should be adjusted to whatever constitutes normal or cruise climb.

From this point on, the short-field takeoff and climb becomes just another takeoff and climb.

Chapter 18

VI. AREA OF OPERATION:
CROSS–COUNTRY FLYING

A. TASK: PILOTAGE AND DEAD RECKONING (AMEL)

NOTE: Refer to the Private Pilot – Airplane Single–Engine Land Practical Test Standard.

B. TASK: RADIO NAVIGATION (AMEL)

NOTE: Refer to the Private Pilot – Airplane Single–Engine Land Practical Test Standard.

C. TASK: DIVERSION TO ALTERNATE (AMEL)

NOTE: Refer to the Private Pilot – Airplane Single–Engine Land Practical Test Standard.

D. TASK: **LOST PROCEDURES** (AMEL)

NOTE: Refer to the Private Pilot – Airplane Single–Engine Land Practical Test Standard.

Chapter 19

VII. AREA OF OPERATION:
FLIGHT BY REFERENCE TO INSTRU–MENTS

A. TASK: STRAIGHT–AND–LEVEL FLIGHT (AMEL)

NOTE: Refer to the Private Pilot – Airplane Single–Engine Land Practical Test Standard.

B. TASK: STRAIGHT, CONSTANT–AIRSPEED CLIMBS (AMEL)

NOTE: Refer to the Private Pilot – Airplane Single–Engine Land Practical Test Standard.

C. TASK: STRAIGHT, CONSTANT–AIRSPEED DESCENTS (AMEL)

NOTE: Refer to the Private Pilot –

Airplane Single–Engine Land
Practical Test Standard.

D. TASK: TURNS TO HEADINGS (AMEL)

> **NOTE:**   Refer to the Private Pilot –
> Airplane Single–Engine Land
> Practical Test Standard.

E. TASK: CRITICAL FLIGHT ATTITUDES
(AMEL)

> **NOTE:**   Refer to the Private Pilot –
> Airplane Single –Engine
> Land Practical Test
> Standard.

* **F. TASK: RADIO AIDS AND
RADAR SERVICES** (AMEL)   *

> **NOTE:**   Refer to the Private Pilot –
> Airplane Single –Engine
> Land Practical Test
> Standard.

Chapter 20

VIII. AREA OF OPERATION:
INSTRUMENT FLIGHT

NOTE: If an applicant holds a private pilot certificate with an airplane single–engine land and instrument rating and seeks to add an airplane multiengine land rating, the applicant is required to demonstrate competency in all TASKS of AREA OF OPERATION VIII.

If the applicant elects not to demonstrate competency in instrument flight, the applicant's multiengine privileges will be limited to VFR only. To remove this restriction, the pilot must demonstrate competency in this area of operation.

If the applicant elects to demonstrate competency in the TASKS of AREA OF OPERATION VIII, then fails one or more of those TASKS, the applicant will have failed the practical test. After the test is initiated, the applicant will not be permitted to revert to the "VFR only" option.

A. TASK: ENGINE FAILURE DURING STRAIGHT–AND–LEVEL FLIGHT AND TURNS (AMEL)

PILOT OPERATION – 10

REFERENCES: AC 61–21, AC 61–27.

1. **Objective.** To determine that the applicant:

   a. Exhibits adequate knowledge by explaining the reasons for the procedures used if engine failure occurs during straight–and–level flight and turns while on instruments.

   b. Recognizes engine failure promptly during straight–and–level flight and during standard–rate turns.

   c. Sets the engine controls, reduces drag, and identifies and verifies the inoperative engine.

   d. Establishes the best engine inoperative airspeed and trims the airplane.

   e. Verifies the prescribed checklist procedures for securing the inoperative engine.

   f. Establishes and maintains a bank toward the operating engine as required for best performance in straight–and–level flight.

   g. Maintains a bank angle as required for best performance in a turn of approximately standard rate.

   h. Attempts to determine the reason for the engine malfunction.

   i. Maintains an altitude or a minimum sink rate sufficient to continue flight considering –

      (1) density altitude.
      (2) service ceiling.
      (3) gross weight.
      (4) elevation of terrain and obstructions.

   j. Monitors the operating engine and makes

necessary adjustments.

k. Maintains the desired altitude ±100 feet, if within the airplane's capability, the desired airspeed ±10 knots, and the desired heading ±10° if in straight flight.

l. Recognizes the airplane's performance capability and decides an appropriate action to ensure a safe landing.

m. Avoids imminent loss of control or attempted flight contrary to the single–engine operating limitations of the airplane.

2. Action. The examiner will:

a. Ask the applicant to explain the reasons for the procedures used if engine failure occurs during straight–and–level flight and turns.

b. Reduce power to zero thrust on an engine during straight–and–level flight and during a standard–rate turn, and determine that the applicant's performance meets the objective.

c. Place emphasis on the applicant's correct performance of emergency procedures on instruments including maintaining the turn if engine failure occurs during this maneuver.

Objective: What's expected of the applicant regarding flight solely by reference to instruments.

Exhibiting Knowledge through Explanation. If you are simply adding the multiengine airplane rating to your Private Pilot Certificate, and you do not hold an instrument rating, then you will be expected to provide no more than is required for the single engine airplane explanation of instrument flight. In such a case, the examiner will probably ask only those questions that would be asked of any private pilot applicant, i.e., queries regarding how you would handle flying into bad weather inadvertently. Your explanation will be restricted mainly to what would be required in order to do a 180-degree turn and get back to where the weather was VFR. If you elect to add a demonstration of competence in instrument flying, you should refer to a manual on instrument flight checks in addition to reading the FAA material on Practical Test Standards. Such material is too comprehensive to be included in a guide for a private pilot's license and will not be included here. Instead, it is recommended that you consult one of the excellent TAB manuals on instrument flight.

Demonstrating Competence. For the multiengine rating for the Private Pilot Certificate, you would be expected to demonstrate those items that are called for in the Flight By Reference to Instruments Only portion of the single engine section of this guide. Since multiengine as well as single engine pilots can inadvertently find themselves in weather below VFR minima, the examiner needs to know that you have the knowledge and skills to extricate yourself from such a situation. Consequently, you will probably be called on to do a little straight-and-level flight, climbs and descents, and turns with all mills going. These maneuvers have been described in the single engine section and you may refer to that section to review what you will be called on to do while under the hood.

Engine Failure during Straight-and-Level and Turns. During that part of the practical test in which you're demonstrating your capabilities in hood work, you will probably be given some engine-out practice. The Task that is described in the FAA Practical Test Standards is not intended precisely for you. However, reviewing parts of the Objective may be of some help to you. Even though you will not be checked to the extent that an instrument pilot applicant would, the items listed can provide some guidance. While under the hood, you would be expected to recognize engine failure as you would on any other occasion by noting the direction of yaw (toward the dead engine) and the extra rudder pressure that needs to be exerted on the operating engine side.

From this point on, you would go through essentially the same procedures that you went through while flying visually. The Objective lists the essentials, setting engine controls appropriately, establishing and maintaining the proper airspeed, establishing a bank of at least five degrees toward the good engine, etc. As you know from having practiced this during training, these matters become more challenging during hood work because of the need for closely monitoring the attitude indicator, DG, altimeter, and airspeed indicator more closely while performing all the tasks required for transitioning to and maintaining flight with an engine inoperative.

Regarding the Explanation. Prior to putting you under the hood, the examiner will ask you some questions regarding flight solely by reference to instruments. These will be related to such matters as how to recognize having lost an engine when you have no outside references, and what the appropriate response to such a dilemma would be. He/she will not require you to respond in the way an instrument applicant would. Your examiner will be satisfied by responses that indicate that the signs of engine failure are the same whether in VFR conditions or below minima. What he/she will expect is for you to recognize that you are not an instrument pilot, that you're not on an instrument flight plan, and that you probably don't know whether or not the airplane is legal for instrument flight. All of this means that the examiner wants you to explain how you'd get out of the situation if you inadvertently flew into bad weather and lost an engine while trying to extricate yourself.

The Performance. You'll be called on to demonstrate that you can fly that light twin straight and level while under the hood. You'll also be required to do some climbs and descents and turns with the airplane in various configurations, just as single engine applicants have to do. At some point during this performance, you can expect the examiner to reduce power to zero thrust on one of the engines—probably the critical engine—and have you perform a similar set of maneuvers after going through the appropriate engine-out procedures for your airplane.

The Emphasis. The focus for this hood work will be on your prompt recognition of and correct response to engine failure. Following this, the emphasis is going to be solely on your ability to control the airplane both with all mills churning and with an engine out while you are under the hood.

The following excerpts from the FAA's Private Pilot Practical Test Standards are included only as a rough reference and because they are a part of the FAA guide. However, since they refer to the requirements for an instrument rating, which are too complex for a Private Pilot Practical Test Guide of this type, no explanations will be provided here.

B. TASK: INSTRUMENT APPROACH – ALL ENGINES OPERATING
(AMEL)

PILOT OPERATION – 6

REFERENCES: AC 61–21, AC 61–27.

1. **Objective.** To determine that the applicant:

   a. Exhibits adequate knowledge of cockpit management by explaining the multiengine procedures used for a published instrument approach with all engines operating.

   b. Requests and receives an actual or a simulated clearance for an instrument approach.

   c. Follows instructions and instrument approach procedures correctly.

   d. Determines the appropriate rate of descent considering wind and the designated missed approach point.

 * **e.** Descends on course so as to arrive at the * DH or MDA, whichever is appropriate, in a position from which a normal landing can be made straight–in or circling.

   f. Maintains the desired airspeed, ± 10 knots.

 * **g.** Avoids full scale deflection on the CDI or * glide slope indicators, descent below minimums, or exceeding the radius of turn as dictated by the visibility minimums.

   h. Executes a missed approach at the designated missed approach point and follows appropriate checklist items for airplane cleanup.

   i. Communicates with ATC properly.

2. **Action.** The examiner will:

   a. Ask the applicant to explain the multiengine

313

procedures used for an instrument approach with all engines operating.

b. Ask the applicant to perform an instrument approach and missed approach with all engines operating, and determine that the applicant's performance meets the objective.

c. Place emphasis on the applicant's positive control of the airplane during an instrument approach.

C. TASK: INSTRUMENT APPROACH — ONE ENGINE INOPERATIVE
(AMEL)

PILOT OPERATION – 10

REFERENCES: AC 61–21, AC 61–27.

1. **Objective.** To determine that the applicant:

   a. Exhibits adequate knowledge by explaining the multiengine procedures used during a published instrument approach with one engine inoperative.

   b. Recognizes engine failure promptly.

   c. Sets the engine controls, reduces drag, and identifies and verifies the inoperative engine.

   d. Establishes the best engine–inoperative airspeed and trims the airplane.

   e. Verifies the prescribed checklist procedures for securing the inoperative engine.

   f. Establishes and maintains a bank toward the operating engine as required for best performance.

   g. Attempts to determine the reason for the engine malfunction.

   h. Requests and receives an actual or simulated clearance for a published instrument approach with one engine inoperative.

   i. Follows instructions and instrument approach procedures correctly.

   j. Recites the missed approach procedure and decides on the point at which the approach will continue or discontinue considering the performance capability of the airplane.

   k. Descends on course so as to arrive at the DH or MDA, whichever is appropriate, in a

position from which a normal landing can
be made straight–in or circling. ✶

l. Maintains the desired airspeed, ±10 knots.
m. Avoids full–scale deflection on the CDI or
glide slope indicators, descent below
minimums, or exceeding the radius of turn
as dictated by the visibility minimums. ✶
n. Communicates with ATC properly.
o. Completes a safe landing.

2. Action. The examiner will –

a. Ask the applicant to explain the
multiengine procedures used during an
instrument approach with one engine
inoperative.
b. Ask the applicant to perform an approach,
simulate an engine failure, by setting one
engine at zero thrust, and determine that
the applicant's performance meets the
objective.
c. Place emphasis on the applicant's positive
control of the airplane during an
instrument approach with one engine
inoperative.

Chapter 21

IX. AREA OF OPERATION:
FLIGHT AT CRITICALLY SLOW AIRSPEEDS

❋**NOTE:** No stall will be performed with one engine throttled or inoperative and the other engine(s) developing effective power.   ❋

Full stalls using high–power settings have been deleted from the multiengine practical test because of excessive high pitch angles necessary to induce these stalls which may result in uncontrollable flight.

❋   Examiners and instructors should be alert to the possible development of high sink rates when performing stalls in multiengine airplanes with high wing loadings; therefore, a maximum loss of 50 feet during entries has been incorporated in these TASKS.   ❋

A. TASK: STALLS,GEAR–UP AND FLAPS–UP (AMEL)

PILOT OPERATION – 4
REFERENCE: AC 61–21.

1. **Objective.**   To determine that the applicant:

   a. Exhibits adequate knowledge by explaining the aerodynamic factors associated with stalls, gear up and flaps up, and an awareness of stall speed in the configuration, power, pitch, and bank required, and the procedure for resuming normal flight.

   b. Selects an entry altitude that will allow recoveries to be completed no lower than 3,000 feet AGL.

   c. Stabilize the airplane at approach airspeed in level flight with a gear–up, flaps–up configuration and appropriate power setting.

   d. Establishes a pitch attitude, straight ahead and in 20° (±10°) bank turns, that will induce a stall with a power setting to maintain altitude +150 feet, –50 feet, during stall entry.

   e. Applies proper control to maintain coordinated flight.

   f. Recognizes and recovers from stalls at the first indication of buffeting or decay of control effectiveness by immediately reducing angle of attack and increasing power.

   g. Returns to entry airspeed and configuration.

   h. Avoids full stalls, excessive pitch change, excessive altitude loss, spirals, spins, or flight below 3,000 feet AGL.

2. **Action.**   The examiner will:

   a. Ask the applicant to explain the aerodynamic factors associated with stalls, gear up and flaps up.

   b. Ask the applicant to perform stalls with

gear up and flaps up in straight flight and turning flight, and determine that the applicant's performance meets the objective.

c. Place emphasis on the applicant's ability to promptly recognize and recover from stalls with gear up and flaps up.

Objective: What's expected of the applicant regarding stalls with gear and flaps up.

Exhibiting Knowledge through Explanation. You must demonstrate familiarity with the stall characteristics of the airplane being flown. The point of such familiarity is not to produce a pilot who has developed expertise in performing stalls. It is to assure that pilots recognize the signs of an imminent stall and respond appropriately. The series of stalls with the multiengine airplane clean (landing gear and flaps retracted) simulates stalls occurring during normal or cruising flight or with the airplane in the configuration of normal flight. The explanation of the aerodynamic factors associated with stalls that is provided for single engine stalls with the airplane clean are applicable as well to multiengine airplanes.

The procedures involved are also essentially the same for multiengine as for single engine airplanes. However, your explanation should indicate your understanding that multiengine airplanes, being larger and heavier, will respond more slowly to recovery procedures. Also, the multiengine airplanes, being more complex, give the pilot more to do and to observe. You will be expected to state the stalling airspeed for a given configuration, power setting, and bank and to describe the appropriate recovery procedures. The procedures are essentially the same as for single engine airplanes, i.e., reducing the angle of attack, leveling the wings, and increasing power. However, for your explanations you should rely on the descriptions of stalls and stall recovery provided in the operating handbook for your airplane.

Entry Altitude. Notice that the objective calls for selecting an altitude permitting recovery completion 3000 feet AGL or higher. This is related to the fact that the heavier airplanes respond more slowly, resulting in greater altitude loss during stall maneuvers.

Preparing for the Stall. The first series of stalls will be performed with the airplane clean. You will establish the same entry airspeed for all stall maneuvers, the approach airspeed for your airplane. For clean stalls, you need do nothing about configuration. Prior to "setting up," however, you will have done clearing turns to the left and right. Then get your approach airspeed by adding back pressure to the yoke. To avoid "ballooning," reduce the power to about 65 percent, or whatever is required for your airplane.

Performing the Stall. Most likely your initial stalls will be straight ahead. When the airspeed becomes stabilized at approach airspeed, begin gradually to apply back pressure on the yoke to raise the nose sufficiently to induce a stall. The pitch change should not be abrupt, only enough to reduce the airspeed by about one knot per second. This will avoid abnormally nose-high attitudes. Clean stalls will also be performed from turns. In these instances, prior to starting the application of back pressure on the yoke, the airplane will be gradually rolled into a coordinated turn with a bank of about 20 degrees. Then, when the bank and turn are stabilized, back pressure will be applied sufficiently to induce a stall. You will most likely be required to perform imminent stalls from turns in both directions.

Maintaining Proper Control. As with single engine airplanes, the ball should be centered throughout the maneuver. The objective's reference to maintaining controlled flight means avoid slipping or skidding that might result in spirals or spins should a full stall occur during the demonstration. An excessively nose-high attitude coupled with a slip or skid could result in uncontrollable flight. A part of the coordination of controls also includes engine and propeller controls. Stall demonstrations are to be conducted with all engines going. Therefore, power applications to all engines will be the same. This, too, is to avoid the risk of uncontrollable flight. Examiners do not like to experience terror on practical tests.

Recovery. Unlike stall demonstrations in single engine airplanes, the multiengine demonstrations do not require full stalls. Consequently, instead of waiting for a break to occur, the recovery procedures are initiated when you get the first indications of a stall, or when the yoke is all the way back. The first thing you'll do, of course, is lower the nose to immediately reduce the angle of attack. If the imminent stall has been conducted with the airplane banked and turning, the wings will be leveled.

Return to Entry Speed and Configuration. The changes in attitude should be accomplished immediately, but not abruptly. Throughout the stall maneuvers, controls should be handled smoothly and with coordination. After the nose has been lowered to "unstall" the wings, and the wings leveled, the airplane should be returned to an attitude that produces the airspeed used for entering the stall procedures.

Avoiding Excesses. The final item should require no explanation. It has already been made clear that these are to be imminent and not full stalls. Suggestions were made as to how to avoid excessive pitch changes. If recovery is initiated promptly, altitude loss will be kept to a minimum. Spirals and spins can be avoided by maintaining controlled and coordinated flight. The latter can be avoided by attention to power settings and monitoring instruments to prevent slipping and skidding.

B. TASK: STALLS, GEAR DOWN AND APPROACH FLAPS (AMEL)

PILOT OPERATION – 4

REFERENCE: AC 61–21.

1. **Objective.** To determine that the applicant:

   a. Exhibits adequate knowledge by explaining the aerodynamic factors associated with stalls, gear down and approach flaps, and an awareness of stall speed in the configuration, power, pitch, and bank required, and the procedure for resuming normal flight.

   b. Selects an entry altitude that will allow recoveries to be completed no lower than 3,000 feet AGL.

   c. Stabilizes the airplane at approach airspeed in level flight with a gear down and approach flap configuration and appropriate power setting.

   ✽ d. Establishes a pitch attitude straight ahead, and in 20°, ±10°, bank turns, that will induce a stall with a power setting to maintain altitude +150 feet, –50 feet, during stall entries. ✽

   e. Applies proper control to maintain coordinated flight.

   f. Recognizes and recovers from stalls at the first indication of buffeting or decay of control effectiveness by immediately reducing angle of attack and increasing power.

   g. Returns to entry airspeed and configuration.

   h. Avoids full stalls, excessive pitch change, excessive altitude loss, spirals, spins, or flight below 3,000 feet AGL.

2. **Action.** The examiner will:

a. Ask the applicant to explain aerodynamic factors associated with stalls, gear down and approach flaps.

b. Ask the applicant to perform stalls with gear down and approach flaps in straight flight and turning flight, and determine that the applicant's performance meets the objective.

c. Place emphasis on the applicant's ability to promptly recognize and recover from stalls with gear down and approach flaps.

Objective: What's expected of the applicant regarding stalls with gear and flaps extended.

Exhibiting Knowledge through Explanation. Very little will need to be added to the prior explanation. You'll already have covered the essentials of aerodynamics and other matters. What needs to be added here are the items that distinguish these from clean stalls. Explain that lowering the gear does not affect the stalling speed: it simply slows the airplane more, reducing the airspeed to stalling speed more quickly. The addition of flap extension will alter the stalling airspeed. You will need to consult the operating handbook of your airplane for this information. Having landing gear and flaps extended will also alter the recovery procedures. Again, consult the operating handbook of your airplane for these procedures, although, generally, they will be the same as for single engine airplanes, i.e., retraction of flaps and then gear. This could be altered by circumstances, however, necessitating your being familiar with the manufacturer's requirements.

Selecting Altitude and Preparing the Airplane. The altitude selection requirement is no different here. As for preparing the airplane, you will need to establish the approach airspeed with gear and flaps extended. Begin by slowing the airplane until you are able to extend the landing gear and then the flaps. Flaps are to be extended only to the setting used for approaches. (Consult the operating handbook for flap setting.) With the airplane properly configured, apply only enough back pressure to raise the nose sufficiently to establish approach airspeed. This should be accomplished with essentially the same power setting used for the previous imminent stalls.

Performing the Stall. Again, imminent stalls will be induced with a very gradual change in pitch, or attitude, and will be accomplished both straight ahead and from turns in both directions. As with the previous stalls, you'll be expected to maintain controlled and coordinated flight throughout.

Recovery. Once again, at the first signs of an impending stall, recovery procedures should be initiated. As with any stall, the first step is getting the nose down to reduce the angle of attack. If in a turn, level the wings.

Follow this with the application of power. All of these procedures should be accomplished quickly but not abruptly. Finally, the airplane should be cleaned up—generally flaps first, then gear. Circumstances can alter cases, however, and you should consult the operating handbook to be able to respond to whatever the examiner is simulating. There may be a difference in what you'd do, depending on whether you're simulating an imminent stall while turning from base to final, or an imminent stall occurring as you're instituting a go-around after "crossing the fence."

The Rest of It. From this point on, the stall recovery and return to normal flight involves the same procedures as for the preceding stall maneuvers.

C. TASK: STALLS, GEAR DOWN AND FULL FLAPS (AMEL)

PILOT OPERATION – 4

REFERENCE: AC 61–21.

1. **Objective.** To determine that the applicant:

   a. Exhibits adequate knowledge by explaining the aerodynamic factors associated with stalls, gear down and full flaps, and an awareness of stall speed in the configuration, power, pitch, and bank required, and the procedure for resuming normal flight.

   b. Selects an entry altitude that will allow recoveries to be completed no lower than 3,000 feet AGL.

   c. Stabilizes the airplane at approach airspeed in level flight with a gear down and full flaps configuration and appropriate power setting.

   d. Establishes a pitch attitude straight ahead, and in 20°, ±10°, bank turns, that will induce a stall with a power setting to maintain altitude +150 feet, –50 feet, during stall entry. ✳

   e. Applies proper control to maintain coordinated flight.

   f. Recognizes and recovers from stalls at the first indication of buffeting or decay of control effectiveness by immediately reducing angle of attack and increasing power.

   g. Returns to entry airspeed and configuration.

   h. Avoids full stalls, excessive pitch change, excessive altitude loss, spirals, spins, or flight below 3,000 feet AGL.

2. **Action.** The examiner will:

   a. Ask the applicant to explain the aerodynamic

factors associated with stalls, gear down and full flaps.

b. Ask the applicant to perform stalls with gear down and full flaps in straight flight and turning flight, and determine that the applicant's performance meets the objective.

c. Place emphasis on the applicant's ability to promptly recognize and recover from stalls with gear down and full flaps.

Objective: What's expected of the applicant regarding stalls with landing gear down and full flaps.

Exhibiting Knowledge through Explanation. There'll be little for you to add this time. Obviously, there will be a different set of stalling speeds because of your having flaps fully extended. Recovery might take slightly longer as a consequence of your having to retract the flaps from their full setting. And, depending on circumstances, you might be required to retract them in increments to avoid abrupt and excessive changes in pitch.

Performing the Stall. This series of stalls will be so similar to the preceding stalls that there is no need to repeat the procedures.

D. TASK: MANEUVERING AT MINIMUM CONTROLLABLE AIRSPEED
(AMEL)

PILOT OPERATION – 4

REFERENCE: AC 61–21.

NOTE: Examiners, instructors, and applicants should be cautioned that maneuvering at minimum controllable airpeed may be at a speed below V_{MC}, and should be alert to recovery procedures if an engine fails at this speed.

1. **Objective.** To determine that the applicant:

   a. Exhibits adequate knowledge by explaining the flight characteristics and controllability associated with maneuvering at minimum controllable airspeeds.

   b. Selects an entry altitude that will allow the maneuver to be performed no lower than 3,000 feet AGL.

   c. Establishes and maintains the airspeed at which any further increase in angle of attack, resulting from an increase in load factor or reduction in power, would result in an immediate stall or the activation of a stall warning device while –

      (1) in coordinated straight and turning flight in various configurations and bank angles, and

      (2) in coordinated departure climbs and landing approach descents in various configurations.

   d. Maintains the desired altitude, ±100 feet, when a constant altitude is specified, and level off from climbs and descents, ±100 feet.

   e. Maintains the desired heading during straight flight ±10°.

f. Maintains the specified bank angle ±10° in coordinated flight.

g. Maintains minimum controllable airspeed + 5, –0 knots.

h. Recognizes buffet if it occurs and recovers immediately.

2. **Action.** The examiner will:

a. Ask the applicant to explain the flight characteristics and controllability involved in flight at minimum controllable airspeed.

b. Ask the applicant to perform flight at minimum controllable airspeed, specifying the configuration and maneuver, and determine that the applicant's performance meets the objective.

c. Place emphasis on the applicant's ability to recognize minimum controllable airspeed and to maintain correct airplane control.

Objective: What's expected of the applicant regarding maneuvering at minimum controllable airspeed.

Exhibiting Knowledge through Explanation. Your explanation of flight at minimum controllable airspeeds in a multiengine airplane will not differ greatly from that offered for single engine craft. The flight attitude of the airplane is similar, namely nose-high, and as with single engine airplanes, control effectiveness diminishes and the airplane responds more sluggishly. There is one significant difference, however, and you must let the examiner know that you realize this. During flight at minimum controllable airspeeds in a multiengine airplane, the airspeed becomes more critical simply because it may be less than V_{mc}. If you let the examiner know that you understand this, he/she will breathe somewhat easier during this part of the checkride. If your explanation includes the procedures for responding to losing an engine while performing this maneuver, then he/she may be positively relaxed.

Selecting an Altitude. While you're up there doing stalls, you'll be at an appropriate altitude for flight at minimum controllable airspeed. So, when directed, or after the last stall, climb back up to the altitude you used for entries to stalls and you'll be ready for this demonstration. Well, if you're not ready, the altitude will be right, anyway.

Establishing Minimum Controllable Airspeed. With the power reduced to maintain altitude, apply back pressure to the yoke and begin to reduce your airspeed. As with stalls, this change in attitude and the resulting decrease in airspeed should be gradual. The speed should be decreased to about 5 to 10 knots above stalling airspeed. The objective calls for an airspeed at which any further increase in angle of attack would result in either a stall or the activation of a stall warning device. Since most stall warning devices are set to go off at about five knots above the published stalling speed for the airplane, you'll need to remain above that airspeed.

With the airspeed stabilized, and the airplane clean, you'll be required to fly straight and level and in turns. You'll also be expected to initiate and maintain departure climbs and approach descents at that same airspeed.

When you've demonstrated that you can perform those maneuvers at minimum controllable airspeed with the airplane clean, you'll then be required to go through the same maneuvers with various flaps settings. You'll also be required to do the maneuvers with landing gear extended. And you will be expected to perform straight-and-level flight, turns, climbs, and descents in various combinations of gear and flap extensions.

Maintaining Desired Altitude. While you're performing the straight and level and turning maneuvers in various configurations, still maintaining something acceptably near the minimum controllable airspeed, you'll also be expected to hold altitude within a range of plus or minus 100 feet. And when called on to do the climbs and descents, you'll need to level off within plus or minus 100 feet of the specified altitude.

Maintaining Heading. As though all of the above weren't enough, you'll also be expected to wander no farther off a heading than 10 degrees in either direction.

Maintaining Bank Angles. With everything else going on, you must also, during turns, stay within 10 degrees of the bank angle that the examiner specifies.

Maintaining Minimum Controllable Airspeed. While accomplishing all of the above—straight-and-level flight and turns, climbs, and descents, all done with airplane clean as well as with various combinations of gear down and flaps extended—the examiner will expect you to exceed the minimum controllable airspeed by no more than about five knots. You can't let the airspeed drop below the established airspeed because you're supposed to do all of the maneuvering without any horns going off or the airplane stalling.

Recovering, If Necessary. If any signs of an imminent stall appear, you must recover immediately. Having already performed all of those stalls, you know all the proper procedures for stall recovery. But suppose, in the midst of all this, one of the engines decides to stop churning. Since you're probably already below V_{mc}, *you must immediately reduce power on the operating engine and bank toward that engine.* That will help you to maintain control. The next stop, of course, is to lower the nose in order to increase the airspeed above V_{mc}. The rest of the procedure will be detailed in the following set of tasks.

Chapter 22

X. AREA OF OPERATION:
TURN MANEUVERS

A. TASK: CONSTANT–ALTITUDE TURNS (AMEL)

PILOT OPERATION – 2

REFERENCE: AC 61–21.

1. **Objective.** To determine that the applicant:

   a. Exhibits adequate knowledge by explaining the performance factors associated with constant–altitude turns including increased load factors, power required, and overbanking tendency.

   b. Selects an altitude that will allow the maneuver to be performed no lower than 3,000 feet AGL.

   c. Establishes an airspeed which does not exceed the airplane's design maneuvering airspeed.

d. Enters a 180° or 360° turn maintaining a bank angle of 40° to 50° in coordinated flight.
   e. Divides attention between airplane control and orientation.
   f. Rolls out ±20° of the desired heading.
   g. Maintains the desired altitude, ±200 feet, and airspeed, ±10 knots.

2. Action. The examiner will:

   a. Ask the applicant to explain the performance factors associated with constant–altitude turns.
   b. Ask the applicant to perform constant–altitude turns and specify amount of turn and roll–out heading, and determine that the applicant's performance meets the objective.
   c. Place emphasis on the applicant's ability to control pitch and bank, and maintain coordinated flight.

Objective: What's expected of the applicant regarding turn maneuvers. **Exhibiting Knowledge through Explanation.** Turns in a multiengine airplane are not significantly different than turns in the single engine trainer you probably first learned to fly. At any rate, the aerodynamic factors are the same. Consequently, the explanations that served for the single engine section will do as well here. Load factors increase in turns whether in a single engine or multiengine airplane. Since load factors increase, it may be necessary to add power to overcome the extra "weight" imposed by turning maneuvers and avoid altitude loss.

Considering that the constant-altitude turns will involve steep banks, the multiengine airplane, just like the single engine plane, will have a tendency to continue to roll when the bank is established, i.e., to overbank. This tendency is overcome in the same way whether you are in a single engine or a multiengine airplane.

One small addition may be made to the explanation presented in the single engine section: In the multiengine airplane, it will be more important to retrim for each change in attitude or power setting during the turn maneuvers. It will make your job of maintaining a constant altitude easier because you'll be fighting the airplane less. Make sure that your explanation clarifies that you understand that this is more a factor of increased weight than of the number of engines.

Selecting an Altitude. Only the constant-altitude turns will be performed at or above 3000 feet AGL. All the other turn maneuvers will be at the altitudes used for single engine demonstrations.

Establishing Airspeed. You will need to check the operating handbook for your airplane for guidance in establishing the appropriate airspeed. In some airplanes, you may be able to perform the steep turns at normal cruising airspeeds. In others, this would exceed the maneuvering airspeed, requiring that you use this rather than normal cruising airspeed. Check it out.

Establishing the Bank and Turn. After clearing the area, you'll roll into a bank of about 45 degrees, adding a touch of power to overcome the "weight" added by centrifugal force and to keep the altitude constant. Hopefully, your practice for the checkride will have made you thoroughly familiar with the airplane's attitude in relation to outside references during these maneuvers. You'll probably be required to do some steep 180-degree turns in both directions, followed by steep 360-degree turns in both directions. If you've learned to fly the airplane by attitude, these turns should not present a problem. As long as you maintain the same slightly increased power setting and keep the nose of the airplane at the same spot in relation to the horizon all the way through the turn, you should have no difficulty with either altitude or airspeed.

Dividing Your Attention. The number of engines makes no difference here, except for the number of inside references. Most of your attention should be on the outside of the airplane where you'll monitor the airplane's position in relation to the horizon. But you'll also need to make periodic checks of what's going on inside. Monitor the instruments to see that your bank is constant, your altitude is what it should be, and your airspeed remains steady. The scanning of the instruments is to back up what the outside references are telling you.

Rolling Out on the Heading. You know that it's necessary to begin to roll out of the turn prior to reaching the desired heading whether you're in a single engine trainer or a light twin. Since the twin is larger and heavier, response will be a little slower. This simply means that you begin the rollout a few degrees ahead of where you'd begin it in the single engine trainer. But since you're given a 20-degree leeway on either side of the heading, you should not experience difficulty.

Maintaining Altitude and Airspeed. During the steep turns, you're required to stay within 10 knots of the desired airspeed, a function of attitude, and within 200 feet in either direction of the desired altitude, and that's a function of power setting. The latter means adding a little power as you roll into the turn and remembering to reduce it as you're rolling out.

B. TASK: **DESCENDING TURNS** (AMEL)

> **NOTE:** Refer to the Private Pilot –
> Airplane Single–Engine Land
> Practical Test Standard.

Chapter 23

XI. AREA OF OPERATION:
FLIGHT MANEUVERING BY REFER–
ENCE TO GROUND OBJECTS

A. TASK: RECTANGULAR COURSE
(AMEL)

NOTE: Refer to the Private Pilot –
Airplane Single–Engine Land
Practical Test Standard.

B. TASK: S–TURNS ACROSS A ROAD
(AMEL)

NOTE: Refer to the Private Pilot –
Airplane Single–Engine Land
Practical Test Standard.

C. TASK: TURNS AROUND A POINT
(AMEL)

NOTE: Refer to the Private Pilot –
Airplane Single–Engine Land
Practical Test Standard.

Chapter 24

XII. AREA OF OPERATION: *NIGHT FLIGHT OPERATIONS*

A. TASK: PREPARATION AND EQUIPMENT (AMEL)

> **NOTE:** Refer to the Private Pilot – Airplane Single–Engine Land Practical Test Standard.

B. TASK: NIGHT FLIGHT (AMEL)

> **NOTE:** Refer to the Private Pilot – Airplane Single–Engine Land Practical Test Standard.

Chapter 25

XIII. AREA OF OPERATION:
EMERGENCY OPERATIONS

A. TASK: SYSTEMS AND EQUIPMENT MALFUNCTIONS (AMEL)

PILOT OPERATION – 10

REFERENCES: AC 61–21; Pilot's Operating Handbook and FAA–Approved Airplane Flight Manual.

1. **Objective.** To determine that the applicant:

   a. Exhibits adequate knowledge by explaining causes, indications, and pilot actions for various systems and equipment malfunctions.
   b. Takes appropriate action for simulated emergencies such as –

      (1) partial power loss.
      (2) engine roughness or overheat.
      (3) loss of oil pressure.
      (4) carburetor or induction icing.

    (5) fuel starvation.
    (6) engine compartment fire.
    (7) electrical system malfunction.
    (8) hydraulic system malfunction.
    (9) landing gear or wing flap malfunction.
  (10) door opening in flight.
  (11) trim inoperative.
  (12) pressurization system malfunction.
  (13) other malfunctions.

2. Action.   The examiner will:

a. Ask the applicant to explain causes, indications, and remedial action for various systems and equipment malfunctions.

b. Simulate various equipment malfunctions, and determine that the applicant's per−formance meets the objective.

c. Place emphasis on the applicant's ability to analyze the situation and take action appropriate to the simulated emergency.

Objective: What's expected of the applicant regarding systems and equipment malfunctions.

Exhibiting Knowledge through Explanation. The list of possible systems and equipment malfunctions listed in the objective is the same for multiengine as for single engine airplanes. Causes and indications would similarly be the same. In all instances, partial power loss, engine roughness or overheat, loss of oil pressure and the rest, the pilot's action would be essentially the same whether he/she were flying a single engine or a multiengine airplane. Regardless of the number of engines, there is not an item on the list that would be handled differently up to a point. Obviously, the multiengine airplane does offer the advantage of one's being able to respond to engine-related emergencies by shutting down the affected engine while still maintaining controlled flight. Consequently, the additional factor added to one's explanation would be, in some instances, to shut down and secure an engine while using the remaining power to continue flight to the nearest airport for a controlled, precautionary landing.

Taking Action. There is little point to repeating in this section all those items that were previously covered in the section dealing with single engine airplane procedures. Do not assume that you will be expected to memorize the list of emergencies and have a ready explanation for each. It's extremely unlikely that an examiner would attempt to simulate all the emergencies on the list. You will be expected, however, to be able to react appropriately to any items on the list that the examiner cares to simulate.

For some simulations—such as certain examples of partial power loss, engine roughness, electrical system malfunction, etc.—it would be possible for you actually to go through the appropriate procedures. Some of these will be dealt with specifically in succeeding parts of this area of operations. Other simulations, however, such as an engine compartment fire, would not permit your actually performing all the pilot actions, and you'd need to settle for simply describing your actions while pointing out or touching each item involved in the response.

For this part of the emergency operations, it should be sufficient to review the similar part of the single engine airplane section on systems and equipment malfunctions. Beyond this, as with other operations, you will also be expected to be familiar with any requirements particular to the airplane which you're flying for the practical test. To be prepared for this, compare the list of "emergencies" provided in the objective with the index of the operating handbook for your particular airplane and then study those sections prior to the test.

B. TASK: MANEUVERING WITH ONE ENGINE INOPERATIVE (AMEL)

PILOT OPERATION – 10

REFERENCES: AC 61–21; Pilot's Operating Handbook and FAA–Approved Flight Manual.

NOTE: The feathering of one propeller should be demonstrated in any multiengine airplane equipped with propellers which can be safely feathered and unfeathered in flight. Feathering for pilot flight test purposes should be performed only under such conditions and at such altitudes (no lower than 3,000 feet above the surface) and positions where safe landings on established airports can be readily accomplished in the event difficulty is encountered in unfeathering. At altitudes lower than 3,000 feet above the surface simulated engine failure will be performed by throttling the engine to zero thrust.

In the event a propeller cannot be unfeathered during the practical test, it should be treated as an emergency.

1. **Objective.** To determine that the applicant:

    a. Exhibits adequate knowledge by explaining the flight characteristics and controllability associated with maneuvering with one engine inoperative.

    b. Sets the engine controls, reduces drag, identifies and verifies the inoperative engine after simulated engine failure.

c. Attains the best engine inoperative airspeed and trims the airplane. ✢

d. Maintains control of the airplane.

e. Attempts to determine the reason for the engine malfunction.

f. Follows the prescribed checklist to verify procedures for securing the inoperative engine.

g. Estabilshes a bank toward the operating engine as required for best performance.

h. Turns toward the nearest suitable airport.

i. Monitors the operating engine and makes necessary adjustments.

j. Demonstrates coordinated flight with one engine inoperative (propeller feathered, if possible) including –

    (1) straight–and–level flight.
    (2) turns in both directions.
    (3) descents to assigned altitudes.
    (4) climb to assigned altitudes, if airplane is capable of climbs under existing conditions.

k. Maintains the desired altitude, ±100 feet, when a constant altitude is specified, and levels off from climbs and descents, ±100 feet.

l. Maintains the desired heading during straight flight, ±15°.

m. Maintains the specified bank angle, ±10°, during turns.

n. Divides attention between coordinated control, flightpath, and orientation.

o. Demonstrates engine restart in accordance with prescribed procedures.

2. Action. The examiner will:

a. Ask the applicant to explain the flight characteristics and controllability involved in flight with one engine inoperative.

b. Simulate engine failure and observe the procedures, and determine that the applicant's performance meets the objective.

c. Place emphasis on the applicant's ability to control airspeed and follow prescribed procedures.

Objective: What's expected of the applicant regarding maneuvering with one engine inoperative.

Exhibiting Knowledge through Explanation. The examiner may briefly review with you the flight characteristics and controllability associated with maneuvering with an engine out. However, most of this will have been covered in some detail in the oral phase of the practical test. Therefore, although there will certainly be some discussion of engine-out procedures prior to performance, the emphasis at this stage of the test is going to be on actual performance. Be prepared, however, to discuss the particulars of handling the airplane with an engine inoperative as these procedures are presented in the operating handbook for your airplane. This initial part of the engine inoperative maneuvers will deal with general requirements of losing an engine. Later parts will simulate emergencies in particular situations. Consequently, the discussion at this point will be on the general, or initial, response to an engine failure.

Setting Controls after Simulated Engine Failure. At a safe altitude, and within landing distance of a suitable airport, the examiner may shut down an engine with the mixture control or fuel selector. Or he/she may simply simulate an engine out by reducing power, setting the throttle to zero thrust. You will then set both mixture and propeller controls for maximum power to maintain at least V_{mc}. Reduce drag by retracting landing gear and wing flaps. Finally, verify which engine you've lost.

Keep in mind that you will not be able to identify the dead engine by checking the tachometers. Some slight change may occur, but the propeller of the dead engine will be windmilling and the governor will flatten the prop blades to keep the rpm constant until the low pitch limit is reached. Also, the windmilling propeller will keep the engine acting as a pump, resulting in the manifold pressure tending to stay at its regular indication. However, the airplane will yaw into the dead engine and you will automatically attempt to correct the yaw with rudder pressure. Use whatever mnemonic device your instructor has taught you to correctly identify the dead engine: Best foot forward; Working foot—working engine; Dead foot—dead engine; Loafing foot—loafing engine.

Identify the inoperative engine as quickly as you can but do not be hasty. The greatest single error is that of the pilot's *incorrectly* identifying the dead engine and shutting down *all* power. Having identified the inoperative engine, tell the examiner which engine you've identified. Then, before you do anything else, pull the throttle of the dead engine back. If nothing happens, your selection was correct and you can continue with the rest of the procedure. If you've made an error, you'll recognize it as soon as you retard the throttle and you can correct your mistake. It will not be disqualifying to make such an error so long as you catch it promptly yourself. It will be a little embarrassing, though.

Attaining Appropriate Airspeed. Quickly adjust the pitch of the airplane to attain at least V_{mc}. Actually, the appropriate airspeed will be that which is called for in the operating handbook for your airplane. Since this initial engine-out procedure will probably occur in normal cruise, you may use the best enroute engine-inoperative-airspeed. When the airspeed has been stabilized, retrim the airplane. Don't guess at it. Use the controls to establish the desired attitude and then trim away as much of the pressure as you can to maintain that attitude.

Controlling the Airplane. You will be expected to maintain something close to the original heading and to maintain a constant altitude, or to hold gradual altitude loss to a minimum. You should also maintain the bank angle that will be mentioned further down the list.

Attempting to Determine the Reason for the Engine Malfunction. This is important, because it determines whether you attempt a restart or secure the engine. If you check it out and you see that the examiner has reduced the mixture to idle cutoff, or turned the fuel valve to OFF, identify it. "Some scoundrel shut off the fuel to my engine." Unless you identify the problem, the examiner could get the impression that you failed to recognize the reason your engine quit. If it's something so obvious as the throttle or mixture control being pulled back and you fail to identify it, you will have created a very bad impression. After you've correctly identified the examiner's mischief, he/she will probably acknowledge that this is a simulation and will have you proceed with the rest of the list.

Using the Checklist. All the manuals include a checklist for dealing with an inoperative engine. They generally indicate that you should: (1) Pull the throttle back to idle; (2) Reduce mixture to idle cutoff; (3) Pull the prop control back into the feather detent; (4) Set fuel selector to OFF; (5) Turn aux fuel pump off; (6) Turn mag switches; (7) Set alternator switch off; (8) Set cowl flap closed. Before relying on this checklist, make sure it agrees with the checklist in the operating handbook for your airplane. Then, with the dead engine secured, you give your attention to the operating engine by setting power, mixture, and prop control as required. Also do the same for the fuel selector, aux fuel pump (ON), and cowl flap. Retrim the airplane to take some of the workload off you. Decrease the electrical load. Again, this list will vary somewhat from one make and model airplane to another, so it's essential that you follow the checklist for your airplane.

Establishing a Bank. Remember that we mentioned this under controlling the airplane? It was also mentioned in the oral examination part. Now you'll do it; bank about 5 to 10 degrees into the operating engine. Again, the operating handbook for your airplane will most likely specify the angle of this bank.

Looking for an Airport. I certainly hope that through all of this you've maintained your spatial orientation. After the airplane is set up for single-engine flight, you'll be expected to head for the nearest airport. Don't rack the airplane around. All your maneuvers, including turning toward the nearest airport, should be gentle and smooth. In heading toward the nearest airport, can you turn in the direction of the dead engine? Of course you can. As a matter of fact, you'll be doing it for this part of the test. Just keep in mind that because of the absence of the propeller airflow over the wing, recovery from turns toward the dead engine will be somewhat slower.

Monitoring the Operating Engine. Well, here you are on a multiengine checkride performing as a single-engine pilot. But you're not the pilot of an airplane with a single engine, so you do have some additional duties in order to avoid becoming the pilot of a multiengine glider. When the preceding items are completed, your operating engine must get your attention.

To avoid possible abuse, you can increase the airflow over the engine and/or provide a richer mixture. Monitor the instruments that can help keep you informed, the oil temperature gauge, the cylinder head temperature gauge. You can also open the cowl flap. If you notice that the operating engine is beginning to heat up, you may have little choice but to reduce power and dive the airplane slightly in order to get more air flowing over the engine.

Demonstrating Coordinated Flight. Now that the airplane is set up for single-engine flight, you'll perform straight-and-level flight if the airplane is capable of that. If it's incapable at whatever your present altitude is, it may be necessary gradually to descend until you reach an altitude where level flight can be sustained. You'll also be required to make turns in both directions. (There goes the myth that you can't ever turn into a dead engine.) Controlled descents to assigned altitudes must also be made. Some examiners may include turning maneuvers with these descents, simulating entering flying a traffic pattern just as you would make an approach for a landing. If the airplane is capable under existing conditions of altitude and density altitude, climbs to specified altitudes may also be made.

Altitude, Heading and Bank Angle Requirements. The tolerance for maintaining altitude or climbing to or descending to specified altitudes is 100 feet on either side of the assigned altitude. You will be expected to stay within 15 degrees of the specified heading and—although the objective doesn't mention it—to roll out within reasonable limits on the assigned heading. Throughout the turning maneuvers, you should also maintain a relatively constant bank. All of these requirements are essentially the same as for single engine airplanes, though you get a little more tolerance in this case.

Demonstrating Engine Restart. You must follow the procedures set forth in the operating handbook, but there are some generalizations that are applicable. The mag switches must be turned on, along with the fuel selector on main. Ease the throttle forward about an inch. Set the mixture control for the altitude at which you're flying. The propeller control should be forward of the feathering detent. Then go through the normal starting procedures. When the engine comes to life, power should remain reduced until the engine has warmed sufficiently. The FAA's AC61-21A calls for 200 degrees Fahrenheit. Cowl flaps will need to be appropriately adjusted and the alternator turned on.

What's been described is a very general procedure. Do not use it as a substitute for the unfeathering and restarting procedures described in the operating handbook for your airplane. When the objective speaks of "prescribed procedures," it means those prescribed by the manufacturer of *your* airplane, not by the FAA.

C. TASK: ENGINE INOPERATIVE LOSS OF DIRECTIONAL CONTROL DEMONSTRATION (AMEL)

PILOT OPERATION – 10

REFERENCES: AC 61–21; Pilot's Operating Handbook and FAA–Approved Flight Manual.

NOTE: There is a density altitude above which the stalling speed is higher than the engine inoperative minimum control speed. When this density altitude exists close to the ground because of high elevations and/or high temperatures, an effective flight demonstration of loss of directional control may be hazardous and should not be attempted. If it is determined prior to flight that the stall speed is higher than V_{MC} and this flight demonstration is impracticable, the significance of the engine inoperative minimum control speed should be emphasized through oral questioning, including the results of attempting engine inoperative flight below this speed, the recognition of loss of directional control, and proper recovery techniques.

To conserve altitude during the engine inoperative loss of directional control demonstration, recovery should be made by reducing angle of attack and resuming controlled flight. If a situation exists where reduction of power on the operating engine is necessary to maintain airplane control, the decision to reduce power must be made by the pilot to avoid uncontrolled flight. Emphasis should be placed on conservation of altitude but not at the expense of uncontrolled flight.

Recoveries should never be made by increasing power on the simulated failed engine.

The practice of entering this maneuver by increasing pitch attitude to a high point with both engines operating and then reducing power on the critical engine should be avoided because the airplane may become uncontrollable when the power on the critical engine is reduced.

1. **Objective.** To determine that the applicant:

   a. Exhibits adequate knowledge by explaining the causes of loss of directional control at airspeeds less than V_{MC} (minimum engine inoperative control speed), the factors affecting V_{MC}, and the safe recovery procedures.
   b. Selects an entry altitude that will allow recoveries to be completed no lower than 3,000 feet AGL.
   c. Establishes the airplane's configuration with −

      (1) propeller set to high RPM.
      (2) landing gear retracted.
      (3) flaps set in takeoff position.

(4) cowl flaps set in takeoff position.
(5) engines set to rated takeoff power or as recommended.
(6) trim set for takeoff.
(7) power on the critical engine reduced to idle (avoid abrupt power reduction).

d. Establishes a single engine climb attitude (inoperative engine propeller windmilling) with the airspeed representative of that following a normal takeoff.
e. Establishes a bank toward the operating engine as required for best performance.
f. Reduces the airspeed slowly with the elevators while applying rudder pressure to maintain directional control until full rudder is applied.
g. Recognizes the indications of loss of directional control.
h. Recovers promptly by reducing the angle of attack to regain control and, if necessary, adjusts power on operating engine sufficiently to maintain control with minimum loss of altitude.
i. Recovers within 15° of the entry heading.

2. **Action.** The examiner will:

a. Ask the applicant to explain the causes of loss of directional control, the factors affecting V_{MC}, and safe recovery procedures.
b. Ask the applicant to demonstrate engine inoperative loss of directional control, and determine that the applicant's performance meets the objective.
c. Place emphasis on the applicant's recognition of and safe recovery from loss of control, and knowledge of the factors contributing to loss of directional control with one engine inoperative.

347

Objective: What's expected of the applicant regarding loss of directional control demonstration.

Exhibiting Knowledge through Explanation. Much of the explanation related to engine-out loss of directional control will have been covered during the oral examination phase. It's unlikely that you'll be called on to repeat the material about the airflow across the rudder that is necessary to maintain directional control being reduced by low airspeed to the point where control is lost. You'll already have explained the meaning of V_{mc} as well.

As for the factors affecting V_{mc}, these may be related to the particular airplane you'll be flying and the conditions of flight. As you will recall from the oral examination portion, the V_{mc} can be affected by the location of the center of gravity, with the V_{mc} increasing as the CG is moved further aft. A higher altitude, on the other hand, lowers V_{mc} in nonsupercharged airplanes, since power decreases with altitude, diminishing the thrust moment of the operating engine. There is an altitude, therefore, above which the V_{mc} is lower than the stalling speed. Density altitude can bring this critical altitude close to the ground, making such demonstrations impossible in areas of higher elevations and/or temperatures. As the FAA Standards point out, if this situation obtains when you take your practical test, you'd better be prepared to give a detailed and lengthy description of loss of directional control at airspeed less than V_{mc}.

Selecting an Entry Altitude. Altitude is particularly critical for this demonstration, since it will involve the actual (rather than a simulated) loss of directional control of the airplane. Even though the loss of directional control is brief and planned, it is important to allow a safe margin for the loss of altitude that will occur as a part of the demonstration. Consequently, your entry altitude must be sufficiently high to assure recovery above 3000 feet AGL. Some instructors recommend that the demonstration be commenced at the highest altitude where takeoff power can be developed. However, keep in mind that as altitude increases, V_{mc} decreases until it is less than stalling speed. As with other maneuvers, a check of the operating handbook for your airplane may give more specific guidance in selecting an appropriate altitude.

Establishing the Airplane's Configuration. The objective specifies the configuration that is to be used for the demonstration. The particulars of wing and cowl flap settings and power settings will need to be determined from the operating handbook. A caution regarding the final item—power reduction on the critical engine—is in order. The power should be reduced very gradually until the throttle is at idle, in order to diminish the rolling tendency away from the operating engine. At idle, the propeller on the inoperative engine will still be windmilling.

Establishing Climb Altitude. For getting at the proper climb altitude, you can use outside references to set the nose in the position, in relation to the horizon, that is normally used for takeoffs. This should produce an airspeed between V_{xse} and V_{yse}.

Establishing a Bank Angle. With the airplane properly configured and at the appropriate pitch, or attitude, you should now roll into a bank of between 5 and 10 degrees toward the operating engine. As you will recall from the oral phase, this is to ensure that the airplane will remain controllable above published V_{mc}, that drag will be minimized and the stall characteristics will not be degraded. The operating handbook may specify the angle of bank to be used, so check it out.

Reducing Airspeed. Gradually increase the back pressure on the yoke. This increase should be sufficient to produce a reduction in airspeed of about one knot per second and no more. Keep in mind that too great a reduction in airspeed can cause a violent rolling tendency away from the operating engine to develop. The same thing can occur if the airplane stalls before reaching V_{mc}. Should this occur, you must immediately reduce the power on the operating engine and also reduce the angle of attack by lowering the nose of the airplane. Otherwise, the airplane will spin. As the airspeed is reduced, it will be necessary to apply increasing rudder pressure in order to maintain directional control. The very gradual reduction in airspeed should continue until the rudder is fully deflected.

Recognition of the Loss of Directional Control. Obviously, the loss of directional control will be indicated by the airplane's tendency to yaw in the direction of the dead engine despite your holding the rudder in a fully deflected position. Do not begin the recovery, however, until the signs of loss of control are positive. Recover too early and you'll simply have to go through the whole procedure again. Generally, if you hold the attitude until the nose has yawed about five degrees, that will be sufficient evidence of loss of directional control yet will still permit recovery within the allowable limit.

Recovery. The recovery, of course, will be by simultaneously lowering the nose to reduce the angle of attack and reducing the power on the operating engine. However, the power should be reduced only enough to regain control since altitude loss is to be held to a minimum.

Recovery Limit. The allowable limit for recovery, mentioned above, is within 15 degrees of the airplane's heading at the entry to the maneuver.

D. TASK: DEMONSTRATING THE EFFECTS OF VARIOUS AIRSPEEDS AND CONFIGURATIONS DURING ENGINE INOPERATIVE PERFORMANCE (AMEL)

PILOT OPERATION – 10

REFERENCES: AC 61–21; Pilot's Operating Handbook, and FAA–Approved Airplane Flight Manual.

1. **Objective.** To determine that the applicant:

   a. Exhibits adequate knowledge by explaining the effects of various airspeeds and configurations on performance during engine–inoperative operation.
   b. Selects an entry altitude that will allow recoveries to be completed no lower than 3,000 feet AGL.
   c. Establishes V_{YSE} with critical engine at zero thrust.
   d. Varies the airspeed from V_{YSE} and demonstrates the effect of the airspeed changes on performance.
   e. Maintains V_{YSE} and demonstrates the effect of each of the following on performance –

      (1) extension of landing gear.
      (2) extension of wing flaps.
      (3) extension of both landing gear and wing flaps.
      (4) windmilling of propeller on the critical engine.

2. **Action.** The examiner will:

   a. Ask the applicant to explain the effects of various airspeeds and various configurations on performance during engine inoperative operation.

b. Ask the applicant to demonstrate the effects of various airspeeds and various configurations on performance, and determine that the applicant's performance meets the objective.

c. Place emphasis on the applicant's ability to recognize the critical effects of various airspeeds and various configurations on airplane performance.

Objective: What's expected of the applicant regarding demonstrating the effects of airspeeds and configurations.

Exhibiting Knowledge through Explanation. This will be a rather easy part of the engine inoperative performance. The explanation required will be a recitation of the data that is given in the operating handbook for your airplane. Consequently, you should check the figures given for the effects of landing gear and/or wing flap extension on the performance of the airplane with an engine out. Do the same thing for a windmilling propeller on the critical engine. This information will be provided in tables and charts, or in the descriptive section of engine-out procedures.

Selecting an Entry Altitude. Since you'll already be at attitude for inoperative engine demonstrations, there is no special concern for this part of the demonstration.

Establishing the Airspeed. For one part of the test, the throttle of the critical engine will be pulled back to idle to produce zero thrust. Nothing else needs to be done with the configuration of the airplane at this stage. With the critical engine at zero thrust, you'll need simply to establish the altitude that produces V_{yse}.

Varying the Airspeed. After the airspeed is stabilized at V_{yse}, you'll be assigned particular airspeeds, such as V_{xse}, V_{sse}, and required to maneuver the airplane. This simply demonstrates the variations in control as the airspeed is reduced or increased—not much challenge here.

Demonstrating the Effects of Varying Configurations. Once again, the airspeed will be stabilized at V_{yse}, and various configurations assigned. You'll explain and demonstrate the effects on airspeed and directional control, including climbs, for the configurations listed in the objective. This part of the practical test is not intended to test you but to demonstrate the importance of cleaning up the airplane and feathering a dead engine for engine-out maneuvers.

E. TASK: ENGINE FAILURE EN ROUTE
(AMEL)

PILOT OPERATION – 10

REFERENCE: AC 61–21.

1. **Objective.** To determine that the applicant:

   a. Exhibits adequate knowledge by explaining the techniques and procedures used if engine failure occurs while en route .

   b. Sets the engine controls, reduces drag, and identifies and verifies the inoperative engine after simulated engine failure.

   c. Attains the best engine inoperative airspeed and trims the airplane.

   d. Maintains control of the airplane.

   e. Attempts to determine the reason for the engine malfunction.

   f. Follows the prescribed checklist to verify procedures for securing the inoperative engine.

   g. Establishes a bank toward the operating engine as required for best performance.

   h. Turns toward nearest suitable airport.

   i. Maintains an altitude or a minimum sink rate sufficient to continue flight considering –

      (1) density altitude.
      (2) service ceiling.
      (3) gross weight.
      (4) elevation of terrain and obstructions.

   j. Monitors the operating engine and makes necessary adjustments.

   k. Maintains the desired altitude, ±100 feet, if within the airplane's capability, the desired heading, ±15°, and the desired airspeed, ±5 knots.

   l. Divides attention between coordinated airplane control, flightpath, and orientation.

   m. Contacts appropriate facility for assistance, if necessary.

2. **Action.** The examiner will:

    a. Ask the applicant to explain the techniques and procedures used for engine failure en route.

    b. Simulate an engine failure while en route and observe the applicant's ability to follow prescribed procedures, and determine that the applicant's performance meets the objective.

    c. Place emphasis on the applicant's correct performance of emergency procedures required during simulated engine failure en route.

Objective: What's expected of the applicant regarding enroute engine failure.

Exhibiting Knowledge through Explanation. Much of the description required for this pat of the practical test will already have been covered in the oral examination phase and during the initial part of the emergency operations section of the practical test, when you demonstrated maneuvering with one engine inoperative. As a matter of fact, some examiners may consider this part of the test already to have been covered by that earlier task.

There are some additional items that can be covered here, if they have not been taken care of during other phases of the test. For example, the cruising altitude will certainly have an impact on the techniques and procedures. You might, for example, need to discuss the "drifting down" technique should an engine fail while you are cruising above the single-engine service ceiling for your airplane. The examiner may call on you to explain such factors as density altitude, gross weight, and the like.

Clarify for the examiner your understanding that an engine failure enroute is less critical than in other circumstances of flight. Even if your airplane is at gross weight and above the service ceiling, an engine failure does not need to spell disaster. Certainly, under the conditions mentioned, the airplane is probably going to descend. I say "probably" because whether or not the airplane descends depends on its absolute ceiling.

Remember that at its service ceiling, your airplane is still capable of climbing at 50 fpm. If you've been airborne for some time, burning off fuel, then the airplane will be at less than gross weight and able to maintain an even higher altitude. But even if the airplane does descend, it is not going to plummet out of the sky and will descend only to its absolute ceiling. Besides, the rate of descent can be held to a minimum, providing the capability of covering considerable distance and reaching an airport where a safe landing can be made. Of course, elevation of terrain will make a difference. If the height of the terrain is greater than the absolute (not service) ceiling of your airplane, you would have a very unhappy day.

Procedures. What's required of the pilot who experiences an engine failure enroute has already been covered in the earlier part of Emergency Operations. The setting of engine controls, airplane configuration, attempting to determine the reason for the engine failure, securing the dead engine, and caring for the operating engine have all been covered previously.

About the only possible addition to the list of concerns would be the item that refers to maintaining altitude or a minimum sink rate. There's a good chance that your enroute altitude would be higher than either the service ceiling or the absolute ceiling for your airplane. You will need to know these, of course.

The density altitude along the elevation of terrain and obstructions would certainly be factors in your conducting the flight with an engine inoperative. However, the absolute ceiling of your airplane coupled with the drift-down rate would probably mean that you would be within range of an airport regardless of where in the U.S. you experienced engine failure. And, as you descended toward the absolute ceiling, the sink rate would be constantly decreasing until it disappeared at the absolute ceiling for your airplane. The airspeed which you would maintain for this drift-down would be V_{yse}. All of the other items listed under the objective were covered previously and require no repetition here.

The objective does include one item that is new to the list, though it has been mentioned before in this book. A part of the engine failure emergency procedure is to contact the appropriate facility, not only for assistance, but to let others know of your predicament. The appropriate facility, of course, depends on the circumstances of your flight. It might mean simply informing whoever you were in radio contact with while enroute. Or it might mean contacting the Approach Control or tower of a nearby airport. But radio communication of your problem should be a part of your normal procedures, after the other items more directly related to flight have been taken care of.

F. TASK: ENGINE FAILURE ON TAKEOFF BEFORE V$_{MC}$ (AMEL)

PILOT OPERATION – 10

REFERENCE: AC 61–21.

1. **Objective.** To determine that the applicant:

   a. Exhibits adequate knowledge by explaining the reasons for the procedures used for engine failure on takeoff before V$_{MC}$ including related safety factors.
   b. Aligns the airplane on the runway centerline.
   c. Advances the throttles smoothly to maximum allowable power.
   d. Checks the engines' instruments.
   e. Maintains directional control on the runway centerline.
   f. Closes throttles smoothly and promptly when engine failure occurs.
   g. Maintains directional control and applies braking as necessary.

2. **Action.** The examiner will:

   a. Ask the applicant to explain the reasons for the procedures used for engine failure on takeoff before V$_{MC}$ including related safety factors.
   b. Ask the applicant to perform a takeoff and will reduce power on an engine before reaching 60 percent V$_{MC}$, and determine that the applicant's performance meets the objective.
   c. Place emphasis on the applicant's prompt and accurate performance of the emergency procedure and correct airplane control.

Objective What's expected of the applicant regarding engine failure on takeoff before V$_{mc}$.

Exhibiting Knowledge through Explanation. This explanation is

355

rather simple. When you lose an engine prior to liftoff, there is not even a decision to be made. You simply close the throttles and remain on the ground. A thought enters your head: "But what if . . . " No Butwhatifs—*you stay on the ground.* "But, just suppose . . . " No Justsupposes—*stay on the ground.* "Yeh, but . . . " *Stay on the ground.* The objective mentions engine failure on takeoff before V_{mc}. You know, of course, that you are not going to rotate to lift off until V_{mc} + 5. Hence, below V_{mc} means you're still on the runway and would not lift off because directional control could not be maintained. Explain that there aren't any alternatives; the airplane stays on the ground.

Aligning the Airplane. This takeoff will begin like any other. One of the reasons is that, as far as you're concerned, it *is* just another takeoff. So line up on that runway centerline as you would for any takeoff.

Advancing the Throttles. It's still just another takeoff, so you advance the throttles steadily and smoothly to what the manufacturer of your airplane lists as the maximum allowable power.

Checking the Gauges. This, too, was covered way back when takeoffs were discussed in the single engine section. You simply have some additional instruments to check now.

Maintaining Directional Control. Although you're flying a light twin, directional control will be maintained with the rudder and steerable nosewheel, just as it was with a single engine airplane. In the very unlikely case that you're taking off in a taildragging twin, you'll lock the tailwheel as soon as you've rolled straight for a few feet.

When Engine Failure Occurs. While you're concentrating on aligning, advancing, checking, staying straight, the examiner is going to make this takeoff different from the others. At about 60 percent V_{mc}, he/she will pull something to reduce power on an engine. You must promptly, immediately, but smoothly close the throttles—quick-like, before that operating engine has a chance to thrust you off the runway and embarrass you.

Maintaining Directional Control. You know how to do this. You use the rudder pedals. No chance of using differential power now, because you don't have any power. However, in this situation, you can use some differential braking. You'll still avoid jamming brakes on, however, braking lightly and only as necessary. Then you'll taxi back and try it again.

G. TASK: ENGINE FAILURE AFTER LIFT–OFF (AMEL)

PILOT OPERATION – 10

REFERENCE: AC 61–21.

1. **Objective.** To determine that the applicant:

   a. Exhibits adequate knowledge by explaining the reasons for the procedures used if engine failure occurs after lift–off including related safety factors.

   b. Recognizes engine failure promptly.

   c. Sets the engine controls, reduces drag, and identifies and verifies the inoperative engine after simulated engine failure.

   d. Establishes V_{YSE} if there are no obstructions; if obstructions are present, establishes V_{XSE} or V_{MC} +5, whichever is greater, until obstructions are cleared, then V_{YSE} and trims the airplane.

   e. Maintains control of the airplane.

   f. Follows the prescribed checklist to verify procedures for securing the inoperative engine.

   g. Establishes a bank toward the operating engine as required for best performance.

   h. Recognizes the airplane's performance capability; if a climb is impossible, maintains V_{YSE} and initiates an approach to the most suitable landing area.

   i. Attempts to determine the reason for the engine malfunction.

   j. Monitors the operating engine and makes necessary adjustments.

   k. Maintains the desired heading, $\pm 20°$, and the desired airspeed, ± 5 knots.

   l. Divides attention between coordinated airplane control, flightpath, and orientation.

   m. Contacts the appropriate facility for assistance, if necessary.

2. **Action.** The examiner will:

    a. Ask the applicant to explain the reasons for the procedures used for engine failure after lift–off including related safety factors.

    b. Simulate engine failure after lift–off, considering all safety factors, by retarding the throttle to zero thrust, and determine that the applicant's performance meets the objective.

    c. Place emphasis on the applicant's prompt and accurate performance of the procedure and correct airplane control.

Objective: What's expected of the applicant regarding engine failure after liftoff.

Exhibiting Knowledge through Explanation. You will be expected to recognize that an engine failure after liftoff does require decision-making; in fact, you'll be faced with some fast decision-making. Your decision(s) will need to be made in terms of the airplane you're flying and the circumstances you're experiencing when the failure occurs. This combination means that a book could be filled on possible decisions. However, there are some generalizations that you'll be expected to provide.

In the first place, if liftoff has occurred, then the airspeed must be at or above $V_{mc} + 5$. Does that mean that you'd necessarily continue flying? Of course not. If you've lifted off and the airspeed is below V_{xse} and the landing gear has not been retracted, you put the airplane back on the runway and start through the after landing checklist. If you've lifted off, achieved V_{xse}, and the landing gear is in the retract cycle, then you probably would continue to climb until obstruction clearance altitude is achieved, at which time you'd try to achieve V_{yse}, all the while retracting flaps and landing gear. But suppose you've got liftoff and have achieved V_{xse} with gear coming up, but the terrain off the end of the runway goes up faster than your airplane goes up at V_{xse}. Then you'd better figure that it's better to belly it in with the airplane under your control than to risk attempting flight and losing control. See what I mean about circumstances altering decisions?

Take another case: Suppose you're departing an airport with runways that stretch almost out of sight. You lift off, get to V_{xse}—or even V_{yse}—lose and engine and are faced with a decision. There's still plenty of runway left to put the airplane down on and get it slowed to taxiing speed before reaching the end. Since you've got a safe airspeed, do your continue the flight? Of course not. If you can avoid flight with an engine out, you'd be silly to go simply because you've achieved the "go" airspeeds. So you put it down, do your after-landing checklist, taxi back to the hanger, and have someone find out what went wrong.

For this part of the checkride, have your plan worked out. First, check the operating handbook for all you need to know about your airplane. Regardless of what the instructional manuals say, if your airplane has the hydraulic pump only on the left engine, and you're faced with a loss of the critical engine, and having to pump up flaps and gear by hand in an airplane that won't climb with everything hanging down and a windmilling prop, your decision may simply be about where to put it. Your plan would specify the speed(s) and/or circumstances that would have to be met before you would attempt to continue flying, what action you'd be taking if the flight did continue, with your plan including airspeeds, direction of flight, pilot actions, and the like.

"I will align the airplane on the runway centerline and apply maximum allowable power (*specify for your airplane*). During the takeoff roll, I will monitor (*specify instruments*). If an engine fails before V_{mc}, (*specify for your airplane*), I will close both throttles and do the after-landing checklist. If liftoff occurs and I am below V_{xse}, (*specify for your airplane*), and the landing gear are still down, I will close both throttles and abandon the takeoff immediately. Or, if I have lifted off and sufficient runway remains, (*specify the point*), I will close the throttles and abandon the takeoff regardless of the airspeed attained. If I have become airborne, have achieved V_{xse} and landing gear are retracting, I will continue to climb straight ahead and, after reaching obstacle clearance altitude, (*specify for your airport*), I will reduce the angle of attack to achieve V_{yse} while I retract flaps, landing gear, identify the dead engine, and perform the engine out checklist," etc. You can write out such a plan, memorize it, and recite it for the examiner as your exhibition of knowledge by explanation for this part of the practical test. Why such a method for handling this part of the test? Because it's generally the most critical time to lose an engine, with its combination of drastic reduction in power, low altitude, and little time for pondering a decision and taking action.

Recognizing Engine Failure Promptly. Hopefully, by now, your practice will have been sufficient to make it nearly automatic for you to associate the failed engine with the dead foot. Since your altitude will be critically low on takeoff, and the airplane will still have the greatest tendency to yaw into the dead engine, since you're at takeoff power, it's vital to immediately recognize the dead engine and begin to take appropriate action.

Setting the Airplane Up. The first action is to make sure that all engine controls are forward—mixture, prop, and throttle—to maximum permissible power settings. Flaps would generally be retracted next, followed by landing gear retraction. The reason for flap retraction first is that flaps produce significantly more drag than do the wheels. However, circumstances can alter cases, so check your operating handbook and take into account the conditions of your airport. With the airplane cleaned up, you "verify the inoperative engine" by retarding the throttle on the failed engine. As you bring it back, nothing should change. If, as you retard that throttle, things do begin to change, everything goes forward again because you misidentified the dead engine.

Establishing the Correct Airspeed. The correct airspeed depends on your airplane and the airport environment. You know that as quickly as possible, you should attempt to achieve V_{yse}. *This airspeed for your airplane should be imprinted on your nervous system.* Whether or not you can go for it depends on whether or not you can afford to sacrifice the altitude needed to achieve it. At this stage, altitude is generally more important than airspeed, so you may need to settle for V_{xse} until you've reached an altitude at which you can safely maneuver.

You must also know whether, under your particular circumstances (airplane and airport conditions), V_{xse} is more or less than V_{mc}. If V_{xse} is the smaller number, then you have no option and must go with $V_{mc} + 5$. When you get the attitude to produce the appropriate airspeed, trim the pressure off to enable you to fly the airplane without undue strain.

Maintaining Control. Essentially, what this means is sitting there with your leg straining, if necessary, to hold sufficient pressure against the rudder pedal to keep the airplane moving in a straight line. It also means that you've trimmed the airplane.

Securing the Dead Engine. Under actual conditions you would go through the checklist to shut everything off and feather the dead engine. The latter is very important because of the drag created by a windmilling engine; it's usually greater than the drag created by extended landing gear. But on the practical test, the engine failure will be simulated, so you will simply read off each item on the checklist, touch or indicate the item to be manipulated or adjusted, and announce what's required to your examiner. You do this to demonstrate that you are picking the right set of controls. The securing, including feathering, will be simulated only, of course, because you must keep the simulated dead engine available in case it's needed. You certainly would not want to turn a simulated emergency into a real one.

Banking into the Operating Engine. This is pretty far down the list. Some would suggest that it should be up there as a part of item "b" on the objective list. Since you already have one hand on the yoke and both feet on the rudder pedals, it requires nothing extra to roll the airplane about 5 to 10 degrees into the operating engine. It provides an extra margin of control, which is vital at that stage. Some would suggest that this be a part of item "c" on the objective list, at the very latest. So if you do it the FAA way, don't be surprised if the examiner makes a friendly suggestion about how this procedure really should be handled.

Recognizing the Airplane's Capability. You'll have learned about this, long before the moment that you need to know it, by reading about it in the operating handbook. Obviously, if the airplane won't climb, you try to maintain V_{yse} because that will keep you in the air the longest while you look for a place nearly straight ahead to get the airplane back on the ground. But keep in mind that although the airplane may not be able to climb out of the situation, neither will it plummet to the ground. So have your plan ready and announce it to the examiner

Getting at the Reason. In the midst of this crisis, after everything else has been taken care of, you can try to make some judgement about what caused the malfunction. Since you've already secured the dead engine, this may be a little difficult unless you're able to go through an entire restarting procedure, including unfeathering the dead engine. The objective includes it, so talk about it with your examiner. He/she may suggest simply getting back to the departure airport as promptly and as safely as you can and letting someone else—such as an A&P—do the analysis.

Monitoring the Operating Engine. In any engine-out emergency, it's important to take good care of the only thing sustaining your flight (besides good fortune). The procedures here are the same as for other engine-out emergencies that you've already demonstrated.

Maintaining Heading and Airspeed. These should require no explanation. The objective clearly states the parameters for your heading and airspeed. Most examiners would prefer that you stay on the plus side of that five knots, even though the standard provides an allowance on either side.

Dividing Attention. Your principal concern for this phase of the practical test is the same as for every other part of the flight check. The first thing that claims your attention is *fly the airplane.* However, coordination is meaningful for this part of the test, but it means something different than for normal flight. Generally, you'd be concerned about the sort of coordination that keeps the ball in the center of the turn-and-slip indicator. But with an engine out, holding the ball in the center can significantly increase the V_{mc}. With the ball centered, the airplane would be in a sideslip toward the inoperative engine, increasing the asymmetric moment caused by having a dead engine, degrading stall characteristics, and requiring greater rudder deflection, which would cause even more drag. So coordination here means holding a bank into the operating engine along with rudder deflection to keep the nose from yawing toward the dead engine.

Now, with all that taken care of—that is, with the airplane under control, and with your control also producing the best possible performance under these conditions—you can now attend to maintaining the flight path, which will be as nearly straight out as possible until the airplane has reached a safe maneuvering altitude. Then you may turn—*gently*—to fly a pattern that will take you back to the airport of departure for your landing. Orientation speaks for itself. It means not only knowing which end is up, a vital matter, but also keeping track of your position in relation to the airport so that you can return and land.

Communicating. At last, everything is as under control as you can get it under the circumstances and you're on your way to the approach end of the runway. Now pick up the mike and let someone know your predicament. This is more important than some may realize. If others know about the fix you're in, you're less likely to be faced with the prospects of a single-engine go-around because someone has cut you off in the pattern or taxied onto the runway when you're on final.

H. TASK: APPROACH AND LANDING WITH AN INOPERATIVE ENGINE (AMEL)

PILOT OPERATION – 10

REFERENCE: AC 61–21.

1. **Objective.** To determine that the applicant:

   a. Exhibits adequate knowledge by explaining the procedure used during an approach and landing with an inoperative engine.
   b. Sets the engine controls, reduces drag, and identifies and verifies inoperative engine after simulated engine failure.
   c. Establishes the recommended airspeed and trims the airplane.
   d. Follows the prescribed checklist to verify procedures for securing the inoperative engine and completes pre–landing checklist.
   e. Establishes a bank toward the operating engine as required for best performance.
   f. Maintains proper track on final approach.
   g. Establishes the approach and landing configuration and power.
   h. Maintains a stabilized descent angle and the recommended final approach airspeed (not less than V_{YSE}) until landing is assured.
   i. Touches down smoothly beyond and within 500 feet of a specified point, with no appreciable drift and the longitudinal axis aligned with the runway centerline.
   j. Maintains correct control during after–landing roll.

2. **Action.** The examiner will:

   a. Ask the applicant to explain the procedures used during an approach and landing with an inoperative engine.

b. Simulate an engine failure by setting one engine at zero thrust, and determine that the applicant's performance meets the objective.

c. Place emphasis on the applicant's prompt and accurate performance of emergency procedure and correct airplane control.

Objective: What's expected of the applicant regarding approaches and landings with an engine out.

Exhibiting Knowledge through Explanation. It's important that you let the examiner know that you recognize that an approach and landing with an engine inoperative is to be done in a manner as nearly as normal as a pilot can make it. This means that you're not going to fly significantly higher, wider, closer in, or faster than you normally do. But there are some things that must be kept in mind that make this approach and landing a little different.

In the first place, all maneuvering is going to be gentle. Also, flaps and gear may not be extended at the same place and/or time as during a normal approach, since you don't want to extend either until you're sure that you've got the field made and a go-around will not be required. Demonstrate your understanding that you're also going to use V_{yse} until you've got the runway assured. It's a little easier to get rid of some slightly excessive airspeed than it is to get it back after it's gone.

Setting the Airplane Up. What you do with the engine controls will depend on when the engine "fails." You may already have set them while you were taking off. That is to say, the examiner may have had you take it around on a single engine. If not, then you'd go through exactly the same procedures that you've used for every other engine-out simulation. If this is the completion of a single-engine go-around, then you still should run over the list, touching or indicating each control to assure that the controls are properly set. It wouldn't even hurt to repeat essentially what you've already said earlier: "I have engine number (*blank*) inoperative."

Establishing the Airspeed. You may have had different pieces of advice on this. Checking instructional manuals produced three different recommendations: Use V_{mc} as your approach airspeed; use the normal approach speed; use V_{yse} for your approach speed. What you'll do is check the operating handbook for your airplane. Then you'll use either that recommended airspeed, or the published V_{yse}, whichever is greater. The reasons for using V_{yse} are: It gives you better performance, it gives you better control, and it has you prepared in the event that a go-around is necessary. An exception to this use of V_{yse} might be made in the case of a need to land on a relatively short runway, when the use of V_{yse} might cause floating, which would use up too much of the runway for a safe landing. In such a situation, V_{xse}, or V_{mc}, might be used as the approach airspeed. When the attitude is established that gives you the appropriate approach airspeed, trim the airplane to maintain that airspeed.

There's also divided opinion on whether or not the rudder should be retrimmed. Some advise retrimming the rudder to diminish your workload under these demanding circumstances. They suggest neutralizing the rudder and holding the necessary pressure with your foot, so that when the power is off, the rudder will be in trim. Others warn against such retrimming because of the complications that could be created in the event that a go-around is necessary. A go-around would add the need for quickly trimming the rudder to the list of items to be performed. The best advice: Check the operating handbook for your airplane.

Using the Checklist. This may be somewhat superfluous if the approach with an engine inoperative is part of the procedure that started on takeoff. On the other hand, it may be good practice to redo the engine-out checklist, touching or indicating each item as you mention it, just to be assured that everything has been done. Keep in mind that this will be a simulation only, with the "failed" engine merely throttled back, so don't start actually performing the checklist. You don't need to *create* an emergency. The exception to this, of course, is the normal pre-landing checklist; that will be completed as it would be for any landing.

Establishing the Bank. Once again, here comes this item far down on the list. If this approach is the end of what started as engine failure on takeoff, then you already have the bank established. If you got your "failed" engine on the way in then, hopefully, the bank was established after you identified the "dead" engine.

Maintaining the Proper Track. Your track on final should, as with all landings, be aligned with the centerline of the runway. This is where all is revealed. On engine-out maneuvers at altitude, you thought you were holding headings pretty well. At least, the DG didn't seem to drift too far off. But on final, a little can be a lot. When you're staring down the centerline of the runway, a great deal is revealed about your directional control. What seemed a tiny "oops" at altitude becomes a gross error on final. Hang in there and do your best while the examiner keeps repeating, "Keep it lined up! Keep it lined up!"

Establishing Approach Configuration and Power. Unlike an approach with everything going, where you would probably start putting flaps down on downwind, it's generally recommended that flaps and gear remain in place until you have the field made. Once you're committed, it could prove disastrous to a go-around if you suddenly had to change your mind, particularly if you had to crank or pump everything up by hand while trying to lumber back into the sky on one mill. Regardless of what you're flying, it's a pretty safe bet that you won't be able to climb out with everything hanging out. And keep in mind that your inoperative engine may be the one that pumps the hydraulic fluid if you were of a mind to go around and try to get everything cleaned up. So hold off as long as you can before dropping the flaps and the gear, but allow yourself enough time to get everything down. Since this is a simulation, you'll merely discuss with your examiner the possible need for manually putting down flaps and gear.

As for the power, the ideal approach would be one that would permit you to gradually reduce power all the way in until you went to idle just prior to setting down. The problem with giving advice about this is that there is such variation among light twins. Back to the operating handbook. Of course, you checked that a long time ago, so you have been using the recommended power setting with an engine inoperative all the way in. Good.

Maintaining a Stabilized Descent Angle and Approach Airspeed. Notice that the FAA calls for you to maintain V_{yse} until you have the runway made. As for the descent angle, you will avoid long, low approaches with the operating engine lugging at maximum. The descent angle should not be appreciably different than it is for a normal approach. Some recommend a slightly steeper approach under these circumstances. Still, coming in a little higher with a steeper descent might bring you in a little too high and a little too hot, causing a lot of float, or worse yet—horror of horrors—a go-around on one engine from a critical point of the approach. Better check that operating handbook for your airplane again and, unless that says to come in higher, make as nearly normal an approach as possible.

Touchdown. Notice all the leeway you get on this one. You've got to touch the runway within 500 feet of the point selected. Now, the following may not work for your airplane; check it out. What some recommend in order to stay within the limitation is that you make your approach clean, aiming for the second half of the runway. Then, when you're sure that you can set down on the second half, get the flaps down and you'll land well within the first half and within the 500 feet of your point, unless your airport has extremely long runways. Also, as with every other landing and despite the fact that your approach has been with one engine gone, you must be aligned with the centerline of the runway when you touch down.

Maintaining the Correct Control During Rollout. Well, now you can really relax and settle down into that puddle of sweat someone poured into your seat. After getting through all this engine-out business, keeping that airplane under control on the ground is just a piece of cake.

Chapter 26

XIV. AREA OF OPERATION:
APPROACHES AND LANDINGS

A. TASK: NORMAL APPROACH AND LANDING (AMEL)

PILOT OPERATION – 5

REFERENCE: AC 61–21.

1. **Objective.** To determine that the applicant:

a. Exhibits adequate knowledge by explaining the elements of a normal approach and landing including airspeeds, configurations, and related safety factors.
b. Maintains the proper ground track on final approach.
c. Establishes the approach and landing configuration and power required.
d. Maintains a stabilized descent angle and the recommended approach airspeed, ±5 knots.

367

e. Makes smooth, timely, and correct control application during final approach and transition from approach to landing roundout (flare).

f. Touches down smoothly beyond and within 500 feet of a specified point, with no appreciable drift, and the airplane's longitudinal axis aligned with the runway centerline.

g. Maintains directional control during the after-landing roll.

2. Action. The examiner will:

a. Ask the applicant to explain the elements of a normal approach and landing including airspeeds, configurations, and related safety factors.

b. Ask the applicant to perform a normal approach and landing, and determine that the applicant's performance meets the objective.

c. Place emphasis on the applicant's demonstration of correct airplane control particularly during the after-landing roll.

Objective: What's expected of the applicant regarding normal approaches and landings.

Exhibiting Knowledge through Explanation. There are some differences between landing a light twin and landing the single engine trainer that the examiner will expect you to be familiar with. In the first place, the pre-landing checklist will be a little longer because the airplane is more complex. And because the airplane is more complex, you should have the pre-landing checklist completed by the time you are on the base leg to enable you to concentrate on final approach and landing. The only items then remaining would be those related to flap and gear extension and airspeed.

Another difference is that the multiengine airplane generally has a higher wing loading, requiring that you make your approaches carrying some power. In fact, some pilots prefer to maintain some power until touchdown. In addition to the above differences, there is also the matter of approach airspeed. In the single engine airplane, you figured it in relation to stalling speed with the airplane configured for landing ($1.3 \times V_{so}$). In the multiengine airplane, you must use V_{mc} as the absolute minimum approach speed, although V_{yse} is generally preferred.

Aside from these differences, the approach and landing will be much like that in a single engine airplane. The examiner will expect you to specify the points at which you'll extend landing gear and flaps, and the airspeeds to be aimed for on each leg of the pattern. All of these matters need to be specified for the airplane which you're flying, so once again, it's necessary to consult the operating handbook for the particulars.

Maintaining Proper Ground Track. The objective seems to start with you on the final leg of the approach. You won't be able to start there on the practical test. You'll need to consider when to put down the landing gear (i.e., at what airspeed and where), what to do about power, and such things long before you get on final. It doesn't seem to make much sense for the FAA to have put this item about ground track here, but we'll go ahead and accept it and remember that on final approach, the proper ground track means alignment with the centerline of the runway.

Establishing Configuration and Power. Well, now we're getting to what really needs to be done. If you really waited until you were on final to begin this, you might be in a little trouble. Generally, you can extend the landing gear and check for green lights on downwind. You can also begin to extend flaps. On base, check the gear again, and put down a little more flap. You'll be slowing the airplane to V_{yse} during all of this.

As for the power setting, the reduction in power would also have begun on downwind. Now, here's where we get into some further differences. There are pilots who wait until they're on final to go to high rpm on the prop controls. I prefer to do that on downwind. In fact, before beginning to reduce power, I go to high rpm because then I can hear the pitch changing. I know what my prop setting is. If I wait until power is reduced on final, I can't hear that change and it becomes an item of faith, so it's forward on the prop control and then reduce power. To what? You reduce power to whatever the operating handbook calls for. The power reduction begins, as in a single engine airplane, opposite the numbers, when you are ready to start the descent.

Understand that what has been presented so far is not exhaustive, i.e., it doesn't cover the entire checklist. That will vary from one make and model to another, so a complete checklist cannot be presented here.

Maintaining a Stabilized Angle of Descent. As with any other airplane, you'll use the airplane's attitude to control the airspeed. The attitude will change as you put down additional flaps, just as it occurs with a single engine airplane. The throttles will be used to control the rate of descent, or descent angle. You'll be carrying sufficient power to keep the descent angle from becoming too steep. Any changes in attitude or in power setting that may be required during the approach should be smooth and gradual rather than abrupt.

Making the Transition from Approach to Landing. On final, you'll extend full flaps when the landing is assured. Rotation will begin as you reach the end of the runway in order to further slow the airplane. If you've been using V_{yse} for your approach airspeed, some recommend slowing to V_{mc} "over the fence." Check the operating handbook to see what's appropriate for your airplane.

You may still be carrying power. Some pilots reduce the power setting to idle when they begin the landing flare. Others continue to hold power until actual touchdown, reducing the setting to idle only when they feel the main wheels on the runway. Certainly, the latter makes for a smooth touchdown, but you should consult the operating handbook for the manufacturer's recommendation.

Touching Down. Hopefully, you'll touch down lightly. However, don't turn to the examiner and say, "Are we down yet?" He/she may not have that kind of sense of humor. If you have not already got the power off, pull it off when you feel the main wheels touch the runway. You should touch down in a slightly nose-high position with no drift and with the airplane's longitudinal axis aligned with the runway centerline.

The Rollout. Now that you're down, it's just another airplane. Control the airplane with rudder and nosewheel and, if necessary, just a touch of brake now and again.

B. TASK: GO–AROUND FROM A REJECTED LANDING (AMEL)

PILOT OPERATION – 5

REFERENCE: AC 61–21.

1. **Objective.** To determine that the applicant:

   a. Exhibits adequate knowledge by explaining the elements of the go–around procedure including timely decision, recommended airspeeds, drag effect of wing flaps and landing gear, and coping with undesirable pitch and yaw tendencies.

   b. Makes a timely decision to go–around from a rejected landing.

   c. Applies takeoff power and establishes the proper pitch attitude to attain the recommended airspeed.

   d. Retracts the wing flaps as recommended, or at a safe altitude, and establishes V_Y.

   e. Retracts the landing gear after a positive rate of climb has been established.

   f. Trims the airplane and climbs at V_Y, ± 5 knots, and maintains the proper track. ❋

2. **Action.** The examiner will:

   a. Ask the applicant to explain the elements of a go–around from a rejected landing including timely decisions, recommended airspeeds, drag effect of wing flaps and landing gear, and coping with undesirable pitch and roll tendencies.

   b. Set up a situation in which a go–around from a rejected landing would be required, and determine that the applicant's performance meets the objective.

   c. Place emphasis on the applicant's judgment, prompt action, and ability to maintain correct airplane control during the go–around.

Objective: What's expected of the applicant regarding go-arounds.

Exhibiting Knowledge through Explanation. You'll be expected to clarify your understanding that a go-around from a rejected landing is a critical maneuver because it occurs at a very low altitude with the airplane trimmed for landing and with a configuration and power setting also appropriate for landing. A go-around can be required at any point, of course, but the earlier the decision can be made, the more safely the maneuver can be executed. Therefore, the decision to reject a landing should never be delayed unnecessarily. As with a single engine airplane, if there is doubt, start the go-around procedures immediately.

You should also demonstrate your understanding of the effects on flight of having the airplane in landing configuration with full flaps and landing gear extended. With some airplanes, climbing in this configuration is not impressive, yet retracting flaps too early and/or too quickly could be a costly error. Also, the rather sudden application of power from the approach/landing power setting to maximum allowable power can cause significant changes in attitude and very strong yawing tendencies.

You should also be able to explain what the approximate airspeed of your airplane would be at the time of the go-around decision, and what airspeed would be required in order to initiate the climb from a rejected landing as well as what would be required in order to achieve this airspeed.

Decision Time. A timely decision is one that is made as early as possible, as soon as it becomes evident that the landing must be rejected. Indeed, as suggested above, if the situation even becomes uncertain, it's probably best to initiate the go-around from that point rather than delaying while you remain indecisive about whether or not the situation really warrants rejecting the landing. It's obviously much safer to make the decision early than to wait until the airplane is in a landing flare attitude and about to touch down. So, when in doubt, do the safest thing; go around.

Applying Takeoff Power. As soon as the decision is made, the throttles must be advanced to maximum allowable power. Going to maximum power immediately does not mean jamming the throttles ahead, however. Some engines could be flooded this way, creating a real problem; but there should be no delay in applying maximum power. At the same time, the pitch of the airplane must be altered to check the descent while control is exercised to prevent an undesirable pitch-up of the nose of the airplane. Similarly, the pilot must be prepared for the strong tendency for the airplane to yaw to the left with this fairly sudden shift from approach/landing power setting to maximum power.

Retracting Flaps. Flap retraction must be handled carefully. In the first place, you must be guided by the procedures specified for your airplane in the operating handbook. Some airplanes require that the flap setting be altered to the takeoff position when the go-around is initiated. However, if flaps are retracted too early, or too quickly, or too far, the result could be embarrassing at best. At too low an airspeed, the retraction of flaps could result in a stall, or an unanticipated and undesirable loss of altitude.

Even at a safe airspeed, and with proper retraction of flaps at the appropriate altitude, it will be necessary to correspondingly alter the pitch of the airplane in order to attain the recommended airspeed. When the objective mentions "recommended airspeed," that refers to the manufacturer's recommendation, the one in the operating handbook. That airspeed is whatever V_y is for your airplane.

Retracting Landing Gear. When the flaps are in takeoff position and the airspeed is V_y, the go-around from a rejected landing becomes merely another takeoff. So the requirements regarding retracting the landing gear remain the same. After a positive rate of climb is established, and you've run out of runway to put the airplane down again, get the gear up.

Trimming and Tracking. Now you're simply making another takeoff. The airplane should be cleaned up by this time, so you complete the job by establishing the proper attitude and trimming to maintain $V_y + 5$. The objective doesn't mention it, but you'll also establish the appropriate power setting for climbing out, since this may differ from the takeoff power setting. Finally, you simply fly the appropriate traffic pattern to go around and try it again.

C. TASK: CROSSWIND APPROACH AND LANDING (AMEL)

PILOT OPERATION – 5

REFERENCE: AC 61–21.

1. **Objective.** To determine that the applicant:

   a. Exhibits adequate knowledge by explaining the elements of a crosswind approach and landing, including crosswind limitations, and related safety factors.

   b. Maintains proper ground track on final approach.

   c. Establishes the approach and landing configuration and power required.

   d. Maintains a stabilized descent angle and the recommended approach airspeed, ±5 knots.

   e. Makes smooth, timely, and correct control application during the final approach and transition from approach to landing roundout (flare).

   f. Touches down smoothly beyond and within 500 feet of a specified point, with no appreciable drift and the airplane's longitudinal axis aligned with the runway centerline.

   g. Maintains directional control by increasing aileron deflection into the wind and using differential power as necessary during the after–landing roll.

2. **Action.** The examiner will:

   a. Ask the applicant to explain the elements of a crosswind approach and landing, including crosswind limitations and related safety factors.

   b. Ask the applicant to perform a crosswind approach and landing, and determine that the applicant's performance meets the objective. (Note: If a crosswind condition does not exist, the applicant's knowledge of the TASK will be evaluated through oral questioning.)

c. Place emphasis on the applicant's control of wind drift during the approach and landing.

Objective: What's expected of the applicant regarding crosswind approaches and landings.

Exhibiting Knowledge through Explanation. Crosswind approaches and landings in a multiengine airplane are not significantly different from those in single engine planes. The explanation that was offered in the single engine section serves as well for this requirement, so you are referred to that section. You might, in addition to that explanation, simply add that you understand that differential power setting is *not* used to maintain directional control on final.

Maintaining Proper Ground Track. Well, here we are on final already. That's all right this time because up to this point, everything will be the same as for any other approach to a landing. As a matter of fact, the same things that you do in any other airplane will be done in your multiengine airplane to maintain a ground track that keeps you aligned with the centerline of the runway. You use either the wing low (sideslipping) or the crabbing approach, or a combination of these.

Approach and Landing Configuration and Power. Again, this will probably not differ from any other landing. Flap settings and power settings will generally be the same. However, you could check the operating handbook to ascertain this for the airplane you're flying.

Maintaining a Stabilized Descent Angle and Approach Airspeed. Nothing will be changed here, either. It's still application of power to control descent and pitch, or attitude, to control airspeed. The airspeed will be that which you normally use, or that which is specifically recommended by the operating handbook for your airplane.

Transitioning from Approach to Landing. What you do here will depend on what you've been doing on the approach to control drift. If you've been using a crabbing approach, then you'll take out the crab at the last moment before touchdown in order to land with the airplane's longitudinal axis lined up with the centerline of the runway. If you've been using the sideslip (wing low) approach, then you may continue to hold that same attitude right through the roundout (flare) to the touchdown, with the upwind main wheel touching down first.

Touching Down. Your touchdown should occur within 500 feet of a point specified by you or the examiner. The touchdown should occur with a nose-high attitude, the main wheels touching down first. Further, the touchdown should occur with no sideways drift and with the airplane's longitudinal axis lined up with the runway centerline. As you know, this is precisely the same as the requirement for single engine airplanes.

Maintaining Directional Control. To some extent, directional control will be maintained as it is in a single engine airplane, with increasing aileron deflection into the wind, using rudder pressure and the steerable nosewheel. In multiengine airplanes, you can also use differential power, an advantage over the single engine plane.

D. TASK: SHORT–FIELD APPROACH AND LANDING (AMEL)

PILOT OPERATION – 8

REFERENCE: AC 61–21.

1. **Objective.** To determine that the applicant:

   a. Exhibits adequate knowledge by explaining the elements of a short–field approach and landing including airspeeds, configurations, and related safety factors.
   b. Considers obstructions, landing surface, and wind conditions.
   c. Selects the suitable touchdown point.
   d. Maintains proper track on final approach.
   e. Establishes the short–field approach and landing configuration, recommended airspeed, and descent angle.
   f. Maintains a stabilized descent angle and the recommended airspeed, ±5 knots.
   g. Touches down beyond and within 200 feet of a specified point, with minimum float and no appreciable drift and the airplane's longitudinal axis aligned with the runway centerline.
   h. Maintains directional control during after–landing roll.
   i. Applies braking and controls, as necessary, to stop in the shortest distance consistent with safety.

2. **Action.** The examiner will:

   a. Ask the applicant to explain the elements of a short–field approach and landing including airspeeds, configurations, and related safety factors.
   b. Ask the applicant to perform a short–field approach and landing, and determine that the applicant's performance meets the objective.

c. Place emphasis on the applicant's control of descent angle, airspeed, braking, and use of flight controls.

Objective: What's expected of the applicant regarding short-field approaches and landings.

Exhibiting Knowledge through Explanation. That part of the explanation that has to do with short-field approaches would not differ from any other approach for the most part. It differs from that offered for single engine airplanes a bit in that the single engine job does not pose the same problems of control that one faces in multiengine craft. Although the approach in a single can be made at a significantly lower approach airspeed, relying on power to "drag" the airplane in, the same procedures cannot be used in multiengine approaches.

The configurations and related safety factors during the short-field approach and landing are essentially the same as for any other landing in the multiengine airplane. There can be some difference in airspeed, however. At some point on final, the normal approach airspeed can be reduced from V_{yse} to V_{mc}. That will enable you to land the airplane with minimal floating. If that airspeed won't work for a particular airport, then that airport is not for your airplane.

Considering the Factors. The short-field approach must take into account the particular, specific factors of the airport you're using. You must plan on sufficient altitude to clear all obstacles and make a descent steep enough to touch down as close to the approach end of the runway as is safely possible. However, that descent angle cannot be much different than normal, since the heavier multiengine airplane is susceptible to damage if there is not sufficient flare before touchdown. And keep in mind that the extra weight means a slower response.

The effects of wind conditions are obvious and need not be reviewed here. The surface on which the landing is to be made is also significant, since sod strips, for example, will not require as great a distance for the rollout after touchdown as would be required on a hard surface.

Selecting a Suitable Touchdown Point. Taking these factors into account, you should identify a point beyond which a landing cannot be safely made as well as a point at which a go-around would be initiated. "As soon as I see that I am not going to be able to touch down by (*the identified point*), I will execute a go-around."

Maintaining Proper Track on Final. You know what this is, of course: alignment with the centerline of the runway.

Establishing Configuration, Airspeed, and Descent Angle. The configuration for the short-field approach will be no different than that for any other approach, unless the operating handbook for your particular airplane specifies otherwise. The airspeed for most of the approach will be the same as for any other landing. However, as was mentioned above, at some (safe) point on final, the airspeed may be reduced from the normal V_{yse} to V_{mc}. The matter of the descent angle has already been addressed above.

Maintaining the Descent Angle and Approach Airspeed. In view of the items listed and discussed above, this item on the objective list seems somewhat superflous. It will not differ appreciably from the approach used for other landings, except as specified. Once again, we could remind you that the descent angle will be controlled with power and the airspeed with attitude.

Touching Down. All those requirements that apply in the case of other landings are equally applicable here. However, on the short-field approach there is not room for floating. Consequently, it's generally recommended that the airplane be slowed to V_{mc} while still maintaining a power setting that will keep the final descent angle relatively shallow. This may mean that at touchdown, the nose of the airplane will be slightly higher than normal.

Maintaining Directional Control. This aspect of the short field landing is identical to that for any other landing.

Stopping Short. Immediately cut power completely when the main wheels touch the runway. If it's an exceptionally short field, you'll find yourself applying "body English reverse thrusters." As soon as the power is cut, flaps should be retracted. (Stay away from the landing gear control!) Retracting flaps will make braking more effective, so after getting the flaps up, apply moderate braking to stop in the shortest distance possible "consistent with safety."

Appendix

APPLICANT'S PRACTICAL TEST CHECKLIST

(Suggested)

APPOINTMENT WITH INSPECTOR OR EXAMINER:

*NAME*_____

*TIME/DATE*_____

ACCEPTABLE AIRCRAFT

- ☐ View-limiting device (if applicable)
- ☐ Aircraft Documents:
    - Airworthiness Certificate
    - Registration Certificate
    - Operating Limitations
- ☐ Aircraft Maintenance Records:
    - Airworthiness Inspections
- ☐ FCC Station License

PERSONAL EQUIPMENT

- ☐ Current Aeronautical Charts
- ☐ Computer and Plotter
- ☐ Flight Plan Form
- ☐ Flight Logs
- ☐ Current AIM

PERSONAL RECORDS

- ☐ Pilot Certificate
- ☐ Medical Certificate
- ☐ Completed Application for an Airman Certificate And/Or Rating (FAA Form 8710-1)
- ☐ Airman Written Test Report (AC Form 8080-2)
- ☐ Logbook with Instructor's Endorsement
- ☐ Notice of Disapproval (if applicable)
- ☐ Approved School Graduation Certificate (if applicable)
- ☐ FCC Radiotelephone Operator Permit
- ☐ Examiner's Fee (if applicable)

PRACTICAL TEST CHECKLIST (ASEL)

(SUGGESTED)

APPLICANT'S NAME_____

EXAMINER'S NAME_____

DATE_____

TYPE CHECK_____

I. PREFLIGHT PREPARATION

- ☐ **A.** Certificates And Documents
- ☐ **B.** Obtaining Weather Information
- ☐ **C.** Determining Performance And Limitations
- ☐ **D.** Cross–Country Flight Planning
- ✱ ☐ **E.** Airplane Systems   ✱

II. GROUND OPERATIONS

- ☐ **A.** Visual Inspection
- ☐ **B.** Cockpit Management
- ☐ **C.** Starting Engine
- ☐ **D.** Taxiing
- ☐ **E.** Pre–Takeoff Check

III. AIRPORT AND TRAFFIC PATTERN OPERATIONS

- ☐ **A.** Radio Communications And ATC Light Signals
- ☐ **B.** Traffic Pattern Operations
- ☐ **C.** Airport And Runway Marking And Lighting

IV. TAKEOFFS AND CLIMBS

- ☐ **A.** Normal Takeoff And Climb
- ☐ **B.** Crosswind Takeoff And Climb
- ☐ **C.** Short–Field Takeoff And Climb
- ☐ **D.** Soft–Field Takeoff And Climb

V. CROSS–COUNTRY FLYING

- ☐ **A.** Pilotage And Dead Reckoning
- ☐ **B.** Radio Navigation
- ☐ **C.** Diversion To Alternate
- ☐ **D.** Lost Procedures

VI. FLIGHT BY REFERENCE TO INSTRUMENTS

- [ ] **A.** Straight–And–Level Flight
- [ ] **B.** Straight, Constant Airspeed Climbs
- [ ] **C.** Straight, Constant Airspeed Descents
- [ ] **D.** Turns To Headings
- [ ] **E.** Critical Flight Attitudes
- [ ] **F.** Radio Aids And Radar Services

VII. FLIGHT AT CRITICALLY SLOW AIRSPEEDS

- [ ] **A.** Full Stalls – Power Off
- [ ] **B.** Full Stalls – Power On
- [ ] **C.** Imminent Stalls – Power On And Power Off
- [ ] **D.** Maneuvering At Minimum Controllable Airspeed

VIII. TURN MANEUVERS

- [ ] **A.** Constant Altitude Turns
- [ ] **B.** Descending Turns

IX. FLIGHT MANEUVERING BY REFERENCE TO GROUND OBJECTS

- [ ] **A.** Rectangular Course
- [ ] **B.** S–Turns Across A Road
- [ ] **C.** Turns Around A Point

X. NIGHT FLIGHT OPERATIONS

- [ ] **A.** Preparation And Equipment
- [ ] **B.** Night Flight

XI. EMERGENCY OPERATIONS

- [ ] **A.** Emergency Approach And Landing (Simulated)
- [ ] **B.** Systems And Equipment Malfunctions

XII. APPROACHES AND LANDINGS

- [ ] **A.** Normal Approach And Landing
- [ ] **B.** Forward Slips To Landing
- [ ] **C.** Go–Around From A Rejected Landing
- [ ] **D.** Crosswind Approach And Landing
- [ ] **E.** Short–Field Approach And Landing
- [ ] **F.** Soft–Field Approach And Landing

PRACTICAL TEST CHECKLIST

(AMEL)

(SUGGESTED)

APPLICANT'S NAME_____

EXAMINER'S NAME_____

DATE_____

TYPE CHECK_____

I. PREFLIGHT PREPARATION

- ☐ **A.** Certificates And Documents
- ☐ **B.** Obtaining Weather Information
- ☐ **C.** Cross–Country Flight Planning

II. MULTIENGINE OPERATION

- ☐ **A.** Airplane Systems
- ☐ **B.** Emergency Procedures
- ☐ **C.** Normal Procedures
- ☐ **D.** Determining Performance And Flight Planning
- ☐ **E.** Weight And Balance/Equipment List
- ☐ **F.** Flight Principles – Engine Inoperative

III. GROUND OPERATIONS

- ☐ **A.** Visual Inspection
- ☐ **B.** Cockpit Management
- ☐ **C.** Starting Engines
- ☐ **D.** Taxiing
- ☐ **E.** Pre–Takeoff Check

IV. AIRPORT AND TRAFFIC PATTERN OPERATION

- ☐ **A.** Radio Communications And ATC Light Signals
- ☐ **B.** Traffic Pattern Operations
- ☐ **C.** Airport And Runway Marking And Lighting

V.   TAKEOFFS AND CLIMBS

- ☐ **A.** Normal Takeoff And Climb
- ☐ **B.** Cross–Wind Takeoff And Climb
- ☐ **C.** Short–Field Takeoff And Climb

VI.   CROSS–COUNTRY FLYING

- ☐ **A.** Pilotage And Dead Reckoning
- ☐ **B.** Radio Navigation
- ☐ **C.** Diversion To Alternate
- ☐ **D.** Lost Procedures

VII.   FLIGHT BY REFERENCE TO INSTRUMENTS

- ☐ **A.** Straight–And–Level Flight
- ☐ **B.** Straight, Constant Airspeed Climbs
- ☐ **C.** Straight, Constant Airspeed Descents
- ☐ **D.** Turns To Headings
- ☐ **E.** Critical Flight Attitudes
- ❋ ☐ **F.** Radio Aids and Radar Services.   ❋

VIII.   INSTRUMENT FLIGHT

- ☐ **A.** Engine Failure During Straight–And–Level Flight And Turns
- ☐ **B.** Instrument Approach – All Engines Operating
- ☐ **C.** Instrument Approach – One Engine Inoperative

IX.   FLIGHT AT CRITICALLY SLOW AIRSPEEDS

- ☐ **A.** Stalls, Gear–Up And Flaps–Up
- ☐ **B.** Stalls, Gear Down And Approach Flaps
- ☐ **C.** Stalls, Gear Down And Full Flaps
- ☐ **D.** Maneuvering At Minimum Controllable Airspeed

X.   TURN MANEUVERS

- ☐ **A.** Constant Altitude Turns
- ☐ **B.** Descending Turns

XI.   FLIGHT MANEUVERING BY REFERENCE TO GROUND OBJECTS

- ☐ **A.** Rectangular Course

☐ **B.** S–Turns Across A Road
☐ **C.** Turns Around A Point

XII. NIGHT FLIGHT OPERATIONS

☐ **A.** Preparation And Equipment
☐ **B.** Night Flight

XIII. EMERGENCY OPERATIONS

☐ **A.** Systems Or Equipment Malfunctions
☐ **B.** Maneuvering With One Engine Inoperative
*☐ **C.** Engine Inoperative Loss Of Directional
       Control Demonstration
☐ **D.** Demonstrating The Effects Of Various
       Airspeeds and Configurations During
       Engine Inoperative Performance   *
☐ **E.** Engine Failure En Route
☐ **F.** Engine Failure On Takeoff Before V_{MC}
☐ **G.** Engine Failure After Lift–Off
☐ **H.** Approach And Landing With An Inoperative Engine

XIV. APPROACHES AND LANDINGS

☐ **A.** Normal Approach And Landing
☐ **B.** Go–Around From A Rejected Landing
☐ **C.** Crosswind Approach And Landing
☐ **D.** Short–Field Approach And Landing

Index